Life's Healing Setups

Guidance to transform struggles Into peace and live beyond your ego

D'ANN ROHRBACH

Cover design by Alayne Speltz: alaynespeltz@aol.com
Content consultation & editing by Robert M. Wier
robertmweir.com
Published by CreateSpace, an Amazon Company

ISBN: 1502466783
ISBN-13: 978-1502466785

*This book is dedicated to
all people who seek a more fulfilling, spiritually
enriched life. May our inner light brighten to engulf
all humanity with hope and truth.*

CONTENTS

ACKNOWLEDGMENTS

Our lives are so entwined that truly nothing is ever accomplished alone. We live as families, groups, communities, and nations as well as individuals, and we all affect each other. Recognizing a divine plan behind this human backdrop allows us to see larger patterns, learn more, and heal more authentically. We are who we are because of our soul's relationships and experiences, alone and together throughout time. The help we give and receive from each other and the roles we play, whether through positive or other kinds of examples and events, benefit us enormously. Therefore, it is impossible to thank everyone who has contributed to my life and this project.

I am indebted to God and to the entire hierarchy of Holy Beings I have attuned to through the years and who have given me their loyalty, constancy, guidance, and love. I continue to be nearly overwhelmed by their magnificence.

My husband, Fred, and children, Amy and Dale, have been there for me during the best and worst of times. My children were volunteer subjects in the early years of my counseling practice, despite their natural questionings of what was happening and what results would be. As adults, they each do uniquely focused energy readings that are significantly insightful and effective, and they are a constant support to me. I could not have stayed with this process and ministry without their loving cooperation and endorsement. They, my sister, Louise Wyman, and many incredible friends have provided listening ears, valuable insights, and gentle encouragement.

Edgar Cayce's readings and the Association for Research and Enlightenment (A.R.E.) played a vital role in tutoring me on a spiritual path. Their course on meditation prepared me for my soul's purpose. Dear friends Kelly and Natalie Hale gifted me with the quartz crystal, Felix, which facilitated my first spiritual breakthrough. I don't know how else my path would have been so obviously and powerfully stimulated and guided had these two life-transforming resources not been available for me. I am profoundly grateful.

So many gifted friends and Light workers have served me in my spiritual development. Through readings, massage, healings, or simple light-bulb statements, they aided my current proficiency. Carleton Ryding, Margarete Kammer, Louis Reeves, and Dr. Margaret Dwyer have been advocates for me and HVT from the very beginning, and I am grateful for their prayers, assistance, and referrals.

Most especially do I express heartfelt love and appreciation to every single person who has ever had a Harmonic Vibrational Therapy®, (HVT)® session. Whether they attended only one appointment, many sessions, or returned regularly to reach a point of profound evolution, these clients have contributed tremendously to this book, which would not have been written without them. In fact, many of them directly requested that I write a book. I thank all of them for their trust, support, and vision. Their dedication, encouragement, experiences, feedback, input, and referrals have kept me going all these years.

This book needed additional talented people to provide their skills to supplement mine. I particularly thank Anne Marie Blake, my first assistant, and then Claudia Skewes and Emilie Rohrbach for their computer abilities and willingness to do anything necessary or helpful for this project to manifest. Roger Brown has been a constant support and assisted me in business matters that made the difference in this book coming to fruition. My editor, Robert M. Weir, worked with me in ways that improved my grammatical and technical abilities; his expertise brought the manuscript to a professional level. Quite literally, divine synchronicity brought these people to me.

I thank Patti Bannasch, Kathy Haskins, Marcia Luther, George Martell, and Margaret Valade for their willingness to be my focus reading group and offer comments, suggestions, and corrections. Kathy Zader has been a continuous support to me, and helped immeasurably with my web site and keeping up with contacts and book update notices. I also thank my talented cover designer, Alayne Speltz, photographer, Peggy Tittle, layout consultant & designer, Amy Rohrbach, consultants Matt Allen and Aimee Goff who enhanced the book's cover copy, and Carrie Zaatar for her practical inspirations.

I ask God to bless all of these souls and countless others who have inspired, modeled, taught, challenged, and aided me. May we all seek to spread Light wherever we are.

PREFACE

I write this book with a deep sense of caring and dedication. I share from the depths of my heart to your heart. My intent is that each reader will benefit from exposure to this material.

Life's Healing Setups unveils and explains the powerful energies behind our life dramas, which I identify as *setups*[1]—an arrangement of people, settings, and parts of a situation that God brings together to *set up*[2] a particular holistic life and karmic *healing*[3] opportunity. *Life's Healing Setups*, then, offers powerful spiritual resolutions to apparently human-related events.

The information and stories in this text originate from *divine guidance*,[4] my personal experiences and observations, professional background, and client feedback during thousands of healing sessions since 1987. From these, I have been able to assess my viewpoint of Source-based information and form insights that serve as guidelines for spiritual growth.

---

[1] **setup** or **spiritual setup:** a spiritually planned, unexpectedly triggered, interactive issue-healing crisis, that is perfectly orchestrated for all involved to push specific buttons, stimulate acute emotions, and provoke intense dramas

[2] **set up:** to put someone or something in a particular place, order, or condition

[3] **healing:** improvement or resolution in any aspect of a person, including the holistic mind/body/spirit connection, and the karmic roots of past and current life experiences

[4] **divine guidance or guidance:** timely, appropriate, and beneficial awareness, messages, inspiration, or advice that originate from beyond conscious, logical thought

Some or much of the information I present might strike you as unusual. That's okay. For many people, the knowledge presented here is outside the norm of what we've been taught by the current traditions of social and religious culture. But I know that the information in this book comes from reliable spiritual guides, beings, angels, and the *Higher Self*,[5] as well as the *Akashic Records*,[6] which are the histories of every soul and every lifetime.

Your experiences, opinions, beliefs, and *interpretations*[7] might be different from what I present here. By keeping an open mind to the *perspective*[8] of others, we enhance our personal growth. I do not intend to change your belief system, but rather to present additional and enriching views and options for your life. Ideally you will be able to see and interpret situations more fully and make wiser, more appropriate, and better self-empowering decisions.

As you read this book, you may want to turn down corners of pages or highlight what you find to be fascinating and important information for future reference. Then when you find yourself going through a difficult time, you will easily find relevant guidelines, suggestions, and inspirational insight that will have necessary, applicable, and beneficial support for your current circumstance and situation. Even my editor, Robert Weir, after going through the manuscript several times, became aware

---

[5] **Higher Self:** an inborn, divinely attuned essence that is a single portion of Source

[6] **Akashic Records:** a high dimensional energetic library that stores all histories of all souls and all lives

[7] **interpretation:** the meaning one derives from personal experiences, events, observations, and understandings

[8] **perspective:** the point of view from which a person sees a situation, experience, event, or even life itself

of divine synchronicities between what was going on in his life and specific sections of text he was editing that, prior to that time, was just "information." This could also happen for you.

If you find that the material becomes too deep for easy reading, please scan through those sections rather than put the book aside. You might also choose to read one section or subsection at a sitting and allow time for thinking and processing before continuing. You will probably find Etheric Energy in Section 2 of the first Chapter uniquely fascinating. Chapter 7 is the most encouraging and uplifting portion of the book because it addresses the benefits and blessings that result from energetic healing. This information could be strongly motivating, and you will not want to shortchange your spiritual growth by missing what you could learn near the end of the work. You could even read it first if you like.

Some of the included spiritual principles might be accessible in other resources, yet my viewpoint might phrase or interpret them differently. Without standardized spiritual vocabulary, other words can be equally appropriate for certain concepts, and some terms might have different or even occasionally contradictory definitions. Portions of this text might disagree with other published, well known material. No one has all of life's answers. My hope is to share what I have learned that has been so profoundly effective in my experience, knowing others' experiences might be equally valid, even if they appear to disclaim what is presented here.

Our perception of Truth is constantly evolving. Therefore, if something stated does not resonate with you or seems irrelevant, out of date, or in error, please disregard that part and continue on with the remaining material.

Because we are all unique, nothing fits everyone equally well. Keep an open mind and be careful of self-diagnosis. Information from books, observations, statistics, and theories should not be blindly or wholly accepted and personally applied without careful thought and prayer. Individual assessment and treatment are vitally and often critically important. You might be atypical. Also, anything is possible, exceptions occur frequently, there seems to be no "never" or "always," God can and does intervene, and miracles do happen.

People's lives improve and heal as a result of regressions, past life therapies, and energy healings. Even if there is no Truth to these tenets, something life changing happens that warrants personal investigation. Dr Richard Bartlett, Founder and Author of "Matrix Energetics," states, "I do not know what the truth about reincarnation is, but the idea of past lives can at the very least be a useful fiction that may allow you to dissolve chronic patterns of energy that cannot even be approached by any other means. If people are not comfortable with the idea of reincarnation, I call this a Parallel Dimensional Expression, or PDE." No belief in reincarnation is required for energy healing , only an open mind. In these turbulent times, it is more essential than ever to understand the energetic setup of everyday life. Learning about and accepting these unseen schematics and using vibrational healing techniques will improve emotional stability and clarity. It will create a grounded centering in which you can be safely sheltered during life's storms.

ABOUT THIS BOOK

Life's Healing Setups is a guidebook to help us on our spiritual journey, and I've employed certain conventions to facilitate your understanding.

One convention is the use of both a lowercase letter followed by the same letter, capitalized, at the beginning of the words: *t/Truth, r/Reality, k/Knowledge, k/Know, and l/Light.*

Truth[9] with a capital T refers to eternal spiritual concepts, attributes, procedures, and potentials that are inherent in God and available within the core of human consciousness. A lower case t on *truth*[10] refers to our emotions, experiences, and what we have learned about life. Because each person has his or her own experience of truth/Truth, I use the blended word *t/Truth.*

This notation also applies to: *reality*, which is based on human truths, and *Reality*, which is based on divine, universal Truth—blended as *r/Reality; knowledge*, which we have consciously learned in life, and *Knowledge*, which we inherently realize from Truth—blended as *k/Knowledge;* the related verb *know* and *Know*—blended as *k/Know;* and *light*, as in a light bulb moment, and *Light*, as the essence of our soul, blended as *l/Light.*

To progress spiritually, we need to clear out our stored emotional reality, open and shift our knowledge of how life works, and come to know that we needed our specific

---

[9] **Truth (capital T):** the ultimate, universal, and transcendent Reality that is miraculously accessible to all

[10] **truth (lowercase t):** the conclusions that we, as humans, have come to accept as reality in our individual lives

experiences—our healing spiritual **setups**—in order to learn what we have learned. To grow, we need to work through our personal truths so that we can reach and reveal our core Light that holds our Truth, comprehend Reality, and gain Knowledge.

~ ~ ~

I also employ symbols to facilitate information presentation.

When you see this design of three tildes, ~ ~ ~, it provides visual breathing room for the text and separates stories or different material of the section.

OM means Creation, a reflection of the absolute reality, and the vibration of the Supreme. The OM symbol, ॐ, is used throughout the text as a visible energetic marker. It indicates that the following passage is a noteworthy illustration or that it delves into a related, yet more advanced concept.

The OM symbol itself emanates a portion of profound energy that assists our integration with *Source*.[11] The affect you receive from this essence will depend on your vibrational rate: the higher your average vibration, the more benefit you will absorb. ॐ will stimulate and enhance deeper personal *understandings*[12] and awakenings; it will fertilize your system to embrace, integrate, and radiate a more spiritually abundant and blessed life.

When I offer directions to indicate an action for you to take or a step for you to follow, I utilize a pointing chevron, ➤. When you use this book for healing reference later, the chevron will

---

[11] *Source:* the Prime Energy of our creation, a portion of which remains eternally accessible whether we are incarnated or not

[12] *understandings:* concepts, perceptions, and assumptions intended to guide, assist, and enrich life, individually accepted and applied, and effortlessly revised and expanded

help you quickly find these instructions.

~ ~ ~

I use many stories to illustrate practical examples of the text and to bring the entire message into greater clarity. Most of these stories involve my interaction with past or present clients and the events or situations they told to me, or therapy results we experienced together. Some of these stories may not have complete or hoped for endings because the client either didn't return for more sessions, gave no feedback, or we moved on to other issues. I relate all of these in the third person, using fictitious names for the clients to honor their privacy and referring to myself with my name. A few stories relate to my clients' previous interaction with other therapists whom I do not identify.

Throughout the narrative text, when I refer to myself, I speak to you directly with the personal pronoun I.

~ ~ ~

Throughout *Life's Healing Setups*, my intent is to encourage, inspire, and facilitate spiritual understanding and soul growth as simply yet broadly as possible. The beginning of Chapter 1, From Source to E/go, addresses preliminary concepts with minimal attention to detail. You might have many questions about the information that is covered there, but I ask you to please accept that my primary purpose for that section is to explain the larger picture. Some specifics are included, but excessive details at that point would distract from the stated intent. As you progress through the book, you will encounter new concepts—some of them evolutionary—which I will explain in depth, and you will see how the information in this early section serves as a foundation for that. Therefore, this initial portion is historical and generic. The rest of the book is personally applicable and relevant; it includes over one hundred real life anecdotes that illustrate how the explained spiritual principles manifested in clients' lives.

ABOUT
YOU AND YOUR E/GO

We are eternal *souls*[13] who chose to leave the love and protection of God, our Source, in order to have diverse life experiences.

At the moment of separation from God, before the existence of time, we brought with us an internal guiding companion called *Ego,*[14] which is the state of empowered consciousness that is attuned to God. Because we realized we were no longer safely sheltered in God's abode, a small, individual segment of our essence—called *ego*[15], with a lowercase e—volunteered to take control of our life, to protect us, and to manage our experiences.

This ego, a lower vibrational form that separated from Ego, assumed responsibility for our physical survival. Our ego wrote its own new job description, which was based on fear and isolation, and assumed the role as the rational, linear dictator of our conscious life. Our ego devolved to be the least spiritually developed portion of our eternal life system. It became the conscious filter through which we process all our historical experiences, beliefs, life management techniques, emotions, thoughts, and interpretations about all aspects of our present life. Our ego's exclusive focus on our human survival is so thorough and all encompassing that we have forgotten that our—and its—

---

[13] *soul:* our unique, eternal Source energy that animates life

[14] *Ego:* the congruent state of empowered consciousness attuned to God

[15] *ego:* a small segment of our divine core that is responsible for our safety but which also functions exclusively with a rational, limited identity as though it were disconnected from Source

divine core is rooted in Source.

When we choose to advance beyond rudimentary human living and stop listening to our all-too-basic and restrictive ego voice, we then out-Source ego's job to the higher power, God and our Ego. While this sounds simple in theory, it is very hard to accomplish because our ego has done such a superlative job of

> *Our ego's exclusive focus on our human survival is so thorough and all encompassing that we have forgotten that our—and its —divine core is rooted in Source.*

controlling us, that it is not willing to abdicate its role even to support our spiritual growth. This is the nature of ego's self-absorbed, limited view, which resists evolving and uses diversionary tactics to remain in *control*[16] of our life, leaving us in a state of struggle rather than *peace*[17]

To comprehend why and how to live beyond our ego, we need to understand what ego is.

First of all, the word *ego,* with a lowercase e—written as E/go if it begins a sentence—in some psychological and psychiatric literature refers to an individual's traits of superiority or inferiority compared to others. This concept is similar to the context in which I use the word ego in *Life's Healing Setups.* Through my therapeutic spiritual energy practice with clients and my knowledge of the Akashic Records, I've come to see ego as an energetically immature state of human consciousness in

---

[16] **control:** exercising command over inner and outer aspects of life, causing disharmony, urgency, incongruency, anxiety, and other disturbing emotions

[17] **peace:** a state of harmony within oneself and in personal relations between people or groups; absence of urgency; congruent acceptance of all aspects of life

which we are unaware of our core oneness with God. E/go's home is the primal, reptilian part of our brain. It causes us to exclusively identify with earth-bound functions and then apply that physical paradigm to all possibilities, overlooking our connection with God. This is the ego that is most often described in this book and the ego we want to live beyond.

However, the word *Ego,* with a capital E, also appears in the book. This Ego refers to our potential empowered state of consciousness that originates from our soul's innate and eternal association with God and is presently, but too often unconsciously, within us. This Ego recognizes and identifies with our unity and love for all souls and all creatures. This Ego employs our whole brain and all of our being, enabling us to function as a finely tuned unit with all of God's divine energy and attributes. When we operate within the realm of Ego, we are multi-sensory, multi-dimensional, whole-brained Light beings. We are authentic. We are One with God.

The self-centered ego and the God-based Ego are both one-and-the-same and, simultaneously, distinct and at odds with each other. The ego, we might say, is a fallen version of its original Ego … or ego identifies with our material needs and life, while Ego focuses on our spiritual evolution first.

> *Your decision to apply energetic concepts in order to seek an expanded consciousness and divine Truth will incrementally discharge your ego's authority and allow its original spiritual identity to override its survival mentality.*

The struggles in our life originate when we turn our attention primarily or exclusively toward the ego-focused, physical world and turn our back on God's messages of guidance, which can be delivered to us through personal inspiration or other means.

Our spiritual goal in life is to live beyond our ego so that we completely and totally identify with God as our Source of all spiritual and life energy. We want our ego, with its limited management of our material life, to merge with our Ego, in a state through which God manages our whole life, and we awaken to our personal union with all creation—as God intended.

When we operate under ego influence, we operate and manage—or cope—our way through life at low-vibration energies. Instead, we want to function and excel with the exalted levels of spiritual energy that we know as *empowerment,*[18] a state of being that defines and describes our unified and co-creative connection with God.

Your decision to apply energetic concepts in order to seek an expanded consciousness and divine Truth will incrementally discharge your ego's authority and allow its original spiritual identity to override its survival mentality. Your single conscious decision to spiritually develop, along with continuing supportive techniques and follow-up, as presented in *Life's Healing Setups*, will transform your life into radiance and empowerment.

As you evolve in this manner, you—and your ego—will come to recognize a new Reality. Neither you nor your ego will disappear or fade into nothingness, as ego fears, but will actually *merge*[19]—or re-merge—into oneness with Source. You and your

---

[18] **empowerment:** the benefits of incremental integration of ego into Ego that stimulates whole brained functioning and manifests Source congruency in our will, thoughts, emotions, decisions, and actions

[19] **merge:** to gradually blend our limited ego into a whole brained Ego as our new personal identity

ego will re-gain the Knowledge that you and it are not separate and isolated from Love, but are blessed with and part of God's eternal and universal Love.

Life's Healing Setups will address the fact that life can be fraught—set up—with difficulties that are intended to help us grow spiritually. These difficulties are nearly always painful. They might also be shocking and alarming because sometimes we need to be shocked in order to wake up and realize our divine, spiritual potential that ego does not want us to know about. We seem to grow most when out of our comfort zone.

So welcome, or at least accept, the difficulties. See the pains and shocks as opportunistic, powerful, and obvious means for you to reinterpret your experiences. Be open to guidance. Allow yourself to see and enjoy more options and wiser responses. Give yourself permission to easily and significantly heal your life.

Life's Healing Setups then, is about the process of reinterpreting life's dramas to actuate personal enlightenment. To do this, we focus on the spiritual patterning behind and within everyday life. As we enlarge our perspective and interpretation of personal experiences and events, we become aware of deeper, hidden, life-improving potentials. It is time for us to discover the subtle yet profound aspects of ego that influence, limit, and block our individual and group happiness and development. My intention is to demonstrate how you can unravel ego's ploys and move to empowerment. By clearing your ego's command of your life, you are embarking on a sacred journey. Our future presents magnified capabilities, expanding possibilities, greater potentials, and incredible discoveries. May we embrace our destiny!

Turn the page and begin to discover a new you. Go with God.

CHAPTER 1:
FUNDAMENTALS

God is the *Foundation of Life,*[20] our Source, the source of all. God is our Prime Energy.

All that we receive from God is *divine:*[21] divine opportunity, divine potential, divine empowerment, and so many other divine gifts.

With this in mind, we will start at the beginning of life.

1: FROM SOURCE TO E/GO

In the beginning was Prime Energy. All creation originated from within this incomprehensible Love. As pure souls, we were unified with Source and unencumbered by any physical or material awareness. We moved about instinctively and immediately, mingling with any and all other souls. We might have existed for eons in this unstructured and blissful state.

Gradually our unique awareness emerged into thoughts and we became thought beings. At some point in distant prehistoric ages, souls chose to leave Source for individual discoveries. There might have been many reasons for this decision, and perhaps that is why there are various and diverse ideas and theories about the beginning of life.

The consequence of abandoning Prime Energy launched each soul into a state of apparent separation from Source, which

---

[20] *Foundation of Life:* the Source of all that is, commonly referred to as God, Allah, or Yahweh in ancient religions, and with words such as Creator, Prime Energy, or Universal Energy in modern times

[21] *divine:* that which pertains to or comes from God; Godlike

created a condition of *fear*,[22] a paralyzing emotion based on the absence of trust. Yet, God allowed each soul to take with it the empowered identity of Ego, which contains guidance and other inherent aspects of Source.

Ego Consciousness

From this Ego, we, now being fearful, extracted a small and confined self-identity known as *ego consciousness*.[23] This ego consciousness is, therefore, a remnant of our divine identity, but it is more associated with the fearful domain of our ego rather than the Source-provided Ego. With its primary concerns being our safety, ego consciousness assumed responsibility for our physical survival as well as the self-serving agendas we created through our individualized thoughts.

Because ego consciousness excludes us from consciously connecting with Source-based soul life, it eventually caused us to forget our divine origins. It is as though ego created a metal wall between our conscious awareness and our now unconscious God awareness, resembling the membrane separating the two parts of our brain, that functions as a wall effectively stopping *God's Light*[24] from being readily available to us. Eventually, our awareness so focused on ego consciousness that we assumed this diminished and isolated identity as if it were our only true self.

Gradually we began to experiment with different life forms that we might assume. In the vastness of creation, other planes of existence, such as organisms within mineral, water, and some

---

[22] *fear:* absence of trust, the foundation of ego, a paralyzing emotion

[23] *ego consciousness:* our exclusive awareness of and reliance on the self-created remnant of our divine identity, that is more associated with fear and protection of the human form and mind than with Source energy

[24] *Light, God's Light, or Source Light:* the actual radiant Source essence of all life, centered physically in the solar plexus

form of plants, offered various states of materiality into which our beings—still only thoughts at that time—could hazily and temporarily evolve into matter. Emerging physical creatures with independently moving bodies, such as insects, snakes, and birds, especially tantalized us. Desiring additional growth opportunities, our souls were attracted to these diverse universes, domains, and dimensions. Over time, we finally fully incarnated into material forms, adapted to having a life span, and explored unfamiliar worlds. In all likelihood, our explorations included *transmigration*[25] through which we incarnated and moved from one realm to another.

After living in various locations and forms, we eventually entered early versions of human bodies on earth. At that time, life on this planet was profoundly simple and rugged. Individuals faced physical needs with fear, crudeness, and diligence. Yes, we still had thoughts, but physical life was so harsh that it led us to enduringly conclude that what is in front of our eyes is more important than what is behind them. Because we had lost our original memory and sight of the divine, we identified with ego-based physicality. Spiritual awareness and growth were rare, if not impossible, at this level of existence.

This fragment of our self, originally in union with Source, recognized its isolation from

> *Humanity's exclusive reliance on visual, logical, and experiential input created ego eyes that have governed our views and viewpoints for millennia.*

God, but seemed incapable of doing anything about it even if we had the desire to do so. We needed to focus our whole attention on *three-dimensional*[26] survival. Humanity's exclusive reliance on visual, logical, and experiential input created ego eyes that

---

[25] ***transmigration:*** incarnating from one kingdom to another

have governed our views and viewpoints for millennia.

This primordial history shaped humanity's development through various stages of spiritual immaturity. Our ego-driven priorities necessitated that we be judgmental and controlling and that we employ certain *ego management techniques*[27] in order to handle our daily life. We know that today, "to be a manager" depicts a higher supervisory role in business, which will continue to be necessary. "To manage" in our personal life depicts non-productivity in regard to spiritual evolution. An example would be a woman who is extremely unhappy with her husband but chooses to remain in the marriage for specific practical reasons, such as for the children, or because she has little or no employment skills. Although not wrong, she is placing her personal life on hold until some future time when she may or may not activate a more fulfilling life. This decision is the equivalent of getting by or making do rather than moving forward. This is why our earthly trials actually complicate, limit, and confuse life and set the stage for more difficulties. As a result, we have been accruing incomplete, harsh life experiences throughout time.

> *Our views and interpretations of life are reduced misrepresentations of the greater whole.*

When we employ ego management techniques, we operate in the state of ego consciousness, and we filter all our experiences through distorted lenses. Our views and

---

[26] ***three-dimensional:*** a view of life based exclusively on that which can be seen, touched, and measured, and which compels and directs human activities; this outlook represents spiritual immaturity

[27] ***ego management techniques:*** three-dimensional interpretive and response skills through which a person maintains an ego-induced façade of being in control of his or her life, but which actually signifies that ego is in control

interpretations of life are reduced misrepresentations of the greater whole. Our lives are missing a sense of flow and satisfaction because we no longer remember our spiritual foundation. At best, our conclusions are insufficient and not adequately accurate.

Although not required, it might take a crisis or a miracle to wake us up to our True, Source-based identity and stop us from continuing to hinder or harm ourselves both physically and spiritually during our human lifetimes.

God Consciousness

An encouraging sign is that significant individuals throughout recorded history—the prophets and sages and holy people—have been aware that ego consciousness causes a sense of dissatisfaction, a feeling of unidentified longing, or that something is missing, insufficient, and inaccurate. Throughout the world, the number of individuals with this awareness of the detrimental aspects of ego consciousness and the corresponding benefits of *God consciousness*[28] is growing. More and more people are now peering through ego's seemingly impenetrable wall and seeing that, even though ego consciousness caused us to have journeyed far from Source, divine love never lets us truly lose our connection with God.

Our awareness of our connection to God is often rekindled or strengthened through *divine intervention,*[29] which is an unexpected conversation, event, or message that causes us to perk up and pay attention to seemingly improbable circumstances or experiences. Divine intervention might occur

---

[28] *God consciousness:* our awareness and integration of Source attributes, energetic resonance, and Knowing that transcend present life limitations and awaken empowerment

[29] *divine intervention:* God's active involvement in life, either directly or through an angel or a messenger; often considered to be a miracle

quietly and in the simplest of ways, as the next story demonstrates.

> Roxanne had been raised in a conservative family with traditional values and perspectives on life. Searching for more advanced and meaningful spiritual Truths had not been in her consciousness. One day, she had an unplanned, in-depth discussion with a new friend about topics that were completely new to her including *reincarnation*,[30] chakras, auras, and energy healing. She was fascinated. From that time on, she frequently reflected on these new ideas but didn't know what to do about them or how to learn about them further.
>
> A few weeks after that conversation, Roxanne walked into a library to get some books for her grandchildren. Her eyes immediately focused on a book about energy healing at the checkout desk. She knew she had to read it. Both the original conversation with her new friend and the "coincidental" experience of easily and surprisingly finding a pertinent book launched a major shift in her life and priorities. As a result of these simple experiences, Roxanne looks at herself and others very differently. She is now on a *spiritual path*[31] to evolve.

---

[30] *reincarnation:* rebirth of a soul in a new body to clear karma, learn lessons, foster new experiences, serve others, and spiritually evolve

[31] *spiritual path:* seeking development of an inner divine nature

2: ENERGY

Science has proven that everything is energy. Energy cannot be destroyed; it is eternal. Energy can change form and shape; it can be charged or neutralized. As a foundation to understanding how our ego attempts to manipulate our energy, it's important that we understand how energy appears in and affects so much of our existence.

Soul Energy

Our souls are eternal energy. We are an eternal soul within a temporary body.

Our souls are eternal energy. We are an eternal soul within a temporary body rather than a body with a soul. This statement alone represents a major shift in how we interpret and view life. If we think that our current body is the only physical form that our soul will ever inhabit, we may focus all our life efforts to leave a lasting legacy, may not invest in serious pursuits, or may tend to put a lot of pressure on ourselves to perform in our very best way during this one-and-only opportunity to "get it right." But when we realize our soul has chosen this body for a divine purpose during this lifetime, which is just one of many lifetimes, we bless the body for the role it will play to facilitate our soul's growth at this time.

We then see great reason and importance for our numerous periods of life on earth. From this largest perspective, we understand that each lifetime represents only a few stitches in our soul's very large experiential tapestry. We can then somewhat relax, attempting to do the best we can while knowing that our soul intends to benefit in one way or another from every incarnation.

Spirit Energy

When the body dies, our soul does not cease to exist. Rather, we simply set aside our bodily form and return to a purely energetic state of being, freed from physical limitations.

Most souls immediately leave earth and reconnect with kindred souls. Some souls, however, linger close to earth as paranormal *spirits*, [32] which are conscious energy fields only one step removed from their physical body. These spirits do not continue to progress beyond their recent life because they are caught in some earth-bound, unresolved dilemma; they might not even fully realize or accept the fact that they died.

We call these spirits "ghosts" and refer to their paranormal activities as "hauntings." These spirits need to be liberated by a person skilled with this type of energy intervention so that they may progress beyond this most recent lifetime. On the other side of life, there are layers of soul development even in between lives on earth, as well as lives elsewhere in other dimensions.

Thought Energy

🕉 When we think, we consciously create energy. We broadcast every mental process to the universe. The force and repetition of our messages is the volume control. We are so powerful that we create our own reality. Frequently thinking, "I am so sick of my job," could eventually manifest as illness unless we change our thought, viewpoint, feeling, circumstance, or employment. We are what we think. There is, however, an undergirding and permeating agenda that skews and limits our ability to manifest our

> *We are so powerful that we create our own reality.*

---

[32] *spirits:* souls that are earth-bound and only one level beyond physical life

36

life's desires: our soul-chosen *karmic* or *life script,*[33] also known as our *life blueprint,*[34] which has a higher priority than ego consciousness.

Etheric Energy

Some electronic equipment can pick up subtle energies, a fact I've learned by providing a recording of each session for my clients. During one client's session, I saw an *etheric*[35] on-and-off switch. I explained what it meant to my client and then turned the switch on. Neither I nor the client heard anything at the time, but when we later listened to the recording, we heard a distinct click, as though a physical switch had been moved, at the precise second the etheric switch changed positions.

This is but one example of the unusual electronic awarenesses and situations with which I have been impressed and felt too often plagued during my whole career. Sometimes, after first recording the client's name and date, the rest of the recording was completely blank or only the first and last few minutes of the session were actually recorded. A few times, a high-pitched buzz was present most of the way through. Occasionally, neither my words nor my client's words were on the recording but background noises were audible: an ambulance, lawn mower, or thunder. Experimenting with different microphones, recording devices, and even the assessment from an audio professional who attended a session with his own instruments did not remedy the complication.

---

[33] *karmic* or *life script:* soul-chosen areas to address in the upcoming life

[34] *life blueprint:* the unseen energetic configuration of life that offers healing opportunities and generates visible effects; how the karmic script functions

[35] *etheric:* a non-physical, energetic, intangible state or existence

I have concluded that extremely high energy overloads my equipment. This dilemma has somewhat stabilized over the years when I started to use an electromagnetic field absorber on my recorder, but I still need to have it repaired unusually often. The repairman's typical comment is, "We've never seen this happen before." I now accept the situation as a consequence of working with powerful energies.

Aura Energy

Vibrational frequencies[36] exist in everything created. When a frequency originates from any apparent life force, such as a person, animal, or plant, it exudes beyond the physical form and is called the *aura, prana, or chi (qi).*[37]

> *Inherent traits and emerging challenges appear in the energy field before they manifest consciously or physically.*

This aura essence surrounds the body and is more subtle, sensitive, and responsive to influences than is the body's denser physical form. Our aura is not under our conscious control but reflects aspects of our personality, life, and body. The human aura has colors and shapes, and contains both physical and spiritual information. Inherent traits and emerging challenges appear in the energy field before they manifest consciously or physically. An intuitive who can read auras might see a person's issues, interests, and possible health concerns before symptoms are apparent.

---

[36] *vibrational frequencies:* scientifically measurable oscillations that emanate from all divine and human creations; frequencies increase as we spiritually develop

[37] *aura, prana, chi (qi):* a vital essence that arises from and surrounds all life forms

Human Energy

ॐ Energy flows between people. It is invisible, instinctive, and spontaneous, and it ultimately determines the baseline quality of a relationship or an interaction. When we become aware of and look for these subtle energy transactions, we sense what we

> *Energy flows between people.*
> *Living beings are eternal.*

would otherwise miss. We learn to appreciate people more than things because material items are transient, while only living beings are eternal. From this more elevated vantage point, our observations and opinions of others' physical appearances, such as ethnicity, stature, clothing, and grooming, become less important. We apply the old adage: "Don't judge a book by its cover." With a deeper and fuller focus, we will nonjudgmentally receive more meaningful impressions of others that will provide wiser, gentler, and more empathetic interpretations of and reactions to them.

Physical intimacy blends the energies of each partner. This partially explains why couples grow to physically resemble each other over time.

Larry had been divorced for more than twenty years and had come close to remarrying twice. His first serious relationship was with "Jeanne," who had epilepsy and, for many years, had been taking Dilantin® (phenytoin), a prescription drug to control seizures.

While dating Jeanne, Larry discovered a spiritual path that deepened his life. He began to seek complementary healing modalities as a component of his new and fulfilling life direction. As a typical engineer who deals with situations that involve logic, methodology, and organizational skills, Larry was not especially interested in psychics. He was therefore delighted to find a *Light worker*[38] who used an advanced computer-generated healing program that energetically assesses, diagnoses, and treats physical conditions. In his first session, the assessment identified Dilantin® in his system. He was stunned. He certainly had never taken one of Jeanne's pills and had never even held one. How could it possibly have entered his system?

As of yet, there is no verifiable allopathic medical explanation for Larry's fascinating computer assessment. Energetic diagnosis of cross contamination from sexual relations is not yet widely recognized, accepted, or endorsed. And additional technological breakthroughs might be necessary in order for allopathic and integrative practitioners to process the implications of what happened within Larry's body.

Scientifically and metaphysically, however, we do know that energy moves instantly, but the physical body is slow to respond due to its high density and relatively low vibration. Therefore, the body can be immediately imprinted, programmed, or tainted by energy that might not show its effects for many years. Similarly, the body can also be instantly energetically healed from these low-vibration frequencies, but these effects might also take time to manifest physically.

It is likely that every sexual encounter, even a one-night stand, transfers energetic residue between partners. A person

---

[38] *Light worker:* a person who contributes to humanity's energetic advancement

who is promiscuous might be carrying a heavy accumulation of unknown, foreign energies. Unless they are cleansed, these mingled energies remain with the body until all the cells regenerate, which happens constantly but requires about seven years to complete. Perhaps the far-reaching physical and energy benefits of abstinence or fidelity, unrecognized by pleasure seekers today, are behind the wisdom of mystics, ascetics, monastics, and cultures that promote monogamy.

Healing Energy

Energy is subtle yet potent. It resembles gentle drops of water hitting a rock, causing the rock, over time, to wear away. In the same way, illness starts to manifest at an energetic level before obvious physical symptoms appear. Identifying and treating conditions at this tier might eliminate further development and/or appearance of poor health or disease.

Skeptics have an especially difficult time accepting this healing concept because they think that if there are no symptoms, there is no reason to believe anything detrimental is happening internally. They usually maintain that there is no way to prove the presence of disease until symptoms manifest. The consequences of their opinion, although not wrong, are only a partial view, and will require them to physically process and deal with conditions or symptoms when they become apparent. However, the longer illness is in the body's system, the more complications it can cause and the longer it generally takes or the more difficult it is to heal.

Although the person in the following story was not skeptical, she was aware of something not making sense in her healing regimen.

> Patty was energetically diagnosed with malaria by a healer using a biofeedback computer software program that identifies, prioritizes,

and treats energetic challenges. Because she had no physical symptoms for malaria, she was shocked by what she heard and had no idea she was carrying such a potentially serious illness. She had, however, been in a rain forest a few years earlier and been bitten by a few mosquitoes. So, unfortunately, the presence of this condition was possibly true.

Patty had been diligently practicing many types of alternative healing modalities to enhance other parts of her body and life, but had not noticed any improvements in those areas. Apparently, her body was directing most or all of the alternative therapeutic energies toward containment of malarial organisms and keeping symptoms of that disease at bay.

After the infecting energies were removed, additional healing sessions finally manifested improvements in other areas of her life.

Energy Resonance

Anyone who has been moved to tears by beautiful art, music, photography, or nature is resonating, beyond appearances, to energy dispersing through the air. This deeper essence, rooted in Source, is so nurturing to our being that even one such experience augments our discernment of quality. From grandeur to simplicity, on its own or combined with innate giftedness, this inherent energy enhances and transports creative effects. Everything less energetically vibrant pales by comparison. As we evolve, we will be inclined to seek out personal items that are both functional, such as a lovely water pitcher, and decorative, such as wall art, that resonate to our core. The energetic internal and external congruency strengthens and enriches our quality and fulfillment of life.

Energetic discord restricts and diminishes the purest energy. Thoughts, feelings, and behaviors that stem from *ego agendas*[39] impede *Source energies*[40] and generate resistance and agitation. Disturbed energies captivate our attention, tarnish our clarity, distract us from a larger awareness, and minimize the size of our *life lens*[41] on the world. With a smaller lens, our energy exchange is reduced to a percentage of what would otherwise be possible. Our ability to receive inspiration and blessings and to manifest Source attributes is compromised. An example of a small lens would be a man looking at life exclusively from a financial bottom line. He would be minimally aware of the potential benefits that wise spending could personally offer him, and would likely part with his hard earned money with some level of resentment. This feeling would minimize and taint his enjoyment and appreciation of the value of his purchase. He would be highly unlikely to seek a spiritual path because he would see no tangible benefits to gain from the expense. With this example, a large lens focus would allow a person to instinctively see advantages from a purchase that seem well worth the cost. Life can flow better with a larger lens.

The Energy of Giving

One of the most direct ways to set aside our ego agendas, open our life lens, and charge our personal batteries is to freely and joyfully give to others. As we give, we make room to

---

[39] *ego agendas:* self-serving views and behaviors

[40] *Source energy:* divine vitality that feeds the soul and provides guidance and opportunities to enhance spiritual evolution

[41] *life lens:* the filtering system, preset with our karmic issues, through which we view and process our life and world; this filter skews our behavior and limits internal and external support, ease, and blessings

receive. The more we lovingly give, serve, volunteer, or donate to others, with no strings attached, the more we open up our own availability and capacity to receive. However, the pivotal words are *freely* and *joyfully*. Buying a gift because it is expected, owed, or if we are more concerned with appearances or what others will think of it or us are signs of an ego agenda that shrinks the size of our receiving lens. So does giving anything for the sole purpose of personal gain. Any ulterior motive, sense of sacrifice, or expectation of appreciation or compensation inhibits lens size, even if it had formerly been expanded.

The size of our life lens fluctuates in response to energy purity. The energy benefits of cheerful giving can present themselves in several ways. As we become aware of more blessings in our own life, we might attain higher levels of personal contentment and happiness, feel more peace, have more hope, see improved personal relationships, and notice more kindness and support within our own world.

> Lisa loves to buy gifts for friends and family even if there is no special occasion. She is an instinctive shopper and often finds new items for close to garage sale prices. In giving so freely and without any thought of tallying, personal benefit, or expectation of outcome, she is blessed with unusually dear and supportive friends. These close companions respond to her generosity with constant invitations for social and cultural events, dining, and other enjoyable opportunities. She realizes how fortunate she is to have so many loving relationships.
>
> One spiritual concept says that we cannot out-give God. Without intending to, Lisa has

activated the benefits from this principle. Blessings return to her in unexpected and diverse ways, and because her actions stem from love and joy, the gifts she receives hold an even higher vibration than the gifts she gives.

Attitudes and Energy

Positive thoughts, words, and deeds extend uplifting energy that can have a remarkable effect on our ability to set aside ego agendas.

> Diane was driving to work one morning and needed to go around a trash truck in her neighborhood. As she slowly moved past, she caught the eye of the worker and smiled at him. He instantly showed surprise, then total delight. He returned the largest smile possible. Diane felt unusually blessed by that simple interaction.

ॐ In contrast, negative thoughts, words, and actions can diminish or even harm others and us. We have all received a demeaning comment and felt the instant assault to our mood and day. Imagine how Diane's day and that of the worker would have been if she had given him a disgusted look or gesture for being in her way.

Attitudes affect energy. Someone with a chip on his or her shoulder can ruin an enjoyable conversation. Sometimes it only takes one person with a sunny disposition to brighten everyone's day. The following quote is from a sermon by Charles Swindoll, Senior Pastor of Stonebriar Community Church in Frisco, Texas:

> *Attitudes affect energy.*

"The longer I live, the more I realize the impact of attitude on life. Attitude, to me, is more important than facts. It is more important than the past, than education, than money, than circumstances, than failures, than successes, than what other people think, or say, or do. It is more important than appearances, giftedness, or skill. It will make or break a company … a church … a home. The remarkable thing is we have a choice every day regarding the attitude we will embrace for the day. We cannot change our past. We cannot change the fact that people will act in a certain way. We cannot change the inevitable. The only thing we can do is play on the one string we have, and that is our attitude. … I am convinced that life is 10% what happens to me and 90% how I react to it. And so it is with you. … We are in charge of our attitudes."

~ ~ ~

We all know people who are incredibly positive. They have admirable dispositions and remain upbeat and buoyant no matter what transpires around them. Their greater problem is their inability to release management and control and to be authentic. Therefore, overly positive people have an inner desire to be more

> *Overly positive people have an inner desire to be more honest about their need to heal as much as someone who is always pessimistic.*

honest about their need to heal as much as someone who is

always pessimistic. Unfortunately, fear or other issues might prevent or delay their progress.

Todd was a very successful businessman when he came for his first session. Although he believed in God and was seeking a stronger connection, his unsubstantial spiritual relationship was working well enough for him at the time. He was not willing to give up control in his own life, which he felt was fine just the way it was. He could not imagine living his life any other way, and could see no reason to change. He had determined to keep his positive façade in place and to protect and manage his own life so all outcomes would be as good as possible. He had an extreme control issue even though it manifested in an overly positive way. During his session, guidance told him he was, "Nauseatingly optimistic." He and D'Ann had a good laugh.

Because Todd was so outstanding in his ability to manage his feelings, he was rarely able to address his own issues and he felt no need to verbally admit or emotionally give in to anything unpleasant. He was barely aware of a less positive, weaker, and more vulnerable inner self. He declined the opportunity to release his ego and *surrender*[42] his life to God.

For weeks after his session, Todd continued to mull over the idea of surrendering. He decided

---

[42] ***surrender:*** to release three-dimensional ego processes, functioning, allegiance, identity, and resulting outcomes in order to expedite empowerment

to review his extensive and lengthy spiritual history to glean insights. He concluded he was ready to take a major step forward.

When he returned for his second appointment, he willingly surrendered his life to God. As a result of this empowering decision, internal and external components of his life opened and rearranged. This began a lengthy healing process as well as the release of emotional disturbances due to buried feelings.

Todd is still predominantly optimistic and positive but is now much more in touch with his own emotions and those of others. He responds more sensitively and appropriately. Having begun to integrate Source energies, he receives guidance. He is a revised and advanced model of the man he was. He felt led to study a healing modality and feels incredibly blessed and privileged to now assist others with their spiritual growth. He is more authentically able to walk his talk.

To date, Todd has been the only client who initially refused to surrender his life to God and yet returned for more sessions. His soul was ready to heal, although it took additional supportive efforts and synchronicities for him to relax, open up, and let go of his ego management techniques. His brave decision enhanced his life in unimaginable ways.

~ ~ ~

Attitudes affect not only people but also animals and inanimate objects.

Craig had recently purchased hearing aids. He was angry about getting old and resented the cost, nuisance, and need to rely on two small pieces of equipment stuck into his ears for the rest of his life.

Craig often took an afternoon nap and would place his hearing aids on a nearby table. One day when he awoke from his rest, he could find only one hearing aid. He searched everywhere. Later that day, he noticed some odd pieces of something on the floor in another room. He was stunned then furious to discover his dog had tried to eat his hearing aid.

He paid for a replacement and felt even more resentful of his situation. Those little things kept getting lost. In a motel, one seemed to disappear while he was walking between the registration desk and his room. After searching for over thirty minutes, he found it in a fold of his coat. Another time, he drove forty-five minutes back to a store where he thought they might have fallen out, but they were not in the store. Days later, he examined his car for the fourth time and found them wedged near his seat.

Craig's frustration was mounting. Finally his wife, Jane, suggested that his attitude might be pushing the hearing aids away. He initially thought the idea was ridiculous, but they talked at length about his whole physical and emotional situation. Within a few days, Craig decided to change his viewpoint and be grateful that such instruments could assist his hearing and interaction with people.

Since his attitude adjustment a few years ago, there have only been a few occasions when he has briefly misplaced them. The pattern change was immediately obvious to both Craig and Jane.

3: VIBRATIONS

Physicists say all life is moving, always gaining or losing, growing or shrinking. Everything that appears solid, such as a wooden table or car engine, contains molecules with vibrating energy and vast amounts of space. All creation has a vibrational frequency that can be measured scientifically. In humans, the approximate range is 40 to 70 MHz with healthy bodies vibrating in the 60 to 70 MHz range, and death beginning when the frequency drops to 25 MHz.[*] The numbers are not constant but fluctuate in response to external and internal influences.

Energies are in every cell of our bodies, and various cells in various organs have various frequencies. A knee vibrates at a different rate than a liver, for example. Physical challenges, injuries, or inherited conditions cause lower vibrations than in healthier areas of the body. Psychological, emotional, and life issue challenges also cause low vibrations, and material objects are vibrationally dense and slow relative to our souls.

> *Developing empowerment is a process of raising our energetic vibrations.*

---

[*] "Vibrational Frequency List," Just a List, http://justalist.blogspot.in/2008/03/vibrational-frequency-list.html (accessed July 30, 2014).

The vibrational rate within each person is similar to scholastic test scores that average out at the end of a semester. We are the sum of our frequencies divided by the number of parts. The average is automatically raised each time a low frequency is removed or a high frequency is added. We can drop a low vibration by releasing disturbed emotions, healing an issue, finally making an important life decision, forgiving someone, or generating some other thought or action that proactively addresses our everyday hindrances. We can add higher frequencies by improving the quality and freshness of our food intake, wearing lighter and more energetically congruent colors, listening to uplifting music, using healing tools that emit frequencies, such as quartz crystals and therapeutic oils, and in many other ways. This text focuses on eliminating low vibrations to facilitate spiritual development.

Unlike quantitative test averages that linger throughout a course or semester, however, the actual numerical value of our vibrational rate is irrelevant except as a general indicator of directionality. As energetic and spiritual beings, we seek the highest vibrational rate we can attain in order to access, be available to, and activate our soul attributes. The higher we vibrate, the greater our spiritual awareness and the more intuitively awake, alive, and energetically sensitive and proficient we become. We need only an overall understanding of vibrations and how to raise them to effectively target spiritual growth. Removing low vibrations efficiently and powerfully promotes our personal as well as humanity's evolution. Developing empowerment is a process of raising our energetic vibrations.

ॐ Our vibrational rate ascends in response to energetic uplifts, but these do not occur solely as a result of learning. We need to do more for ourselves than *merely know* spiritual concepts. Everything in our life is processed from our limited consciousness, and we have the responsibility to take initiative to learn, but that is only the first step. We must also act. Consider, for example, that anyone can read about how to climb a mountain, but actually climbing it is an entirely different matter.

Except for meditation, seekers have typically addressed spiritual growth almost exclusively from outside sources. Reading books, attending lectures, classes, and retreats, and having intuitive readings are standard activities. Some people are called to follow a spiritual guru. Others relentlessly attend workshops, pursuing a more fulfilling life at seminars and conferences. They believe if they could only learn what to do, their lives would improve.

Although we need external resources to assist our development, *living our t/Truths* benefits our life most powerfully. While we readily acknowledge the results and advantages of personal experience, we often settle for mere learning, without application. Even though there are great Truths to learn, rarely has this approach been spiritually effective enough. Too frequently, we, and even long-time spiritual seekers, leave out the dedication and effort to activate what we already know could improve our life. To truly learn, we need to remember the information, use our will power and self-discipline to practice recommended techniques, and apply what we know. This learning process has been the historic, slow, and deliberate method for humankind, and it requires commitment and effort to accomplish our goals. Fortunately, Source is revealing newer, more powerful, and easier ways to spiritual leaders to assist our soul development and enhance our personal lives.

> *E/go can justify almost any action and any lack of action.*

We might think we have good reasons for not utilizing life-changing ideas. Some people even delude themselves into thinking that they are either exempt from the need to do so or that they have already accomplished their spiritual goal. All of this sidestepping is nothing more than ego processing. E/go can justify almost any action and any lack of action.

Head knowledge without individual practice and experience has severe shortcomings. The need for practical application is essential for spiritual growth, which is less about learning and more about

> *To derive intended benefits, we need to apply Truths and learn through experience.*

utilizing. To derive intended benefits, we need to apply Truths and learn through experience. Experiencing something adds a fuller and deeper integration of a skill or concept. This is because we rarely forget experiences, and we incorporate what we learn at a deeper than factual level.

Once we understand that we are already empowered at our core and are willing to accept responsibility for and make energetic changes in our life to promote spiritual

> *Once we understand that we are already empowered at our core... we will shift from an outer learning to an inner spiritual focus.*

growth, we will shift from an outer learning to an inner spiritual focus. The need for self-discipline will diminish. As we address and remove our energetic barricades, we will raise our vibrational rate. We will, no doubt, continue to read, learn, and seek assistance, but we will also become more discerning of what information and experiences energetically attract us, and which are timely and appropriate to boost our development.

4: RESONATOR

Even though souls once, long ago, chose to live in the

physical world, thinking they would "separate" from Source, the connection was never severed and divine love continues to kindle inside us. This love is Source energy. It is our Source Light. More than just a component of Source, Source Light is the very *essence* of Source, the very essence of God.

The physical headquarters for Source energy is the solar plexus. Located in the stomach area, it's about one and a half inches above the navel. As the primary location of our Source Light, this contains all our empowered attributes. It is our divine ally, our idling spiritual engine.

One facet of this core functions by continuously scanning, receiving, and responding to external input. It reads energy from outside and offers an inner response, reaction, insight, or guidance. We refer to this operating component as the *resonator*,[43] which is a continuously functioning component of our Source-based Ego. Operating similar to a metal detector that generates a more obvious signal when near a metal object, the resonator responds more strongly in the presence of more crucial energetic input.

Gut Instincts

Most people have had an occasional, spontaneous gut instinct. When this rare flash of inspiration happens, it is significant and the timing is ideal. The signal is telling us what we need at the critical moment when we need to know it. The input is strong enough that we can't help but hear and then, hopefully, follow its direction. In retrospect, we find that the guidance was accurate and beneficial even if it seemed illogical or mysterious at the time.

Sometimes this guidance is received unconsciously, and we

---

[43] *resonator:* an internal energy detector that alerts us to timely and/or critical messages that originate beyond our conscious scope

are unaware that our action is driven by something more powerful than our own thoughts.

Amanda has always lived with financial strain. The bulk of her discretionary money came from her yearly tax refund. One year, she decided to take this surplus and buy shares in an electronic technology company because the stock was growing substantially. Without consulting anyone and not seeking intuitive guidance, she invested $1,000.

She is very close to her only sibling, Wendy, and they talk a few times each week. Several years after her purchase, Wendy mentioned to Amanda that she was thinking about transferring some of her investments in order to receive a higher interest rate. Amanda said she would recommend a company that had performed very well and she would call Wendy back with the information. Normally, Amanda would have called back that day with the company's phone number, but she didn't.

The two sisters continued to talk regularly on the phone. Amanda did not bring up the subject, and Wendy decided she was in no rush, so she didn't ask for it.

Months later, curiously out of the blue, Amanda casually mentioned that she had the company name and phone number for Wendy's investment. As soon as they hung up, Wendy phoned the stockbroker. When she asked about the stock, he said, "It's really interesting that you should call right now. We were just sitting here talking about that specific company, and we think it peaked yesterday." Wendy asked what he meant by "peaked." He said that it had reached its apex of value, not for this week or this month, but permanently.

Wendy thanked him, hung up, immediately called Amanda, and relayed the conversation. As a result, Amanda promptly called and placed an order for sale of the stock. That day was, in fact, the beginning of the steep decline for technology companies.

Amanda received a payment that was many times the cost of her original investment. She had not consciously heard guidance to call Wendy that day, and she had not been tracking or even suspected what was happening in the financial market. Rather, she intuitively responded to an inner nudging from the resonator and received the largest financial windfall she had ever experienced.

Urgent Messages

Initially, when some danger is imminent, the resonator preempts our standard *ego mechanics*.[44] Our thoughts are interrupted with an urgent message that alerts us to a critical outcome that could be averted if we immediately change our behavior or action.

One morning, while Kevin was backing out of his garage, he unexpectedly heard an internal command to "Stop!" He put his foot on his brakes and looked in the rear view mirror. He

---

[44] *ego mechanics:* thought processes that create disturbing emotions, defy spiritual growth, and perpetuate spiritual immaturity

saw nothing unusual, so he continued to back up. He again heard, "Stop!" He did so, and, after checking the mirror and seeing nothing out of the ordinary, he took the car out of gear and got out to see what might be wrong. Two little children, not visible in his mirror, were sitting and playing in his driveway within a few feet of the car. He was deeply shaken, appalled by what could have happened, and incredibly relieved.

Kevin is an ordinary man in that he is not seeking, receiving, or working with spiritual principles in his life. This experience was unprecedented and monumentally critical. He will feel forever grateful for the guidance he received that day.

~ ~ ~

Communication from the resonator does not constantly override or intrude on our thoughts. Over time, as we become more fluent with resonator messages, the transmitted information seems to become increasingly available. Should you ever be in conflict between what your head tells you and the message you receive from the resonator, trust your gut. It will never lead you

> *If we do not know about or are consciously unaware of healing occasions, we do not look for them, cooperate with them, or benefit from them.*

astray. Even if the results are not what you think they would or should be, there is a larger purpose behind what is happening.

The resonator continues to serve us throughout life, and it

can be a life saving mechanism. However, if we only allow it to override our standard *ego input* [45]without developing more subtle guidance recognition awareness, we reinforce ego input as our *default method of operating*[46] and will continue to rarely see other options than our usual choices. If we do not know about or are consciously unaware of healing occasions, we do not look for them, cooperate with them, or benefit from them. Fortunately, we have an alternative, covered in detail later on in the book.

5: CONGRUENCY

When ego withdrew our conscious connection from Source, we were cast into an *incongruent*[47] state. Now, as we evolve, it is up to us to restore the hidden connection and develop our inherent capacity to more consciously receive Source's subtle messages. We can do this in concert with the resonator.

But we must do more than simply depend on the resonator. We need to raise our vibrational rate and take advantage of our countless opportunities to become more energetically and spiritually *congruent*[48] with Source.

To stimulate and strengthen the pathway to Source, we can

---

[45] *ego input:* consciously processed, unenlightened messages that are based solely on what we've learned from our past three-dimensional experiences

[46] *default method of operating, default system, default response(s), default executive system:* uniquely developed, well-practiced, automatically triggered, three-dimensional coping strategies and self-management techniques that we formed through karmic issues and present life emotions and experiences, in order to survive life's stresses and challenges

[47] *incongruent or incongruency*: portions of inner emotions, thoughts, and functioning that significantly differ from each other and require ego management to handle

[48] *congruent or congruency:* a state of mental, emotional, physical, and spiritual integration in which all facets of our functioning align with Source Truths

send our thoughts and questions to the solar plexus, seeking a response, then sit quietly in meditation or contemplative

The more we desire, seek, and work with guidance we receive from the resonator, the more we will receive obvious, powerful, and frequent guidance.

thought to learn what messages Source sends to us. The more we desire, seek, and work with the guidance we receive from the resonator, the more we will receive obvious, powerful, and frequent guidance.

~ ~ ~

Becoming spiritually and internally congruent is a process of clearing out old programmed energies. Similar to spring-cleaning, we can look at what is there and proceed with decisions and actions that eliminate discordant patterns and blocks. A necessary stage of personal development requires that we recognize, express, and release emotions that we have allowed to accumulate as a byproduct of merely managing life.

A necessary stage of personal development requires that we recognize, express, and release emotions that we have allowed to accumulate as a byproduct of merely managing life.

ॐ As we accept how we truly feel in a situation, we need to include input from the resonator as a component of our reasoning and response. Most of us need to release our strong opinions and feelings and adopt wiser, more healing ways. These upgraded behaviors allow energetic clearing, but the changes will likely cause confusing and emotionally uncomfortable situations to arise. We might find that initial efforts at congruency are discouraging or difficult. They might appear to be unproductive. However, with practice, our developing skills will advance and produce obvious and rewarding results. We will know ourselves more fully and discover formerly unrecognized spiritual blessings. As we remove blocks from our energy fields, we become more effectively integrated with Source.

Mary managed a department in a growing company. The dominating focus of business prevented serious or lengthy personal conversations. When a coworker would ask Mary how she was, she would always say, "Fine," or another similar short response.

At the beginning of a session, D'Ann asked Mary how she was doing. She said, "Fine." A few minutes later, Mary admitted she had had a migraine headache for two days. When D'Ann questioned her earlier response, Mary said, "Well, no one wants to know how I really feel," thus admitting that she had chosen to hide her true feelings.

Mary soon learned there were healthier ways to become more congruent to her reality without acting, and that she could speak truthfully without sounding like she was complaining or being negative. She was encouraged to practice phrases that were more honest, such as: "Not as good as I'd like to be," "I'll be better tomorrow," "Only okay. Thanks for asking," "This is not a good time for me right now," or "I have a headache today."

When Mary attempted to verbalize the first phrase, she found that she literally could not speak. Then she burst out laughing. She realized how much she had programmed herself to ignore her physical reality. As she practiced and applied her t/Truth in everyday life, this block cleared very quickly. She began to be more congruent with herself.

Expressing our t/Truth supports empowerment. Living this way promotes clearing and merging of our ego identity with the wholeness of our

> *Expressing our t/Truth supports empowerment.*

being. Congruency allows us to live in harmony with Source and to receive and understand guidance.

6: WHITE LIGHT

We are all aware of the value we place on light. It makes darkness manageable, brightens a gloomy room, helps us read, and illuminates our path. We say: "The light just went on," when we grasp an idea; "You light up my life," when we feel happier; and, "Shine some light on this for me," when we seek further understanding.

Using *White Light*[49] is one of the most basic spiritual techniques to know and develop. It is a powerful protection, comfort, and blessing that can be used anytime, anywhere, by anyone, and around anything, living or inanimate. No equipment is needed, and its use can be repeated whenever desired. Distance is irrelevant.

There is no single right way to work with White Light. It is

---

[49] *White Light:* an intentionally visualized, milky-white energy field placed around an object, life form, or person for protection, comfort, and blessing

generated from our thoughts, third eye, heart, or hand merely by intent. Using this substance is as simple as imagining, visualizing, or pantomiming milky White Light swirled, poured, or formed into an energy ball around the recipient. You need not be concerned about the technique because your intention, supported by physical action, carries and determines effectiveness. This process is effortlessly and immediately externally effective, but it does take several minutes to produce internal benefits.

Ideally, we will surround all of our loved ones, cars, homes, rooms, businesses, pets, concerns, causes, and anyone or anything else with White Light. Place a bubble of it in a doorway to coat everyone who walks through. Use it around an ambulance, the patient, driver, and medical technicians. Spread it around strangers, colleagues, clients, customers, and people nearby in public places. When someone is ill or in difficulty, use White Light around them. Use it in offices to improve the atmosphere.

ॐ There are no bulletproof vests in spiritual work, but White Light can do miraculous things. If a person is scripted to die that day in a plane crash, White Light will probably not prevent the accident or the death. However, the person's transition would be helped in some way. White Light is not a guarantee that everything will go well, that we'll always be happy, or that we'll never be injured. But its use will modify or benefit some aspect of the situation.

~ ~ ~

White Light Stories

The following eight stories illustrate the effects of using White Light in various circumstances. Each person noted an immediate benefit from this simple, yet powerful technique.

~ ~ ~

This White Light protection provided a logically impossible, miraculous outcome.

> Sally was driving the 45-mile per hour speed limit in the slow lane of a divided eight-lane highway. She was intuitively guided to change lanes about a block before the next traffic signal. This was easy to do because not many cars were on the road. There was no need for her to slow down before the light turned green.
>
> She felt a sudden and surreal sense of slow motion and threw White Light around her car. At the intersection, one car from the left and another from the right both ran the red light. They collided and actually sprang apart just as Sally drove through the miraculous opening between them. When she looked in her rear view mirror, there didn't appear to be room for her car to have fit through. It was unbelievable. Listening to guidance and using White Light prevented Sally from being involved in the accident.
>
> After calming down emotionally, she saw cosmic humor in how much angel work it must have taken to insure no one was seriously injured or killed.

~ ~ ~

God's omniscience and White Light worked together to spare a life.

> Brian had been able to hear guidance and use

White Light for many years. He worked in a town forty miles from his home, and when it was safe, set his cruise control for 72 miles per hour on the freeway.

As he was leaving the house to go to work one day, he noticed that he was instinctively placing White Light around himself and his car even though he had not consciously decided nor heard guidance to do so. This experience was unprecedented. He said aloud, "What's this about needing more White Light?" Not hearing any answer, he completed the process and forgot about it.

About thirty minutes later, he was in the middle lane of the freeway in heavy traffic but still driving his usual 72 miles per hour. As he crested a hill, he saw that the cars ahead were at a standstill. He could not stop in time. He would die if he stayed in his lane or moved right. His only option was the fast lane to his left. He quickly glanced in his side mirror and saw about five cars there. He also noticed a rare and unexpected paved shoulder. He veered left. As he did so, each driver in that left lane moved onto the shoulder and never even blew their horn, a surprising lack of reaction.

When Brian had safely returned to the middle lane, he remembered the White Light experience at his home that morning. He spoke his deepest gratefulness to God for sparing his life. God had known precisely where Brian's car, traveling at his usual 72 miles per hour, would be thirty minutes later. Had Brian chosen to drive 71 miles per hour, he would have been one-half mile shy of the crest of the hill where the traffic backlog would have been visible. At 73 miles per hour, he would have been one-half mile ahead of the potential accident. God had known even this critical difference. Although it took many hours to calm down, Brian knew he had received a miraculous intervention.

~ ~ ~

White Light can minimize emotional reactions to unpleasant experiences.

Hank chose to attend a music concert in a building where he used to be employed, and his position had ended painfully several years earlier. He knew that going there would bring up unpleasant memories, but felt willing to finally face them. Just after getting into his car to drive there, he swirled White Light around himself a few times.

When he arrived at his destination, he felt absolutely nothing. No pleasure, fear, emotional pain, or unhappiness. It was as though Hank was wrapped in the thickest emotional blanket he could imagine. He perceived accurately, could respond naturally, yet felt completely free of emotions. The evening was unique, successful, and memorable.

A person does not need to know about or believe in White Light to be helped by it.

> Sam swirled White Light around his wife the morning she was to go on trial in court for a family dispute with their daughter. She knew nothing about White Light, so was not looking for an extraordinary experience.
>
> She phoned Sam at the lunch break and expressed her delight and surprise to be so composed, unemotional, and clear-headed. She was impressed and perplexed. Sam did not tell her what he had done.

~ ~ ~

ॐ White Light can have far-reaching benefits that might be beyond our ability to realize.

> Brenda and her husband, Mike, had an unusual experience when they rented a car for an extended road trip. As soon as they returned home from the rental agency, Brenda tried to place, swirl, or throw White Light around the car, but her actions seemed blocked. Not knowing why or what else to do, she simply drew larger White Light circles around the car. The couple left town the next morning.
>
> Less than half an hour from home, a truck tire threw a stone that chipped the windshield. A few hours later, the portable electric cooler plugged into the cigarette lighter socket caused a fuse in the auto's electrical circuitry to blow and the couple needed to find an auto dealer to

replace it. They bought a new, smaller portable cooler that evening. The next morning in a motel, they were packing their suitcases when Brenda realized she had left her purse, which held all their cash and credit cards, in the breakfast room. Heart pounding, she ran back to their table. A female guest sitting at the next table told her she had found the purse, not opened it, and had turned it in to the front desk. The clerk returned it to Brenda who found that its entire contents were undisturbed.

While loading the car that same morning, Brenda discovered that they had left the driver's window open all night. They had many personal items inside, but everything was safe and dry. That evening in the next motel room before going to bed, Mike discovered he had left a brand new, electronic device in the first motel room. When he called and asked about it, the staff there was able to retrieve it and forward it to Mike.

About thirty-six hours after leaving home, this series of odd events ceased. Brenda thought that, perhaps, a previous renter had significantly altered the rental car's energy and it must have taken that long for the effects of that negative energy to wear off and the energy of the White Light to saturate the car. Only God knows what else would have happened without that effective protection.

~ ~ ~

The earth's elevating energies facilitate White Light's ease and potency. Also, as more and more people become aware of White Light, they are wrapping it around their loved ones, even without telling them. Thus it is now possible to overdose. If this happens, the effect is not serious, dangerous, or permanent.

> Gary and Cindy were on their way to the airport to catch a flight. Before leaving home, Cindy had placed White Light around them, their luggage, and the airplane. They both commented while driving how smoothly everything was going. The couple easily found a parking spot, and the shuttle came immediately. The general security line was short.
>
> Once they were seated on the plane, they noticed they were talking more slowly and felt as though they had taken strong tranquilizers. Cindy then realized they had been overdosed. She presumed their son, daughter, and her brother had also used White Light on them. The effects were laughable and more obvious than they had ever been, and they gradually dissipated a few hours later.

~ ~ ~

White Light works instantly and can be profoundly effective in an emergency situation.

> Vicki has a house on a busy street corner with a stop sign. She was in the backyard with her dog, Coco. The dog spotted a squirrel across the street in front of the house and started to chase after it.

Although Vicki couldn't see or hear a car, she intuitively knew one was coming and that it would hit Coco if the dog were to dart into the street. After ineffectively screaming the dog's name three times and just as Coco was bolting across the sidewalk toward the street, Vicki threw White Light around the dog. Coco not only instantly stopped running, she actually sat down, and turned her head around to look at Vicki, just as the car came to a stop at the intersection.

~ ~ ~

If loud noises, thunder, or fireworks distress a pet, swirl White Light around him or her a few times. Because time is needed for a body to internally absorb the frequencies, ten to fifteen minutes might elapse before this treatment becomes effective, but it lasts for a few hours.

Marsha was in Hawaii on New Year's Eve. The tradition there is for families to ignite fireworks at midnight. Her hosts had a large dog that would typically shake intensely from the noise.

Marsha placed White Light around the dog about 10:00 that evening. He was completely unaffected by the celebration two hours later. The hosts were impressed and grateful.

Experiment with White Light anytime you think of it. You might see immediate results, or you might never be aware of the difference it makes, but using it always generates a spiritual and energetic benefit for the recipient.

CHAPTER 2:
SOUL SCRIPTS

Energy from past lives affects our current life. Some of the energy that our souls carry forward from past lives is known as *dharma*,[50] and some is called *karma*.[51]

Dharma is rewarding past life energies that manifest as abundant blessings that are often obvious and present as talents, gifts, and favorable qualities and situations. Dharma energy is apparent, unencumbered, readily available, and comes to us with no mandates to correct or clear any old or outstanding soul issues.

The primary exception to working with these assets occurs when a beneficial dharma resource is entangled with a detrimental karmic issue that would cause it to misfire and not produce satisfaction and ease. An example of this is the soul attribute of a desire to be generous. When this dharma blessing incarnates entwined with a karmic issue such as selflessness, it manifests as excessive, sacrificial, and perhaps inappropriate generosity. The giver is then taken advantage of and unappreciated by those he or she helps. The conflicting energy of this issue will continue until it is cleared. After clearing, fortunately, the person will gradually become aware of previously unnoticed options and gain the flexibility to choose to give or not, have freedom and ease to select when, to whom, and how much to give, and thus receive more appreciation for or feel better about his or her efforts.

---

[50] *dharma:* personal blessings, advantages, qualities, and traits that manifest from past life attainments

[51] *karma:* unreleased and unresolved issues and emotions from past lifetimes

Karma, in contrast, is our unfortunate, unfinished business that generally comes from our previous lifetimes on earth, but it might also stem from our experiences elsewhere in some other life form on a different planet or dimension. Additional energetic emotional debris also collects from experiences in this present lifetime. Because energies are eternal, unless we remove this debris while we are still living now, they will remain with our soul after our death and become karma for us to clear in some future lifetime.

Karma is energetically charged and programmed into our body. It is typically the theme of our soul's life script, which defines our primary purpose for being born into this incarnation, and becomes the first order of healing business for us to address on earth.

Therefore, the major focus of this book is to help us reinterpret and clear our karma and present life collection of emotional debris created by our mandated karmic experiences, because they are the source of our distressful and resistant challenges. We will learn and understand how past lives shape present lives, how energy is the spiritual design behind everyday experiences, and how using healing techniques described in later chapters will directly benefit present life issues, relationships, qualities, outcomes, and happiness.

~ ~ ~

The effects of karma are known as *issues* or *life issues*.[52] We usually interpret these issues as being unwanted and negative.

In *Life's Healing Setups* and my work with clients, I refrain from using the words "negative" and "positive" as much as possible because of their dualistic connotations. I've come to

---

[52] *issue(s) or life issues:* karmically caused recurring challenges that trigger illogically harsh emotions and elude permanent resolution

realize that situations we initially view as having a downside are really opportunities for us to learn uplifting lessons that will help our soul evolve and advance on its spiritual path. It all depends on how we look at our issues.

Because karma originated in our past lives and is the cause of issues in our current life, it might seem logical to look into the past first. But I've found that's not the case. Most people, until becoming familiar with their past lives, see only the present, especially if the present is filled with trouble and fear. Indeed, many people don't even believe in past lives or the concept of reincarnation. Therefore, I've found that the impetus to seek and explore the cause begins with a focus on the effect, that is, the issues that are glaringly staring us in the face every day.

So we begin this chapter by examining life issues first in the next few pages, then delve into their karmic causes after that. The third section in this chapter will help us understand reincarnation as a necessary event that enables us to remove karma. The fourth section defines scripted roles

> *Karmic life issues manifest primarily in three ways: as repeating challenges, as illogical or strongly felt emotions, and/or as uniquely predictable decisions and reactions.*

that people play in our current life and the roles those same souls played in past lives. We will go on from there to see how we are all helping each other reduce karma and resolve issues—even when it seems that we are not. We will see how much greater understanding we acquire when we look beyond the small cubicle of issues in this lifetime, and view those issues from the broader historical perspective of many lifetimes.

7: LIFE ISSUES

Karmic life issues manifest primarily in three ways: as repeating challenges, as illogical or strongly felt emotions, and/or as uniquely predictable decisions and reactions.

Repeating challenges are difficult situations with similar themes that arise in diverse settings, locations, and timings, and involve a variety of participants. The actors might change, but the same issues are provoked. A person rarely understands why these conflicts keep happening, what they mean, or how to improve or eliminate them.

Illogical or strongly felt emotions arise from perplexing, confusing, and intense emotional reactions that cause recognizable overreactions. When a person does all that he or she can to rise above and manage the inner emotional chaos, life seems to work out better.

Uniquely predictable decisions and reactions stem from perspectives, interpretations, and replies to personal situations that are based on soul-chosen, karmically scripted roles. Each person has dealt with these certain issues many times throughout his or her life, and has learned a somewhat efficient coping strategy. When faced with the next round of strife, this default method of operating takes over and carries the person through the event. In this state, there appears to be no way to minimize or prevent these situations from randomly occurring.

ॐ Life issues elicit recurring challenges in order to inform us of their energetic presence inside us, and provide stimulation and opportunity for energy liberation. They establish our unique viewpoint and

> *Life issues elicit recurring challenges in order to inform us of their energetic presence inside us, and provide stimulation and opportunity for energy liberation.*

interpretation of experiences, which promote default responses, more challenges, and emotional turbulence. Our soul syllabus, however, prevents awareness of additional and more effective response options, and we continue to make decisions that align with and reinforce our issues. For example, a person who lives in fear of poverty will make decisions that focus excessively on money. In spite of this compulsion, the fear will remain and perpetuate the pattern even if the person becomes wealthy. This is why clearing our karmic life issues is our first order of spiritual business.

Identifying Specific Issues

Personalities are formed by many factors and influences, but the foundation is issue-based.

> ➢ When you dislike someone or a person says or does something that triggers a strong mental and

> *Your "messenger" has displayed your own issues in the same, or the exact opposite, way that you are working on them.*

emotional response within you, make a list of every behavior he or she exhibits that annoys you. Be as thorough and honest as possible.

When completed, you will see that your "messenger" has displayed your own issues in the same, or the exact opposite, way that you are working on them. For example, if you feel the "culprit" is always self-centered, your issue is either that you are also too self-absorbed, or too selfless. This written activity can be sobering, but you will finally see in black and white what issues have been relatively invisible up to that point in your life.

Likewise, blaming others is a sign that something internal is happening that *you* need to recognize and release because it is holding you back from evolving. Most often, this reaction stems from your *judgment*[53] or *expectations*[54] of the other person.

> When you are tempted to blame others, look within yourself for the same traits you see in other people.

> Besides self-assessment, you can ask someone you trust for input and feedback about your issues.

What you learn through these practices could be enlightening and life changing. Noticing what disturbs you will help reveal your life challenges. Identifying your issues gets easier with education and practice.

> *Noticing what disturbs you will help reveal your life challenges. Identifying your issues gets easier with education and practice.*

~ ~ ~

---

[53] *judgment:* the act or practice of screening life through a filter that depicts all events, circumstances, and issues as good/bad, right/wrong, black/white

[54] *expectations:* deeming that the actions, responses, or results of someone or something should conform to our self-defined interpretation of rightness or appropriateness

Our life issues manifest in one of the four positions represented by a flipped coin that lands heads up, tails up, wobbles, or stands securely on its edge. The coin's position for each issue we bring into our present life coincides with our soul's past life experiences, our karmic needs, and the best challenging actions by each role-playing soul in our life script.

When the coin is *heads up,* the energies in the present life are *in the same arrangement* as they were in a prior life. For example, an extrovert in an earlier life is an extrovert again; someone who couldn't trust others in a previous life continues to distrust.

When the coin is *tails up,* the issue energies in the present life are *in the exact opposite position* as they were in a prior life. A former extrovert is now an introvert; someone who couldn't trust before is excessively trusting or gullible.

When the coin *wobbles,* the *issue energies vacillate.* Sometimes a person is the life of the party and at other times a wallflower; another person is sometimes trusting and sometimes leery. These people know they fluctuate but can neither predict, prevent, nor change their behavior.

When the coin is *standing firmly on its side,* the *issue energies pull in contrary directions simultaneously.* This pattern defies logic, which says that a person can't be extroverted and introverted at the same time, or trusting while also being suspicious. Yet this arrangement does exist and can manifest with any issue.

People who have several issues with the dualistic, coin-firmly-on-its-side position are typically in long-term counseling or seek help early in life. They need professional assistance to understand and resolve their significant confusion. Because there is a reason—a cause to this effect—in their karmic experiences, past life therapy is a benefit for nearly everyone and can be especially helpful, revealing, and healing in these seemingly illogical cases.

~ ~ ~

The following case shows the "tails up" karmic position for a person who was convicted for certain crimes in this life that he condemned others for in a previous life.

> Dwight has a sex addiction and criminal record as a peeping tom. In a previous life in the 1800s, he was a fire-and-brimstone preacher in the southern United States. As a fundamentalist, he taught parents to take complete authority and control over their children's lives, not to "spare the rod and spoil the child." He condemned sin and would go on verbal tirades against excesses of the flesh.

> After his first session, he was addiction free for the thirty-nine days before his second appointment. The karmic clearing removed the energies his soul had brought into his current life from that specific past lifetime and allowed him to reduce his sexual thoughts and urges. During those addiction-free days, he did not seem to need extra will power to override his long-term sexual pattern. His previous degree of self-control was able to override the lower level impulses. He had never experienced such relief before in his adult life.

> When he came for a second session, a different past life focused on the related but separate

issue of excessive control. Yet he did not book
any additional appointments.

After the first session, Dwight was able to obviously see the
profound change in his life from the removal of the first and
most powerful layer of karmic energies involved with his sexual
addiction. This made it possible for the next layer of control to
become available to be addressed and cleared in the second
session. The order in which these issues emerged during his
therapy session demonstrates that a person's Higher Self
determines what issue is covered in each session. This is the
process of incremental karmic clearing that literally can
transform a present life. Had Dwight been willing to continue
energy therapy, he would have noticed regular, significant
healing.

There could be many possible reasons for his decision not to
return for a third session, but it was likely because there was at
least one more significant past life still in his system waiting to
be cleared that was triggering his present addiction. Very
possibly, he simply wasn't yet ready to clear the karmic effects
of that life. Nevertheless, the information he learned and the new
awareness of his past life offers Dwight a needed opportunity to
potentially heal his judgment and control issues—when he is
ready.

Life Script Variations

ॐ Many possible script variations are present within any
one life. A soul might desire to completely address and release a
significant issue or issues within a single life. Or the soul might
select to clear a smaller or variable part of a particular major
issue. This latter example often occurs if the soul has gone back
and forth, playing a "heads up" position and a "tails up" position
in many lifetimes or has had experiences with the coins in all
four positions. Those scenarios over many lifetimes tend to make

it difficult for a soul to clear its issues, so selecting a smaller, more specific part of the larger issue can provide a long-sought healing benefit. One small bit of progress can open the path for significant gain.

When addressing a specific issue to heal, a soul can select a variety of approaches. If the issue is miserliness, it could stem from a soul's history of being either excessively generous or stingy or resentful of giving help, love, time, energy, or money to others.

Using the idea of the coin being either heads up or tails up, some possible alterations of a life script for a soul who was a miser in a past life are:

- playing the role of miser again, or being overly generous again;

- incarnating into an impoverished life, or one of great wealth;

- living at the receiving end of stinginess, or the giving end of generosity.

With the coin wobbling, the person would sometimes give generously and sometimes hold onto help, love, time, energy, or money stingily even under similar circumstances.

And with the coin standing firmly on edge, the person might give generously while, at the same time, wishing that he were not so generous, or be a tightwad while simultaneously wishing to be more generous. Specific experiences could include:

- receiving a large inheritance, or struggling to earn a living;

- being careful with money, or making unwise

spending decisions;

- overspending and buying compulsively, or being greedy.

A miser could also face continuous financial insecurities and challenges, require financial rescuing for others or self, invest unwisely, or be taken advantage of or not equitably compensated by family, friends, or in business partnerships.

In addition to the issue of miserliness, some of this soul's challenges might also target other issues such as dependence, isolation, betrayal, responsibility, or fear. The breadth of the above list of possible issue variations demonstrates the intricate and delicate karmic balance that each soul so carefully plans before birth.

By becoming aware of a larger array of potential karmic possibilities, we can gain the wisdom to explore the depths of issues—about ourselves and others—and not jump to seemingly obvious conclusions based merely on "logical" three-dimensional perspectives.

8: KARMA

The *tenet of karma*[55] is traditionally known as: "An eye for an eye, and a tooth for a tooth;" "You reap what you sow;" "What goes around comes around;" and the Golden Rule, "Do unto others as you would have them do unto you." If we love or serve others, we will receive love or be served. If we attack and abuse, we will be attacked and abused.

Our soul knows our karmic issues when we are born and usually retains conscious past life memories into infanthood and

---

[55] *tenet of karma:* the principle of "cause and effect" that directly influences, molds, and restricts our present existence due to unreleased and unresolved past life energies

even the toddler stages of life. However, we become disadvantaged as we grow into our earthly environment and tend to forget our past lives. Yet, this knowledge continues to exist unconsciously and also as invisible emotionally charged energies that operate in the background, much like factory-installed software programming in a new computer. Physically, we can store this karmically programmed energy throughout our body, although it is primarily centered across the chest as a thin band about five inches above the waist.

Although we are very familiar with the effects of our programming, we are consciously unaware of how our life has been energetically designed. The simple reality is that our intangible energies function like a magnet that continuously attracts to us people, circumstances, and events that push the same *buttons.*[56] These recurring, all too familiar, intense, and illogical happenings appear as problems that are difficult, painful, and confusing. They appear to be undeserved, certainly unwanted, most often take us by surprise, and elicit an immediate, overly strong emotional and mental response. The best we can seem to do is muddle and manage our way through the episodes. However, managing our life issues generates more emotional reactions than we allow ourselves to release, and we

> *Our intangible energies function like a magnet that continuously attracts to us people, circumstances, and events that push the same buttons.*

---

[56] **button:** an energetically charged issue that is emotionally inflamed and easily provoked

energetically store the excess in *emotional trash bags*.[57] These trash bags reside mostly in the chest area and they accumulate in doses that raise the energetic ante.

Some people store their karmic emotional trash bags in other parts of the body. We do not consciously select emotional and energetic storage locations. Rather, the locations are automatically determined according to our soul script and other unique factors or criteria. These factors could include: genetics; the nature of the karma, especially if a previous life ended with physical violence or trauma which would tend to attract physical challenges to the area of the earlier fatal wound(s); weaknesses in our physical structure due to environmental issues, health challenges, injuries, or areas of the body with limited functionality.

Certain three-dimensional life characteristics or personality traits also influence where karmic energy is programmed and accrues. For example, anger is most often held in the liver. Suppression of inner t/Truth in favor of always saying politically correct responses might cause frequent sore throats, stiff necks, or other symptoms in the vocal cords, throat, neck, or even shoulders. Feeling fear might manifest as ulcers, poor digestion, or stomach issues.

~ ~ ~

Imagine the following scenario. Your boss assigns additional responsibilities that you don't want and have no time to do. Likely, you will decide it is not smart to tell him what you really think or to explode at him in anger or frustration. So you force yourself to rise above your natural reaction. If you are great at managing your emotions, you will bury your anger, perhaps

---

[57] *emotional trash bags:* the energetically charged emotional accumulation from the present life that is typically stored in the chest area with little or no apparent physical implications

mildly state your opinion, give a convincing performance of acceptance and cooperation, and resume your former activity. After the boss leaves, you might release some of your feelings by complaining, throwing papers, or some other subtler means of expression.

But no matter what you do, the situation probably generated more emotion within you than you released. Any excess unwanted emotion, not just anger, becomes *emotional debris*,[58] which you typically store in emotional trash bags, and remains energized and active even when you bury it. This becomes *energetic debris*.[59] The next time a situation triggers the same response, more unwanted emotions will rise to the surface. Every time a person, situation, or event pushes your button and you generate more negative energies that you don't release, you raise the ante and intensify the next emotional drama.

> *If you don't understand how energetic setups work and don't proactively release and heal your stockpiled emotions, these energies become more and more concentrated and toxic with each additional deposit.*

If you don't understand how energetic setups work and don't proactively release and heal your stockpiled emotions, these energies become more and more concentrated and toxic with

---

[58] *emotional debris:* a collection of unreleased, unresolved emotions from present life experiences accrued from merely managing challenges and minimizing, avoiding, or denying reactive feelings; these might be stowed anywhere in the physical body and create symptoms or health challenges

[59] *energetic debris:* any undesired, unreleased, and unresolved energies in our system; these can be karmic or emotional, but might also include other "low energies" such as environmental residue and strongly persistent, limiting mental filters that manifest as three-dimensional thoughts, habits, beliefs, judgments, and so on

each additional deposit.

Every time a challenging incident triggers our emotions, it provides incentive for us to release inflamed emotions and remove some of the stored toxic energies. Through ego eyes, these difficulties appear as perplexing, random, undeserved hardships with no apparent permanent solution.

ॐ With greater vision and understanding, however, our soul knows differently. If we are open to our feelings, we know we have something that needs to be cleared

> *We need to operate under the tenet of karma only until we incrementally and energetically release its mandates.*

from our operating system, and that we need to operate under the tenet of karma only until we incrementally and energetically release its mandates.

The process that creates karma involves accumulating emotional debris lifetime after lifetime until we neutralize it. Historically, due to lack of understanding about how karma works on earth, we have required several or many lifetimes to remove it, but, in actuality, we can create potential future karma and clear both it and soul-chosen karma in the same lifetime.

Before-Birth Decisions

Before incarnating into a given lifetime, each soul meets with a group of divine *beings*[60] who help us plan our karmic life script,

> *Because we create karma in groups, we tend to reincarnate as groups to resolve our collective and individual issues.*

---

[60] *beings:* advanced spiritual entities or souls, not presently incarnated on earth, who promote divine intervention and/or assistance for humanity

and show us the major social issues and significant personal and world events that are likely to happen on earth during our upcoming life. We select our country, ethnicity, environment, gender, genetics, and religion. We determine the souls who will be in our birth family and, in some cases, our adoptive family. We also select the souls who will be our family members when we are an adult. The souls of most of these people have been with us in former lives, and we nearly always have unfinished business with them. Because we create karma in groups, we tend to reincarnate as groups to resolve our collective and individual issues.

After selecting the souls who will star in our life dramas, we visit our buffet table of karma where energetic leftovers from all of our prior lifetimes are stored. We choose our present life issues and *roles*[61] according to our uncompleted past life experiences with each family member, our own unfinished emotional business, and unique agendas we need to address for our *soul growth*.[62]

> *Besides karma, our life script contains many factors.*

Besides karma, our life script contains many factors. As an energetic template or design of our soul's selected issues, it functions like a checklist of things to heal and accomplish in an upcoming life.

ॐ Scripted possibilities that assist in our soul development are:

---

[61] *roles:* soul-scripted behavior

[62] *soul growth:* the process of healing, evolving, and blossoming into our potential divine empowerment

- lessons we have yet to learn;

- qualities we are to cultivate, such as kindness or responsibility;

- mistakes we need to rectify;

- new specific experiences for us to attain, such as traveling or higher education;

- abilities and talents we are to develop;

- service to humanity we are to perform through invention, research, inspiration, or countless other ways; and,

- most especially at this transformational time, our soul evolution.

Our first spiritual priority is to neutralize and clear karma that has determined our challenging present life issues, roles, and relationships. Each individual determines, at the soul level, what is on the remainder of their script and how most appropriately to address this syllabus.

God approves each soul-scripted plan, and each soul gives this agenda to the beings who were involved

> *Our first spiritual priority is to neutralize and clear karma.*

in its development who see that it is filed in the Hall of Records, a different area near where the Akashic Records are stored. The final karmic script first addresses the primary soul business of clearing karma. To accomplish this goal, the script programs our uniquely needed challenges, and limits or prevents us from creating all that might seem like a full, rich, or satisfying life that we might consciously desire, according to the world's physical standards.

Eventually, we learn that until our soul clears these initial requirements of this life, the energetic mandates of karma block us from accomplishing other, more rewarding soul goals on earth. Fortunately, as we heal karma, we gradually become aware of more options, more ease, and our greater capability to develop more rewarding life potentials.

ॐ Karma influences and shapes the quality and scope of our activities, agendas, abilities, and emotions. This shape is metaphorically like a mold for gelatin, and our present life is the gel. If we attempt to change and improve our life while we are still in the mold, it's no wonder that personal growth is so slow, resistant, and difficult. To launch significant life improvement, we need to set ourselves free from the karmic mold. But even when we accomplish that, we find that our gel is still in the same shape as it has been, which means that our present life issues remain. Fortunately, however, the restrictions of the preset mold will no longer thwart our further attempts to heal. We will then notice that the previously rigid gel softens so that shifts, changes, and improvements come more easily, and that significant transformation is possible.

Spiritual Healing Setups

Even though issues arrive with us at birth, we usually become more aware of and disturbed by their presence as we grow older. Karmic spiritual setups are situations that occur with unique timing to bring issues to our attention as needed, to enable us to release and heal the charged emotions. These are opportunities we need to emotionally provoke us into action. If we fail to act or to "learn our lesson," we up the ante and continue the game. Because the accumulating ante intensifies with each healing opportunity, life's dramas grow into melodramas.

ॐ Life provides many opportunities for us to heal. They present themselves as frequent, repeating quandaries that we do not seem able to prevent. When a person, circumstance, or event causes us to feel strong or severe agitation, that's a sign that an issue is emerging to be released or a major life lesson is being presented. We are familiar with the resulting disturbed emotions because they have often erupted before. Reinterpreting our assessment of what is transpiring, and releasing our emotions in a safe, timely, and appropriate way will facilitate our healing.

> *When a person, circumstance, or event causes us to feel strong or severe agitation, that's a sign that an issue is emerging to be released or a major life lesson is being presented.*

ॐ These spiritual setups have three significant variables: their rate of recurrence, intensity, and duration. An issue generally manifests more often than we would like, is painfully obvious, and lasts longer than we think it should. While experiencing a spiritual setup, it seems as though we have little true control nor helpful alternatives. But that's not true. We have the power to reinterpret these experiences, address our responses with spiritual understandings, clear our emotions, and exercise our God-given *free will*.[63]

Karma and Free Will

It is rather common, when we first learn about how karma works, to blame ourselves for making soul decisions that affect our life so harshly. True, we are responsible, but we are not to

---

[63] *free will:* the ability to make choices in life, which expands as we remove karma and address our soul script

blame. The issues that our soul selects before birth appear to be easily fixable when we are in that disembodied state, but they can be hard to accomplish when we are actually alive in our body, living within the karmic mold of limitation. Our limited conscious understandings don't provide much to work with or draw on when tough times happen in the physical world and we experience frustrations in key areas of our life.

ॐ We are only able to see, process, and connect with potentials in our life that are not hidden by *karmic restrictions, barriers,* or *energy blocks.*[64] By reducing access to additional resources that would facilitate a more rewarding and satisfying life, these soul mandates inhibit full expression of our free will and assist us in staying on track, according to our soul script, to heal.

The story below tells a past life lesson and consequence, which is still occurring, that has resisted all conventional efforts to resolve. Because the issue is karmic, only energy healing will clear it.

> In a previous life, Daryl had been a general in the U.S. Army in Europe during World War I. He was diligent, responsible, and well respected. He carried the heavy burden of being responsible for the lives of those he commanded. During a battle, he made a fatal strategic decision that claimed the lives of all his soldiers. Although he was also mortally injured, he physically lingered about twenty minutes. During that excruciating time, he felt

---

[64] ***karmic restrictions, barriers,*** or ***energy blocks:*** soul-mandated requirements imposed by karma that, until they are energetically cleared, prevent us from attaining some specific desired accomplishments or attributes in this life

abject despair and rued his disastrous mistake that had caused such a tragic end for so many men and sorrow for their families.

In this current life, Daryl is a very hard worker with high standards. However, he cannot make important personal or family decisions. He follows the easiest course and stoically copes with the results of his actions or inactions. Daryl has no substantial ability to take initiative to help others, to improve his own circumstances, or to see or find any better possibilities to help improve his life.

Gloria, his wife of many years, is aggravated by his cowardly behavior but has suppressed and stored her anger and frustration throughout their married years. This has created so much stress that it has generated physical symptoms within her. Gloria also needs to clear these emotional hurts in order to promote her physical healing.

During a joint therapy session, D'Ann encouraged her to release her feelings daily in any safe and available way. Daryl realized, from his unveiled past life, why he had been incapable of making serious decisions. He agreed to take more initiative in order to heal that karmic wound and to improve his relationship with his wife. The couple, wanting to improve this lifelong issue between them, resolved to focus on a path of energetic healing.

As this case exemplifies, learning about pertinent, past life background that affects our present life will usually open our minds and shift our understanding. Then, we can activate more free will and make wiser and more meaningful options to improve the quality of our life and our relationships.

Our Eternal Soul

Our souls choose to enter countless dimensions and locations to spiritually grow and evolve. Because a soul is eternal, it experiences a continuous stream of life even between incarnations. This is called *life between lives.*[65] Rarely do we remember our experiences in-between lifetimes or any of our past lives. This memory block makes us impressionable and vulnerable to the environmental circumstances and relationships of this life.

There is a blessing in not consciously knowing our life agenda, of being unaware of a divine plan for our life. If we had not accomplished our goals in many earlier lifetimes, we could be overwhelmed with the burden and hopelessness of all we have to do during this one lifetime.

As we humans evolve energetically, spiritual therapists and mediums are helping us acquire greater knowledge of the Akashic Records and past lives. Fortunately, we are also gaining the higher vibrational energy we require to beneficially handle this valuable knowledge. And a tiny percentage of people on earth are already capable of remembering their prior incarnations without professional assistance.

> Just before Bonnie incarnated into this life, she did not drink from the river of forgetfulness. Her open memory gives her full recall of all her past lives, various and repetitive

---

[65] *life between lives:* multi-dimensional, continuous stream of soul life between incarnations

relationships, and lives between lives.

Bonnie knows all of her past relationships with everyone in her present life. She and her father, for example, have had hundreds of lifetimes together. This knowledge is not easy for her to live with, and it promotes frustrations in more obvious and intense ways than it would otherwise have been without her total awareness.

Because the issues with each person have not been cleared through so many prior incarnations, she finds it daunting to think that, during this one life, she could possibly accomplish and resolve everything from the past. For this reason, Bonnie's life has been extremely difficult, burdened, and overwhelming.

Nevertheless, she has gone into spiritual healing work, is very effective at it, and receives validation and satisfaction through her occupation. Her emotional and energetic releases are improving her outlook and contentment. In spite of the challenges, her overall life is happier, clearer, and easier because she has focused on serving others.

> *Although helpful, it is not essential to know our past lives, only how to clear our soul script*

🕉 Living without past life memory might seem to be a problem or a temporary gift, depending on our viewpoint, yet our goal is to become aware and awake. Although helpful, it is not essential to know our past lives, only how to clear our soul script.

Karmic Choices

Each karmic life script brings with it unique possibilities, intensities, and variations for *karmic clearing*.[66] At the soul level, we predetermine the degree of our *issue potencies*[67] and their likely effects in our upcoming incarnation. We have no free will choice other than to live within these mandates because they have a higher priority for our soul than different, easier, and more desirable conscious life options. Most souls select a moderate degree of karmic restrictions or barriers that allows a rather typical quality of life with some problems but also enjoyable occasions, favorable employment, some discretionary income, good friends, and health.

Some souls choose a *karmic reward*[68] lifetime. They appear to live a happy, successful, and relatively easy life, and most everything works well for them.

A few souls incarnate with self-chosen *karmic retribution*[69] for some past misdeed that offers constant opportunities to finally learn their critical life lesson. For example, if they had been pompous and insensitive before, they might be homeless, handicapped, or impoverished in this life. Or if they had been abusive to others, they could be abused in this life.

---

[66] *karmic clearing:* removing the low energy vibrations of karma to enable spiritual evolution

[67] *issue potencies:* the force or concentration of a karmic issue that presets the prevalence of button pushing and intensity of emotional reaction

[68] *karmic reward:* an infrequent soul-selected lifetime to enjoy blessings with a minimum or absence of karma

[69] *karmic retribution:* a self-chosen life circumstance in which a situation we posed on others in a previous life is imposed on us in this lifetime

Some souls select a difficult *karmic burn*[70] life in which they can clear enormous amounts of backlogged issues. A few examples would be serious birth defects or long-time chronic or life-threatening illnesses, whether physical, mental, or emotional. As difficult as these lifetimes can be for the person and his or her family, the greater Truth is that the experience is nearly always soul-serving for all concerned and is hardly ever happenstance, accidental, or fruitless. These disadvantaged people are actually playing a role for their families as much as their families are for them, thus fulfilling their agreements according to their soul scripts. Fortunately, with advancing awareness of karmic therapies, the persons involved with such a setup can utilize energy healings to provide at least some minimal shifts as well as beneficial understanding in the physical world.

ॐ Knowing that their souls made a choice to have that type of life position and experience does not give the rest of us cause to ignore or dismiss their plight. Rather, challenging situations are opportunities to work on many soul-needed attributes. If someone with such challenges is in your life, you can be proactively sensitive to their needs and realize that your soul contract with them also serves you.

~ ~ ~

As we work on issues in one lifetime, regardless of our karmic choices, we make varying degrees of progress regarding the issues we entered this life to address, but we often also create additional emotional baggage that we carry over after death into a subsequent lifetime. This is the slow, deliberate, and heavy characteristic of karma, and we are all subject to its effect.

A life spent addressing energy healing can offer an effective,

---

[70] *karmic burn:* a soul script that includes all or a difficult portion of accrued karma to address in one lifetime and results in profound, recurring challenges that often prove to be unsolvable through conventional means

relatively quick way of clearing karma. It can also reduce or eliminate additional energetic debris. One focused, spiritual life can remove and heal many lifetimes of issues. However, the healing path is not usually smooth or easy, even for those who choose to live a life purely dedicated to spiritual development.

Oaths and Vows

An *oath* or a *vow*[71] is a strong, definitive statement that can have serious consequences in future lifetimes if not consciously fulfilled or released. Probably the most common vow is that pronounced by a couple during their marriage ceremony to love and cherish "until death do us part." People commonly take an oath of loyalty to a military leader, an organization, or a cause. Sometimes an oath or a vow is spoken as a vendetta or an intention to extract revenge upon another.

All of these decrees are typically in effect only during the period of this lifetime. The marriage vow contains a natural escape clause that terminates with the death of either spouse. An oath to a commander-in-chief, an organization, or a cause generally ends with fulfillment of the term of service, although many people who take such an oath carry that sense of loyalty to their graves and might even be honored at their funeral with a memorial, such as a national flag or an organizational pin or medallion. A vendetta, such as "I'll get you for that," typically ends with the extraction of revenge or a change of heart.

Oaths and vows become karmic and carry over into another lifetime when we make a statement that includes a never-ending clause, such as "I'll *never* let that happen to me again," or "I'll *never* let another person get close to me," or "I'll *never, ever*

---

[71] **oath** or **vow:** a decree or consuming mental commitment, without a fulfillment or expiration clause, made in a previous lifetime or earlier in this lifetime, to do or not do a particular act, that energetically remains active throughout incarnations until the decree is consciously released

trust another person." Without words such as, "for as long as I live," these statements continue into eternal, karmic perpetuity in every life we live anywhere until we consciously release ourselves from them.

ॐ Even vows that seem soul-enhancing can have karmic repercussions. Most of us have had at least one past life as a religious ascetic, yet often those past times were so challenging that we might have been shunned or martyred for our *beliefs*[72] or lifestyle. We might still be living with the financial or sexual effects of vows we made lifetimes ago concerning a life of poverty and chastity. We might have taken other vows that, although appropriate or apparently harmless at the time, continue to impose profound energetic karmic restrictions or barriers that are preventing us from experiencing a potent spiritual life.

In my practice, I've found that, in order to be set free from the mandates of a vow, clients require that the past life, with its particular circumstances that led to the original vow or oath, be unveiled to them. For this reason, karmic energy associated with vows or oaths is best released through the intervention of an energy therapist.

Latent Karma

Latent karma[73] can attract immediate or very quick learning situations and consequences of unwise actions from this lifetime. If we immediately remediate the energetic disturbance, we avert the potential karmic effect. If the energies remain, however, we

---

[72] **beliefs:** resolute, judgmentally screened, and predetermined guidelines that are intended to shape life, and often require allegiance, prescribed behaviors, and self-discipline

[73] **latent karma:** emotional energetic debris acquired during this present life that is unreleased and unresolved

will be presented with more opportunities to purge our emotions. Ideally, we will do this in the current life and not carry them forward for attention in another life.

The following story illustrates a major life experience and lesson that removed potential karma for a future lifetime. It began unexpectedly, occurred quickly, went on hiatus, and was completed two years later.

> Jennifer had just pulled into a parking space in a shopping mall. As she opened her door, a strong gust of wind took it out of her hand and smashed it into the door of the neighboring car. Her heart sank when she saw that the car was brand new, clean, expensive, and beautiful. She felt terrible about it. She didn't know what to do. She had heard that if an accident happens when a driver is not in the car, his or her insurance company would pay without applying a deductible. Feeling disturbed and unhappy, she left the cars and went into the store—without leaving a note.

> Two years later, Jennifer pulled into a parking lot in her own brand new car on a windy day. She was in the store for less than ten minutes. When she came out, her new car had a significant dent from someone else's car door. Jennifer concluded that if ever again she were the cause of damage to another parked vehicle, she would leave a note with her personal information—and an apology.

These two events were truly accidents because all three drivers had done nothing wrong. Jennifer didn't realize how strong the wind was blowing when she opened her car door. She certainly didn't intend to damage someone else's car. She later recognized that the same statements were true for the person whose car door dented hers.

Jennifer immediately caught the karmic connection between the two accidents. Had she left information for the first driver whose car she damaged, and had that person responded to her note with a phone call, Jennifer could have apologized again and followed through to make sure there was no financial burden to him or her. Interestingly enough, she noticed that she had no emotional response whatsoever toward the driver who had unintentionally damaged her own new car. Jennifer's focus was completely on the karmic significance of the two accidents.

From a larger perspective, these two events were spiritual setups intended to clear potential karma. Jennifer had unintentionally caused an accident, but she did intentionally decide not to resolve it at that time. Therefore, the tenet of karma, the process of action and reaction, required that the same type of event happen to her. She was fortunate that the karmic experience cleared in such a relatively short time so she did not carry it over into a future lifetime. Likely her accident would not have needed to happen if she had forgiven herself and asked, in absentia, to be forgiven by the driver for damaging the first car and for not leaving a note. Doing so could have cleared the energetic burden from her own system.

~ ~ ~

The following story is hypothetical, but it contains appropriate concepts for the scenario. A person with this mindset would be unlikely to seek spiritual healing.

> Harry has a karmic issue of trying to beat the system. He frequently feels cheated and believes he is justified in keeping any extra

available perks, samples, or cash he finds. He has not yet realized that his self-serving and greedy conduct is causing him to be shortchanged.

One time when he cashed a check, he received too much money back from the clerk and did not return the excess. The amount of the financial discrepancy is fundamentally irrelevant. He felt good about getting away with more than he deserved. He made his decision consciously, knowing what he had done, but not caring that it was unethical.

Because Harry kept the extra money, a situation developed through which he could eliminate this potential additional karma: he was overcharged when he bought something in a store and did not realize it until much later. He has often suffered other kinds of retribution for greediness: parking meters have taken his coins without registering the time, which resulted in him receiving tickets; and friends have not followed through on commitments, repaid loans, or helped him when he needed their help.

If Harry continues to make the same choices to beat the system, he will continue to be duped. Each experience is an important spiritual setup. These are the recurring scenes that offer potential healing and clearing. When Harry finally realizes the connection between his behavior and its repercussions, he could choose to behave differently. If he decides to be honest, he will reduce his karmic need to be shortchanged. Remaining trustworthy would eventually help to eliminate this issue.

~ ~ ~

When we finally understand that spiritual healing is about clearing the energetic emotional debris of a karmic script, a natural question arises about people who are emotionally detached or mentally ill. A rather common example would be that of a sociopath. People with this mental condition have no conscience or emotional sensitivity, and they bend conventions and laws to suit their own purposes. They acknowledge no wrongdoing, easily defend themselves, and accept little or no responsibility for consequences of their actions. They view life as being exclusively about their opinions, needs, and desires. People living with this dysfunction have karmically selected this role to serve a necessary soul experience. The resulting difficulties of being close to or living with such people are also necessary for all the souls involved with or in relationship with them.

It might appear as though sociopaths would be immune to karma because they are emotionally blind. Unfortunately for them, that is not the case. Lack of emotional awareness and responsibility is a tremendous disadvantage for anyone, but it does not prevent or excuse toxic energy buildup. Due to their inability to clear issues in everyday life, they accumulate an enormous amount of unresolved, latent karmic energies throughout their present lifetime, and they add burdens to close relationships. All of these untouched energies are stored in the person's system and will need to be cleared in future lifetimes, most often with the same souls who are presently playing roles for him or her.

Personal Transformation

Our Higher Self determines which issues come up to be healed. It also sets the timing, circumstance, and situational intensity. Therefore, in order to *transform* or experience a *personal transformation*,[74] we need to reinterpret events in our life and respond more wisely when they occur. By rising above ego consciousness, we enlarge our perspective and improve our interpretation. We then enable ourselves to have clearer and less reactive emotional responses.

> *Our Higher Self determines each issue that arises to be cleared as well as its timing, circumstance, and situational intensity.*

As we expand the context of how we see our world, we come to realize that our enlarged perspective offers a proactive benefit to healing that complements emotional clearing opportunities. This larger and less emotionally entangled view helps us foster wiser decisions. We then come to accept responsibility for attracting the difficult situation, and realize that we need each of those distressing incidents in order to provoke and activate our issue energies. Eventually, we see that these setups offer incentive and motivation for us to release the old, karmic energies.

Then, as we acknowledge the healing intent behind each life challenge and apply both proactive and reactive beneficial responses, we begin to initiate our personal transformation. From this foundation, we can utilize *spiritual principles*[75] to revise

---

[74] ***transform*** or ***personal transformation:*** a gradual energetic healing process that replaces three-dimensional operations with divine functions and attributes

[75] ***spiritual principles:*** energetic virtues, guidelines, and understandings that help us heal and transform

those situations and promote our karmic clearing and healing. As we more effectively respond to our challenges in ways that facilitate spiritual growth, our issues diminish and eventually disappear. Continuing forward, as our energetic awareness expands and our vibrational rate increases, so does our ability to know and apply additional and higher spiritual principles, and instinctively manifest their attributes.

Source is constantly giving us opportunities to release and heal our issues so that we might transform our lives. In order to seize those opportunities, we must be willing to clear our *ego filters*,[76] which are fear-inducing tools that ego uses to stifle our beautiful, God-centered personalities, and reinforce our need for rudimentary, body-based views, values, and

> *When we continue to use old, reliable patterns to cope with difficult situations, we will experience old, reliable outcomes.*

procedures. E/go filters cause us to operate from a position of control, have expectations, be judgmental, react defensively, and place a high premium on our opinions, priorities, and physical security. Our life lessons tell us that we must set aside our ego filters and change our habits, decisions, and actions in order to avoid perpetuating, augmenting, or even re-creating karma.

At the same time, we must be aware of our default method of operating, which is similar to toiling in a rut. We've learned how to survive and function adequately within old, well-ingrained patterns. We might not like our life, but it can feel safer to stay in the rut than leave it for unknown greener pastures. Therefore, it is possible for us to augment or re-create karma even after it was cleared by choosing to follow or return to old patterns when

---

[76] **ego filters:** three-dimensionally programmed screens used to interpret and understand life and curtail higher functioning potentials

better options are known and available. When we continue to use old, reliable patterns to cope with difficult situations, we will experience old, reliable outcomes.

Making personal changes might require bravery, perhaps more than we feel willing or able to generate. Our frustrations might be so significant from previous

> *When we listen to ego, we stall our spiritual progress.*

ineffective efforts to improve that we might choose to give up.

This fearful or lethargic thinking comes from ego, which wants to remain in control of our life and be allowed to trump spiritual energies at least to some degree. When we listen to ego, we stall our spiritual progress. But our soul, with our intended soul script, keeps nudging us along. This internal prodding encourages and supports our

> *Because we are eternal beings, we will have as many lifetimes as necessary to address unfinished business.*

spiritual development. As we evolve, we realize that choosing the option of soul growth increasingly benefits our life. Our free will then becomes our ally and continues to provide the opportunity for us to choose between mere physical survival and evolutionary soul advancement.

The person in the following story made a decision that, although not wrong, will delay her soul growth. Fortunately, because we are eternal beings, she will have as many lifetimes as necessary to address her unfinished business.

Elaine was an extreme people person and had an extensive circle of close friends around whom her life revolved. After a few energy sessions with D'Ann, she began to notice improvements in her life. The changes were effortless and welcome, but she became uncomfortable with what was happening to her social life.

The topics of conversation with her longtime friends now seemed trivial, shallow, and predictable and were not as interesting as they had been before. She loved her friends and wanted to keep such cherished friendships. She didn't know what to do.

Elaine painfully decided to stop session work. She chose to prioritize her friends over personal development.

For your own soul's sake, please do not let the possibility of losing good friends or having relationship challenges in your life as a result of healing stop you from evolving. One of the more difficult ego aspects of life can be over-reliance on being accepted or being seen in good favor by others. If you choose to place less emphasis on ego and pay more attention to Source, you might find it necessary to let go of some previously good friends or change relationships. This step toward continued healing will probably be awkward at first, and you will likely feel sad about not being close to old, familiar companions. But your new, higher-vibrational energy will also attract more rewarding,

> *We attract people, events, situations, and experiences that energetically serve us.*

congruent, and supportive people who will stabilize and enhance your emotional status. You will be eternally grateful for your new friends, and you will also become a better friend.

Karmic Opportunities

🕉 In spite of our interpretations of and reactions to life's affairs or trials, anything important that happens is designed for our benefit in some way or another. We attract people, events, situations, and experiences that energetically serve us.

Whether we created our predicament as a consequence of our action or inaction, or are an innocent participant, our soul intends for us to learn through and from every experience we have. At the very least, challenges or even catastrophes can deepen our appreciation for life and/or the scope of human expression, and they can evoke empathy and compassion for others in similar plights.

🕉 When our Higher Self allows us to experience an adversity that is attracted by karma, that is, a **healing setup**, its intention might be to heighten our awareness and sensitivity to emotions, nudge us to make important or uncomfortable changes, trigger personal advancement, reprioritize our life, change life direction, or develop new abilities.

Other soul growth benefits can be to:

- learn cooperation;

- be a better team player;

- care for, help, or serve others;

- improve communication or interpersonal skills;

- learn to receive help;

- develop strength, stamina, determination, or integrity;

- practice speaking our t/Truth; or

- strengthen foundational attributes such as acceptance, love, trust, and gratitude.

Experiencing and releasing profound grief and anguish will remove accumulated emotional trash bags. Even if there seems to be no possible benefit from the experience, it is helpful to look at it from this view.

> *Not everything that happens on earth is predestined.*
> *~Free will exists~*

With that in mind, we come to realize that not everything that happens on earth is predestined. Life challenges occur for many reasons. Accidents, complications, and events happen, and we need to deal with them. Tires go flat, appliances break down, and bodies age. Free will exists. We make mistakes and poor decisions. We override or choose to avoid divine guidance.

The dilemmas we face are natural results of decisions we have made. If we quit high school, we might be stuck with low-paying jobs. If we don't think for ourselves, we might find it difficult to make decisions and, thus, remain frozen in our tracks. There are often practical lessons to learn, such as if we pay our bills late, we also pay a costly penalty. We might have agreed to take on genetic tendencies or situations that predispose us to conditions not caused by our own actions. For these reasons, it's important that, when assessing life's problems, we allow for other factors—besides karma—as possible influences on the outcome; these could include human error, forgetfulness, or lack of training or education.

Regardless of the factors, as we spiritually evolve, we will notice improvement in the ease with which we move through difficulties. We will

> *Blessings can manifest in infinite ways.*

recognize formerly hidden blessings in timing, conditions, circumstances, cost, opportunities, assistance, and outcomes. We will see that blessings can manifest in infinite ways.

🕉 So how do we distinguish between circumstances that originate from our karmic decisions, free will choices, and those that stem from external factors beyond our control? We can usually be confident they stem from karma if:

- We feel an immediate, strong, and obvious internal reaction;

- The challenge or situation is repetitive, resistant, and emotionally potent;

- We employ a moderately effective management technique that we have developed from similar prior experiences;

- The cause is elusive, unavoidable, and familiar;

- The episodes recur regardless of our efforts to prevent them;

- The situations or circumstances often defy logic; and/or

- The spiritual setup appears bizarre, unreal, "fishy," or so strange that only God could be presenting the situation for our ultimate healing.

Karma once required lifetimes to clear, which is why there is a need for reincarnation. As vibrations on earth continue to intensify, opportunities to heal occur more frequently and with greater urgency. We can now clear issues in weeks or months when we know what to do—and do it.

9: REINCARNATION

Many people don't accept the principle of reincarnation because it seems irrelevant, confusing, or in conflict with their religious beliefs. Some

> *Reincarnation exists.*
> *It is the consequence*
> *of karma.*

dismiss it as too insensible. Others don't want to know about complications that past lives might create in the present. Your or my opinion about reincarnation is irrelevant. It doesn't matter if you know about, understand, believe, want, or reject this concept. Reincarnation exists. It is the consequence of karma.

Reincarnation exists because we can only interpret experiences in linear time as past, present, and future. Memories and knowledge of earlier lifetimes reinforce our impression of linear time. Although quantum physicists tell us that time does not exist, our apparent reality disclaims this. We still rationally see our lives as restricted by time, distance, and three-dimensional limitations. A more elevated insight, however, is that everything happens simultaneously, that all lifetimes are concurrent because there is only now. Eventually, we will evolve and develop the wisdom and ability to interpret and live life both linearly and nonlinearly.

At this time on earth, enlightened individuals tell us that the span of time between lives, measured linearly, is variable for each of us just as we each have unique karmic backgrounds, incarnations, experiences, and number of lifetimes. Edgar Cayce, the greatest psychic of the twentieth century, revealed through his guidance that the average time between incarnations is thirty-three years. Some former Atlanteans stayed away from earth for 10,000 years, and a few cultures attract souls within days of their recent death.

In addition to time, some of our restrictions on earth include gravity, physicality, materiality, duality (light/dark, hot/cold), and seasons. We have no control over these matters and must accept and work within them. It might appear as though we have no way to substantially improve these complications, and, according to our personal earthly experience, that is probably accurate.

We have historically perceived life on earth as basic, slow, and difficult, but it also offers opportunities for exceptional spiritual development greater than during the life between lives. Resembling an accelerated scholastic curriculum, physical life brings to us the precise situations we need in order to heal. The more often we are exposed to personal problems, the greater the possibility that we will see repetitive patterns and spiritually understand the root causes beneath or behind the situations.

Adversities target soul-needed lessons for rapid achievement.

Adversities target soul-needed lessons for rapid achievement. The more limitations and challenges we face, when accompanied with our developing understandings, skills, and inspirations, the more potential we have for

Employing energetic exploration enhances empowerment.

accomplishment and creativity. Employing energetic exploration enhances empowerment. If we learn how to interpret life with energetic understandings and know how to effectively respond in ways to facilitate our growth, we will have countless opportunities to practice remediating and healing our issues. Learning and utilizing energetic concepts can produce significant results that would otherwise be impossible.

ॐ Fortunately, due to the previous soul growth of many individuals and higher frequency energies now coming down to earth, life on our planet is finally at an evolutionary level capable of receiving and sustaining more and more highly advanced energies and entities. Some souls are even now born without karma. This influx of clear beings is escalating as earth is in transformation mode. These wise

> *We need enlightened individuals to create a healthier, more authentic society.*

people are here to serve humanity and model an empowered life. We need these enlightened individuals to create a healthier, more authentic society.

Issue Mandates in Reincarnating

Unless we address and clear karmic energies, we will continue to face repeating challenges that defy permanent resolution.

In a former life, Priscilla lived in Connecticut in the 1800s. She was a daughter in the wealthiest family in town. Her father was a banker. The family had servants and an enviable lifestyle. Her life consisted of lessons, protocol, and etiquette. She had to behave in a charming way, not look down on others, but be very aware of social class. She was not allowed to admit or discuss her emotions, needs, or even ideas.

In this present life, Priscilla married into great wealth. Her lifestyle included a private jet, personal limousine and driver, a nanny, and a six-day, live-in housekeeper. Her husband was not the least bit interested in anything she said,

did, or felt. She was expected to behave and
entertain in certain predetermined ways. Her
present life was hauntingly familiar to her, but
she didn't know why. After being unhappy for
years, she finally divorced her husband.

Priscilla's decision was probably inevitable. Although the
divorce created major upheaval, pain, and enormous turmoil, it
also improved her life by removing her from a strong,
overwhelming karmic situation with little or no room for her to
improve. But unless she pursues additional energy clearing or
significant therapy, she will likely attract another wealthy partner
who will play the same karmic role of domination for her. If she
heals, she can live a happier, more rewarding life with or without
great wealth.

~ ~ ~

After retirement, Franklin and his wife moved
from one state to another about 2,000 miles
away. They rented an apartment for a year
while they built and furnished their new home.
They were delighted with their new location
and found it relaxing and invigorating.

Within two weeks of finally moving into their
new home, however, Franklin became restless,
irritable, and unable to relax or sleep well. He
had never felt this way before and sought
energetic assistance. Through session work, he
learned that he had lived as a Native American
in their new state many lifetimes ago. He had
experienced an emotionally difficult death as a
rather young man, and his body was buried
within twenty miles of their new home. He
was being affected by the close proximity to

his buried bones, which were still holding and emitting residual energy that connected him to the earlier lifetime and his painful demise.

After the karmic energies were removed from him and the bones, he had no more symptoms. He was able to fully enjoy retirement in their new home.

Understanding and accepting spiritual and energetic concepts is important, but it's not the same as removing them. Franklin's healing results are typical when karmic issues are cleared, regardless of the number of past lives spent working on them. Because charged energies created his problem, removing them was necessary in order for him to eliminate his symptoms.

> *Understanding and accepting spiritual and energetic concepts is important, but it's not the same as removing them.*

Karmic Roles in Action

ॐ Reincarnation on our planet means returning to an earth body with essential soul purposes. There are varieties of performers and experiences available in each lifetime we select. People often presume that each successive life is more advanced than former ones. This is an oversimplification. This present life is not necessarily the most elevated we have ever lived. We might have chosen a less spiritually evolved life or one that is physically, emotionally, mentally, socially, or financially challenging if that is the most appropriate way to resolve pressing issues.

We select each life with circumstances, relationships, and issues to address our soul's needs. We might occasionally choose incarnations that offer reprieve from particularly painful issues and people so that we can focus on other, more minor issues that have been awaiting our attention. We often trade or shift relationships with family members from one life time to another to better understand a different perspective and, thus, address karma and learning. A daughter, for example, could have been her parent's mother, father, sibling, child, spouse, business partner, or close friend in an earlier life.

> Sean had a past life as an orphan. He lived in the middle 1800s in Europe and had one older sister and two younger brothers. His mother died during the birth of what would have been a fifth child when he was three, his brothers were toddlers, and his sister was five. His father deserted the family. Sean's sister was emotionally unstable and over reactive.

> Because Sean was the oldest male, even though he was only three years old, he assumed and carried the burden of the small family in the little ways he could. What he actually did for his siblings was less significant than the weight of his burden. For three years, the children survived by begging, stealing, asking for help, and any other means available. Then they ended up in an institution or group home.

> Sean was the primary sibling to calm and assist his sister in her dramas. He was so aware of her challenges that he took an oath that he would never show his own feelings or talk about them, no matter what happened. His almost exclusive attention was on his sister.

> Although he appears to be a very pleasant man

in his present life, the intensity of Sean's oath, which he had never revoked, stimulates his contained emotions to boil over when they are beyond his capacity to control. On occasion, he explodes like a volcano.

Sean is married, and his marriage is working. However, the couple had never been able to reach his forbidden feelings, no matter how hard each of them tried. This block created significant challenges in their relationship.

During a session, this emotional karmic issue came to the surface when Sean could identify and address it as a past life vow. Sean's karmic oath prohibited him from displaying or even admitting his emotions in his present lifetime. With guidance, Sean was able to release his oath and begin to speak a little about some of his emotions.

Afterward, he and his wife began to experience frequent challenges as a result of his new ability to finally express and release his long held feelings. His outpourings were like the opening of floodgates and were, sometimes, more than she wanted to handle. As they worked through and with these interfering, painful, yet necessary difficulties, their communication began to improve. It took some time and continued effort to develop a healthier relationship, yet even during this challenging process, their marriage improved.

As is most often the case, souls incarnate together in this life in order to work through karmic issues that they created together in other lifetimes. In this case, Sean's wife was not in that specific lifetime, although they shared karma from other lifetimes that they are dealing with and which added karmic energy to this situation. However, his former sister, whom he had sacrificially served and protected, is now his mother.

When Sean heard this, he said that explained a lot about her life and their interactions together. His mother's present life script has allowed her to karmically return the favor (!) by doing for him what he did for her back then. Unfortunately, her excessive care has manifested as worrying, bothering, and interfering far too often, which, as you might expect, was a challenging factor within his marriage.

In order to clear the karmic relationship contract between them, Sean would need to forgive his mother. Doing so would release him, and could release both souls, from ever again needing to serve each other, back and forth, with that issue.

Reincarnation Diversity

ॐ Not only have we had diverse relationships and roles with our current family members but most of us have had past lives with disparate roles: fame/solitude; wealth/poverty; happiness/despair; health/sickness; ruler/peasant; hero/culprit; and other scenarios, characters, and positions. The possibilities are nearly endless. We can safely assume that all of us have experienced both genders and we've been members of most religions and ethnicities.

If people knew that everyone has spent lifetimes with various physical characteristics, then gender and sexual orientation bias, discrimination based on the color of a person's skin or religious beliefs, and even jokes that ridicule ethnicities or the handicapped would disappear. We would know that a person targeted for discrimination now has likely either been a discriminator in a past life and switched roles to, in effect, get a taste of his or her own medicine, or has volunteered to face the challenge of abuse in order to assist humanity.

Bullying or denigration of people with homosexual, lesbian, or transgender tendencies has long been common throughout societies and has become more out in the open in modern Western cultures. Those who incarnate with a sexual identity challenge typically have spent a majority of past lives as the opposite gender. Homosexual attraction might be an unavoidable result of these dominating karmic energies and experiences.

Those who incarnate with a sexual identity challenge typically have spent a majority of past lives as the opposite gender.

Becoming aware of these broadening concepts can awaken personal, societal, and global acceptance of others and ourselves. We will come to see life with love and inclusion rather than judgment and condemnation. Instead of categorizing and judging people by physical factors, we can adopt a more evolved and unified view that equalizes the worth of each person and increases the likelihood of success for all people.

We can adopt a more evolved and unified view that equalizes the worth of each person and increases the likelihood of success for all people.

~ ~ ~

Karma is evident in our lives even though we might not understand it or see it. In a sense, when we reincarnate, we pick up energetic backpacks from specifically chosen past lives, and we live with that baggage until we set ourselves free from it.

Wayne had always been very uneasy around fire and never wanted to use the fireplace in his family's home. On the rare occasions when his family enjoyed a fire, he made sure to have a bucket of water nearby. During the night, he would get up several times to make sure the fire was extinguished.

In a past life, Wayne had been burned at the stake as a warlock. Removing those past energies healed his fear of fire. He still did not love to watch one burn, but was comfortable in a way he was never able to be before.

~ ~ ~

Maggie was a complete novice to the spiritual arena when she came for a past life reading and healing. She had lived in Spain in the 1500s as a female gypsy, and was only comfortable when the wagons were all circled for camping at night.

She learned the social rules of her community and family, which included stealing. The whole group she lived and traveled with had no ability to empathize with others. They had no guilt about their behavior and knew fear only when they were pursued, caught, and punished. They were not overly attached to material goods and would sometimes give their stolen items to each other. They would also typically abandon them when they broke camp.

In her early twenties in that life, Maggie was seriously injured and was no longer able to participate in thievery. In spite of her physical condition, she was able to keep herself very busy.

In her present life, Maggie is a single mom, gainfully employed, and keeps extremely busy. As an only child, she is very close to her cousins who, in that former life, had been her extended family. At the end of her session, Maggie revealed that she is the only one in her present family who does not steal!

She told the story that when she moved into her first home, she had a house-warming party. One cousin gave her a towel lifted from a hotel. Another cousin stole medical supplies from his employer and presented them as his gift. Another bragged about how long it took her to collect the complete set of flatware from the cafeteria where she worked. Maggie stated her appreciation for their creativity, made no judgmental retorts about the gifts, but let them know she wished they had purchased, rather than stolen, her gifts. She also told them that she loved them anyway, kept their presents, and used them until she could afford to replace them with new items.

Maggie hired one of her cousins to help paint her new home. When they returned from the paint store, they unpacked her purchases. Then he lifted his shirt and removed his treasures. He told her she had bought cheap supplies but he had taken the good stuff. He proceeded to use his ill-gotten cache, so Maggie did not return anything to the store.

Because stealing had been a pattern in her family throughout her whole life, Maggie was not as surprised by his behavior as someone else would be. She doesn't steal and wishes her family didn't either. She has learned to accept her cousins as goodhearted people in spite of their flaws.

A few weeks after that session, something else clicked into place for Maggie. She realized that, every night in bed, she re-creates the comfortable feeling of a campfire circle in her gypsy life by surrounding herself with a pile of pillows. Although she remained uncertain about reincarnation, she had no explanation for these meaningful coincidences.

Karmic Carryovers

Almost all of us bring *karmic carryovers*[77] into this lifetime. These might appear as benefits or disadvantages, but we need to heal or clear only our difficult issues and challenges. Advantageous skills and talents, favorable circumstances and situations, supportive people, good fortune, abundance, and other blessings also likely derive from earlier lifetimes to enhance our present life and assist with our ability to survive and work through our karmic issues.

Through our many incarnations we have probably developed more dharma capabilities, (as explained at the beginning of Chapter 2,) than we can possibly manifest in any one lifetime. Enjoying and cultivating hobbies and areas of gratification such as cooking, knitting, glass blowing, photography, dancing,

---

[77] ***karmic carryovers:*** issues that have been active in many earlier lifetimes

music, art, writing, or gardening might draw on in-born aptitudes.

Pet peeves or areas of distaste come from both past and present life experiences as well. Some people hate housework, loud talkers, other people's slowness, and so forth. Intense opinions can easily transcend time and stay with us in the future. But because we can't change anyone else, we are left to heal and improve only our own lives.

~ ~ ~

The next four short accounts are further evidence of karmic carryovers that affect current lives. All of these people removed their contaminated energies and experienced release from their anxieties.

> *Because we can't change anyone else, we are left to heal and improve only our own lives.*

Grace had a fear of flying that stemmed from a past life during World War II when she had been a male bomber pilot who died when his plane was shot down.

~ ~ ~

Lauren had a fear of driving that originated from when she had been one of the earliest car accident fatalities in the early 1900s.

~ ~ ~

Bea had a lifelong dread and fear of being institutionalized. Nothing in her present life explained why she felt this way. She had been extremely frustrated because of her inability to get relief from this serious and perplexing anguish. A past life unveiled that Bea had been sent to an establishment for the mentally impaired where she was mistreated and abused for most of her life.

~ ~ ~

Alfred and his wife took a vacation along the California shoreline one summer. He suddenly and unavoidably discovered that he was terrified of heights, curves, and turns. He could not drive into the scenic turnouts along the coastal highway.

In a past life, Alfred had died when he recklessly drove over a cliff. After the karmic energies were removed, the couple successfully repeated the same trip the following summer. Although he did not yearn for the lookouts, he was able to drive into them and enjoy the views.

Introductory Emotional Impressions

When we first meet someone and, for no obvious reason, have a strong reaction, we usually are recognizing past life energies. Sometimes this energy is impersonal, such as when a highly intuitive person picks up the other person's vibrations even if they have not had a past life together.

More often, however, both persons have the same type of spontaneous response, although one might be more affected than the other. A heartwarming emotion reflects a loving and rewarding past together. Fear or discomfort usually indicates unfinished old business. Even though the reason might be unknown, when we have a strong, negative reflex, it's a sign that we need to forgive the other person.

~ ~ ~

The more we recognize in the moment our own emotions and reactive impressions, the more information we have to work with in order to advance understanding of what is occurring and to promote healthier and wiser responses to the situation or circumstance. Proceeding with this additional and more enlightened input facilitates greater appreciation for how life continuously and energetically serves us in all ways.

> Linda decided to attend a national, yearly decorating convention in Texas. About 100 people attended, most of whom she did not know. When she was introduced to the host's wife, Pam, Linda immediately felt profound love, and the two women hugged each other. Linda had never before had such an instantaneous and intense reaction.

> The next day, Linda entered an auditorium and sat near the back. As she looked ahead, she saw Pam sitting with her husband, Joe. They were facing the stage. This was the first time Linda had seen Joe, and she felt overwhelming love toward him as well. The sensation was so strong that she actually cried. This amazing response came about from viewing only the back of his head.

> Linda will never forget the experience and regrets, yet feels strangely peaceful about, having never seen them again.

10: ROLES

William Shakespeare left his mark on history because of his gift with the English language, both written and spoken. His talent also included great insight into human dramas. He was inspired when he wrote in *As You Like It,* "All the world's a stage, And all the men and women merely players; They have their exits and their entrances, And one man in his time plays many parts."

People in our lives play roles for us, and we perform for them. Our cast of characters can include anyone, but the major performers are those closest to us, primarily family

We would not recognize the need to heal and evolve without people in close relationships who highlight and provoke our issues.

members, partners, or colleagues. They are serving us when they play a role blatantly and intensely, and it creates challenges. We identify our issues by experiencing problems. We would not recognize the need to heal and evolve without people in close relationships who highlight and provoke our issues. This is why families can be so dysfunctional. Individual members are intended to mirror issues and push each other's buttons.

People do not blossom in harsh circumstances, and families are rarely happy, healthy, kind, honest, supportive, and loving when playing out dramas. Because we are consciously unaware of this structuring, we do not know how to interpret or effectively work with our dilemmas to maximize our growth. We misinterpret life and miss opportunities that could otherwise offer resolution and transformation. This conscious misinterpretation of the soul's healing agenda is due to our typical ego interpretation of life and its happenings.

Karmic Contracts

The contracted roles we play resemble the parts performed by actors in a melodrama. When our feet touch the floor in the morning, we put on our energetic costume, and it's the last thing we remove at night. We so much believe in the reality of our costume that we also believe that each

> *E/go interprets role-playing as real life. It believes in appearances and actions that are deceiving.*

person in their outfit actually IS the character they are portraying. That's because ego interprets role-playing as real life. It believes in appearances and actions that are deceiving. Our view is accurate, but not valid. We only see the most superficial level of life, and because it resembles a magic act, we fall for the fantasy of appearances without understanding the reality behind the scenes. In the movie *Superman,* Christopher Reeve played the title role so well that a naïve or very young person could assume he would have been capable of such supernatural feats in his personal life.

This is the healing setup. People blindly yet skillfully perform as a cast to create the illusion of dysfunctional reality. Although we consciously wish life were different, repetitions of our costumed roles strengthen rather than diminish our dramas.

> *People blindly yet skillfully perform as a cast to create the illusion of dysfunctional reality.*

We are being exposed to increasingly intense and absurd interactions and events that our soul intended for us to experience in order to edit and unburden our life scripts. When we learn that melodramatic enactments occur to boost healing, and when we then spiritually process life, we finally expedite self-empowerment.

Humanity needs to evolve past ego interpretation to become enlightened.

> *Humanity needs to evolve past ego interpretation to become enlightened.*

~ ~ ~

Due to contracts that our souls make with our family members, roles played for us in childhood set the stage for life dramas to trigger karmic issue buttons. As a child, we might be able to see certain unwanted personality traits, actions, and events around us, but we are not mature enough to recognize patterns or have the capability to heal them.

Most people in a birth family have the same or complementary issues. Because issues determine our perspective in life, experiencing shared issues trains us to see life from the same perspective as that of our family, and to form comparable conclusions based on similar viewpoints. These ideas include shared beliefs, expectations, judgments, values, history, and life management techniques. Family similarities allow members some commonality to understand each other. Sometimes, however, a child is born with different issues than the rest of the family unit. Any member not compliant with the group focus can become problematic.

If a family were sharing an issue of poor self-esteem, for example, their karmic scripts might limit success, abundance, and happiness. They could model complacency and low expectations, or they could be aggressive and demanding. They would likely not have skills to emotionally nurture and support each other. If the exceptional child has great determination and discipline to succeed, the others would not relate and might actually attempt to hold him or her back. This person could conclude that he or she doesn't belong to this family and might suspect he or she was adopted. While human interactions and/or appearances indicate a mismatch between these individuals, in actuality, the soul had specific reasons for selecting this family and these issues.

As an adult, the soul's family members usually pick up and expand the same issues that the birth family modeled. Occasionally, but rarely, there are exceptions or variations to the childhood patterns. For example, if a soul is born as a female who is scripted to learn the role of an enabler, this will be unconsciously but literally modeled by her birth family from her first breath onward in order to consciously teach this life pattern to her. As an adult, she will attract a spouse

> *As an adult, the soul's family members usually pick up and expand the same issues that the birth family modeled.*

and/or situations that will require her to play the enabler role at a cost to her personal freedom and happiness. Or if a soul is born as a male to work on the issue of assuming excessive responsibility, this quality will be modeled in the birth family and continue on in his adult life by souls playing the required roles for him and for each other.

🕉 Sometimes significant issues are not tied into gender roles, but birth issues are perpetuated into adulthood. If a boy suffers abuse, then he will typically become an abuser, continue to be abused, or be devoted to expose and remedy abuse issues for others. A female often marries a man with the same problems and roles as her father. The reverse is true for a man when choosing a wife.

> *Birth issues are perpetuated into adulthood.*

127

Juanita, a woman in her thirties, had been raised in a family that modeled her main issues of not being good enough, being wrong, and not receiving any emotional support. Her parents, especially her father, had been extremely verbally abusive and demanding to her but not to her younger sister, Harriet. Juanita learned how to act pleasantly but keep herself emotionally protected and insensitive. She never felt close to Harriet or either of her parents, and she left home right after finishing high school.

Juanita moved away and needed to financially support herself, so she found an office position and established an independent life. She eventually met Thane online, a man eight years older than she, whose primary issues, patterned by his father, were perfectionism and policing, pointing out where people or things were wrong and how they should be corrected. His mother was inefficient and messy, and Thane had greatly resented his constant need to carry excessive house responsibilities to compensate for her casual homemaking efforts.

Thane had been married one time earlier, divorced, and had full custody of his two children who were under age ten. It took several dates before Juanita was comfortable enough, because of the children, to contemplate becoming more involved with Thane. They eventually married.

Juanita and Thane had one child together, but there were ongoing challenges between Juanita and Thane's children. As the years went by, the family unit became more emotionally agitated and fractured, and both of his children left home as soon as they could.

Thane had been berating Juanita for years, but the intensity and frequency of his verbal abuse increased after his children moved out. He focused his criticism on her sloppy housekeeping standards and tried to teach her how to do things better. She was enormously frustrated. The situation was so incredibly similar to how she was raised and how her parents treated her back then. She didn't know what she had done to deserve or bring about the old feelings of being wrong, not good enough, and not supported. How could she possibly have missed his personality traits that would berate her exactly like her parents had? What could she do about it?

For his part, Thane was exasperated with Juanita because she seemed to behave so much like his mother had when he felt the need to take on house responsibilities that were actually hers. He was perplexed that he had selected a wife who would be such a continuous challenge to him. He believed that he was being reasonable with her, and the problem between them was certainly not of his making.

Thane wanted Juanita to go for marriage counseling with him, but she felt the counselor would just end up being another person who would criticize her and point out her failures. Their efforts to talk through their challenges together did not help either partner change or feel better, and they eventually divorced.

This story, based on real life, is a powerful and clear example of how a person will attract into his or her life exactly who and what is needed to trigger unresolved issues, and it illustrates how the adult family nearly always plays the same role as the birth family. Thane played the part of Juanita's father, who constantly criticized her. Juanita played the role of Thane's mother, who was messy and disorganized.

The intended spiritual benefit behind the difficult marriage was to provide the setting and incentive to emotionally and energetically clear and heal both partners' major karmic issues. Because neither partner understood how life is set up to assist healing, they could only handle so much frustration and anger. Unfortunately, neither one of them healed any of their issues, and divorce seemed to be the only solution. They each decided to remain single, but if they do decide to remarry, they will likely attract a new partner who will play the same roles yet again to offer potential healing.

~ ~ ~

🕉 As adults, we have more freedom, choices, and opportunities to change our lives than we had when we were children. We also have some degree of ability, authority, and independence to remediate our problems and improve our situations. Even with determined personal motivation and effort to work on ourselves, frustrations we encounter with other people, circumstances, and events, ultimately remind us that we can only heal ourselves.

When we spiritually reinterpret how life is setup, we begin to understand that distressing times and people merely provide us with an opportunity to re-experience our issues and release their energies. When we finally grasp this basic concept and cooperate with this essential purpose and plan, we begin to heal. We stop shooting the messenger when we realize that, if one person does not perform in accordance with our scripting and needs, then someone else will. Although the messenger is ultimately held accountable for his or her words and actions, the t/Truth is that the experience brings to us an intended soul benefit.

ॐ When we don't understand what is happening, we feel frustrated and angry. As disagreeable and even wrong as a role-playing partner appears to be, and as demanding and painful as our life with that person might be, we need to accept our own karmic responsibility for helping to create the situation. The natural tendency to blame others distracts us from the larger picture. Blame aborts

> *Blame aborts healing. But freedom from judgment expands and clears our perception.*

healing. But freedom from judgment expands and clears our perception. We will see ourselves more fully and take appropriate responsibility for the consequences of our own words and actions. With this new and deeper understanding, we can improve our lives and relationships, but we must apply dedication, perseverance, and an open mind to excavate the hidden t/Truths of life.

Clearing Karmic Contracts

The need for karmic role-playing arises from the tenet of cause and effect, which states that a result is the natural consequence of an action or event. We have lifetimes on both sides of this equation, alternating irregularly between, for example, being a villain and a victim. Our partnering soul also switches roles with us, and we repeat our drama through many incarnations. This is in accordance with the karmic script that we agreed to play with the other souls in our dramas.

Although more than one soul might occasionally partner with us and play the same role in this or other incarnations, we nullify that karmic contract when we spiritually and energetically forgive our self and our actor partner(s,) which is the intention of our and presumably their soul script(s.) Such spiritual *forgiveness*[78] permanently voids our participation in that particular drama with that particular partner in this life and usually

> *Spiritual forgiveness permanently voids our participation in that particular drama with that particular partner.*

subsequent lives. If we carry additional identical karma with another player, the drama will continue for us until we forgive that partner as well as any additional actors with whom we have the same unfinished business.

You can forgive in the presence of a single, primary, role-playing partner, with or among a group, or acting alone to forgive yourself and any or all supporting cast. Should the other(s) choose not to forgive and release you, they will draft a different soul to play your role either in this life or a future one.

Forgiving both yourself and your role-playing partner takes on a whole new perspective when you realize the back-and-forth role switching you've done over millennia.

Frank had been married to his second wife for

---

[78] *forgiveness*: the process of reinterpreting painful experiences and relationships, and clearing their stored, negatively charged emotional energies

many years. They were each seeking spiritual growth when he realized he had unfinished business with his first wife, Ada. He had not forgiven her for the painful role she had played for him. Contacting her and talking this through would be highly frustrating and ineffective.

He decided to do a spiritual forgiveness session on her. Afterward, he felt relieved, but sensed she had not forgiven him. He did not know what to do about it. When he learned about role switching, he again forgave her for the roles she had played in their previous lives together, and he was finally able to feel peaceful whenever he thought about her. Their relationship remained fundamentally the same, but Frank felt more at ease and emotionally clear whenever they conversed, and he was less agitated afterward. He was delighted with the improvement.

Ada did not know that Frank forgave and released her from their soul contract. Her life did not change just because Frank forgave her, although it would have improved in some way(s) if she had forgiven and released him too. She did notice, however, that he was somewhat more pleasant and less reactive when they spoke. Because Frank chose to no longer participate in Ada's drama, she will need someone else to play his role in her present and future lives until she realizes the need to forgive that person, and does so.

More on forgiveness, including how to forgive, appears later in this book. For now, however, you understand that forgiveness is an integral step in releasing yourself and others from your karmic contracts and debilitating karmic roles.

11: BUTTONS

Issues become aggravated when someone pushes our buttons. These episodes occur to everyone occasionally or frequently, but always unpredictably. Having our buttons pushed is the primary way we learn to identify our challenges and our most basic spiritual opportunity to promote healing.

Button-pushing incidents look like problems. Some event arises or someone says or does something that trips an instant mental and emotional charge in us. We know we do not deserve this treatment and do not want it. We have not only handled this situation before but feel resentful or even angered that it is coming up yet again. Because our buttons have been pushed throughout life and because we so rarely keep our emotional plate clean, we have accumulated a storehouse of energetic debris.

ॐ Due to these earlier dilemmas, we might have had serious consequences such as feeling embittered or being physically ill or depressed. Perhaps we chose to leave jobs, move to new locations, change relationships, or made other life-altering decisions just to get away. We might resort to blame or futility when we have no answers about why these same problems, with only slight variations, continue to happen.

> *Knowing how we react when our buttons are pushed is a preliminary step to healing an issue.*

Knowing how we react when our buttons are pushed is a preliminary step to healing an issue.

Jim and Rachel had been married for many years. Jim's major issue was, "I am always wrong." Rachel's issue was, "Other people always come first."

At the end of a demanding and frustrating summer, Jim and Rachel were determined to finally take at least a one-day road trip. On an early Friday morning, they started to load their car. Their telephone rang a few minutes later, and Rachel answered it. The caller was Jim's sister, Heather, explaining that she had been planning to take their mom to the doctor's office for a checkup that morning but had been unexpectedly called into work.

As Rachel handed the phone to Jim, she was on guard to see how he would handle this predicament. He told Heather not to worry about it, he would be glad to take their mom to the doctor's office. Rachel instantly went into a bizarre emotional rampage. She shouted, "Why are you always putting other people first? When will you value my life and desires too?"

Rachel was appalled at her overreaction, yet it was as though a dam had burst. She went into the kitchen and opened and slammed cupboard doors. Realizing that she had to get out of the house, she slammed the front door as she stormed out.

By the time Rachel reached the driveway, she heard an inner voice say, "Look at what just happened." She continued to walk, more slowly, while new insights bubbled forth. She realized that, because of her karmic contract with Jim, she was required to react in such a way that would cause him to feel, "No matter what I decide to do, I'm going to be wrong."

Because his mom's doctor's appointment was only for a checkup and was not urgent, he acted according to his script, seeming to be aware of only two options: to please his wife and disappoint his sister, or to please his sister and disappoint his wife. In his karmic mind, his only choice was who he would let down. He, no doubt, felt Heather's job had a higher priority than an outing with his wife, even if it was desperately needed, so he made his decision quickly.

Because Rachel's issue was not the same as Jim's, she could come up with several additional alternatives that would have allowed them the free day they had planned: reschedule Jim's mom's appointment; ask his brother, sister-in-law, or a nephew to take her; make arrangements for a cab or the senior transport van; ask one of his mom's neighbors for help; or Jim could take her to the appointment and someone else could bring her home.

Once Rachel understood that both she and Jim were simply acting according to their individually established norms, her anger vanished. She decided to return home and talk to her husband. She told him that she was not mad at him anymore and that he was affected by his decision as much as she had been. They both needed to get away to get some balance in their life after so many weeks of responsibilities.

They defused their emotions further when Rachel decided to go shopping that morning. Jim took his mother to the doctor's appointment. When he returned home, the couple went to a movie. They cleared their schedule for the following day and went on their road trip the next morning.

No matter how much Jim and Rachel wanted and needed to enjoy their day according to their intended plan, this healing drama held a higher spiritual priority. The whole circumstance was a spiritual setup, and this one button-pushing phone call triggered each of their issues, bringing them to the forefront of their attention so they could choose to work together for mutual soul growth.

Almost always, everyone involved in a critical situation, event, or experience will have their perfect button pushed in the precise way they need. It would be exceptional for a dramatic scene to happen that is not perfectly orchestrated for all. This is why button pushing is a spiritual setup that stimulates healing in our lives.

> *Venting emotions reduces the energetic intensity of our issues and can elevate our state of awareness and appreciation for the situation around us.*

ॐ We can also learn from Rachel's radical reactions and her response to the voice she heard in her head. Venting emotions reduces the energetic intensity of our issues and can elevate our state of awareness and appreciation for the situation around us.

Our issues intensify and become more obvious and frustrating as we mature. Even so, we might or might not recognize recurring healing episodes as variations of a theme.

> Ruth, an elderly woman, was furious at Ed, the husband of her best friend. Their relationship had never been good, and she privately thought he was eccentric. In spite of this, Ruth had invited Deb and Ed for a visit.
>
> As a perfectionist, Ruth had carefully and thoroughly cleaned her home. Sometime during the evening, Ed used the restroom. When he came back to the living room, he was gingerly holding something in a tissue. He told Deb he had dropped his comb on the floor and would have to take it home to sterilize it. His extreme response triggered a button in Ruth. She was livid. She had meticulously cleaned that room, and it was not dirty. He was insulting her and her housekeeping abilities.
>
> Ruth vowed to herself that she would never speak to Ed again. The rest of the evening was very uncomfortable, and all three of them were glad when it was over.

None of the players understood how healing works, so they did not realize there was any possibility that something good could come out of the disastrous evening. Ruth and Ed were the stars in this one-act drama. They were both perfectionists: Ruth about cleaning and appearances, and Ed about dirt and germs. What a divinely perfect spiritual setup.

Ruth interpreted this crisis as the opportunity to finally force her to draw a personal boundary line to stop tolerating Ed's behavior. That one evening's agonizing drama and its repercussions created a new working protocol for both women. Although Deb was a passive observer in the actual episode, her peacemaker button was pushed when Ruth told her the next day that she was never going to speak to Ed again. Deb was distraught at Ruth's position and was perplexed about how to handle her best friend versus her husband. They discussed how they could keep their friendship going in spite of this new twist.

They continued to meet occasionally for lunch, and talked frequently on the phone, but they avoided any references to Ed, and the three of them never again met socially. Ed was indifferent to his wife keeping her long-time friend.

Because Ruth chose an ego-based management technique, the three participants did not make soul progress from this experience, but they did have social relief because they did not have to endure any more issue-healing opportunities among them. Ruth's decision to make a vow is an understandable, conscious ego conclusion under the circumstances, but it was not spiritually wise. Her emotional energies were stored as trash bags and will remain active until she intentionally releases them and her vow, either in this life or as karma in some other.

~ ~ ~

Reinterpreting why our buttons get pushed in the first place enables us to cooperate with the intent behind the setup, which is designed to benefit us. We need each event to provoke and stimulate charged emotions. They goad us to release them. When we learn to interpret life without judgment, we begin to live in a state of *grace*.[79] We then maintain a calmer state of mind and

---

[79] **grace:** the ability to allow for the unknown

minimize the need for spiritual setups.

12: MIRRORING AND PROJECTING

We all have blind spots. When trying on new clothes, we need mirrored reflections to give a fuller view and impression. A three-way mirror provides perspectives from other angles that help us make purchasing decisions, yet we still can't see ourselves as others do. *Mirroring*[80] in life happens when others reflect or actively display our own issues back to us. These reflections are a normal part of life, and they occur more commonly and are less episodic and less dramatic than button pushing.

The issue being mirrored might appear as our opinion of the other person's weaknesses, based on our experience and history with them. Yet the greater t/Truth is that the issue being mirrored is the same as ours, the exact opposite, or some variation. If we think someone is extravagant, he or she probably is, but the mirroring is likely to reflect that we might also be or wish to be excessive, or we could be withdrawn or ultra conservative. If we find someone to be too predictable, we might either be stuck in our own ways or, conversely, overly spontaneous and even disorganized. If we see someone as judgmental, we might either display the same characteristic or

> *Mirroring emotionally draws us into the drama so that we may better see our problem.*

feel a need to always defend ourselves against the judgment of others. If we encounter people who must always win, we might be that way also, or we might be dealing with a role of "loser" or "competitor."

---

[80] *mirroring:* grating interactions with others who reflect or display our own issues

Mirroring emotionally draws us into the drama so that we might better see our problem. The severity of our emotional response indicates the extent of our own involvement in the issue. When we observe a drama and have only a mild or neutral response, it means the behavior of the other person likely depicts his or her soul scripting more than ours.

ॐ Although our blind spots prohibit us from objectively seeing ourselves, we readily see what's wrong with other people. Sometimes we laugh or experience frustration when we hear someone criticize a third person because their objection fits our observations about the complainer. The old sayings, "The pot that calls the kettle black," and "A finger pointing at someone else leaves three pointing back at us," illustrate that we are often unable to see our own deficits except when we see them in others —and even then we often don't accept the characteristic as also being one of ours. This folklore wisdom has been in our consciousness for ages, yet we rarely personally apply it.

~ ~ ~

The flip side of mirroring is *projecting*.[81] When we project, we expect the other person to behave or not behave in a certain way because we have determined that way is right or best, and is the way we would behave under the same circumstances. However, the other person's standard operating procedure or management technique might be directing them to behave in their way and not our way.

Projecting is so incredibly common that we only recognize it when we become frustrated with the other person. When we do catch what is happening, we focus exclusively on them and how wrong, predictable, stubborn, foolish, or narrow-minded they

---

[81] *projecting:* inappropriately attributing our opinions and expectations onto another person as his or her own

are. If a person always arrives late, for example, we continue to expect them to be on time, or we reluctantly accept that they will never be punctual. According to our management style, we can be repeatedly surprised, disappointed, or angered. We might continue to blame them for inconveniencing us yet again.

We bring projection into our everyday life in countless possible ways. We can project our opinion about a hairstyle that we find unattractive, activities we deem unhealthy, attitudes we identify as resistant, interests we believe are unimportant, or decisions we categorize as unwise. We might complain about someone who is a complainer, and we might not recognize that we are complaining too, or we might see that trait in ourselves but dismiss it as not being that bad.

Children and teens need to be corrected and guided, but as adults, we each have discretion to live our own life. Projecting actually reflects our irrational attempts to fix others because we think we are right; it is, in

> *Projecting actually reflects our irrational attempts to fix others because we think we are right.*

fact, a childish activity in which adults engage. The irony is that our opinions might be accurate, and perhaps nearly everyone we know would agree with us about the situation. Yet applying our standards onto someone else is unrealistic and rarely effective. Done frequently on the same person, projecting aggravates a dueling game filled with misunderstandings and blame. It creates and reinforces turmoil and strife.

> Everything was always about Sarah. She had no empathy for others, few listening skills, and rarely asked questions of other people. She tilted conversations in her direction and seemed incapable of remembering anyone

else's important events or experiences, even those of her family members. Her relationship with her only sister, Megan, had been intermittent, occasionally difficult, and disappointing for each of them. They both mirrored selfishness to each other.

On one especially frustrating day, Sarah was to pick up Megan to attend a holiday program. Megan took a long time to answer her doorbell and wasn't ready to promptly leave. Sarah realized there was no way they could make the program on time, and she was angry. They got started too late, and when they arrived, the only seats available were at the back of the auditorium.

Sarah was furious about the whole afternoon. She couldn't even enjoy the program. She decided to take Megan home as soon as possible, instead of going out to dinner with her, as they had planned.

The theme of Sarah's conversations over the next few days was about how bad and wrong Megan was. Sarah accused her sister of not appreciating her efforts to take her to the special event, not apologizing for delaying their arrival, not offering to pay for parking, and showing no concern that Sarah was angry. She concluded that Megan was incredibly selfish.

Not only was Sarah self-absorbed, she had issues about these exact matters. Her buttons were: people are to always be on time; kindness I show requires appreciation from others; costs are to be shared equally; my way is the best way; never sit in the back of any room; and my needs, feelings, and efforts are all that matter.

This anecdote is a classic example of a spiritual setup of mirroring and projecting that happens to everyone in the unique way we each need. Unfortunately for Sarah, she never did learn about her issue of selfishness even though everyone who knew her saw it; from experience, they either recognized it would be futile to point out her selfishness to her, or chose not to discuss it because they knew it would only make matters worse. Regrettably, there was no contact between the sisters after that disastrous day together.

~ ~ ~

Once we recognize the hidden benefits behind mirroring and catch ourselves projecting, we become able to claim responsibility for those issues in our own lives and will more clearly identify our karmic soul scripting. Then we can reinterpret what is happening, safely release the stimulated emotional baggage, and proceed more authentically through the situation. In a later chapter, we will learn how to do this, using the Three Pillars of Transformation.

CHAPTER 3:
LIFE'S HEALING SETUPS

At this point in our development, humans seem to require provocation in order to stimulate our ego-managed emotions. Agitation creates the incentive and opportunity for us to release and clear these accrued and unwanted emotions from our system.

This chapter delves into the intricacies of how life is set up to help us reach the deepest level of our emotions and offer the greatest potential for healing. Fortunately, life's challenges contain divine beneficial intentions. We only need to reinterpret a life challenge into that of a healing opportunity.

13: RELATIONSHIPS

Our oneness with Source originates from a baseline of *unconditional love*[82] in and for all people. We are each a part of this whole. We select specific relationships and karmic roles to serve each soul in our incarnations.

The scripts that contain our mandated issues challenge us to rise above low frequencies from past lives. The scripts are also a conundrum. The scripted issues are meant to help us heal. Yet, they also block us from accessing our pure core until we energetically and incrementally release them. In this way, our life script initially sets up a barrier to our integration with Source, then simultaneously intends and nearly forces us to become aware of and stimulate our need to heal.

---

[82] *unconditional love:* an ever-present state of nonjudgmental acceptance, support, and radiance that is embedded in Source and is consistently all encompassing and all forgiving

Healing, then, is incremental, like peeling away layers of an onion to get to the core of our divine identity. The process is like learning mathematics: first we learn numbers, then addition and subtraction, then multiplication and division, then higher math. With the development of each new skill, we advance into deeper onion layers, which represent removing the energy barriers we chose to work on in this life. This gradually opens our ego consciousness to the benefits of spiritual evolution and allows us greater access to and integration with Source.

If it weren't for our close interaction with karmic soul connections, we would be oblivious to our issues. We need people, with all of the resulting dramas and challenges, to keep us on our spiritual healing track.

The role-playing partners we chose for our close karmic relationships target and expose our fundamental challenges. They help us reach and remove our emotional debris with scripted precision.

Relationships can be anything from fleeting to lifelong, casual to life-changing, rewarding to troublesome. We all desire happy, easy lives. We want to be accepted, supported, and loved. However, we are most emotionally and energetically connected to family members because our shared past lives have created deep bonds together. The role-playing partners we chose for our close karmic relationships target and expose our fundamental challenges. They help us reach and remove our emotional debris with scripted precision. Some families provide emotional nurturing. Others model mild to severe dysfunction, drama, and/or abuse.

As a result of our soul contracts with birth, adopted, and adult family members, our life scripts foreordain issues, roles, and the need for enactments. Living spiritually uninformed lives restricts our awareness to visual, experiential, and emotional input. We draw life conclusions based on incomplete evidence. The assumptions and opinions we form calibrate, reinforce, and perpetuate our life patterns.

> *Living spiritually uninformed lives restricts our awareness to visual, experiential, and emotional input.*

ॐ Because we are all inherently part of a singular, universal energy, our actions and thoughts affect everyone. This is why healing ourselves stimulates healing possibilities in others. Resembling the ripple effect of a stone dropped in water, those closest to us receive the strongest inducement to improve their lives as we evolve. Their free will choice allows them to benefit from or reject each auspicious opportunity that we and others present to them.

> *Healing ourselves stimulates healing possibilities in others.*

If relationships were puzzle pieces, the people closest to us are those with whom we connect and interlock. As we heal, our basic shape smooths out, indentations fill in, and protrusions shrink. Our fit with others becomes not as locked-in as before, yet some issues or areas of concern might have improved. As our connections with those nearest to us become more flexible, those people might need to adjust their lives to accommodate our changes. If they are unable or unwilling to adapt, the relationship usually deteriorates, and we might simply slide away from each other or find ourselves face to face with difficult or even excruciating decisions and changes.

As the relationships shift, additional emotional material almost always comes up for us to review and release. Communication is essential, and blame is detrimental. When we address foundational issues, situations in relationships often get worse before they improve. This consequence provides stimulation for us to release accrued emotional energies and facilitates our further healing.

> *Communication is essential, and blame is detrimental. When we address foundational issues, situations in relationships often get worse before they improve.*

~ ~ ~

Other people respond to our healing in essentially three ways: by not changing at all and being angry that we are, by shifting a little bit with us, or by changing to a greater degree as part of our and their souls' life script.

Typically, others continue to behave exactly the same way they always have. If they pushed buttons before, they will still attempt to do so. The critical difference in the relationship is that our emotional reactions to the button pushers will gradually become milder. We will more clearly see that they are pushing our buttons, still wish it were different, and yet recognize the other's role is to help us clear our issue. We will notice that we have growing compassion for and understanding of them. We might actually want to thank them for pushing our buttons and, thus, confirm that our change is beneficial and motivating us to change further. When we realize that we don't need anyone to push our buttons anymore, we will discover wiser and healthier responses to situations that, previously, triggered our highly emotional reactions.

Invariably, our healing will also cause some sort of shift in others around us. People who are stubborn, egotistic, outspoken, and controlling will see our improvement as altering the rules of their game without their permission. They will not be happy about it, claim that we have no right to change or treat them this new way, and might declare that things were fine the way they were before. Unless they come to a self-realization of their own, their behavior will seem to worsen, possibly becoming more vehement or vociferous or even violent, as we heal. This is a sign that

> *Invariably, our healing will also cause some sort of shift in others around us.*

such relationships were undoubtedly not rewarding to begin with, and are now falling apart or intolerable. Some affiliations will need to be severed. Should this occur, we need to practice spiritual forgiveness in order to eliminate future karma with these souls. As painful and difficult as this might be, our decision could begin to heal each life involved in our script.

ॐ It is possible, though unusual, for a person to play a role exclusively for us. At the soul level, he or she was willing to take on the assignment even though it offered no substantial benefit to that individual. Blocked by the limitations of human vision, that person might not even realize he or she is also changing as we heal. As we clear our issue, this soul partner stops playing the old role that used to bring up our strong reaction. As we heal, the other person appears to heal also. We might find this improvement to be perplexing because he or she is not trying to amend his or her life, and we are doing all the work. We will, however, welcome the difference.

~ ~ ~

In the following story, the married couple was enmeshed in soul-scripted and challenging lives that improved because of seemingly discourteous comments from a neighbor. As the wife shifted, so did her husband and her neighbor.

> Dora and Carl had been happily married for many years in spite of some annoying issues between them. The longevity of their marriage was the result of the fact that they were each people pleasers and givers, so they supported each other easily and willingly even when in disagreement. Dora was on a spiritual path, and Carl preferred a proscribed religious practice.
>
> Carl was a wonderful, thoughtful, kind, and helpful man—at least on the surface. He had many friends and would go out of his way to do anything for anyone—albeit at his own pace. He was soft spoken, worked hard to support his family, and was extremely creative. He also had Attention Deficit Hyperactivity Disorder (ADHD,) which resulted in him having an image of low self worth.

His management style was to stay in control of his life as much as possible, to put off for later what could be done earlier, and only do things on his timetable, even though, illogically, he prioritized socializing and others' needs over his own agendas.

It had always been challenging for him to make decisions and complete projects. He had many internal conflicts and his tendency to always have choices at hand created external chaos; as an example, his several bottles of shampoos, conditioners, bubble baths, and bars of soap created clutter around the bathtub.

After the couple was first married, Dora pointed out to him when things were not finished, the mail accumulated, or there was some looming deadline that needed his attention now. Whenever she did this, Carl's response was either anger or withdrawal. Over time, Dora learned not to mention the things that Carl didn't take care of, assumed more of his responsibilities, and worked at minimizing and eliminating judgment from her life. Eventually, even their children would comment that their mom was one of the most accepting people they knew and would give the benefit of the doubt to anyone. However, Dora continued to think blame-filled thoughts about her husband.

Dora's next-door neighbor, Trudy, was a hard-working, fun-loving person. Her life had been difficult, and she was challenged in relationships. She had the karmic role of being a policewoman and would often help others by pointing out what they were doing wrong and what they should do to correct it. Trudy's primary focus had been her adult family, and Dora had only occasionally been the subject of her corrective attention. However, after her divorce, Trudy began to tell Dora what she needed to do in order to change her life.

One red-letter day, for the third phone conversation in a row, Trudy told Dora how hurt she had been yet again by their recent talk and what Dora should have said differently so that Trudy would not have been offended. Dora apologized and hung up as soon as she tactfully could.

Dora found the emotions she was feeling to be just too strange. She asked God for clarity about what was going on. A quiet inner voice said it was time to clear judgment from her life. Dora immediately realized that her neighbor had been doing for her exactly what she had been doing for Carl, except that Trudy was verbalizing her complaints to Dora while Dora held her harsh feelings about Carl inside. Wow and ouch! What a stunning and sobering insight.

Trudy and Carl had each been serving Dora very well to bring this problem of judgment to her attention, and she realized that she was ready to be completely rid of this issue. Never one to procrastinate, Dora immediately forgave each of them and, recognizing her responsibility for this issue, she surrendered it to God.

The next morning over coffee, Carl asked Dora for her opinion about how he could improve his ADHD. This had never happened before in their marriage. As Dora considered this and replied, Carl listened with an open mind, which was also a new occurrence, and they had a fulfilling discussion about the subject. Dora pointed out a few ways that Carl unnecessarily created chaos in their lives, and he was not defensive about her comments. Another unprecedented response.

They each had house chores to do that day, and Carl went to clean the bathroom. A few hours later, Dora went into the room and saw what Carl had done. She was speechless. The tub had only one shampoo, one conditioner, one bar of soap, and one bubble bath. The room looked beautiful. She had not discussed this with him that morning nor asked him to clear things out. He had done this completely of his own volition. She complimented him several times that day and carried around an inner smile, knowing that his change had occurred primarily because of her forgiveness and surrendering.

Dora felt a major shift in her marriage with Carl. For the first time in many years, she felt they were on the same side of the fence, working together in a partnership rather than each fending for themselves. This benefit permanently continued but tapered off somewhat over time.

Dora was able to more quickly and easily catch any judgmental thoughts as they came up and surrendered them each time. This technique was effective in reducing the strength and frequency of her negative thoughts.

The rapport between Trudy and Dora mended, although Dora still sensed a need to do more listening and questioning than discussing or sharing her opinion. Trudy gradually began to address judgment in her own life.

If you have ADHD, or any of a number of other chronic, serious conditions, such as bi-polar, hoarder, or obsessive compulsive disorders, you might have areas of happiness and fulfillment in life, but you have signed up for frustrating challenges and, likely, a spiritually unempowered life that is serving you in some way at the soul level. Medications, support groups, and newer energetic techniques might help you better manage and improve your quality of life. Although it is now unusual, it might become possible to heal these conditions in this incarnation. To do so would require an open mind, professional energetic intervention and modalities, and strong determination to continuously make small personal changes. The more family or professional support you have, the more likely you will conquer this challenge.

If you live with a person with one of these significant conditions, you have a soul contract with him or her, and you are also being served by the agreement. Should you be on a spiritual path, you have probably enlisted for an accelerated course toward empowerment. If not, staying in the relationship might strengthen responsibility, loyalty, or other karmic weaknesses, or it might deter your personal development. As in other partnerships, soul-contract agreements might be revised or ended, if a person is at a high enough vibrational level to do so.

One other important spiritual concept to extract from this story is that things happen *for* us, not *to* us. All things are intended to serve us rather than promote a victim mentality.

> *Things happen for us, not to us.*

14: CHILDREN

ॐ Family interactions began in antiquity, gradually plotting out roles and behaviors that others in the karmic scripts began to expect. In many cases, the ancient family model is still fundamentally intact. However, old familial belief systems and expectations have begun to change radically during the last several decades. Dad no longer has to be the one who takes out the trash. Mom rarely stays home and prepares all meals from scratch. Mom and dad might not be married. There are often step- and half-sisters and brothers. Parents could be a homosexual couple. The definition of family is expanding. Eventually we will have totally revised models of relationships, partnerships, marriages, and families. They will be inclusive, accepting, diverse, and more spiritually congruent.

Because energies are increasing so rapidly and we need assistance to change our inner and outer lives, most, but not all of the children now being born in recent years are old, wise, and attuned souls. These gifted children are here now to compel us to change. They are not all knowing or perfect, but they might make fewer serious mistakes in life due to their inborn spiritual connection, and some of them are pushing the traditional behavior envelope to assist humanity's evolvement. These spiritually advanced children are expediting a re-evaluation of our current family structure and methods of operating. In order to advance personal, societal, and global spiritual development, we need to radically alter family dynamics. These children will be showing us that old patterns, styles, systems, procedures, methods, and interpretations of life and its management are becoming less and less effective.

Family and parenting challenges occur, however, because babies do not come with instruction manuals and adults are left to invent coping and training techniques as necessary. Lacking the awareness, concepts, and skills needed to assist the evolutionary transition, parents are puzzled, overwhelmed, confused, frustrated, and exhausted by the behavior and antics of their spiritually advanced offspring. This essential metamorphic stage for humanity is not easy for anyone, yet it will benefit everyone. These challenging children bring the most profound gift and opportunity available to humankind as a whole. Families are carving out new relationship models that will provide structure and support for empowered beings of all ages in the future.

> *Families are carving out new relationship models that will provide structure and support for empowered beings of all ages in the future.*

These young people with elevated energies have inner radar and are skilled at detecting those who are living shallow, unreflective lives. As a result, it is difficult for them to respect incongruent people, even their parents, and they have difficulty pushing past their spiritual knowingness to play the expected role of a human child. The children seem to resemble a doctoral student living and interacting only with preschoolers who, in turn, are trying to parent and discipline them. Daily life for these children requires that they continually filter, adjust, and simplify their existence. Over time, this wears the child down, withering away that doctoral student persona, as he or she seeks spiritually advanced companionship. This dilemma creates challenging situations and conditions within a family, classroom, and the world at large.

Parents want and need to understand and support their child's energetic potentials, special gifts, and extraordinary needs. Most of today's offspring are unwilling and/or unable to fit the historical model of compliant, authority-dominated children. They demand to be heard and honored, not controlled and punished. They inherently have an academy award winning ability to push buttons and mirror issues for others, especially family members. This causes parents and society to blame them for acting out, not cooperating, and being stubborn.

Parents are perplexed about how to handle their children and, with fatigue and desperation rising, far too often give in to whatever their child wants simply because that seems like the easiest thing to do. This understandable yet undesirable response can shift the dynamic away from healthy family interactions and respect, with the parents raising their children, to a situation in which the child controls the family.

> *Most of today's offspring are unwilling and/or unable to fit the historical model of compliant, authority-dominated children. They demand to be heard and respected, not controlled and punished.*

~ ~ ~

🕉 Perhaps the most basic and essential idea for parents to know is the importance of teaching and modeling consequences of actions. We reap what we sow, and, in practical terms, for every action, there is a reaction or consequence. This is the impersonal, unemotional, nonjudgmental, and factual cosmic tenet of cause and effect, which is a constant in life and generically applicable to all things and in all ways. It is essential for children to learn about, experience, practice, and live within the guidelines of this ordinance. It is up to parents to discuss their thoughts about what this means to them, and to agree on how to employ the principle when directing and disciplining their children.

Developing guidelines, boundaries, structures, routines, expectations, judgment skills, and emotional nurturing sets the necessary backdrop in place. Each one of these areas must be learned in childhood to create the foundation for healthy and responsible adult behaviors. Eventually, we all need to evolve and expand beyond such a fundamentally configured life pattern. When we do, we will find that entire families will find unlimited freedom to grow in ways that few people today can even imagine.

Enlightened parents understand that striving to always make everything easier deprives the child of helpful or needed life experiences. When a child who is old enough to understand throws something and it breaks, it is more beneficial for the adult to explain what happened than to just fix it. Working with the child to mend the item can become a positive reminder of the larger lesson.

The significant difference between consequences for one's actions and punishment is the lack of judgment and accusation on the part of the disciplinarian.

Even the steps of raising a child are progressive. Early on, a parent demonstrates and helps a child make his or her bed.

Gradually, the parents encourage more responsibility by participating less. When a child is older, if he or she displays a rebellious attitude or the parents' expectations are not met, the child needs to be disciplined with some consequence, perhaps not to see a favorite TV program or to sit in a time-out chair— but not administer it as punishment. The significant difference between consequences for one's actions and punishment is the lack of judgment and accusation on the part of the disciplinarian. A child is not wrong because he or she did not listen to the parent or did not cooperate with expectations. The discipline is merely the consequence of the child's action or inaction. And that is actually a healthy growth experience.

~ ~ ~

ॐ Today's evolved children are also extremely intelligent and have much to teach their parents and other adults. They like order in their lives and their home

> *Evolved children are the first major wave of the new humanity.*

environment and might become anxious or have difficulty sleeping in the midst of chaos. They have little patience for what they see as meaningless requirements or procedures, unevolved people, and especially teachers who merely perform traditional roles. They love nature, creativity, and art, and they excel in technology. They are usually telepathic and frequently see other dimensional beings and hear spiritual guidance. Their finely tuned sensitivities are easily overloaded, so they appear to overreact and are often stressed, causing many of them to be labeled as having an attention deficit. They are affected by higher frequencies than most of us are even able to perceive, let alone understand, manage, or eliminate. They might react to people, situations, and events in peculiar ways and for unknown reasons. All of these conditions are challenging for their parents and other adults to live with and handle at this stage of our global spiritual development. However, the potential benefits for these children and those of us who interact with them are boundless and inestimable. These evolved children are the first major wave of the new humanity.

There are some children on earth now who are here to model this new humanity. Even at a young age, they are incredible peacemakers and wise beyond their traditional education. They magnetically attract people to them and offer attention, help, and support to others. They can solve problems and resolve difficulties with instinctive breadth, cohesiveness, and ease. Anyone who knows them is impressed with their beingness.

These advanced souls are serving humanity in selfless ways, but they can easily feel overloaded, exhausted, and taken advantage of. They have difficulty refusing to help anyone, and rarely allow themselves to complain or express their personal challenges. Their life is a priceless treasure to those who know them, and nearly everyone responds to their unique, appealing, and outstandingly gifted personality. We have much to learn from them. As time goes on, there will be more of these souls on earth, and they will derive support from each other.

ॐ Many young children have past life recall. If their family accepts and supports this possibility, parents should ask their children exploratory questions and accept their answers without judgment. Assure them that they can talk about the subject anytime they wish at home but caution them to be selective in discussing these thoughts with others. Society as a whole is not quite ready to acknowledge reincarnation.

More often, past life memories are not understood nor is discussion of that subject wanted in the average family. The child might even be ridiculed for what he or she says when mentioning a past life experience. If this happens, it doesn't take long for the child to stop talking about this subject and much valuable karma or dharma information is lost to both the child and the family.

Eventually, children consciously forget about previous incarnations. However, these energies remain active and accessible in the creative and spiritual side of the brain, from which memories of past lives can be retrieved at any age through hypnosis. Doing so provides tremendous insight and life understanding, and can produce physical and/or emotional healing.

~ ~ ~

Watch young children in action, play, or conversation and look for possible past life references that might provide a clue to soul histories. For example, two youngsters were playing and one said to the other, "Remember when we were up there?" pointing toward the sky. "Yes," the other replied. "All we had to do was wave our hands and everything was done."

Look for former life patterns in present affiliations that can reveal aspects of prior relationships, issues, roles, or experiences that are destined to be played out in this lifetime. Beyond being fascinating, these insights can teach something that will help us more effectively guide and support our young people on their spiritual paths: a son might attempt to control a sibling or parent, even at a young age; a daughter might appear lazy and expect everyone to wait on her.

Realize also that the parents' reactions to these childish characteristics and roles are equally a part of life's dramas. It is entirely possible that, karmically, the child might be scripted to be the star and the parents to be members of the supporting cast.

15: EMOTIONAL TRUTH

Emotions are designed to be a blessing and an insightful gift. Instinctively they keep us on track with our inner k/Knowing by leading us

> *Emotions are designed to be a blessing and an insightful gift.*

toward what is better for us and away from something not helpful or possibly even dangerous. If we sense or feel that we don't want to do a certain thing, go to a particular place, or trust someone, we learn to listen to and apply this input. If we feel happy, encouraged, validated, or any of the more positive feelings, we rely on this input to pursue more of what we are doing. We refer to this inner sensation as our *emotional t/Truth*[83] because it is a sign of our ability to be congruent with our higher, divine energy.

A person who has no emotional reactions is not healthy. Feeling detached from other people and even our own lives leaves us flat, lonely, frustrated, depressed, hopeless, and possibly suicidal or even murderous. We want and need to minimize and eliminate these adverse qualities. It is not our spiritual goal to be overprotective of or exclusively focused on our own feelings, needs, desires, or opinions. It is through releasing our ego experiences, history, and identification that we will become healthfully and emotionally clear and disentangled from dramas.

As we remove emotional debris, our feelings resonate accurately according to our t/Truth. Anytime we speak with congruency, our message includes both levels of truth

> *Healthy emotions help us remain inherently stable, honest, and appropriate to the situation or event.*

---

[83] *emotional t/Truth:* honestly recognizing, admitting, and expressing emotions to assist congruency

and Truth, even if our words are clearly based on emotions. Resolving our feelings as they erupt will keep our emotional plate clean, allowing emotional clarity to function as an additional guidance resource. Healthy emotions help us remain inherently stable, honest, and appropriate to the situation or event. This condition allows us to respond to others with benevolence, grace, and kindness.

However, when our t/Truth is blocked, ignored, denied, distorted, misinterpreted, or challenged, we are left with only ego life views, interpretations, reactions, and emotions. Some people have learned they must react strongly to others in order to be heard or to be included in decision making. Others back down from those who frequently either dominate them or don't listen to or want their input. These are both ego-based responses. E/go might block us from being receptive to help from others. Likewise, ego can block others from being sensitive to our needs, situations, and/or feelings and being willing to help us. We have experientially and painfully discovered that the more emotional we are, the less respect and assistance we receive from others.

Whatever our conclusions, eventually we collect excess emotional baggage that distorts our personal interactions and relationships. All of these energies are highly charged and troublesome. If we had cleared them when they originated, we would not have created issues in the first place. However, we are rarely taught how to effectively and efficiently respond to our disturbed feelings.

> *Controlling our emotions only perpetuates and intensifies them.*

As a result of having no other apparent options, we learn to override and suppress our emotions through management techniques that put a spin on what we really feel. This action might appear to help us in the short term but ends up merely postponing resolution and clearing. Controlling our emotions only perpetuates and intensifies them. As we learn to utilize our emotional truth, we might determine to reject the immediate urge that would have been our automatic reaction in the past and, thus, decide not to behave in the way we are tempted. If, for example, a friend says or does something that hurts or angers us, we might quickly evaluate our initial, negative response and decide to do or say something kinder or more compassionate than we would have otherwise.

This skill of responding in a calmer manner is socially encouraged and seems helpful to the overall relationship and situation. But if ego is still involved, then we discover, deep down inside, that offering only a gentle response works well for everyone else, but is incongruent with our true inner feelings. Although it is often beneficial to be kind and helpful, totally ignoring our real emotions is not authentic and reinforces our need to only manage ourselves better. Ideally, we will rise above ego when we accept how we feel and use that as a factor in deciding what to do or how to respond. The result is then more genuine.

There are people, however, who have no filter in their head to screen what comes out of their mouth. They have no regard for anyone else's reaction and frequently spew their self-righteous, angry opinions and tumultuous emotions onto others. People with these behaviors are not emotionally healthy. Their karmic lessons are probably to become more sensitive to others, learn how to be supportive, and develop compassion, empathy, and other higher soul qualities.

If you or someone in your life is wired this way, you probably already know that close relationships are dramatic and difficult. The spiritual component to remember, however, is that those involved with these dramas are living their karmic script; they signed on for the challenge, and have something potentially rewarding to benefit from it.

If you are an adult living with someone with these issues, you are not required to maintain the relationship merely because it is in your script. As you evolve, you can move beyond the need to stay in old patterns. This idea is not an easy or quick opt-out for unpleasant relationships, but, after intense or prolonged difficulties and doing all you energetically and honestly can to help the other person and to heal yourself, leaving allows a fresh opportunity for you to clear, restabilize, and start again. Your departure might also be a welcome break for the other person or people in the unhealthy relationship.

As long as you understand how you benefited from the relationship issues, have worked things out as well as you can with the person or people involved, and have spiritually forgiven them, you might be able to sever the ties and be freed from any further karmic role-playing. You might then be better able to facilitate your own soul growth or help other, new friends with their soul growth in ways that are beyond the realm of your current circumstances. If you sense that is the case, then take this concept into your heart and your intuitive consciousness and ask for divine guidance. Then, if appropriate, give yourself permission to leave, and do so as pleasantly and honestly as possible.

Being True to Our t/Truth

We all carry around unpleasant emotions. Although it is always appropriate to be tactful, presenting a corrupted

> *We do not become congruent until we are purely honest.*

version of our t/Truth compromises our integrity. We do not become congruent until we are purely honest. We need to recognize and accept the emotions we feel no matter how distressingly familiar, uncomfortable, difficult, confusing, irreversible, wrong, or painful they might seem to be.

We need to safely express our emotions. At first, we might do this only when we are alone or with an understanding friend. Later, and with practice, we will learn that we must be willing to speak our t/Truth appropriately in the moment to those who push our buttons. We need to know our emotional truth and give it a voice. Until we come to terms with our life and emotions, we are stuck merely managing them, which often means hiding or suppressing them.

> *Until we come to terms with our life and emotions, we are stuck merely managing them.*

~ ~ ~

To heal and release emotions, we move the low-vibration energies up and out of our system. The vacated space then becomes unprogrammed, allowing more room for God's Light to enter within and providing us with more internal congruency and wiser behavior options. As we heal one issue, a related or connected issue has its opportunity to surface and break apart also. As we work with this process, our life might not get easier initially, but it will incrementally improve.

> Theresa was seeking spiritual development. She had worked as a nail technician in a salon for many years. Her life issues of betrayal and rejection were peaking, practically begging to be released and cleared.
>
> Theresa needed a hip replacement, so she

referred her clients to other technicians during her sick leave. When she was able to come back to work after the operation, all of her customers except one returned to her. Although she could have perceived the high number of returning clients as a positive acceptance of her skill and personality, she felt betrayed and rejected by this one woman's lack of support. This holdout's decision caused Theresa to have an uncontrollable, over-the-top reaction, and she cried for days. Even during that excruciating time, Theresa knew that her buttons had been pushed and she was overreacting, but nothing could stop her tears.

A few weeks later, this former client confided to Theresa that she had not wanted to offend the substitute by leaving her. After Theresa explained the standard protocol for temporary support by professionals in her field, her customer returned. When the situation resolved, Theresa recognized how her tears expedited healing, and she saw cosmic humor in the event. Now she literally laughs about all of it.

ॐ If each soul was a towel, we would incarnate with it being emotionally saturated and unable to naturally drip dry or evaporate. Our goal is to leave life with the driest, fluffiest towel possible, one that is energetically wrung out. Whenever we finally stand up for our own inner t/Truth and say or do what is honest for us, we wring one end of the towel, and the situation or reactions of others nearly always deteriorate. When this happens, it is as though another hand is wringing the other end of the towel. The towel does get drier, but the wringing from both ends also heightens our emotional distress.

This towel-wringing practice is intended to maximize release of our emotional energy, and allowing our frustration and anger to come out, as Theresa did, will promote actual healing of our issue. Not doing so aborts this opportunity, delays healing, intensifies the issue, and requires stronger personal management, which, of course, only prolongs the problem.

If we are unaware that Source wants us to wring our towel until it is dry, we only know our human feelings, and we witness the apparent outcomes of dealing with our issues only with human eyes. We learn how to use ego management techniques to handle our internal disturbances, and doing so appears to minimize external negative consequences—for a time. So we logically conclude that we should not be honest again because it only makes things worse. When we do this, we resolve to continue managing our issue, which only reinforces it and leaves a great deal of moisture in our metaphorical towel.

~ ~ ~

When you begin to be more honest in relationships and when your buttons are pushed, plan on outcomes being more difficult for a while. Also, do not continue to fall for the illusion that managing and perpetuating the old habit is helpful.

> Nancy is a hard worker and determined to succeed at everything she undertakes. She has turned out to be a wonderful, caring mother who handles a lot of responsibility. She is also dominating, judgmental, and controlling. She developed these traits as a defensive management style to compensate for her life issues of rejection and abandonment. Others with these same difficulties might use different

coping techniques.

Susan is Nancy's mother-in-law. She is generous, kind, giving, and fun loving. Susan's issues have been to avoid confrontation, compromise her feelings to prevent arguments, and have others like her. She had learned how to live with and manage these issues yet would usually feel the need to talk about what was wrong only with a third party rather than directly to the person involved. This behavior perpetuated and intensified her challenges because she avoided facing and clearing her emotions.

Nancy lived rent-free with Susan's family to complete college before she married Susan's son. As soon as she moved into the house, she told Susan that the food on a particular cupboard shelf was hers and the family was not to use it. Nancy, however, helped herself to the family's food. For the sake of the relationship, Susan complied with Nancy's mandate. Although she was very disturbed, she said nothing about it to Nancy because she did not want to create problems for herself, her son, or her future daughter-in-law. She did, however, talk about Nancy behind her back, with other friends and family.

Nancy's issues seemed to worsen and extend as the years went by. Even after marriage, she felt entitled and was full of expectations and demands. Susan and her husband were normally outgoing people, but they withdrew from conversation when Nancy was around in order to avoid her emotional landmines.

One day, Nancy asked Susan to take her younger daughter to weekly counseling many miles away. Susan has never been a confident driver and the commitment would have taken most of one day each week. In spite of how much she loved her grandchildren, regularly babysat for them, and knew there could be potentially devastating fallout, she absolutely could not back down anymore. This was the final straw. She had to say no. It was not even the driving that was the main dilemma, although she could have explained it as that. Her decision was based on her needs to be a fully interactive partner in relationships and to speak her t/Truth.

Knowing she had to speak to Nancy in person, Susan surrendered everything about the encounter before she went to see her. The scene was painful and traumatic. Nancy even accused Susan of being a bad grandmother and told her to leave. Susan went to her car, sat there, and cried her heart out. When Susan stopped crying, she realized that, in spite of this terrible experience, she did not regret finally speaking up, finally expressing her emotional truth.

Nancy decided to avoid all contact between her family and Susan's. It was excruciating for Susan to not see or talk to her grandchildren. Nancy and her family were not invited to the next birthday celebration held at a brother's home. When Nancy's birthday came along, Susan sent her a card with a check. A few days later, Nancy texted Susan to thank her for the gift. The two women went out to lunch a few times. The conversations were awkward and tentative, yet these were the baby steps they needed to take to build a healthier relationship.

Although Nancy and Susan did not fully discuss nor resolve the episode itself, they did gradually work through some of their issues. The families resumed seeing each other, and there was a noticeable improvement in their interactions and relationship. Susan benefited from a major life growth and now frequently speaks her t/Truth, regardless of what she thinks the response might be. Nancy is more open about her challenges but still seems unwilling to examine her life, take personal responsibility, and make changes to evolve. It is still easier for her to blame others. Nancy will continue to have interactions that push her buttons to assist her with healing her issues, but, of course, it is her choice to embrace or reject them.

Claiming Responsibility

Sometimes the best way to deal with emotions is simply to honestly recognize the facts of the situation, both within us and within the other person or people who are engaged in the conflict. Seeking spiritual guidance can help us see through emotional curtains.

Rita is married to Leo and has a professional but low-income career. They have modest means but, due to other family circumstances, own a newer second home. After several years, Rita felt that this vacation residence needed interior painting. Leo, however, felt it would be fine for several more years and was not willing to consider the idea nor pay for it.

Rita also knew it was time to begin a few larger house projects in preparation for their retirement when their income would drop. While at the vacation residence with Leo for a long weekend, Rita obtained estimates from three painters. Afterward, the couple had a heart-to-heart talk about this undertaking. Leo did not change his mind about not paying for the work and insisted that if the project went ahead, they were to keep exactly the same colors they presently had throughout the whole house.

At one point in the discussion, Leo told Rita he did not want her opinion. She was stunned, and didn't know what to say. In fact, she didn't know how to talk to him at all. If a husband does not want his wife's input and opinions, there can be no relationship. She left the room and took a shower to cool off her emotions.

Rita cried and prayed extensively during the shower. She called for spiritual help, asking for ideas to move forward in this relationship. She needed to develop some foundation for conversation but sensed that was not possible. Instead, she realized that she had to be truthful in the moment. Although this Source input didn't seem at all helpful, she reflected on her and Leo's life issues and what was energetically presenting itself.

She could clearly see that Leo had control and money issues. She realized that she always preferred to avoid confrontation. A perfect healing setup. Because their long and solid relationship seemed to be on the line, she didn't know what to do or how to proceed.

After redressing, Rita told Leo to return to the living room so they could talk. She said she no longer knew what to say to him and would probably be uncommunicative for a while. She said she didn't deserve to be treated this way and that his position was unbelievable and stubborn. In spite of this, she claimed full responsibility for what had happened because she understood there was some, as yet unknown, benefit behind this crisis. Leo said he didn't understand what she meant and didn't care.

At the end of the weekend and after two days of minimal conversation, Leo asked if this was the way things were going to be between them from now on. Rita had no answer to give. On their drive home the following day, they had several hours of discussion in the car. Based on that, she decided to go ahead with the painting, paying the whole cost from her meager savings and keeping the original colors.

Rita discovered she was no longer willing to back away from confrontations. Although she does not instigate arguments, she now works through a problem to attain some level of agreement between them. This action is not always easy, but it is necessary and helpful.

This spiritual setup began when Leo unknowingly pushed a button that provided a healing opportunity for them both. Although he is not seeking healing and does not want to hear about such matters, Rita no longer hesitates to point out, factually rather than emotionally, when he is closed, resistant, uncooperative, and controlling. Over time, they have both made adjustments, and their marriage has actually improved.

Communication Is Essential

The most basic level of expressing our emotional truth is self-serving and myopic. Speaking our feelings in anger with no regard for their effects or consequences on others can be a short-term stage of opening up, but that is not our goal.

> *Speaking our feelings in anger with no regard for their effects or consequences on others can be a short-term stage of opening up, but that is not our goal.*

Living this way creates relationship challenges and provokes more painful and volatile emotions. It is an endless, repeating, futile cycle. Something needs to change in order to improve outcomes.

Anita had an emotional breakdown after an argument with her husband. She blamed him for the problem and her reaction. In her mind, he was absolutely wrong, and, she cried all day.

By the next day, Anita realized that as long as she continued to look at their relationship the way she always had, she was emotionally stuck. Unless she shifted her position and interacted differently with her husband, nothing was going to improve. She accepted and took responsibility for her excessive emotional reaction to what had happened. She let go of her anger and blame by forgiving him and determined she would do whatever she could to facilitate healing in her own life and in their relationship.

Although Anita still needed to follow up and work things out with her husband, her release of blame made a noticeable difference. Her husband felt less defensive and cooperated with her better than he had before her change. They were finally able to talk more constructively about their problems and began to make critical, although seemingly small improvements in their relationship.

Clearing Emotions for Authenticity

Everyday life has dramatically emotional highs and lows. We are accustomed to this. Even in a marriage, there are usually far too many emotional episodes. The honeymoon stage typifies the elevated glow of new and insatiable love, which settles into ordinary life about one or two years later. Eventually, more than half of today's American marriages result in divorce.

> *As we release our emotionally based karmic relationship chains, ... we do not become doormats, but express ourselves t/Truthfully, live in attunement with others, attract positive and more evolved people in relationships, make wiser decisions, and have conciliatory and authentic responses.*

As we release our emotionally based karmic relationship chains, we rid ourselves of the need to frequently experience widely fluctuating feelings and dramas. Then as we develop into our spiritual potential, we grow beyond the need for management techniques and, instead, choose internal and external congruency. From this new position, our feelings are neutralized, cleared, and more healthfully tuned in to events and people and emotions around us. At that point, we love life more genuinely. We exude unconditional love and have boundless compassion, deep caring, and a desire to serve others. We do not become doormats, but express ourselves t/Truthfully, live in attunement with others, attract positive and more evolved people in relationships, make wiser decisions, and have conciliatory and authentic responses. This highly evolved processing promotes living the healthiest, most empowered emotional state possible.

16: FINANCES

Much has been written about finances and abundance. Because we all need money to survive, most people have issues with these topics that they must come to terms with in one way or another. Those who are blessed with abundance have it easier in some ways, but they also seem to have as many life challenges as those who struggle financially. Their problems might play out differently but are just as emotionally volatile as those who have fewer resources. In fact, wealth often breaks families apart and does not necessarily minimize or prevent serious issues.

Those with long-term financial difficulties almost always have chosen this in their karmic script. Financial challenges can offer important and necessary, yet unrecognized and consciously undesired, soul experiences. This lifetime of poverty might be balancing a former life of wealth in order for the person to learn compassion for fiscal plights and lifestyles, or it might help prevent the person from experiencing a frivolous, extravagant, or spiritually unproductive life. Limited income can aid appreciation of more meaningful life qualities such as friendship, kindness, and thoughtfulness. Many souls took vows of poverty in past lives that continue to prohibit abundance until those energies are removed. Even when eliminated, it takes intentional effort, time, and corrective decisions and behaviors to improve financial stability.

It is common for other primary issues, such as low self-esteem, inability to handle responsibilities well, victim identity, excessive anger, or inflated confidence with inferior training or skills, to cause financial problems.

Insufficiency can also be the result of present life factors. Poor spending habits, living beyond one's means, and addictions will likely catch up with a person sooner or later. Carelessness about job responsibilities could cause repeated firings. After a loss of employment, pride motivates some people to refuse taking a lower level job than they previously held, thus causing additional financial detriment. This theme has many variations. In these cases and others, it is up to the individual to claim responsibility for, address, and correct the situation.

> *We are already worthy in the eyes of God, regardless of our definition of material success.*

Our society has made materialism, consumerism, and money our gods. As a culture, we excessively prioritize topics and items that are transient, unnecessary, extravagant, and ultimately meaningless. We need to revise our values. When all else has failed to redirect our lives, we might receive a spiritually powerful financial crash. Bankruptcy, extended loss of professional or rewarding employment, serious health crises or accidents, mortgage foreclosures, and other critical experiences might energetically serve us. Earning self-worth through things and appearances, such as designer clothing, a prestigious car, or the large home we require for a prosperous image, might spiritually deprive us of a deeper and more fulfilling life path. We are already worthy in the eyes of God, regardless of our definition of material success, but ego life interpretation blocks us from understanding this.

Finances are often a major problem in marriage and can lead to divorce. There are no right or wrong generic guidelines to prevent these challenges, although communication, cooperation, and understanding of each other's views and needs are essential in a partnership. If the relationship has been otherwise healthy, seeking professional assistance could help. Also, allowing for past life issues to arise between the partners presents additional information to work with.

Financial dilemmas ultimately come down to a lack of trust in ourselves, each other, life, or God. But, in Truth, God is the Source of all we need. The only lack we experience is self-generated through ego eyes.

> *God is the Source of all we need. The only lack we experience is self-generated through ego eyes.*

17: MARRIAGE AND DIVORCE

The historic, cultural requirement for marriage was to provide a setting for children, to give birth to more hands to share responsibilities, especially in primitive hunter and then later agrarian societies, and to assure family assistance and loyalty in times of crisis. The relationship was based on survival needs, and producing enough offspring to allow for some to die of childhood diseases was essential for society. Hopefully, the process of conception and child raising included at least some rapport between partners.

Eventually marriage evolved into a union frequently based on love. However, there always have been exceptions, deceptions, and abuse within this system. Increasingly more couples are delaying or avoiding the commitment of marriage. Many factors play into this trend. Our technological revolution has freed most of us from prolonged and demanding hard labor. Improvements in quality-of-life resources allow choices and independence based more on desires and ease. And some people are simply afraid of marriage, which is a complex arrangement with endless varieties of issues, roles, goals, and interactions.

Nevertheless, marriages are soul-contracted partnerships. Although occasional unions are lovingly supportive, most often karmic issues permeate the alliance and become painfully obvious as time goes by. The relationship might have a scripted expiration, which does not necessitate divorce, but offers the chance to either end or extend the contract.

Severing the connection might providentially allow greater healing experiences for each partner. However, if the two have not adequately accomplished their soul lessons and karmic clearing, they will need to do more work. It might be helpful for the couple to change the setting and cast of supporting characters; they might need to edit their roles and enactments to stimulate additional opportunities for soul growth.

Unless the couple substantially diffuses their karmic magnets, future intimate partners will likely present similar issues and roles. If there is an extended lapse between commitments after a divorce or breakup, the individual might have healed, shifted, and matured significantly enough to attract a happier, healthier relationship. Whether with the original partner or with another, personal growth and development will usually reduce issue potencies, which, as we learned in an earlier chapter, are those forces or concentrations of a karmic issue that precipitate button pushing and emotional reactions.

~ ~ ~

A marriage ceremony carries great significance. It marks a new commitment, arrangement, and chapter in life. It also activates and intensifies the deepest soul-needed issues.

> Janet and Lloyd lived together for several years before marrying, decades before this became a common occurrence. They thought they knew each other well enough to ensure a solid future. They were aware of each other's faults but felt they knew how to live with and work through their challenges.
>
> The morning after they married, Janet realized everything had changed. Lloyd no longer seemed willing to cooperate with her. He resisted her input and ignored her attempts to clear the air and improve their relationship.
>
> They stayed together their whole lifetime but were miserable, blamed each other, and led separate and independent lives. Janet was depressed and felt overwhelmed by her circumstances. She was starved for attention and affection. But she was unable to leave Lloyd because dealing with the practicalities of life was beyond her. She felt it had been a mistake to marry him in the first place.

Janet and Lloyd's high degree of emotional entanglement and pain did not promote growth in any way. It did strengthen endurance and self-sufficiency, which are ego management techniques, but it also generated blame, misery, and victimhood.

Their life together would have been spiritually more advantageous if they could have addressed personal concerns, claimed their individual share of responsibility for their karmic needs, and taken necessary steps to improve their relationship. Ending the marriage could have attracted better opportunities to heal and offered more fulfillment for each of them.

~ ~ ~

Sometimes, the health of a relationship is affected by timing: the timing to leave and the timing to become involved again. Sometimes, we just need time to connect with our inner self.

> Martin was unhappy in his third marriage. Because his prior divorces had apparently not assured him of happier unions, he was perplexed about what action to take. During a session with D'Ann, divine guidance told him that his soul contract with his current wife, Doris, was for twenty years. They had been together exactly that long. Neither of them had been happy for some time, and they had done all that they knew to do to try and heal their marriage. So when Martin realized this spiritual insight, they decided to legally separate but not divorce so she and their two sons could remain covered by his insurance policy. He bought another home and moved out.
>
> Martin and Doris were frequently in contact with each other, and he assisted with their sons as often as possible. Over the next two years, he continued to energetically clear his emotions and worked at understanding a larger life view. Martin and Doris eventually chose

to reunite. He moved back in, sold his other home, and legally voided their separation.

They were like honeymooners again. Over time, their original issues reappeared, but Martin knew how to more effectively address their challenges. They are now happier and more committed to each other than before.

The improvement in their marriage is significantly due to Martin's more expansive and advanced interpretation of life. He has more awareness of setups and knows how to apply more effective healing actions and responses. He initiates more conversations with Doris to work through their issues together. Martin can now connect the dots in his life that continue to enhance his empowerment.

~ ~ ~

Integrity fosters and deceitfulness diminishes our connection to Source. Therefore, a promise, whether officially sanctioned or casually personal, ethically requires that

> *Integrity fosters and deceitfulness diminishes our connection to Source.*

we honor it. However, it is also possible for us to alter or void the commitment, publicly or privately. Unless or until we do that, our marriage vows or relationship promises take priority over any passionate thoughts or actions we might have or take toward anyone other than our partner. This is not only a matter of societal mores or legislated or common law; it is an energetic, spiritual Truth.

A betrayal of loyalty or act of unfaithfulness affects us at many levels, especially energetically. Although the behavior often feels disturbing to the betrayer and is usually excruciatingly painful for the mate when he or she finds out, it is possible that this specific issue was a healing setup. The partner being violated might have been unfaithful in a past life, perhaps with this same mate. This view does not excuse the action or diminish the consequences, but it does broaden the interpretation. Genuinely asking to be forgiven and recommitting to the relationship might release the psychological, emotional, and spiritual damage of the infidelity. Spiritual forgiveness might produce a miracle.

~ ~ ~

Divorce is not necessarily a sign that either party is a failure. Yet, because it marks the official demise of a commitment, it is natural to interpret it that way. As one life chapter closes, another one opens. The all-too-typical mistake ex-spouses make is to harbor blame and hatred toward their former partner. Some bitter people actively do or say things to berate, hurt, and retaliate. Unfortunately, children are often the pawns in this drama. These actions intensify and perpetuate issues.

> *Divorce is not necessarily a sign that either party is a failure.*

Every negative action, word, and even thought about someone else harms the thinker who holds onto that negativity more than it does the other person. Each occurrence resembles taking a knife and stabbing ourselves. Fortunately, we can find resolution through karmic understandings, spiritual forgiveness, and releasing

> *Every negative action, word, and even thought about someone else harms the thinker who holds onto that negativity more than it does the other person.*

judgment. With continued effort, life and soul growth does improve in some very important ways.

~ ~ ~

So often in life, we feel like we don't know what to do: stay together or separate. When ego takes over, vengeance and hatred might seem like the necessary things to feel. In reality, the best course of action is always to seek understanding at the soul level. Then to foster acceptance and forgiveness, move on with whichever course we choose, and rid ourselves of energetic debris we might still carry in emotional trash bags. Sometimes the results from this course of action are astounding.

> After ten years of marriage and with three sons, Hannah and Ken divorced. They went through the usual legal, financial, physical, and emotional stages and adjustments that most couples experience. They communicated minimally and avoided contact as often as possible.
>
> After a few years, Hannah remarried and had a daughter. This marriage was manageable, but after more than thirty years, she and her second husband divorced. Shortly afterward, Hannah decided to visit the large and thriving church where she had originally met Ken all of those years ago. He had since married Gail, and they regularly attended this same church. Hannah and Ken's sons also occasionally went to services there.
>
> Over months and years, the blended families spent time together, and Hannah and Gail became good friends. They all sat together at

church and often spent holidays at one of their homes. The level of healing was so obvious, unusual, and deep that the family occasionally commented on it. They felt profoundly blessed.

CHAPTER 4:
UNIVERSAL
TRANSFORMATION

Most people are frustrated by their inability to stay on top of their life. They may feel lost because their well-honed personal management techniques are less effective than ever. Some people also feel backed into a corner by rage and desperation because they no longer have answers to previously answerable questions.

Even those whose life seems to be fulfilling and not problematic still have internal karmic energies that they seem to be well able to rise above. We may think of these rare individuals as winners, yet there is still soul business for them to take care of in this lifetime. They might have brought in only a few areas of strong karma, or perhaps they are in a karmic reward life with a tiny dose of it.

This chapter explores and explains components of how and why life as we have known it appears to be disintegrating and is becoming more chaotic, confusing, difficult, stressful, painful, and unstable. Although these symptoms are widespread and unfortunately too common, there are steps each of us can take to relieve this situation and promote healing more effectively and quickly than has ever been possible before. We'll come to appreciate these changes when we see that all life experiences are assisting the evolution of a new and more spiritually advanced species of humanity. We will learn that we can all benefit through these most trying times.

18: E/GO LIFE

E/go is the most proficiently functioning yet least spiritually evolved part of our being. Typical ego thoughts are at least 90 percent negative, meaningless, and redundant. Its energy is usually headquartered in the left-brain for right-handed people and the right brain for left-handed people; for ease of understanding, we refer to its standard placement as being in the left brain.

> *E/go is the most proficiently functioning yet least spiritually evolved part of our being. Typical ego thoughts are at least 90 percent negative, meaningless, and redundant.*

When we allow ego to dominate our thoughts, we become like a person who resides in a foreign land and learns to dress, walk, talk, and live like the local inhabitants. Yet there remains within us an inner identification with original roots of our homeland, even if we attempt to ignore those roots. When we forget our spiritual beginnings and listen to ego more than Source, we create dissonance and turmoil within ourselves and within our relationships. That's because, regardless of what seems to happen in our lives, our core energy is still connected to Source, just as memories from our early youth will always connect us to the locale of our birth.

To understand this, think of God as an ocean and each person as a drop of water. We are miniature portions of God. Having been created in God's image, our core is therefore

> *Think of God as an ocean and each person as a drop of water. We are miniature portions of God.*

divine, and it holds profound attributes, such as unconditional love, wisdom, authenticity, trust, and wholeness. The historical human dilemma has been our inability to connect with, integrate, and manifest these desirable qualities into daily life. E/go has effectively prevented us from knowing peace.

E/go Identity

Our ego identity is not about intelligence or education. E/go is who we think we are in our perceived separateness from Source. We acquire an ego identity as a result of processing life through our ego filters. E/go specializes in survival, self-agendas, intellectual rationality, materiality, management, control, judgment, and appearances. Although important and in many ways necessary, exclusive reliance on these factors locks us into perspectives and cycles that merely perpetuate their own existence. Spiritual empowerment appears to be unavailable, and we become confined to logically restrictive interpretations of human input and experience.

We have developed our method of operating from karma, life experiences, and our rudimentary translation of outer appearances based on insufficient context. By default, we function almost exclusively from our limited, linear ego. The primary exceptions occur when we engage with creativity, inspiration, and guidance. Otherwise, we handle life with the smallest

> *We have developed our method of operating from karma, life experiences, and our rudimentary translation of outer appearances based on insufficient context.*

view of reality, a skill that we've diligently practiced and honed by everyday living. However, that skill also brings additional seemingly impossible self-improvement responsibilities and recurring challenges that require further management. Our restricted interpretations and management techniques create repercussions and complications that lead us either in an upward spiral of increasingly intensive pressure to perform, or into a downward spiral of defeat and despair.

The three-dimensional ploys that ego uses to perpetuate its existence as well as our karmic issues include humanity's efforts to: handle emotions in an immature manner; be belligerently assertive or submissive; strive to be right without admitting mistakes; apologize excessively; continuously look for what's wrong and blame others or ourselves; and stay in control or futilely give up no matter what happens. When we remain in the state of ego consciousness, we wish life were easier and more rewarding, but we are reluctant to revise what we have proven to be essential, albeit ineffective, methods of conducting our life.

E/go does not want to relinquish its command in our life and is crafty in its ability to survive. It relies on its own agendas and devices to provoke dramas that reinforce its own viewpoints. By exerting its authority, it prevents us from seeing a

> *E/go eyes see with judgment and examine the contrast between what it determines it wants or deserves versus what it appears to receive.*

larger perspective with additional and wiser options for decision-making. E/go eyes see with judgment and examine the contrast between what it determines it wants or deserves versus what it appears to receive.

E/go is alert for any internal and external discrepancies that it views as a danger to itself, which it then reports to our mind as a situation that is unfair to us. Because life rarely balances out fairly on a regular basis, this viewpoint and method of processing frequently stimulates an eruption of an array of landmine emotions that require management. The resulting conclusions, which seem logical from our three-dimensional experiences and appearances, perpetuate chaos and disturbance, snagging us and holding us back from moving on to a more rewarding life as well as spiritual development.

~ ~ ~

No holds are barred when ego restrains and distracts us from more constructive, especially Source-based, thoughts and actions. E/go knows that diversion is sabotage, so it will attempt to derail our attention from the larger picture of what is

> *E/go knows that diversion is sabotage. ... The three most basic tactics ego uses to snag our attention are crisis, fear, and emotional turmoil.*

occurring or is possible. Like a two-year-old, ego will use whatever devices it can to distract us from our spiritual goal, however, the three most basic tactics ego uses to snag our attention are crisis, fear, and emotional turmoil. Because ego consciousness is our default system of operating, we can fall into diversionary traps automatically, unless we are alert for ego's ingenious methods.

E/go management frequently attracts karmic setups and dramas. It dredges up disturbing emotions and fears to create crisis. E/go generates fear by instilling our minds with strong and repetitive self-doubts, negative thoughts, and possible disastrous consequences to something we ultimately have little or no control over. E/go then immobilizes us in emotional turmoil by getting us stuck on a myriad of unnecessary facts or details, requiring that all questions be answered before we take the next step, or by refusing to reinterpret our recurring healing dramas. This can cause us to frequently change our minds, live in the past, procrastinate, complain, and use excuses to reinforce energetic stagnation. To perpetuate its authority in our life, ego sends messages that demean or exaggerate our abilities or confidence. Vincent van Gogh stated, "If you hear a voice within you saying, 'You are not a painter,' then by all means paint, and that voice will be silenced." That voice is ego.

E/go Traits

Not following through on what we know we should do is a very common, widespread, deviously effective, sabotaging, and natural ego trait that delays or stops our development. This circumnavigation pattern has many contributing components such as

> "If you hear a voice within you saying, 'You are not a painter,' then by all means paint, and that voice will be silenced." —Vincent van Gogh

disinterest, rebellion, addictions, poor self-esteem, lack of self-discipline, avoidance, denial, or complacency concerning commitments, projects, or goals. Resembling a car in neutral, we will not get anywhere unless we shift into action. Not doing so holds us back from healing and growth in any area, and spiritually prevents us from becoming authentic and walking our talk.

Expectations and entitlements are premeditated resentments that generate conflict. Typically, when we have expectations or feel entitled, we focus on a specific, predetermined outcome. It is as though we hold out our hand waiting for the response we believe is correct.

> *Expectations and entitlements are premeditated resentments that generate conflict.*

If we do not receive what we think we should, we feel like our hand is being slapped, and we resent the person who we deem to be uncooperative. It would be far better for us to release our expectations of required outcomes and maintain inner peace.

> *E/go is a partitioned, spiritually immature, and limited identity in the head that has not yet reintegrated with the more powerful and underused remainder of our brain.*

E/go's diversionary plots are extremely successful in distracting our attention from a larger context, thus detaining our growth. Because we are so enmeshed with ego as our identity and its tactics are so familiar, we rarely "catch" what is happening unless someone more spiritually attuned points it out to us.

This inner mental duality of ego versus Source identity might seem to imply schizophrenia, but ego is not a mental illness. E/go is a partitioned, spiritually immature, and limited identity in the head that has not yet reintegrated with the more powerful and underused remainder of our brain. It functions with a three-dimensional, material, and physical regimen that resists spiritual development.

E/go Games

When playing out our soul-scripted life roles, we routinely engage in *ego games*[84] in which we play our standard role and receive a familiar yet usually undesirable response. Our reaction to the game will show up primarily in one of two ways: either internally as irritation, resentment, or anger because we didn't want to do what was needed or didn't get the response we wanted; or externally as a disappointing or complicating result of our actions. We then rebound away from the other player or players in the ego game, which usually is painful or difficult. Our conclusion will be that we don't understand why this problem keeps occurring, we wish things were better, and we don't want to deal with the other person anymore. We might be able to get through the immediate concern or situation, but no healing will have taken place.

This is a circular cycle, similar to eating food or making a bed. The results are only temporary, so the action needs to be repeated. E/go games continue to play out until we see what is happening and make a change. Nothing

> *It is completely up to us to heal our ego's shenanigans.*

improves unless we take constructive action. Doing so will reduce ego's grip in our life. Not changing will perpetuate the old pattern. It is completely up to us to heal our ego's shenanigans.

We have all seen a frustrated parent trying to calm down his or her loud, misbehaving youngster. Eventually the parent shouts some variation of "Be Quiet!" This game was triggered by the noisy, insistent child, consists of exchanges volleyed back and

---

[84] **ego games:** repetitive roles and behaviors that stimulate repetitive responses and dramas

forth, and continues until the adult ends it. Although this interaction gives the adult management or control of the situation, the child cooperates only temporarily.

Fortunately, most children outgrow this demonstrative behavior, but some go on to learn more devious or manipulative ways of getting attention, controlling, or even winning the game. Those children continue game playing throughout life with any person or in any situation or event until they outgrow or heal beyond the need to play the game. Then the person, now an adult, will begin to notice other people playing their games and exercise a free will choice to play along or not.

> Connie and two of her spiritual friends were going out to dinner. She had been looking forward to this evening since it was planned because the group always has lively, interesting, and oftentimes inspiring conversations. She was sitting in the back seat of the car, and her friends were in front.
>
> At one point, Connie realized that their conversation was unusual. It took a few seconds before she realized what was happening. There was nothing wrong with what they were saying, but the topic was totally frivolous and ego-based. How uniquely peculiar for them! She could have played along and contributed her views, but she consciously chose to remain quiet until the subject changed to something more profound and appealing.

As bite-sized as this insight was, it represented a brief ego clearing moment for Connie during which she could glimpse what had previously been hidden from her awareness. Much of what is said in conversation is repetitive filler words on the same old topics. Its meaninglessness wastes time and energy. Connie determined that, in the future, she would do what she could to avoid spending time with people who seemed to be stuck, or being in situations in which she would be merely spinning her wheels. This awareness was new and fascinating for Connie. Her good friends had unintentionally taught her a valuable lesson.

~ ~ ~

Everyday life encourages ego games. We rarely see what is happening, and our ignorance perpetuates our unfulfilling and repetitive experiences.

> Ian has a razor sharp ability to identify and target other people's weakest areas. He thinks nothing of telling others when and where they are wrong or how they could be better if only they would listen to him. His personality makes him challenging to be around.

> Alexa is a spiritually advanced friend who often questions why she maintains her relationship with Ian. Whenever he goes into a verbal tirade and corrects her, she notices that she becomes defensive. She is pulled into this ego game even when she clearly understands what is happening. The conflict between them is more obvious to her because their relationship is such a sharp contrast to her other friendships.

> The rest of Alexa's friends are supportive, kind, and caring. Ian thinks all of his friends are okay and is unable to qualitatively distinguish variations among them. He

behaves the same way with all of them. He does notice Alexa is more patient with him but acknowledges no responsibility for being difficult with her.

The point of this story is to highlight how different Alexa feels and behaves when she is with Ian rather than when she is with her other friends. When he provokes her, she is distracted from her Higher Self and the attributes she so highly values. Alexa does not feel good about her thoughts, emotions, reactions, and sometimes behavior when she is with Ian. His low energies pull her down to his level, and it takes days for her to restabilize and re-enter her spiritual zone.

Alexa has tried many solutions to help the situation: praying for understanding, patience, and wisdom; surrendering her protective and defensive ego responses; forgiving Ian and herself; and adjusting her attitude whenever possible. When she has tried gently talking to Ian about his shortcomings or his poor interpersonal skills, he either closes her down or, if he does briefly admit his problems, does nothing to work on improving himself. She has had limited success with him because she is only half of the relationship equation.

Eventually, unless Ian makes great personal changes, Alexa will likely decide that she is expending too much effort to maintain such a tenuous, draining, lopsided, frustrating, and unrewarding bond. She will likely terminate the friendship.

Releasing E/go

E/go can be thought of as a ball made of overlapping Velcro strips, and every ego filter is an individual band. These bands adhere together, supporting each other and impeding our integration with Source. We increase the strength and size of the ball with each repetitive, developing, and expanding ego thought

197

we have or ego action we take. To facilitate our spiritual advancement, we need to prevent additional strips from accumulating and also remove those that are already in place.

While under the auspices of ego dictatorship, we all have life issues to heal, and clearing them can be a long process. Sometimes we feel discouraged because we seem to have so little control of our thoughts, feelings, and habits. However, diligence in seeking spiritual growth rewards us with incremental success, even as we continue to notice a seemingly endless lineup of personal challenges we would like to release.

It helps to remember the analogy about our test scores. Every time we delete a low-frequency score, we raise our overall vibrational rate and move in the direction of greater authenticity and empowerment. We pull a strip of Velcro from the ball.

Conceptually, we might wonder how we can gain sufficient knowledge and wisdom in order to implement these analogies. Those answers will emerge throughout this text as we cover practical ideas and steps to promote ego integration with Source.

The next story exemplifies ego's shrewdness as well as the relatively simple ease with which we can release ourselves from debilitating ego patterns.

> Guy had been on a spiritual path for many years and knew how to interpret, work with, and release almost everything that came along in his life. But he had always had an issue of being stressed over time. No matter what he did, his intrusive thoughts about time made him continuously aware of how long the endeavor was taking. He attempted to spend as little time as possible on any project so that he could either be finished or go on to the next

job. Although he valued a quality result from his efforts, the pressure of needing to accomplish his responsibilities with limited time was a burden.

Even though Guy was spiritually advanced, this issue was still presenting itself and becoming more apparent, frustrating, and difficult for him to handle. He had done all of the techniques he knew to heal his thoughts, actions, and issues. He had tried to change his views, interpretations, and methods of management. Although all of these efforts had greatly assisted and improved other areas of his life, this time issue had not budged.

One day, Guy received guidance from his inner voice that identified the culprit as ego-generated thoughts. He saw that his thoughts had relentlessly focused on time restrictions, provoked and aggravated this issue, and delayed his spiritual growth by holding him captive to feelings of limitation and lack in regard to available time. He had fallen for this strategy because it had become so familiar and habitual. Guy decided that he needed to end his repetitive, disturbed, and stressful ego entanglement.

Once Guy understood what was happening, he began to catch the many times he fell for ego manipulation. At each occurrence, he surrendered the issue and mentally or verbally reinforced his position that the old habit of distraction and agitation was over. He would tell himself that he was free to do what he wanted and needed to do and when he determined to do so. He confirmed within himself that he would spend the appropriate amount of time that each task required without carrying the burden of time in his consciousness.

He often repeated several different phrases: "A task takes as long as it takes." "I have all the time I need." "All is in divine order." "I will no longer fall for ego maneuverings; that habit is gone." "This issue has no control over me anymore." He was forceful in his attitude and daily repeated these declarative statements many, many times, defying the paralyzing ego grip. Within a few weeks, he noticed incredible internal freedom in his workaday life.

We all live relatively hypnotic lives on autopilot, and it is easy and natural to succumb to our normal routines. When we consciously affirm a different reality, as Guy did, we begin to change. We peel away a strip of Velcro. We drop a low test score and increase the average of our vibrational energy and efficiency.

~ ~ ~

Many spiritual leaders and business consultants promote the use of affirmations as a self-advancement technique, and those people who are able to tap into some upper dimensions can benefit from using affirmations very easily and relatively quickly. I have found, however, that there are a variety of other processes now available that promote deep life-change. Affirmations can be powerful reinforcements to assist in changing our behavior, but they seem to function best as an auxiliary support to other, more efficient and stronger healing techniques. The three primary techniques I recommend are surrendering, forgiving, and *ego vacuuming*,[85] which are covered later in this text and presented as the Three Pillars of Transformation.

If we can get to a point where we become open to new possibilities and release ego's familiar experiential and interpretive choke hold, then we can begin to heal. With healing, we will see new ideas and possibilities take hold, and we can then better utilize positive affirmations to gradually manifest internal shifting and opening.

~ ~ ~

In order to release ego, it is critical to understand, as clearly as possible, the distinction between thoughts that originate in our head and inspiration that comes from Source.

Anything determined exclusively in the head, no matter how good or wise it is, has a lower vibration than Source-based transmissions. Applying spiritual principles and concepts only from *head authority*[86] minimizes and/or delays our self-empowerment.

> *Spiritual growth is about clearing our head of ego agendas.*

---

[85] ***ego vacuum***: an etheric tool that suctions out ego mechanics, trash bags, and energetic emotional congestion, instantly neutralizes all removed energies, and raises vibrational rates

[86] ***head authority:*** the habitual ego voice that overrides and masquerades as genuine guidance, and which we often choose to obey

In contrast, *Source wisdom*[87] represents our life essences and energetic fuel, an endowment from God to our soul. *Soul endowments,*[88] therefore, are qualities that emanate from Source energies that drive our thoughts, awareness, and conduct.

Spiritual growth, then, is about clearing our head of ego agendas, and doing so will incrementally upgrade our identity. As we get our head out of our own way, Source energies and essences take over.

> *In the empowered world, life and soul growth are not about seeking to know as much as possible but about getting beyond the need to know.*

God's Light, shining within us, will be brightest when we exude spiritual essences from our core.

ॐ In the empowered world, life and soul growth are not about seeking to know as much as possible but about getting beyond the need to know. When we are in that empowered state, we will attune to Source wisdom more than ego head authority, and we will receive what we need to know when we need to know it. We will still accomplish tasks, but we will also enjoy the flow of life because our head will be responding to the higher vibrational frequencies of Source, rather than operating on our own definition of earthly knowledge. We will then be authentic and live in a state of grace and trust. This sought-after condition has sometimes been referred to as living in God's shopping cart.

Then, as we spiritually mature, we will continue to use cognitive functions such as memory, logic, and skills as appropriate. Physical needs will remain, education will still be

---

[87] **Source wisdom or input:** synonyms for divine guidance; antonym for head authority

[88] **soul endowments:** attributes that emanate from Source to enhance our soul and life evolution

necessary, and rational and scientific processes and development will continue to be important. However, we will see that we need to evolve away from our absolute and exclusive dependence on these standard

> *Spiritual attributes are not accomplishments; they are states of being.*

essentials of the material world for all things in everyday life. We will come to realize that spiritual attributes are not accomplishments; they are states of being.

We will then gradually escalate our connection with Source input, which are the divine messages we receive from God, and wean ourselves from total reliance on earthly, head authority influences. We will expand from ego's linear functioning to allow subtler and more powerful vibrations, inspirations, and higher dimensions to enter our evolving consciousness. Source insight and wisdom will enhance and amplify all areas and processes of our lives, enabling us to stimulate internal and external transformation.

We will seem to flow more easily in the material world. Here's a simple example.

> Previously, whenever Lawrence lost or misplaced an item, he would throw his hands up in the air and exclaim in disgust, "Now where in the world did I put that?" And he would search high and low in numerous places, often for an extended period of time, his frustration growing. Eventually, he would find the object of his search and frequently it was in rather obvious sight or even in a place where he had already looked.

One day, he received the insight to begin his search in a Source-wisdom manner. He would take a breath and calmly say, "Where is …?" or "Where did I put …?" and name the object. He would not demand to know but merely politely ask for information from the all-cognizant energy sources around and within him.

Often, he would merely look up and see the object on a shelf in front of him. Or he would walk into a room a few moments later, glance sideways out of the corner of his eye and see it in a relatively obscure place. He might receive a thought such as, "It's in your car, fallen under the seat," And he would go there and immediately find it. Each time this occurred, he was amazed at how easily this way of tapping into Source wisdom simplified his life.

~ ~ ~

The more we know about something, the more effective we can be, but merely in the ego world. In everyday life, we have all learned more than we can possibly remember or use, yet our own lives have generally remained the way they have always been. This personal bypass occurs when we rely on head-determined action for rational, effort-based, and concrete results. Accomplishing something requires intentional action, with some degree of effort and self-discipline. We need to get things done and will complete our learning process only when we can actually perform the task we want to learn, whether it be washing clothes, riding a bicycle, or living as a *Light being*.[89]

---

[89] **Light being:** a person who exudes the glow of his or her divinity

Kelsey is a charming, warm, generous, social, and delightful person. She is married and has four children. Her positive approach to life is so obvious that she magnetically attracts people to her. She even admits that she cannot handle any more friendships; her plate is full. However, this blessing comes with a major karmic challenge: she is an excessive helper and giver.

Kelsey was adopted as an infant and raised with one brother, who was also adopted. As the only daughter, she felt that she needed to be perfect. Kelsey learned early on through her experiences that doing things for others made them happy. This management technique worked superbly well for everyone else, but not so well for her. Whenever she attempted to do what she wanted for her own happiness, things around her worsened. As a result, her emotionally sacrificial and nearly exclusive focus has been to help others.

Too many of her extended family and friends are emotionally and financially needy. Giving to so many people drains her energy and vitality. She would enjoy giving if she could freely choose to do so, but instead she feels constantly obligated. It is too hard to resist helping when she is so blessed. If she does not help, her emotional disturbance is even worse than usual.

Because these issues establish inequitable relationships, she plays a constant benefactor role. Regardless of the setting or participants, she is always the primary listener, instigator, fixer, helper, and positive force. She gives, and others receive. When she needs help, she does not receive anything close to reciprocal support. Even though she often thinks about how unfair her life is, her words and behavior rarely even hint that she feels that way.

As an advanced spiritual seeker, Kelsey came to realize that she was actually raised with many spiritual concepts. Her thoughts and actions have been well practiced to serve others, turn her other cheek, avoid conflict, detach from the immoderate need for material things, and have a generous and pleasant spirit.

Even though all of these traits are desirable, they are head-based, persistent, and pervasive. Kelsey constantly felt that, in order to be liked by others, she had to bury her personal, more honest thoughts, opinions, and emotions. She continuously struggled with her preferences versus her expected roles. Her major challenge then was to override this head-determined good behavior toward others with what she would really prefer to do – to be more honest.

At a critical healing juncture, Kelsey felt fatigue, depression, and hopelessness. In spite of all of her efforts, people around her continued to be unceasingly needy. She had given to the point of exhaustion, was stuck, and saw no solutions. She could no longer keep up her relentless giving. She needed support from others. Where were they when she needed them?

Kelsey learned through session work with D'Ann that her behavior had been established by karma and reinforced with accrued beliefs and expectations. By this point her karmic energies had been released, but the remaining present life effects still remained. These energies required continual self-discipline, determination, and forced effort. Her dilemma both perplexed and disgusted her. Her life experience had taught her that: If she did not do what others expected, she would be wrong; When she did give to others, she would be right. Yet acting in that manner merely perpetuated her issue.

Kelsey also discovered that the energy driving her unwanted behavior was actually low-octane ego fuel. Switching to a Source based life by using the Three Pillars of Healing would gradually reduce the excessive giving role. Eventually she would feel less constant need to help. She would gain the freedom and ability to choose from additional response options, such as saying no, giving less, honestly expressing her own emotions and needs, and revising relationships.

Although Kelsey had surrendered this issue before, she had not known what follow-up steps to take to facilitate continued high-vibrational healing, and she had reverted back to carrying her burden alone. This time, however, she had more conscious pieces to work with. She surrendered over-giving again. She watched out for her emotions and inner needs when in the old situational patterns. She instantly surrendered them all in the moment and gave herself permission to release her feelings. She had more talks with God about her perspectives and actions.

When she found herself caught in her usual, repetitive ego mechanics, she claimed freedom from the need to obey them. She also forgave each needy person, energetically released them from her system, and began to be more forthright in conversations. Within days of Kelsey's new awareness, a life healing setup occurred.

Kelsey had recently lost a family member and was still in mourning. She was in such turmoil that she could barely sustain everyday activities. Not able to release enough pent up and current emotions, she was having nighttime panic attacks that prevented her from sleeping. Karen, a very close friend, called and skipped over the usual courtesy of asking how Kelsey was, if it was convenient to talk right then, or if she could possibly help. Instead, Karen immediately launched into a list of several things she needed Kelsey to do for her that day.

Unexpectedly and without thinking, Kelsey finally spoke her truth. She had reached a point of no return. She was no longer able to rise above her ego-managed routine and prioritize everyone else's life over her own. She would not continue to do what she thought the other person wanted and, fundamentally, did not care what Karen's response might be. She told Karen that there was no way she could possibly help her, that she had always done everything she could for her, and that she now needed help herself. Interestingly, Karen did not get angry or defensive. She immediately apologized and admitted how insensitive she had been. Although she offered to help Kelsey, there seemed to be nothing she could do at that time.

In effect, Kelsey had helped herself. She felt validated in her new approach of handling requests for help. This experience was a major shift in her life and her interactions with others, and she was then able to better address and manifest healing in her present life issues and roles.

If someone had been videotaping Kelsey's daily life before and after this healing setup, the recording would show similar or even identical actions. Both before and after, she seemed to have her act together and be extremely blessed. Although this is accurate from facts and appearances, inner programming and emotions rarely or minimally show up on an electronic recording of activities. Inside, Kelsey was quite different.

> *As internal processing and sensitivity heal into compatibility , the ease and effect of every effort is enhanced.*

ॐ As internal processing and sensitivity heal into compatibility, the ease and effect of every effort is enhanced. We might all continue to perform our typical activities, but the higher vibrations driving them result in empowerment. Even if it doesn't show, we feel better about ourselves when we are aware of our inherent connection with Source.

Outgrowing E/go

E/go is always on alert for its own endeavors, which more often than not differ to some degree from what is really happening. This conscious, critical, inner ego voice nitpicks everything and is only

> *E/go needs retraining to appreciate a much larger scope of life experiences.*

temporarily satisfied when life responds according to its expectations, thoughts, and agendas. E/go needs retraining to appreciate a much larger scope of life experiences. Beyond that, we ultimately desire for ego to recognize its God-centered origins, give up its head authority ways, and accept Source wisdom. Retraining is a step in that process, and *gratitude*[90] is a tool with which we can facilitate it.

Gratitude is the greatest magnet for happiness. Feeling grateful places us in an emotional position to experience blessings by

> *Gratitude is the greatest magnet for happiness.*

attracting to us people, circumstances, and events that will make our hearts sing. We might not feel grateful in a certain situation, but intentionally focusing on appreciation will give us practice in reducing ego's message of dissatisfaction. This is one of the few instances in which "fake it until we make it" is helpful.

---

[90] **gratitude:** feeling and expressing emotional and mental appreciation

Because we can only take the next step from where we are at the moment, we likely will feel deceitful about or dismissive of such initial efforts to change our view. The way to dance around this dilemma is to first admit, verbally or silently, how we really feel about something. We need to tell and remind ourselves that we want to interpret situations differently, even if we don't know what or how to do that yet. Then we will end up with an improved version of the experience that takes us closer and closer to genuine gratitude and opens the gates to receive more gifts from God.

Jake was in business for himself. He enjoyed his job, but there was always so much work to do that he usually felt burdened and unhappy. Because he dealt with the public, he would have his professional, upbeat persona when conversing with a customer but, afterward, revert back to his distressed baseline. He determined one day that he wanted to enjoy his life and needed to make a change in himself.

Because he was his own boss, he could alter anything he wanted. Jake rearranged his office and replaced a few outdated items. He relaxed his work hours and dressed more comfortably. He bought an attractive storage container for all of the current paperwork that had been sitting on his desk. Jake reminded himself many times a day that he enjoyed his job, liked people, and did not have to feel miserable about the necessary paperwork and bookkeeping.

Repeating this new intention, Jake began to

shift his life off the old center into an inner appreciation for his professional endeavors. He grew to be more grateful for his career. Frustrations did not affect him as deeply as they had before, and he came to terms with the tedious and required tasks he had formerly resented. As a result of these upgrades, his business began to improve, became more rewarding, and his days had a better rhythm and flow.

> *Expressing gratitude may not initially feel authentic, but it will incrementally move us toward a more fulfilling life.*

Expressing gratitude might not initially feel authentic, but it will incrementally move us toward a more fulfilling life.

~ ~ ~

So many daily activities and responsibilities are essential to support physical life. We attempt to reduce stress and burdens in our days, create ease and flow, and have success and happiness. Obviously, daily life will continue to need upkeep, and we will never enjoy all the activities in which we engage. However, when we continue to release ego from its survival assignment so that it can gradually merge back with Source, we will see over time that the inner resistance and dissonance from lower vibrational levels will no longer exist. Our life perspectives, interpretations, emotions, and actions will become congruent. E/go games and agendas will resolve, and we will move in harmony with *divine timing*.[91] This evolved method of operating is only possible when we, including our ego, are integrating with Source.

Because our whole conscious identity has been associated with ego, we haven't known who we are underneath our façade. Therefore, diminishing ego's influence and healing ourselves is usually a chaotic, prolonged, painful, and challenging process. We feel as though we are jumping into a deep lake and don't know how to swim. There is no tangible, spiritual global positioning system to lead us to our empowered destination. However, we are being assisted in

> *It is in divine timing that healing opportunities are happening now, and the intensity of our difficulties maximizes the energetic releases that elevate our advancement further and faster than ever before.*

our transformation by our Higher Self and by means of profound external energies that unceasingly boost us forward at an unprecedented rate. It is in divine timing that healing opportunities are happening now, and the intensity of our difficulties maximizes the energetic releases that elevate our advancement further and faster than ever before.

We begin to feel as though we are riding in a glass elevator on the outside of a skyscraper. As we lift from the ground floor, we rise above old limitations that are represented by the shorter buildings that had blocked our view. Our vision expands to take in an entirely unfamiliar vista. We feel as though an entirely new life will present itself when the elevator door opens again and we emerge in the penthouse.

---

[91] ***divine timing:*** synchronistic experiences that occur at the best possible moment to maximize potential benefits or outcomes

19: FIRST FLOOR LIVING

A fifty-story building represents an energetic spectrum of the contrast between ego and Source. Our vibrational level determines the floor we can access at any given time. We are born into and tend to live at the first floor. This ground level has only one small window through which we can look out at daily life. Although our view is accurate, this limited perspective causes us to miss the greater, more important context of our surroundings. A significant vibrational boost advances us up to the next floor. As we are lifted, we see that every higher level has progressively larger, wider windows. At the fiftieth floor, we experience a 360-degree panorama of expanded horizons, plus the limitless sky. This expansive perspective fosters empowered beings with abundantly endowed lives. Whether we realize it or not, all souls eventually seek this top level of spiritual attainment.

Yet, our day-to-day pursuits take place at the ground level. Earning an income, washing clothes, and interacting with people continue regardless of spiritual development. This limited, ego-based, and head-ruled view leads us to resolute but incomplete

> *We have unknowingly but consciously created some of our personal and social problems as a result of insufficient understanding, misinterpretation, poor choices, and mistakes.*

conclusions about life. We have unknowingly but consciously created some of our personal and social problems as a result of insufficient understanding, misinterpretation, poor choices, and mistakes. These factors are constants under ego leadership, and they reinforce our primary, first floor views.

Our activity at the first floor is ruled, restricted, and biased by karma. These are soul-scripted mandates that require us to be involved with roles, dramas, and dysfunctions as well as employ linear and rational life management techniques. Our emotions become tainted as a result of our frustrating experiences, and we often end up engaging in or working to rise above anger, hatred, blame, revenge, and other strongly negative feelings.

First floor life has a baseline of separation, aloneness, and fear. We see chaos, confusion, discordance, and conflict all around. We carry the responsibility to defend, decide, accomplish, protect, judge, compete, tolerate, sacrifice, and expend great effort to rise above challenges and be successful. Our view of fairness is skewed from our life conclusions and opinions.

> *Unenlightened humanity spiritually operates at a preschool*

All of these components are low vibrations that cover and block Source energies. Seeing with three-dimensional ego eyes is vibrationally at the developmental stage of a two- or three-year-old child. Even today, unenlightened humanity spiritually operates at a preschool level.

First floor protocol requires that we utilize a judgmental filter, which can be toxic. We all know people who are incredibly judgmental, and they are uncomfortable to be around. Very little misses their critical assessment, and we need to be ready to defend ourselves at any time, as in the story of Ian and Alexa stated earlier. As children, we quickly discover the importance of learning right from wrong, and that knowledge serves us well until it stops working for us. Eventually, our interactions within this black-and-white view, coupled with the ego management skills we employ to survive on the human physical and emotional levels, prohibit us from evolving. Yet, somehow within our inner self, we truly know that, as we release judgment, which includes the concept of right and wrong, we can manifest grace and compassion.

Three currencies in the first-floor world are expectations, judgments, and unfairness. If we treat someone kindly, we expect that we should be treated similarly. When we are not, we judge that we have been treated unfairly. We become disappointed or sometimes outraged when a person deals with us unfairly, that is, in a way we feel we don't deserve, or when someone does not behave according to our well thought-out policies.

> Sharon always sent her brother a birthday card. He rarely reciprocated. When he did occasionally mail one to her, it was always late. Every year, she was disturbed about his thoughtlessness. Because of her expectations, she had trouble understanding how he could know the date and yet keep forgetting. She always remembered his birthday. How unfair!

> One year, Sharon's frustration, based on her judgments of her brother, was so sharp that she rethought their relationship. He obviously was not going to change. She either had to keep dealing with her aggravation or change something about her interpretation and reaction. She eventually decided to forgive him and gave herself permission to stop sending cards to him, unless she genuinely wanted to. Over time, she began to appreciate having a brother in her life and their relationship smoothed out. When she occasionally did get a card from him, she felt as though she were receiving a special, heartfelt hug.

Sharon had looked at her situation the way most of us do, from the first floor. Her views were based on expectations, social conventions, and judgments. Although her personal opinions were not wrong, they did not assist her spiritual growth other than to highlight, by agitation, what she needed to heal.

~ ~ ~

First-floor limited views require that we play roles, which elicit emotional reactions that often trump more logical decisions or responses. Our inadequate, inappropriate, unwise, or unhealthy thoughts and behaviors in each moment rarely keep our emotional plate clean. We develop techniques and skills to control these feelings. Those techniques eventually take full control of our lives, leaving us, paradoxically, out of control.

> *Although our personal opinions are not wrong, they do not assist our spiritual growth other than to highlight, by agitation, what we need to heal.*

Our society, at the first floor, encourages us to proficiently suppress our personal emotions. We are supposed to smile even though we feel sad. We are supposed to say we feel fine even when we are not. Our current life's history and experiences—our management techniques—have spiritually served us to perfection by bringing to us the precise disturbing encounters we need in order to release our charged karmic emotions and assist our healing. Unfortunately, our ego eyes don't see these encounters as growth opportunities.

Even at the first floor level, we know that we must first determine what is wrong in order to fix it. But how can we figure out what's wrong when ego typically sees more negatives than positives? We do our best to be right, from our perspective, but we so often don't know what is the wisest decision or action to select. Then, when we are wrong, we have even more work to redo. And if we don't, situations will arise to bring additional challenges to our life or relationships. We don't like this. But because we form our hard-earned opinions from limited, intense personal experiences, we uphold our viewpoints even to the extreme. Rather than holding a larger and more inclusive perspective, we end up respecting others only when they meet our personally determined criteria.

The first floor world appears to have so much wrong with it due to the karmic setup of roles and dramas. Ethics, integrity, kindness, and service are in short supply. There are many unsolvable problems at this level, and people live in misery, illness, and dysfunction. Our problems are unwanted, painful, difficult, confusing, and frequent. We often feel isolated, weak, frustrated, fear-filled, anxious, and discouraged. We want to stop our soap opera, but the first floor does not have a director's office where we can turn in our resignation.

We've heard there's an elevator or stairway around here somewhere that can lift us out of this chaos. Where is it? We will find out later in this book.

20: VICTIMHOOD

One of the common roles of first floor living is that of a *victim*.[92] Most people bring into life a low to moderate dose of this issue energy. However, some souls either needed or were willing to take on significant victim experiences in order to fulfill a karmic obligation. The intense demands from this high dose of role scripting prohibit lasting success, happiness, and personal development.

---

[92] *victim:* a person who is abused by life, feels powerless, and is typically unable to foundationally improve or thrive

Victims are born with potent levels of powerlessness, and their earliest memories are of being treated unfairly or punished. These sufferings breed emotional anguish, extreme anger, continuous frustration, and a need to blame others or God for their misfortunes.

Victims seem to continually make unwise decisions, resist change, demonstrate little motivation or will power, might have unrealistic aspirations, and have meager ability to accomplish and sustain even minimal life goals. Some victims carry heavy responsibilities and are inundated with family, health, or other burdens.

Employment is most often difficult, unrewarding, short-term, and/or inadequate. Even with a decent job and an average or better income, a victim's excessive expenses or unwise spending habits create continuous financial challenges. They can't seem to get their life on track and are always struggling in many ways. In order to survive, a victim needs to find help, answers, and solutions on the first floor.

Unfortunately, persons living a victim role have a major disadvantage to healing their life due to being excessively and obsessively focused on first floor ego views, experiences, problems, and insufficiencies. They almost exclusively see what is wrong and what needs to be fixed. Although they believe they have done the best they can with their circumstances, life always seems to work against them. They perceive that none of their problems are their fault, and their anger and frustration seem justifiable to them. They feel they have been abandoned and that no one else understands their plight, knows how desperate they are, or cares enough to help or support them. Even if someone has repeatedly helped, the effects are not sufficiently long lasting to provide independence, and, sooner or later, the helper nearly always encounters emotional and financial burn out.

In spite of the fact that victims' views, interpretations, emotions, and decisions have not improved their life pattern, they are terrified to see anything differently, fear change with a demonstrative passion, and cling to their status quo. This perspective and reaction obstruct alleviating and healing potentials from emerging. The conundrum for victims is that they are desperate for help, yet even when they receive help, they experience no long-lasting or substantial benefit.

With no other resources available to assist them enough, the only logical conclusion is that they must change themselves. However, just as they fear change from the outside, they are unable and/or unwilling to change from within. As long as they resolutely lock in their present life view and limit their perspective to the first floor environment, they will continue to struggle. If victims are going to experience a life change, it will be when they reinterpret their life, open up their radar to screen for other possibilities, and accept, incorporate, and apply new ideas.

Likely, we all know someone or several people living with this difficult role of victimization, and we have probably held typical, harsh, judgmental reactions toward them. In contrast, our own life would benefit if we were to cultivate an attitude of grace toward such individuals. We can hope that our more pleasant energies might help them on the spiritual if not the human

> *In order to heal a karmic life role, victims must disconnect from at least a tiny bit of ego's paralyzing grip.*

level, but certainly setting aside our judgments would encourage compassion to grow within us even if it has little to no affect on the victim.

Primary Constructs

First floor life is only three- or perhaps four-dimensional. In contrast, we now know that enormous multidimensional transformative spiritual energies have become available. Unfortunately, persons trapped and dominated by an adamant ego do not recognize these higher frequencies and, in effect, do not allocate space or time for them to enter their life. In order to heal a karmic life role, victims *must* disconnect from at least a tiny bit of ego's paralyzing grip.

Victims will heal only if, and to the degree, that they can create room for new energies and possibilities to enter. This new, but still very small, breathing space can allow for a slight but essential mental adjustment. It then becomes possible for victims to learn and incorporate something not previously allowed under ego domination. Even a tiny release or brief suspension of ego's dictatorial grip could change their entire life.

> *Working with Primary Constructs appears to be the only healing option presently available to overcome powerlessness.*

To soften, open, and detach ego's choke hold, victims need to insert *primary constructs (PCs)*[93] into their life. PCs allow them to accept a new energetic view and reinterpret their existence and experiences from a higher spiritual perspective. This change in attitude and thinking must be done before contending with incessant first-floor needs. When victims realize there is hope and potential for life to improve, their agony is somewhat relieved. However, these persons still need to release

---

[93] *primary constructs (PCs):* the notion that we can accept an energetic view and apply a spiritual interpretation to our existence and experiences

their cemented perspective on life to substantially amend anything. As difficult as this is to do, working with PCs appears to be the only fundamental healing option presently available to overcome powerlessness.

PCs are comprised of two spiritual Truths. The first is: victims are eternal energy beings who chose to live this difficult role in the present life. This idea is initially overwhelming and incomprehensible, and it can instantly cancel any mental openness they might have had. It takes tremendous determination to heal, but it is possible, over time, for victims to finally resign themselves to accept this premise. At that point, they might remain open long enough to learn the next spiritual Truth: the victim role has been serving them as well as others. While this concept is equally hard to mentally grasp, once recognized, these spiritual t/Truths can penetrate mentally even if only a few drops at a time.

> *Two spiritual truths: Victims are eternal energy beings who chose to live this difficult role in the present life. The victim role has been serving them as well as others.*

ॐ Victim scripting only exists at the first floor of life. When victims embrace and employ these primary constructs, they gain a larger understanding of how life is energetically designed. This more advanced awareness equates to gaining a perspective from a higher floor. The view from this new level provides the opportunity to finally begin to shift thinking, beliefs, and actions toward trusting God rather than continuing to stagnate in ego isolation and despair.

> *Victim scripting only exists at the first floor of life.*

Prolonged Victimization

Nearly everyone has occasional, prolonged episodes of powerlessness and anguish. We all know what it feels like to be a victim even if we are not playing it as a scripted role. The early or unexpected death of a loved one, being unfairly fired from a job or bypassed for a deserved promotion, a friend's betrayal, and so many other painful scenarios fortify our underdog feelings. It can take a long time to recover from excruciating experiences, and some people never do.

If someone continues to carry excess toxic emotions for about two years after such an occurrence, it is not uncommon for that person to develop a serious or life-threatening illness. An essential stage of healing involves going through pain to release and be set free from the disabling emotions. Leaning on supportive family and friends can be very helpful. Utilizing support groups, counseling, therapy, healing sessions, and integrative modalities can offer effective assistance and support. Acceptance of the life event can restore peace and allow recovery.

ॐ Because we are on earth to heal, we should not expect life to be easy, but its quality and flow will improve as a direct benefit of releasing painful emotions and clearing programmed energies. However, even these powerful steps will likely produce minimal improvements in the life of a role-playing victim.

Cindy had relationship problems with everyone. Both she and her twin sister, Gwen, were married with children. Their relationship was close but difficult. They had continual disagreements and occasional fights that involved everyone in both families.

Everyone was working on victim issues,

although only Cindy was seemingly seeking help to improve her life. Even though she had been a client of D'Ann for a long time, she still carried a chip on her shoulder that discouraged pleasant or rewarding relationships at all levels. She and her husband treated each other with civility that masked hostility. Her daughter, who painfully rebelled as an adolescent, felt emotionally unsupported, isolated, lost, and unhappy.

Cindy did not have a close friend, and even coworkers mostly left her alone. Because she didn't like them either, this distancing was fine with her.

As often as she could get away, she would drive to her nearby cottage so she could have her own quiet space. Her personal attention was exclusively focused on handling the negativity being hurled at her. She determined that she had no other choice. Internally, she affirmed that: "Everywhere I turn, there are problems. I am not wrong; everyone else is. I do not deserve to be treated this way by others. I am miserable, and it is entirely everyone else's fault."

Things came to a head one Thanksgiving at Gwen's home. The family was arguing around the dinner table. All of them were concerned exclusively with their own thoughts, views, and pain. They started shouting at each other. Finally exploding, Cindy stood up and yelled at them that if she had a gun, she would kill them all right then and there. She stormed out and went home.

Cindy was still carrying this rage at her next session with D'Ann, many days later. Her tirade at her family only started to vent a small portion of her anger. She did not know what to do with the rest of it in spite of the fact that this topic had been discussed many times in previous sessions.

D'Ann reviewed karmic patterning, role-playing, and how to safely and energetically release emotions. Unfortunately, Cindy was not willing to suspend her furor for even a few moments, which would have given her a brief opportunity to look at her life differently and attain some degree of larger understanding and acceptance. She was adamant that she would never forgive her family. Her pretense of therapy ended a few sessions later when she walked out early, shaking her head that she did not want to hear any more about forgiveness.

Although Cindy is very intelligent, she was fixated on how difficult her life was relative to how she wanted it to be, which is the standard view through ego eyes. She had learned a variety of ways to interpret her life differently, so she could have responded more wisely and authentically, and thus felt better. She knew the karmic issues in her family and how to heal by ceasing judgment, releasing emotions, and forgiving. However, her unwillingness to actually forgive will block her from improving her own life. Her decision will perpetuate and exacerbate her victim experiences. It might take her future lifetimes to heal, but eventually she will.

Victimized by Adversity

ॐ Catastrophic events happen on earth. So often these tragedies occur in impoverished countries where the quality of life is minimal to begin with. Losing everything, especially friends and family members, in a disaster or having an accident that leaves lifelong handicaps is agonizing. When people are victimized by severe adversity, whether through a mishap or intentional deed, their whole life changes. They need help at every level. Complete recovery might not happen. Only God knows why these tragedies occur. Basically, as difficult as this might be, trusting God provides the greatest possibility for acceptance and peace.

A spiritual view might provide more insight into what is happening behind such challenging events. Each soul learns before birth what life on earth will be like during the upcoming incarnation. Some souls need and others are willing to experience difficulties for specific reasons. Every involved soul was either willing or scripted to undergo the calamity and gain some lesson from it or to possibly end life because of it. It might seem insensitive, illogical, or even cruel to presume that there could possibly be any positive result from physical crises or an early death. The benefit might seem minuscule in comparison to the outer devastation and/or inner pain, but there is still some higher purpose behind every occurrence. The calamitous accident was, nearly always, not accidental, unless the person received

> *We do not have a choice about whether to have the misfortune; only how we handle the effects.*

preventive guidance and ignored it.

Physical pain is an enigma. Certainly, it hurts, but it might also enable us to burn off karma and trigger an emotional release. Chronic or mild discomfort might be a way to draw our attention to unresolved present or past life issues. Pain can also result from so many internal and external factors that it might not directly serve us. Unfortunately, however, pain is a part of the human physical experience. Every emotional reaction to physical pain represents a free will choice that can move afflicted persons into deeper, more authentically positive and aware levels of operating, or it can stop them so completely that they become bitter, depressed, and angry. We do not have a choice about whether to have the misfortune; we only have a choice about how we handle the effects. Self-pity and negativity only drive others away and continue the feeling of victimhood.

Surmounting Victimization

For role-playing victims, healing is one of the most difficult things on earth to do. These afflicted people have few skills or capability to make lemonade from their lemons. More than simply interpreting everything more optimistically, they need to adopt the concept of Primary Constructs and change several critical areas of their life, including their views. It is essential for them to reinterpret their own situation, surrender all aspects to God, and maintain constant vigilance and determination to heal. They need to also take personal responsibility for their dilemmas, stop blaming others and using excuses, and forgive others for the roles they each had agreed to perform at the soul level. Ultimately, they must become willing and have the courage necessary to make changes, and this will maximize important healing opportunities.

Victim soul scripts mandate the role throughout a person's life, but there can be spiritual intervention. Victims need help from others and might be able to benefit somewhat from professional guidance and services. Some victims who are determined to improve themselves and their situations can begin to effectively move forward by at least contemplating different life perspectives and scenarios. It is possible for most victims to

227

make some important life changes, but it depends exclusively on their free will choice and proactive participation.

ॐ Throughout this process, it is necessary for both victims and those trying to help them to know that, from the largest universal view, there really are no victims. When we accept this

> *From the largest universal view, there really are no victims.*

understanding, regardless of our starting position, we begin to move away from victimhood and closer to the position of co-creator with Source.

21: JUDGMENT

Nothing is right or wrong. Or everything is right and wrong. If anything, we are exactly where we are supposed to be, working with what our soul determined for us to handle, and life is progressing perfectly according to our needs.

However, we don't like all aspects of our lives and passively wish, or have actively attempted, to make internal and external revisions. So we are frustrated and, at times, feel we are wrong and, thus, keep working very hard to be as right as possible. Even so, issues can be so difficult that we might blame ourselves for taking them on. When we release judgment, we can more thoroughly and clearly begin to appreciate our lives and the healing opportunities, disguised as seemingly insurmountable problems, that are so constantly available to us.

> *Judgment perpetuates karma.*

When evaluating our lives, we must beware of judgment. Judgment perpetuates karma. Only the first floor view of life operates with full power judgment. Screening life from this first floor position draws barriers that inherently divide people and inhibit consensus. Because we each have different and limited scenes at this floor, judgmental opinions and beliefs operate in ways that malign unity and generate ill will, dramas, and even wars. Fortunately, as we incrementally heal, we reduce judgment. Gradually liberating ourselves from judgment raises us up a few floors in our spiritual skyscraper.

Some behaviors or activities are wiser, healthier, and timelier. Others are more detrimental, painful, or negative. We can all agree that some things are, in fact, wrong. It is impossible to condone murder, rape, and so many other violent and reprehensible actions. Yet, we must also realize that there is more going on behind the scenes than just the obvious appearances. Our views and opinions will not completely or permanently alter or stop anyone else's poor behavior. Bad things will continue to happen. However, our expanded understandings will benefit us by providing us and others around us with more acceptance, compassion, peace, and wisdom about each situation and person involved.

Not everyone on earth is scripted to heal in this lifetime. There will still be real life repercussions from poor decisions. Someone

> *Not everyone on earth is scripted to heal in this lifetime.*

who breaks the law will continue to be held accountable and face appropriate consequences. Murderers, rapists, and other hard-core criminals need to be kept away from the population to thwart repeat offenses. They need rehabilitation more than punishment. Their action was not right, but it might have balanced a karmic mandate. Some criminals will not change in this lifetime. Their egos are too badly damaged, and the persons are too filled with blame, hate, and a need to retaliate or defy the social system. They require our entire arsenal of legal and ethical protocols to prevent them from perpetrating more harmful actions.

One of the greatest advantages of understanding and accepting the concept of reincarnation and karma is the progressive elimination of blame. By claiming responsibility for our own life and reinterpreting it with a spiritual understanding, we will naturally shift our judgmental attitude. Berating or condemning others or ourselves is a

> *One of the greatest advantages of understanding and accepting the concept of reincarnation and karma is the progressive elimination of blame.*

futile, ego-based activity. The pattern of continually doing so is inhibiting and energetically damaging.

It is possible, but very difficult to initially accept, that even the most violent criminals and their innocent victims have important roles they are actually fulfilling for each other. How can we possibly comprehend that mass murderers or world wars might have ultimate beneficial justification? But if we could see a large enough view of each violent scenario, we could understand that, in some way, it meets the unique needs of every soul involved.

Enlarging our view of life and releasing judgment will not ignore consequences of actions, nor will it condone, minimize, excuse, or promote tragedies. But our expanded view will enhance our interpretive screen, reveal additional

> *We design our life. Knowing that we entered into a soul contract to have challenges will shift our responses and improve our life quality.*

possibilities and interpretations, and foster a deeper and fuller spiritual understanding and acceptance. Simply stated, we design our life. Knowing that we entered into a soul contract to have challenges will shift our responses and improve our life quality.

~ ~ ~

We make decisions and form opinions from the information available. That is the best we can do. If we had more information to work with, we could respond better to whatever comes along. Living in a state of grace can help suspend standard opinions and decisions based exclusively on appearances, and it can neutralize some of the effects of life's issues, roles, and dramas. This concept is well illustrated in a common story that has been used by several writers and speakers in various forms and also serves our purposes here.

> A man and two young boys got on a bus and took their seats. The boys were loud, fussy, and overactive. They began to run up and down the aisle, disturbing the passengers. The father seemed oblivious to them and continued to stare out the side window. People on the bus were looking at each other, glaring at the father, and becoming increasingly irritated at his lack of control over the boys. What a terrible father! What unruly children! Someone should do something about them!

> Finally, a man sitting near the father tapped him on the shoulder and asked if he was aware that the boys were misbehaving. The dad came awake from his reverie. He apologized and explained that his wife, their mom, had just died, and they were on their way home from the hospital. Instantly, the response of every

person within earshot changed dramatically. Instead of anger, they now felt pity and some measure of compassion.

Had the passengers applied grace, they would have been less judgmental toward the father and his sons, had a softer and kinder interpretation about what was going on, and been somewhat less disturbed even before they learned what had happened. The point is: All people have their story; our role is to, without judgment, accept them even when we don't understand, no matter what their conduct or behavior.

22: FEAR

Our perceived separation from God created fear. The personal, intense, yet generic fear that erupted when our soul originally

> *Our perceived separation from God created fear.*

left Source is still with us even as we live first floor lives.

ॐ Fear predominates at the first floor. From this level, appearances that induce fear might be accurate, but when viewed from higher vibrational dimensions and with advanced understandings, they are irrelevant and deceiving.

This is why fear marks the core of ego's power over us and why we must clear that fear from our consciousness in order to freely walk our path toward reintegration with Source. Walking that path is like ascending the stairs in the skyscraper, one level at a time, from the first floor to the fiftieth floor. It marks our state of transition from low-energy beings into empowered beings.

This is an ongoing process. Throughout many lifetimes and probably in this life too, we have dealt with our issues repeatedly, managed them as efficiently as possible, yet have been unable to significantly improve and heal them. Our lives are not fully the way we want them to be, and problems and frustrations abound. As a result, we have lived first floor lives as though they were real.

We have finally realized that fear will not just disappear in response to our wishes, prayers, or management. To release fear, we

> *"You gain strength, courage, and confidence by every experience in which you really stop to look fear in the face. You must do the thing you think you cannot do."*
> ~ *Eleanor Roosevelt*

must bravely face it and not back down. We must feel fear, experience it, and conquer it. Then, when we win victory over fear, it will have no hold over us. As Eleanor Roosevelt stated, "You gain strength, courage, and confidence by every experience in which you really stop to look fear in the face. You must do the thing you think you cannot do."

The Illusion of Fear

Fear is the most elemental, stunted, and freezing emotion in humankind. The well-known acronym F- E-A-R stands for False Evidence Appearing Real, and this is a universal Truth. When we fall for the first floor illusion of fear, we bypass the opportunity to heal and evolve. When we feel alarm, we employ coping skills to assist us in surviving the seeming threat. But these skills only deal with the problem at the first floor level. In reality, they sidetrack us from our intended growth.

That's because fear is a tool ego uses to distract us from our spiritual development. Conquering fear liberates us from the ego

> *Fear is a tool ego uses to distract us from our spiritual development.*

stranglehold so that we can become conscious of our inherent integration and congruency with Source. When we reinterpret a spiritual setup as an opportunity to heal, we then empower ourselves to handle the situation differently. When we are truly ready to evolve, whether by riding the elevator or taking the staircase up, we will have the internal grounding and awareness to avoid panic; we will focus on trusting God and k/Know that miracles can occur.

As our vibrational healing energies escalate, (as earlier described in Section 3 of Chapter 1,) we are better able to target our fears and assist their release. Then, as we remove theses low energies, we emancipate ourselves from the old, preschool limitations of ego identity, control, and agendas. We clear the path and assist ourselves to form a Source-based identity that enables us to remember our original, still-intact relationship with God.

As a result of cosmic initiative, we are now consciously aware that more fear-evoking issues are happening in our lives at the first floor level. Our anxieties and worries become more grippingly obvious. We see that society's previously working structures appear to be breaking down, demanding to be revised. We don't know what to fix first: families, employment, business, education, law enforcement, religion, food supply, or financial, legal, medical, and political systems. Aspects of human interaction such as stability, security, service, quality, and integrity are also being affected. The pace of deterioration, chaos, and pain is quickening. The potential for greater fear is rising.

Yet, in the midst of this disintegration, unheard of new technologies, healing modalities, and inspiring prospects are also emerging. The good in our world is becoming phenomenally wonderful, while the bad is horrendously difficult. The gap between these two extremes is widening into a chasm. We are at a make-it-or-break-it point. Do we stand still amidst the status quo, jump into the abyss, or leap across the gap?

To remain in the status quo is to be paralyzed with fear. To jump into the abyss is to give in to despair. To leap across the gap is to take a risk and place our trust in God, which is, in Realty, not a risk. The choice we make depends on our spiritual understanding of how life works, and the strength with which we have allowed ego to ensnare us.

E/go grips some excessively logical people very strongly. These persons require more intense or bizarre personal setups to jar themselves loose from the grip of their existing ways. They might need to hit bottom before they wake up, review their life, and make critical, life-improving changes. Other people need to stop blaming everyone else and start taking responsibility for their own conditions. Regardless of where we are on our spiritual path or what floor we have reached, we all have issues and traits that require major demolition, renovation, and/or reconstruction. That is why we are alive, experiencing this earth time in our spiritual evolution.

Having a fear experience resembles taking a final exam for us to choose which voice, ego or Source, we will seek, listen for, and respond to in our life. E/go's baseline effort to control life is overwhelming fear. Source wants us to recall that we are endowed and empowered with God's eternal Truth. Each fearful situation that we encounter is a personal reminder that control is a low-vibration energy that cannot survive the powerful frequencies of empowerment.

> *Control is a low vibration energy that cannot survive the powerful frequencies of empowerment.*

An empowering thought is one through which we remember that all souls desire reunion with Prime Energy. We want to return home. We no longer have to leave physical life behind to be integrated and aligned with Source. It is only ego that is holding us back from a life filled with God's Light. Once we make the decision to go through fear without buying into the first floor setup of limiting appearances and consequences—and to stop buying into the emotional drama—our inner operating system realigns to surrender ego control and trust God.

Fear-Based Responses

Typical responses or reactions to fear range from overwhelming panic and rage to desperation and inaction. People in a state of fear feel frozen in place, knowing they are doomed and can do nothing to prevent an inevitable, horrendous outcome. They hope to survive until the event passes or the situation eases. They might pray for help to survive. They might seek another way out through alcohol or drug abuse to numb their pain. They might physically run away. Or they might negotiate a bargain with God, committing to follow through on the pledge.

In the following stories, the persons involved utilized healing energy therapy to gain understanding about and resolve significant fear-induced physical pain.

> Charlie has been pursuing healing for many years and is spiritually advanced. When a very close sister-in-law died, he had an excruciating, over-the-top period of grief. He thought he probably felt even more pain than his brother, her widower.
>
> He began to have serious heart alarms and

decided to go to a cardiac specialist. The tests results showed no aberrations. In spite of this good news, his symptoms persisted. He started having unprecedented, frequent fearful thoughts about his own death, what his family would do if he were to die, and all of the related concerns and emotions for their well being without him. He was astonished at how dark his thoughts and moods became.

At Charlie's next session, he learned that processing fear is a necessary stage of healing, and he had fallen for ego's diversionary tactic. This was a light-bulb moment for him. After he surrendered his emotions, ego lost its last major hold on his consciousness. Charlie is no longer being held back from transforming into a Light being.

~ ~ ~

Jeff had had two life threatening bouts with brain cancer. He was not afraid of dying but was fearful of the pain and loss he might have to go through before he died. He hated and was not willing to face this fear and did nearly everything he could to ignore or rise above the emotion. He forced himself to stay busy, read, play games, watch movies, attend events, and do anything that would distract his thoughts.

However, for the third time, severe headaches returned and with it came the fear of more brain cancer. This time he sought energetic healing. D'Ann assured him that there was no more cancer at the moment but that he did need to release the toxic fear energies. If the dangerous energy remained, cancer would return.

Immediately after his session, Jeff had two to three weeks of excruciating pain with accompanying exhaustion and panic. He was not able to control, block, or rise above the symptoms in his usual manner. He stayed home, rarely got dressed, cried, became angry, took long baths, prayed, and slept.

When the siege passed, he was a different person. Not only did he experience greater relief from the fear and pain but also the dread and effort it took for him to keep going. He enjoyed a higher quality of life than he had experienced for some years.

After a few months, however, the headaches again returned. This time his fear and pain only manifested for about three hours, a significant improvement from earlier, longer-lasting episodes. His doctor's new diagnosis was incredible: he had gingivitis, not cancer. This was easily and quickly treatable. Jeff had moved through and beyond his fear and had healed physically as well.

Jeff's situation was unique. Not everyone with brain cancer has excess toxic fear or severe headaches. There are many possible physical causes for both the fear and the pain, so professional medical diagnosis and care is essential. Complementary or integrative modalities might also benefit an ill person, and they have a greater potential to actually heal the body rather than just buy more time alive. Holistic therapies might also extend the person's quality and length of life, and/or minimize side effects from allopathic medical treatments.

🕉 Just because a person has cancer does not necessarily mean he or she is soul-scripted to die from that disease. There are other possibilities: remission, cure, other medical conditions, or sudden death such as an accident. Unless a miracle takes place, if a person is scripted to pass from a specific condition, that will be the cause of death. However, the timing of it might be flexible for some people.

~ ~ ~

Fear caused by factors out of our control can be very powerful. When we are able to rise above even those strongest of fears, the results can be amazingly miraculous.

> As a young professional, Jonathan accepted a demanding management position in a local college that had a history of turmoil, competition, and arguments between departments and poor communication throughout the college. Both of the people who held this job before had resigned with serious health issues after brief employment there. The work situation did not improve, but, somehow, Jonathan was able to endure longer than his predecessors. However, his stress level grew more difficult to handle.

> Very early one morning, Jonathan placed an emergency call to D'Ann. Things were at a crisis point. He had just lost a grievance against an opposing department that had earlier won a complaint against his. Jonathan was panicked about his personal safety and

survival. He was terrified that a present or former employee would make an attempt on his life. He felt unsupported and betrayed by upper-level managers who were involved with the situation. He said he was alone, hopeless, and trapped. Even though he was on prescription medicines for anxiety and depression, he was now unable to keep going. He needed help to understand what was spiritually happening and how to proceed.

D'Ann and Jonathan prayed together. They surrendered everything: his life, fear, viewpoints, interpretations, outcomes, opinions, money, and employment needs. While barely possible to accomplish when emotionally so distraught, they offered forgiveness for all involved. They asked for divine intervention from any and all beings who were able to protect him and help in any and all ways. They cast White Light around Jonathan, the building, offices, and all entwined people. They even requested assistance from the spirit of his deceased grandmother, if it were appropriate and available.

The next morning Jonathan saw the custodian, Bart, as he was walking into the building. Bart asked Jonathan, "What happened?" Jonathan didn't know what he meant. Bart said that the window in Jonathan's office had cracked. Jon immediately assumed it was from a bullet or rock. They went to his office together to assess the damage. It was a stress crack, not the result of some missile.

That same day Jonathan had two surprising emails from students praising his methods and assistance. These had been copied and sent to Jonathan's boss. He also received an email from his boss, offering the first-ever support for him and his situation. These validating events helped him see meaningful results from his prayers, but they did not substantially change the work situation.

The building Jonathan worked in was over fifty years old, and the windows had never been replaced. The crack had likely happened sometime during the prior night's crisis when Jonathan had released some of his physical stress and panic. The window represented Jonathan's ability to see and interpret the world from his standard, old view. He recognized that the old energies were displaced by higher frequencies as the result of spiritual intervention and that the energetic contrast was too extreme for the glass to handle. The new window symbolized his newly cleared and improved life view and his upgraded understanding. He could now make wiser interpretations of events and select better response options than he could before the setup.

Jonathan needed to go through this terror to relinquish fear from his life. He was at the end of his tracks and could do nothing else about his work situation with his prior perspective. The situation was a given, and his interpretation had been accurate. He didn't deserve these problems. His emotions were boiling over, and anyone going through his life experience would feel the same way. His concerns were valid because of numerous well-publicized stories about disgruntled employees shooting and killing bosses and coworkers. It can and, tragically, does happen. His feared possible outcome was logically justifiable.

Jonathan was not wrong.

He learned that he was at a major transition stage to leave ego life behind. Yet, he had to get to this juncture in order to stop merely managing his life. Because personal management techniques perpetuate ego authority, we all need some opportunity to shift our control base to Source. Although the problem occurred in his professional world, it was providentially set up to benefit him personally. This crisis targeted Jonathan's feelings of fear, victimization, defeat, hopelessness, and overwhelming powerlessness, and it offered him the chance to shift his perspective and interpretation of life. This major emergency happened so that he could heal.

The results of Jonathan's crisis and the memorable following day shifted a foundational component within him. His enlarged understanding provided somewhat better outcomes at work and improved his emotional reactions. Things are not yet easy or frequently rewarding for him, but he has some degree of emotional disentanglement from the dramas. Jonathan chose to seek spiritual clarification, assistance, and intervention. He remained protected and safe, and he energetically benefited from the hell-like experience. Surrendering his views, opinions, and fears and then inviting spiritual help allowed healing to manifest.

The Fear Setup Equation

ॐ The opportunity behind a fear event enables us to free ourselves from the chains that have bound us to ego, and it is crucial to understand what is happening when we undergo a fear experience. Enduring an excruciating crisis is an essential, briefly debilitating, yet life-transforming stage of the healing process.

> *We must all evolve beyond fear to achieve empowerment.*

We must all evolve beyond fear to achieve empowerment.

There is a linear, first floor formula that will help clarify the components of this extreme, essential, and healing event. The equation of a fear setup is:

Outcome (o) = Perspective (a) + Interpretation (b) + Emotions (c) + Response (x) or o = a + b + c + x

Outcome (o) is the result we know is likely or inevitable, the situation we are compelled to avoid, and the reason for our fear or terror. An outcome might happen immediately, in the short-term, and/or in the long-range future. The outcome appears to be inescapable, and we know that we would do absolutely anything to prevent or minimize our fate. But because we seem to have no recourse, we feel backed into a corner. We know that what we fear can happen and has happened to others or even ourselves before. With every fiber of our being, we loathe the situation we are in.

We begin to determine this conclusion based on ...

... our personal first floor, limited, and habitual *perspective* in life (a), which impacts how we handle all situations, especially the present one. We have looked at life predominately the same way throughout adulthood.

> *The intent behind a fear setup is for God's Light to supersede the ego's foundation of energetic fear, an event that automatically shifts our perspective so we can expand and evolve.*

As long as we continue to have the same vantage point, we block other more insightful and more effective possibilities from our view, which causes us to continue unaware of higher vibrational potentials. The intent behind a fear setup is for God's Light to supersede the ego's foundation of energetic fear, an event that automatically shifts our perspective so we can expand and evolve.

Unfortunately, we have little possibility of effectively adjusting our physical, mental, emotional, or psychological condition during the crisis. Afterward, however, our improved perspective enables us to look back on the situation and place it in a larger context. This provides us with more Source input and assists us in our spiritual development. We eventually come to realize that our perspective needed to be augmented and upgraded to foster our further integration with Source.

To our perspective, we add …

… our resulting *interpretation* from our standard view (b). As long as we keep the same perspective, we reinforce our usual interpretation of life. Our personal history has taught us how our life works and what we must do to survive, manage, and succeed. We have experientially honed our default operating system, and we profoundly resist amending it. However, a Source-based operating system awaits our discovery on the other side of our wall of resistance. Our interpretation automatically enhances as our perspective shifts (a + b).

That opens us up to be more aware of …

… our *emotions* (c), which feel critical, irresolvable, uncontrollable, rigid, stifling, and excruciating. Our ego reacts and we panic, thinking we are at the end of our rope with no options other than to hang on until we are dead. Fear won't let us go. During this crisis, very little except fear mentally computes in our head. We simply cannot convince ourselves of anything constructive, and even our management skills no longer work. We desperately cling to our old version of life without realizing that the best course of action would be to let go and trust God.

We have not consciously comprehended that emotions do not passively dissipate and that we need to actively process and release them so that we can raise our vibrational rate of energy. As our perspective expands and our interpretation advances, our emotions level out (a + b + c).

And that sets the stage for us to select …

… our undetermined *response* (x). This unknown factor represents the only wiggle room we have to break away from ego domination and actually heal our life. Our typical fear response is inaction, which locks us into the inertia of the status quo. We see no efficient or effective way to change or stop the spiritual setup from playing out, and we have no apparent control over the actual outcome.

> *Our undetermined response (x) represents the only wiggle room we have to break away from ego domination and actually heal our life.*

~ ~ ~

🕉 But appearances are deceiving. When we look at the fear setup from a *new perspective* (A), that is, the enlarged context of a major blessing in disguise, the necessary healing opportunity will actually foster trust. Then we *reinterpret* (B) the situation as having a beneficial intent for us even though we do not as yet have any specific and practical answers. Although our *emotions* (C) will continue to be relatively

> *Appearances are deceiving.*

frozen in anguish, (which can be relieved to some degree or other in a crisis by using the Three Pillars of Transformation,) we will then put all of our attention on our *undetermined response* (X).

From this new perspective, reinterpretation, and acceptance

of our fear setup, we can then use more profoundly powerful spiritual techniques and intervention to assist us in achieving an improved and more positive *outcome* (O) than would otherwise have been possible.

We can use prayer and ask for or even demand assistance from divine beings to provide protection, strength, relief, peace, understanding, and the speediest and most spiritually beneficial resolution for all people involved in the situation. We can use White Light everywhere, forgive all people involved, and surrender absolutely everything. After this, we can keep reminding ourselves that we trust God.

When we factor these new, higher values into the equation $(A + B + C + X)$, our energetic steps can lead us to an unanticipated better outcome (O), including infinite miracles.

$\sim \sim \sim$

The purpose of the fear setup is not to end our life. Fear occurs when we believe that we have no options, no way out, no solutions, no hope. The formula of $a + b + c + x$ applies when we are in the state of fear. That state comes to us when we encounter a setup and don't yet realize it is a healing opportunity. This state of fear can happen whether we are generally fearful or are normally courageous and confident in most areas of our life.

> *The purpose of the fear setup is not to end our life. Fear occurs when we believe that we have no options, no way out, no solutions, no hope.*

This state of hopeless fear can last for many weeks or months. Or it can last for a few moments, hours, or days. Fear lasts for as long as we remain fearful.

Once we realize that we have options, we begin to change our perspective, and we invite ourselves to enter into the realm of new possibilities. When this happens, we then apply the formula $A + B + C + X = O$, and allow ourselves to be open to affirmations that will help us climb even further out of the depths of fear.

~ ~ ~

> *Fear lasts for as long as we remain fearful.*

The following list of affirmations offers a few ideas to enlarge your perspective (A) beyond fear and improve your interpretation (B) of an emotional (C) crisis. Collectively, the words here are suggestions to effectively expand and enhance your responses (X) and generate improved outcomes (O).

Affirmations to elevate perspective (A):

- I am intended to benefit from this experience, regardless of what it looks or feels like.

- I am trusting that something more powerful is working for me beyond what I can see at this time.

- I apparently need this event and am ready to receive it even though I don't want it, have no answers as to why it's here, and don't know how to resolve it.

Affirmations to generate enlightened interpretations (B):

- I am intended to survive this experience.

- I know my unwanted and painful emotions have

never served me and they need to be cleared.

- I accept, appreciate, and cooperate with this excruciating and transformative opportunity.

- I have the courage I need to make necessary changes in my life.

Affirmations to reduce emotional anguish and relieve some degree of anxiety (C):

- Everything I feel right now is exactly what I need to experience in order to clear this issue.

- I do not deserve, nor am I wrong, to feel these emotions.

- Underneath my volatile feelings are divine attributes.

- I give myself permission to safely and appropriately release my emotions.

- I am compassionate toward everyone and everything involved in this situation, including and especially myself.

- Although I have no answers, I know that this experience will pass.

Affirmations to improve internal and possibly external responses (X):

- I surrender my ego mechanics, dramas, beliefs, opinions, and all other spiritually immature understandings.

- I face, admit, surrender, and release everything in

my system that is restraining me from evolving.

- I forgive myself for my part in energetically causing this excruciating spiritual setup.

- I forgive all people who appear to be working against me, k/Knowing they are actually serving me.

- I ask for all the spiritual intervention possible to assist me through this difficulty.

- I ask to receive, recognize, and apply guidance and intervention.

- I claim back my authentic power.

- I speak my t/Truth.

- I trust God.

23: FIFTIETH FLOOR LIVING

Looking down from the fiftieth floor of our skyscraper, we can still see objects and events occurring on the first floor, but the additional

> *Our choice to be blindly enmeshed or observantly involved with life's dramas determines whether we align with ego or Source.*

elevation provides greater context and meaning. The enlarged and heightened view is consequentially mesmerizing, profound, and life enhancing. Something extremely unpleasant at the first floor might barely be visible from the top floor.

Even while energetically on the fiftieth floor, we still interact with people and participate in activities on the first floor, but our view and interpretation of what is happening there is significantly enlarged. We can be instantly enmeshed in the emotions of ongoing first floor events, but are less likely to. Or we can, just as instantly, rise above them. It is as though we can be both places at the same time, involved while also observing. Our choice to be blindly enmeshed

> *Our healthier responses and wiser decisions might influence those around us to also rise above the situation.*

or observantly involved in life's dramas determines whether we align with ego or with Source.

As our perspective broadens, our interpretations expand. We are no longer misled by what seems to be taking place in everyday life because we understand there is so much more going on beyond immediate, first floor appearances. The energy we exude because of our broadened awareness on the fiftieth floor promotes miraculous changes at the first floor. We will have healthier responses and make wiser decisions in life, and these, in turn, might very well influence those around us to also rise above the situation to the degree they are able.

~ ~ ~

Just as it is not physically possible for us to be on the first floor and the fiftieth floor at the same time, the following analogy is also not literally possible, but the concept behind it is accurate. With first floor protocol, a painter spends many hours or even days prepping a room or building prior to actually applying the first brushstroke of paint. The painter finds this stage of work to be tedious and time consuming. He would like to avoid doing it, but it is an essential part of the process. When this preliminary step is completed, he then paints, which he thoroughly enjoys doing, and cleans up.

With fiftieth floor awareness, God does all of the prep work. The painter merely shows up and paints. His drudgery is gone, his attitude improves, and he looks forward to his activities because they are so rewarding. This radically reduced and simplified protocol represents the

> *The more we get out of our own way, the more God will enter, prepare our course of action, and improve our life.*

beautiful, empowered operating system that is available to all of us with higher vibrational living. The more we get out of our own way, the more God will enter, prepare our course of action, and improve our life.

~ ~ ~

Attaining higher levels in our fifty-story building resembles a natural stream of water. With ego in charge at the first floor, we have been attempting to walk upstream. The current creates a constant resistance, and if we stop pushing ourselves to accomplish or move forward, we lose ground. Then, just when we think we have things figured out and that our management techniques will help us navigate in the stream, something else comes along that reinforces our need to keep pushing. We might even feel that life just isn't fair.

Once we surrender our life to God, however, we turn around in the stream and the current now gently yet persistently leads and supports our direction. With little external resistance, we don't need to push ourselves as hard as before. We learn that the stream moves us forward to where we need to be for the greatest good of all. With practice and more experience of surrender and trust, we end up floating in the stream and experience the benefit of fiftieth floor blessings. We effortlessly arrive at where we are destined to be, and we find that our effortless "work" is easier and more rewarding.

From a higher view, we see that our reluctance and frustration have turned into joy and play. We profit in direct proportion to how far we have removed ourselves from ego, how far we have risen up the stairway or in the elevator of our fifty-story building. When we reach the fiftieth floor, we also see that we have the option to look down at the action below or straight out at the wondrous horizon in front of us or at higher and more miraculous elevations above. In the optimal world, we will look in all three directions: back at the first floor to appreciate the situations we encountered there and how far we've come, at the horizon to value this higher-level view, and skyward toward the realm of infinite possibilities.

ॐ The fiftieth floor represents the completed activation of our portion of divinity. Unconditional love and soul attributes manifest fully at this exalted vibrational level. E/go, with its limited functionality, has opened, cleared, and reintegrated with Source, thus eliminating from our lives issues, roles, mirroring, dramas, and setups. We identify with the unity of all life so that separation, fear, and anxiety cease to exist. Judgment, expectations, beliefs, life management, and self-agendas have been removed. Problems are eased and life flows.

We consciously, freely, appropriately, and authentically interact with all life. We make congruent responses and enjoy harmonious relationships. Because we have cleared all previously programmed energies, our emotions are appropriate, and we honestly express them in all given situations. Peace and wisdom abound. Guidance, synchronicities, and God's intervention in our life are evident, constant, and profound.

We desire to serve others. Our hearts overflow with

gratitude. We feel blessed and privileged. Intuitive gifts prevail and stimulate unheard of possibilities. Miracles are normal at this multidimensional level. All is well.

Physical life continues to be lived at the first floor, but resembles the openness of a fifty-story atrium. There are no blocks or barriers of any kind to limit unconditional love. We fully exude God's Light from our soul, and we manifest Source qualities in the course of our empowered, everyday experiences. We have blossomed into our divine potential.

24: PLANETARY TRANSFORMATION

ॐ The linear, logical, three-dimensional, conscious, ego-based part of the brain has been scientifically proven to process about eight bits of data per second. The other major portion of the brain, the neocortex, is predominantly spiritual, creative, and multidimensional. It has been scientifically proven to process somewhere around eight billion bits of data per second. Eight versus eight billion!

Historically, we have been living and functioning from the most limited and archaic part of our brain. Our rational interpretations have all been formed from this restricted input. This concept is similar to working today on a computer from the earliest years they were available. Although based on cutting edge technology at the time, they are

When we energetically clear antiquated ego mechanics from our system, we promote transformation.

now antiquated, slow, inefficient, and cumbersome. We would be unable to use current software programs. The old computer would not be wrong, but there would be no reason to use it. Although we cannot replace our brains with state of the art processors, removing old ego programming does allow us to become whole brained. When we energetically clear antiquated ego mechanics from our system, we promote transformation.

~ ~ ~

Since 1987, many vibrational healing shifts, openings, and transmissions have been sent to earth with the intention to boost humanity's development. Although energetically invisible, these episodes have tremendously affected us. Astrologers have highlighted many heavenly events, but especially three profound ones that had never happened before, determined by unique lineups or configurations of planets, constellations, stars, and the sun and moon.

The first occurred on August 16–17, 1987. This was the Harmonic Convergence, which officially ushered in the Age of Aquarius or what was then called the New Age.

The following numbers are not literal, but the examples relate accurate and relevant concepts. Presume humanity has essentially three different levels of electrical wiring capabilities within us: wires that will carry 110 volts, 220 volts, and more than 220 volts.

Our default method of operating on the first floor and engaging in karmic-based activities requires wiring that carries only 110 volts. This number is the standard frequency of electricity for buildings on the American continent. The Harmonic Convergence began to increase the quantity of energy coming to earth. The potency and vibrational rate also began to expand. Over time, the oscillation moved up to 111 volts, 112 volts, 113 volts, and higher. This energetic elevation began to lift us beyond first floor living, whether we consciously knew about it or were ready or not.

Sixteen years later, we arrived at another spiritual mile

marker, the second heavenly event to promote evolution. This was the Harmonic Concordance, which transpired on November 8, 2003. Energy sent to earth at that time was figuratively at 220 volts. The spiritual focus of the Harmonic Concordance was to create internal and external congruence and transformation. As a result, old human systems of operating, both internal and external, began to break apart, causing disruptions. Personal lives and individual management skills, social institutions and structures, weather patterns, and climactic earth events began to more obviously change, erupt, or deteriorate at a pace that elicited fear. The Harmonic Concordance vibrations continued to escalate in force and potency. They have moved up to the metaphorical equivalent of 230 volts, 240 volts, and higher.

Nearly seven more years passed before the occurrence of the third major celestial event, called the Cosmic Cross, Cardinal Cross, or Mayan Portal. This stellar phenomenon happened during July 11–17, 2010, and marked the official beginning of the new human species: multi-sensory, multi-dimensional, whole-brained, empowered Light beings. Many such babies and young children had already incarnated on earth, but they were frontrunners. After 2010, most babies are born with these Source capabilities available and functioning at an appropriate level for their age. Adults, meanwhile, are undergoing energetic renovation and can attain the new high level of operating current by learning what is energetically possible, how to work with and through the resulting challenges, and applying this new information.

As of July 2010, earth began to be flooded with increasingly intensifying multi-dimensional energies. Humanity's old 110 wiring systems, and even newer 220 systems can no longer function and hold together with the elevated power of these higher frequencies. Relatively speaking, very little 110 and only slightly more 220 energy is now available to us. People operating exclusively from ego, with its 110 circuitry, are finding it more difficult to live.

We are all being inundated with tremendous energy forces to stretch and adjust, or break down. This situation upsets the traditional status quo, which was designed to operate at 110 energy, and it precipitates significant fall out. Nearly every aspect of life is crumbling in disruptive, obvious, and possibly calamitous ways. The threats are imminent and the protections are inadequate, just like the little boy who thrust his finger in the dike in attempt to hold back the raging ocean. A person can't avoid hearing about the radical and diverse changes and crises occurring worldwide.

These higher, multi-dimensional energies are targeting and breaking apart our inborn and life-created energetic blocks and barriers. Our hindrances are low-vibration energies that are comprised of karma,

> *Spiritual growth is the removal of what has hindered the blossoming of our inner t/Truth. As we evolve, it becomes more essential for us to make decisions based on our inner t/Truth rather than using the past as our exclusive frame of reference.*

unresolved issues, emotional debris, and ego filters as well as the societal norms we established to function at those low-level vibrational understandings. These hindrances have prevented us from activating our divine potential.

As a result of the multi-dimensional energies, karmic and present life energetic debris is thinning and breaking apart, which enables us to more easily remove them from our lives. As we release our energetic accumulation, we progressively move toward personal empowerment. Spiritual growth is the removal of what has hindered the blossoming of our inner t/Truth. As we evolve, it becomes more essential for us to make decisions based on our inner t/Truth rather than using the past as our exclusive frame of reference. One definition of insanity is doing the same thing and expecting a different result. It takes an open mind, willingness, and courage to upgrade our life processing.

Resembling the concept of reincarnation, this energetic evolutionary process is happening whether we know it, believe it, understand it, want it, or resist it. The purpose behind this cosmic transmission is to hasten our planetary and personal evolution. This energetic deluge will continue and escalate into the foreseeable future. Everything is intensifying. Our issues and frustrations are increasing beyond our ability to manage at the 110, karmic or ego level. To evolve into Light beings, we need to be overwhelmed beyond our ability to manage life on our own so that we allow or even invite God to take over. Our lives and bodies are being impacted to force us to release old, limited programming and to create space for the new to emerge. We are on the brink of stepping into personal empowerment.

Not everyone is feeling the effects of multi-dimensional high energy in the same way, and there are varying degrees of personal sensitivity. We are all consciously aware of ever more random and scattered strange reactions, conditions, and events, but we typically have no understanding of what is causing such rapid upheaval and change. In addition to this general scenario, most people working on a profound spiritual path have physical symptoms and periods of

> *Switching our response from control and management to higher dimensional understandings and reactions that support our growth will produce wonderful personal and social benefits.*

specific difficulties at certain stages of transition. We are living in a chaotic mix of energies that are bizarre, intense, and often painful. Switching our response from control and management to higher dimensional understandings and reactions that support our growth will produce wonderful personal and social benefits.

~ ~ ~

We are a species birthing a new humanity. During labor, a woman cannot continue with her normal routines, has very little capability to focus on other things, has few or no answers to relevant questions, has no actual control over what is happening within her body, and only wants to stop the painful contractions. We feel very much that same way about our present lives at this stage of our evolution. After the birth, however, the new mother is so grateful for her newborn that she would go through it all again. When we manifest God's Light within and allow it to flow forth from us, we will have that appreciative perspective also.

Individually, we will each arrive at a make-it-or-break-it point as energies continue to intensify. This point nearly always involves a fear crisis or happens when our lives have totally fallen apart. We can't avoid this essential stage of development that is not yet conventionally recognized. Our reaction to this healing crisis will be determined by how open, evolved, and trusting we are; where we are on our life path; what we spiritually know; what we need and are ready for; and our life scripting.

> *If we choose to heal, we will notice personal growth and renewal in spite of inner and outer chaos.*

🕉 Our three primary response options are to: shift into being an empowered species; resist, prolong, and worsen our current, painful stage of development; or eventually be unable to keep going and become panicked, enraged, or violent.

If we choose to heal, we will notice personal growth and renewal in spite of inner and outer chaos.

As souls, our goal is to become aware of, integrate, and manifest our portion of God's Light on earth. We are being given a divine opportunity to evolve at this point in time. Every person alive is supposed to be here. We chose this time and this planet because earth is, at least to our consciousness, the most happening place in the Universe. Unbelievable inspirations, understandings, and breakthroughs are occurring at an unprecedented level and pace. This process is taking us into uncharted territory. We will continue to appear the same physically, but we will have advanced wiring, connections, and capabilities that we cannot see externally. This evolution is therefore primarily internal, invisible, energetic, subtle, and yet profoundly life changing.

25: TIME

Humanity has developed linearly and logically throughout the ages. Our predecessors were aware of astronomical movements, seasons, weather, diurnal and nocturnal sequences, and patterns of birth, growth, and death. Early humankind recognized they could not control these events and gave their inner power over to functioning within the requirements of the physical, material world. Survival depended on successful management of their lives within this environment. Their primal concept of time as one second relentlessly following another is still valid at the first floor of life. Linear three- or four-dimensional processing with 110 systems cannot accept any other interpretations or possibilities. Therefore, we live beholden to the clock, and we must fit our activities and responsibilities within this abstract yet binding framework.

> *Events take place within time, yet are beyond time and not bound by it.*

Emerging humanity has a completely revised format of and relationship with time. The more we get out of our own way, the more God, who is eternal and infinite, takes over. The fuller and stronger connection humanity has with Source, the freer we are from time constraints. The same pace of seconds continues, but opening dimensionalities allow us more flexibility in regard to how we interpret and interact with time. Events take place within time, yet are beyond time and not bound by it.

This shift and freedom occurs in exact proportion to ego removal. Instead of

> *We will be where we need to be when we need to be there.*

mental life management, we will seek and embrace energetic attunement. We will be where we need to be when we need to be there. Time restraints will ease. Synchronicities will increase. Our life will flow with lightness and delight.

In the old system of operating, when we placed a load of wet clothes into the dryer, we would set the timer, look at the clock, and then go about our business. We might check the clock once or twice to see how much longer we had before the buzzer would go off. We would plan our activities during the drying process around the predetermined time so we would be there and remove the clothes from the dryer to prevent wrinkling.

The new system of interpreting time is radically improved. When we set the laundry timer, we might or might not look at the clock, and we do not need to keep track of the drying time as we plan and perform other tasks. We are free from carrying the responsibility to be there at the right time. We remain mentally open and able to focus on what we are doing during the preset cycle. At some point, we have a thought that the clothes are dry. When we arrive in the laundry room, we see that the machine has either just turned off or will do so within moments. This occurs because we instinctively attune to a larger energetic arena in which we unconsciously receive and assimilate an empowered, clearer sense of each moment. This connection allows a steady flow of guidance to arise in our lives.

Although impossible according to old paradigms, the pace of time is actually speeding up, allowing us to break through old limits. The quicker tempo is dramatically increasing our stress level. There is too much to do, and we are running to keep up. Life is more frantic and frenetic, less leisurely and enjoyable. Managing time is more problematic because ego control is the core issue that is holding us back. It is as though the old lifestyle must be consumed in flames in order for the new to manifest. Even young children intuitively feel compressed time.

As we continue to receive intensifying and transforming energies on earth, Source reminds us they are spiritually serving us. Our present stage of development is providing us with opportunities to release our traditional experience with time. The steps we take to become congruent with Source will relieve our distress and advance us toward empowerment, which includes freedom from time constraints.

26: BUSINESS

ॐ Conflicts and challenges regularly present themselves in daily life and are considered unwanted but normal. When they occur, we have our well-developed management techniques and style of handling them. Ultimately, we want Source to prevent serious problems, but as long as we lead and interpret life with head-based agendas, we continue to minimize and block Source attributes, inspirations, and blessings. This concept applies to every area of our life, both personal and professional.

> Don is a master at professionally supporting
> people. As the boss, he fluidly shifts job

responsibilities around to those with the most appropriate skills and talents. He gives employees the freedom to work at their own pace and style as long they meet their deadlines. As a result of this somewhat relaxed atmosphere, he is loved and respected by his employees. When challenges arise, he usually resorts to a statement about, "That is not going to happen on my watch. We are going to trust." Don's company is doing extremely well in spite of global, national, and local economic conditions and turndowns. This success is significantly due to his spiritual development and leadership.

Even though Don's position represents a very positive and healthy approach to business, his verbal assertions still originate from his head. He has spiritually revised and upgraded his ego perspective, management, and protocol beyond the vast majority of business owners and policy makers. His advanced insights have improved his company's goals and outcomes, yet his comments only minimally addressed the most powerful resource in business: heartfelt dedication of every employee.

Fortunately, he continued to evolve. Once he understood this deeper, critical, and nearly boundless potential, his interpretive screen enlarged and he restructured many areas of operation. Don's discernment is now so refined that he can tell during a hiring interview whether or not the job applicant is an energetic match with the company. He is molding and modeling an empowered business of the future. In contrast, old operational systems in business, still utilized by most companies, will not survive advancing vibrations.

~ ~ ~

In a small or family-owned business, considerations used to be allowed for an employee's and/or a customer's personal situation. Owners cared almost as much for people as profit. Over time, there were exceptions and revisions to this compassionate policy. Larger and more commercial ventures could not afford to be so caring, and conglomerates almost exclusively focused on output and profit at the expense of individuals.

Conventional business practices have become exclusively rational and linear. They overlook the concept that the workers' personal support fundamentally determines the potential effectiveness of any venture. Defining success exclusively on monetary standards works against genuine service, employee morale, dedication, and personal and professional engagement. When policies are shortsighted and bottom-lined, employees feel less valued as people and they receive reward through their paycheck more than their contributions to the business. This environment leads them to treat their duties exclusively as work, with minimal emotional investment.

A business is only as authentically prosperous as its employees are emotionally committed and connected to its success.

This is very unfortunate and totally a reflection of first floor mentality. In t/Truth, a business is only as authentically prosperous as its employees are emotionally committed and connected to its success. As long as procedures are only factually determined and are based only on quantitative employee output with little or no consideration for the workers' welfare, the company might experience growth and development of skills, knowledge, and achievements, but the essential success component is eclipsed.

When employees are valued as people rather than machines whose only worth is measured in production volume, they are more likely to emotionally invest in the company and offer creative solutions and suggestions. When they feel included as team members, are acknowledged for their efforts, and feel supported in the greater good of their endeavors, creativity, enthusiasm, and productivity can surpass even management's well-envisioned expectations. To overlook or dismiss this personal, most basic resource of business is to miss the main ingredient that can provide business success beyond measure.

~ ~ ~

Due to our inherent oneness with Source and all others, every employee is a vital component of the inclusive whole. Understanding and developing the energetic component of workers could improve business operations and effectiveness and eventually have far-reaching benefits for everyone associated with the business. Each individual's vibration affects a group's identity, function, and success. The total vibrational average of all employees has even more clout in organizational outcomes than flat line, linear policies issued from a management executive and administered by a supervisor.

The prevailing American business model operates at a first floor, low energy vibration and needs to be revised. Enlightened procedures combined with cohesive energies will transcend old business agendas, functions, accomplishments, and profits. Therefore, the key to enhancing long-lasting business success

> *The key to enhancing long-lasting business success substantially rests on the vibrational energy level of each employee as well as the company's group average.*

substantially rests on the vibrational energy level of each employee as well as the company's group average.

More business consultants and resources are becoming available to assist employee and personal development in occupational organizations. The facilitators teach and inspire with new methods and information. Addressing the energetic level of participants in any venture can transform to some degree its approach, procedures, structure, operations, and success. The only exceptions to this concept seem to occur if an organization's intent is criminal, deceitful, deluded, or totally self-serving. In these cases, the people involved would reject personal development anyway.

Raising the collective energetic average in the office place can be challenging, and some employees will not cooperate or be willing to change. A management team who wants to evolve the company will need to discuss and deal with individuals who resist; they will need to make difficult decisions in regard to employees who refuse to cooperate. However, it is possible to collectively address vibrational principles with guidance, inspiration, and supportive people skills.

There is no substitute for genuine care, concern, and respect for the importance of individuals by other workers and especially upper managers and business owners. These moral qualities are in short supply today. The tragic,

> *Businesses must evolve to honor employees, ethics, quality, and service as much as their financial bottom line, or they will not survive the higher frequencies of transformation.*

common practice of terminating a position and walking the employee out the door violates the most fundamental dignity and integrity of a person. Although there is proprietary justification for this kind of action, energetically it is inexcusable. Businesses must evolve to honor employees, ethics, quality, and service as much as their financial bottom line, or they will not survive the higher frequencies of transformation.

CHAPTER 5:
THREE PILLARS OF TRANSFORMATION

As you attempt to manifest personal, long-sought healing and benefits in your life, you might find yourself asking inevitable questions:

- Is it possible to learn something life-changing from a book?

- If change is as easy as it's presented in books, how can I know the solutions work?

- Do I have to memorize and remember what I read?

- Just how hard do I have to work to heal my life?

The answers lie in the three Pillars of Transformation: surrendering, forgiving, and ego vacuuming.

> *The critical key to healing is to* work with *the energy of our challenges.*

In this chapter, you will learn simple and nearly effortless techniques to bring these pillars into your life. You will see that your use of these pillars will profoundly and efficiently remove low-level energies and facilitate your vibrational ascension. Because they are different than the common ego methods of managing challenging situations or physical and emotional symptoms, with frequent use they will help you rise from a first floor existence to the fiftieth floor of enlightenment. The critical key to implementing these pillars in your life is to *work with* the energy of your challenges.

This concept is not new. It's as old as ancient martial art masters who utilized their aggressor's physical prowess to thwart attacks. And yet it is a simple how-to understanding that is missing from the typical advice given by even long-time spiritual seekers today.

So, to answer your questions: Yes, you can learn from *this* book, and you will see that what you learn works. You don't have to memorize because you will learn to easily go with the flow of energy around you.

This chapter gives practical, how-to-walk-your-talk information. It covers, with essential details, exactly why and how to apply the techniques given as well as the benefits of implementing those techniques. If you decide to use these practices, you will speed your transformation process to the greatest degree that is safe for you to handle at any given moment. Even though your life might continue to present or attract challenges for awhile, you will also become aware, over time, of profound, desirable improvements internally that can also manifest externally.

In the next three sections, I present the Three Pillars of Transformation with instructions to:

> ➢ first, surrender to get yourself out of your own way;

> ➢ second, forgive in order to clear relationship challenges; and,

> ➤ third, use the ego vacuum to remove low-level internal energies.

In everyday life, however, there is no order to these but only our awareness of which technique is most appropriate for the immediate situation.

27: SURRENDER

A sign in front of a local church said: "If God is your co-pilot, swap seats." This is a humorous admonishment for first floor consciousness, which requires that we be in control and put God in a secondary position.

Traditional first floor consciousness holds the belief that souls have only one life in which we are to behave and do good, obey all human-crafted laws, serve God, and then, at death, attain Heaven—or, if we don't do good things, perish for eternity in Hell. In Reality, our souls typically reincarnate into bodies many times before eventually coming to realize that we are eternally divine beings who have never completely separated from God.

Based on the belief of only one incarnation, first floor consciousness, usually instilled by our parents and teachers at an early age, would have us accept that life is a blank slate, but with vision and confidence and effort, we can achieve anything. Although this concept sounds uplifting, it is actually a limited and biased perception.

We might think we know what we want, but not what we ultimately need. We might choose to live under the influence of *ego control*,[94] but we will manifest our karmic healing and ultimate soul growth when we learn how to surrender to God's greater power.

---

[94] ***ego control:*** a state of being in which we allow ego to rule our life, distancing us from our inherent trust in God

Why Surrender

The word surrender has come to be synonymous with loss or defeat. On the human level, we don't like to lose or give up voluntarily. We prefer to stay in control of our life as much as possible, and we work even harder at that when things around us appear to be falling apart, spinning out of control—when people seem to be pulling our strings and telling us what to do. But this "control," which we imagine is within our domain, is actually the work of our ego. When we listen to this inferior voice, we merely perpetuate our default system of operating.

The more we seek to control our life—which means to allow ego to control our life—the more we prohibit God from manifesting that which is spiritually most beneficial for us. We think staying in charge is the right thing to do, but that conduct actually reduces our accessibility to and integration of those expansive, multi-dimensional energies that enable us to operate at frequencies above

> *The more we seek to control our life, the more we prohibit God from manifesting that which is spiritually most beneficial to us.*
>
> *...*
>
> *Control restricts our spiritual options and minimizes our soul growth.*

the old 110 structures. In Truth, control restricts our spiritual options and minimizes our soul growth. Surrendering enables our progress.

ॐ Control is like a brake pedal, and trust is the spiritual accelerator. Control blocks trust and prevents us from moving forward in the manner that God

> *Control blocks trust.*

wants for us and Knows we can accomplish.

270

An example of God moving us and others around us forward appears in the movie *42*, which is the story of Jackie Robinson, the first Negro—to use the vernacular of the day—to play baseball at the major league level during his rookie year with the Brooklyn Dodgers in 1947. In a powerful scene when Dodgers' owner Branch Rickey first talks with Robinson about playing for his team, the owner becomes verbally abusive about race to see how the young athlete will react. Angered, Robinson asks, "You want a player who doesn't have the guts to fight back?" And Rickey retorts emphatically, poking his cigar at Robinson's face, "No. I want a player who's got the guts *not* to fight back." In other words, surrender—not to prejudice, delivered through racist taunts—but to the power of God, delivered through the free will of Branch Rickey, to rise above ego-driven prejudice so that other non-white players can play "America's Game" in the majors. With Source-based sincerity, Robinson replies, "Give me a uniform and give me a number on my back [the number 42], and I'll give you the guts."

Robinson's prowess in 1947 earned him Major League Baseball's Rookie of the Year Award. More importantly, he rose above the verbal jeering, the initial snubbing by his teammates, and even the physical danger of hard

> *Surrendering is the most immediately available and powerfully effective response to any difficult event or situation.*

fastballs thrown at his head during the era before batters wore protective helmets. His demeanor provided a heroic, real-life example of the fact that surrendering is the most immediately available and powerfully effective response to any difficult event or situation.

ॐ Surrendering is an all-purpose activity, but it is most beneficial in regard to what is happening in the moment, regardless of your skill level.

> ➤ When emotionally triggered, surrender rather than react.

When you surrender your ego's limited and false interpretation, you get out of your own way. The situation and outcome, as well as your emotions and reactions, open and shift to embrace God's Truth. Your

> *When you surrender your ego's limited and false interpretation, you get out of your own way.*

response position and effect is wiser, and you tend to avoid judgment and defensiveness.

~ ~ ~

ॐ The one, primary technique to jump-start a vital spiritual life is to stop ego from being your dictator and surrender your life to God. By surrendering, you release your

> *To jump-start a vital spiritual life ... surrender your life to God.*

separate, spiritually immature, three-dimensional functioning and controlling ego. It is as though a portion of the sealed, metal chamber that has blocked Source Light from shining into and through ego is removed every time you surrender anything.

That segment of released ego instantly merges back with Source energy, and the ego-based left brain fluidly joins with the empowered, Source-connected right brain so that you become more whole-brained. You gain more integration with Source and the inherent attributes that you have been seeking in other, less effective ways. You choose to operate your life with eight billion bits of data per second, instead of eight bits.

You need not worry about becoming too good too fast, nor is it possible to surrender and lose anything that is valuable and of ultimate benefit. Rather, your free-will decision will, at the exact proper time and way, alter the path you have been on up to this point. Your new direction is more empowering because it progressively

> *It is not possible to surrender and lose anything that is valuable and of ultimate benefit.*

reunites ego with Source by removing ego's authoritative domination.

So do not let fear stop you from making this life-changing decision to embrace the first of the Three Pillars. Instead, know that this is the single most powerful act you can do for yourself.

What to Surrender

You can surrender absolutely anything: your use of ego filters, outcomes of situations about which you are worried, your emotions and opinions, limiting thoughts, your decision-making protocols based on old paradigms, and habits that you no longer want.

Surrender all negativity, worries, the timing of events or appointments, feelings of being late or overwhelmed, your to-do list of desired accomplishments for the day, old problem management techniques, and anything else—even relationships—that cause heartaches or headaches for you. You can shed whatever has been holding you back and eliminate what no longer works.

If life under the influence of ego control were several

> *Be ruthless when cleaning out ego. When in doubt, pitch it out.*

bookcases, every square inch of each shelf would be filled with an accumulation of ego-generated thoughts, processes, and karmically driven energetic clutter. Every time you surrender anything, it is as if you were taking a handful of items from a shelf and creating empty space. The temptation is to put something better in the place that you've now emptied. But you do not want to do that!

> ➢ Leave the vacated area empty and allow God's Light to enter your life.

> ➢ Remember you will not lose anything that ultimately benefits you.

> ➢ Be ruthless when cleaning out ego. When in doubt, pitch it out.

Initially, you might not notice much difference or improvement when you surrender. However, as you become more adept at tossing that which no longer serves your higher good, the results will be more obvious and come more quickly.

Because we are already empowered at our core and have nothing there to surrender, we all have the inherent potential to immediately, completely, and permanently surrender anything. But we need to practice surrendering to develop this magnificent ability.

> *We all have the inherent potential to immediately, completely, and permanently surrender anything.*

How to Surrender

We can choose to surrender on two levels of magnitude. We can surrender our total and whole life to God. We can also surrender everything else about our conscious identity and normal life functioning.

> ➢ Should you choose to make this life change, sit alone somewhere for a few minutes, and go through the following activity.

Total Surrender

ॐ The technique for surrendering your whole life to God is simple and easy. It does not require memorization of lengthy prayers or daily rituals, but utilizes, instead, a natural concept based on our inherent oneness with God.

> ➢ First, repeat out loud: "I surrender my life to God, (Source, Prime Energy, or whatever term you are comfortable with)," many, many times, until you notice some sense of internal and energetic response. This process could take five minutes or more to complete.

What happens during this time resembles digging a tunnel from inside ego toward Source, or, in your body from the crown of your head to your solar plexus. Each surrender statement equates to the removal of one shovel full of dirt from your head and chest, allowing you to take a step ever closer to the Light of your spiritual core. Once you conclude this activity, an internal passage of your portion of God's Light will begin to assist your energetic alignment and fusion with Source.

> ➢ When you have completed this surrender activity, take a few deep breaths to support and integrate this profound life change into your being.

You will most likely then experience a sense of relief, opening, lightness, and hope.

Situational Surrender

Whether you have surrendered your whole life to God or not, situations will occur when you will likely want to surrender the outcome to God.

> ➢ Make a statement, an affirmation, such as: "I am now surrendering this situation to you, God, and I trust You to work this out in a way that benefits all concerned." Or, "I don't know how to handle what is happening, but you do, God. So I surrender this and please work this out to benefit everyone involved." Then stand back and watch what happens. You will likely be pleasantly or even incredibly impressed with the outcome.

After surrendering, you might find that you more instinctively speak your emotional truth with honesty, conviction, and tact. In fact, God will be guiding your actual words to elicit unforeseen and optimal results. The outcome can be better than anything you could have thought of, let alone accomplish on your own. On rare occasions, your greater power, through your reacquaintance with God's Light, could also be challenging to either you or others around you because you are not perpetuating your customary status quo.

> ➢ If you need more emotional relief or a greater degree of comfort, temporarily remove yourself from the company of those with whom you are in a challenging situation, breathe deeply, verbally vent, and/or physically release any further emotions or feelings. When you finish this step, ask your guides to neutralize any negativity in the air and/or room.

➢ Then, if appropriate, return to your compyour calmer state. This is necessary because prot
• usually need to be addressed and worked through
the other person or persons with whom you maint،
some level of relationship.

➢ It will help, as you rejoin the others, to again
remind yourself that you are choosing to surrender all
control and possible outcomes.

~ ~ ~

Regardless of the degree to which you surrender,
surrendering is a skill that improves with use. Practice it as often
as possible on everything. Just state a sentence out loud about
something that you don't want to think about, interpret, feel, or
act upon in the same old way. When you don't know what to do
about something, state whatever issue or problem you are
working on, and express your decision to surrender it to God.

Benefits of Surrendering

As you repeat this process of removing ego stuff, you will
see more and more benefits.
The higher frequencies from
God's Light have a
cumulative effect. With
practice, you will see that it is
continuing to promote

> *Nothing is as important
> as our need to speak our
> t/Truth.*

wholeness within your entire being, including your association
with t/Truth.

🕉 Nothing is as important as our need to speak our t/Truth.
When we do, we incrementally discharge the internal barriers
that we had constructed when we merely managed our emotions.
Every healing opportunity stimulates us to release these energies.
In the rare cases when the short-term result does not seem better

or easier, you will later discover some other overriding, unknown factor that eventually improves through your surrendering.

> Chester needed to have a talk with his mother. As her power of attorney, he had been in charge of her finances for some time, but she had begun making decisions and taking actions that were not in her best interests, a situation that made his life much more difficult than it had been. He did not know how to fix the dilemma.
>
> As he drove to his mother's home one day, Chester talked with God and expressed his feelings, concerns, and perplexity over the need for a specific answer or solution to this problem. He surrendered everything about the encounter: how long the conversation would take, how he and his mother would each feel, what the outcome would be, and, most of all, his uncertainty of what to do and say. As he walked up to the front door, he asked God to speak through him.
>
> Once Chester sat across from his mother in the living room, out of his mouth came, "Mom, I need you to help me better so I can help you more." He was stunned. He would never have come up with that phrase on his own. Because it was stated so simply, authentically, unemotionally, and clearly, his mother did not become defensive and argumentative. She replied that, of course she would help him if doing so would help her. The meeting worked

out in a way far beyond what Chester could have attempted to accomplish on his own.

~ ~ ~

🕉 Sometimes, we find ourselves in situations in which we want to speak our truth, according to our current emotional state, but don't. Even then, surrendering our control, reactions, and emotions over external events, outcomes, and problems works instantly. That is its specialty.

> *Surrendering our control, reactions, and emotions over external events, outcomes, and problems works instantly.*

Gene and Trish hosted some friends one summer, and as a thank you gesture, their two guests took them to a Sunday senior brunch buffet at a local casino where the cost of the meal was moderate.

A few years earlier, Trish had asked a waitress if she was paid by her employer or relied entirely on tips. She said she did receive a wage, but after taxes it was not even minimum wage. Trish thanked her for answering, and told her she would tell her friends and guests to tip more than they normally would for a buffet. This became a practice that Trish followed for several years.

On this day, however, Trish was partway through the meal with her friends before she realized that she had not mentioned anything about tipping. She felt terrible about forgetting something so important for the waitress. She mentally apologized to God and admitted she had blown it. She now had to think about what she could do to make amends for her omission. She could bring up the subject right then, but that would be like asking for more money from her guests, which did not seem appropriate. She could leave the tip herself, perhaps discretely handing it to the waitress on their way out, but that didn't feel valid either. She could detach herself from the outcome and watch how it worked out, but that didn't seem honorable. So she finally decided to surrender the situation to God.

A few minutes later, one of the guests stood up, reached into his pocket, pulled out an amount of money that would be a very generous tip, especially for a buffet, and placed it in the middle of the table. Trish had to stop herself from laughing. "Thank you, God," she thought to herself.

~ ~ ~

When we release ego, we free up space for God to enter our life and manage it for us. Rather than seek personal control, we prioritize God's input and learn over time to trust this higher-level, more divine way of being. This surrendering to God allows us to move in God's flow, interact with and respond to people in more authentic ways, and ultimately manifest *God's will*[95] in our life. Surrendering empowers us to integrate with Source and k/Know that all is well.

---

[95] ***God's will:*** a process, experience, or outcome that comes from God and serves our highest good

Inner Surrender and Outer Success

🕉 It is possible to do our best in life, work very hard, and become successfully rewarded in everyday areas of life such as employment, family, fame, or financial abundance. Many people settle for and are happy with this level of accomplishment. A person's religious beliefs might appear irrelevant when compared to financial success or worldly happiness. Therefore, it's important to remember that achieving our first floor goals does not necessarily violate God's will.

> *Achieving our first floor goals does not necessarily violate God's will.*

However, when we have surrendered our life to God, everything is more on track for our spiritual advancement. Our personality, emotions, value system, goals, relationships, and life itself become more soul satisfying and inspired.

Ernie came for his first session with D'Ann as a result of a friend's suggestion. He had been on a long spiritual path but was ready and looking for the next step, whatever that might be. He acknowledged that his outer life was successful, yet his inner being was in chaos and he had been rejecting his emotions as if they were the plague. D'Ann recommended that he surrender his life to God, taking that life-changing step during the first session with her. After that, he began to realize that, with his old ways, he had been avoiding the feelings of his heart and missing an important component of life.

Sometime later, Ernie's stepmother died and Ernie flew to a different state to attend the funeral. When he arrived at the front door of his father's home, the hired caretaker, who was a relative, told him he could not come into the house without permission from Ernie's brother Fritz. This caretaker even threatened to call the police. Undeterred and convinced he had the right to come inside, Ernie moved past the man and entered anyway. He did not realize that there was an issue with money and inheritance and that he could be a suspect if any items or valuables disappeared. He merely looked around and soon left, taking nothing.

Then he drove to Fritz's nearby home. Fritz had obviously been called by the caretaker and told Ernie that he had acted like a madman when he overrode the demand not to enter their stepmother's home. Fritz then ordered him off his own property.

Ernie was shocked and clueless about the cruel, suspicious, and menacing way he was being treated. Two people had threatened him within a matter of minutes—and for no good reason that he could discern.

Although he was enormously perplexed and disturbed, Ernie did not respond in anger. In the past, he would have been ready for a fight, which is a standard reaction for a person, typically a male, who is not familiar with or receptive to methods for calming violent emotions. Instead, Ernie saw this situation entirely differently than he would have before and rather quickly concluded, as he told D'Ann, "It had nothing to do with me." He decided to leave the drama, fly home immediately, and not attend the funeral.

Ernie acknowledges that surrendering his life has freed him from operating with self-righteous anger across the board. He is now aware of his own emotions and how he expresses them. He can even hear guidance. Everything in his life has improved and deepened since he surrendered his life to God.

~ ~ ~

The following story is a literal and incredible example of a person who surrenders and gets ego out of her way so God could take over. And did He ever!

Veronica was a retired teacher who, when employed, did not relate well to her colleagues. She did not like any of them, and knew they did not like her. Mostly out of curiosity, however, she had planned to attend the celebration for the teachers who were retiring that year. She was going to leave her session with D'Ann and drive directly to the party.

Near the end of Veronica's appointment, she became reluctant to attend the gathering and told D'Ann that she wanted to change her mind. D'Ann encouraged her to go as an experiment, advising that she surrender absolutely everything about the occasion, which they then did together: how she might feel while driving there, during the party, and afterward; whom she would see; how long she would stay; what would happen; and anything else about which she was concerned.

That night, Veronica left a message on D'Ann's voice mail that said, among other things, "Well, maybe God *does* do miracles! I got to the entrance, and people *hugged* me! I went inside, and people came up to *me* to talk! I did not stay the whole time, but maybe God *does* do miracles."

~ ~ ~

One of the most difficult things to surrender is our personal opinion. We have formed our personal opinions through ego eyes, the hard way, from difficult experiences. We didn't understand that our life setups through which we struggled were actually beneficial healing

> *One of the most difficult things to surrender is our personal opinion.*

opportunities. Therefore, we are naturally reluctant to revise our conclusions.

But the more we cling to our old opinions, the more we perpetuate ego's view and permit ego's decision-making power to dominate us. The r/Reality is that we are either willing to change, evolve, and trust God—or we are not. If we are not willing, we will allow old patterns and operating systems to persist and, thus, delay or minimize our progress along our potentially significant spiritual path. We must come to realize that our previous personal opinions were valid—*at those earlier times*—but the time has now come for us to move beyond them.

ॐ Once we learn this spiritual perspective that all occurrences are intended to assist our development, we will want to clear all of our old polished opinions, which are no longer desirable or appropriate energies, from our life. Eventually, when we are significantly more empowered, our opinions will be cohesive with Truth and have validity and obvious beneficial effects. In this manner, we will become co-creators with God, an example of which occurred in this story.

> *When we are significantly more empowered, our opinions will be cohesive with Truth and have validity and obvious beneficial effects. In this manner, we will become co-creators with God.*

Lucy and Vic had been married many years. They had control issues between them. Lucy would give in to whatever Vic wanted in order to avoid a fight. Oddly enough, because they so often disagreed, Vic felt as though he gave in all the time.

They were both very frustrated in spite of the deep love they shared. At different times, they would each rebel and do something or buy something they wanted without concern for the other's opinion. Lucy embraced spiritual practices, but Vic wasn't interested in such things. She had been working with surrender for a few years when a particular incident occurred.

Lucy and Vic's subdivision held a yearly garage sale. Both of them enjoyed shopping for bargains and visiting with neighbors, and during this sale they would occasionally split up to look at different things. One year while shopping, Vic caught up with Lucy and asked her to come with him to look at a collapsible dining room table. They went to see it. Because it was an antique style with dark wood, Lucy didn't care for it. They already had a beautiful dining room table and did not need any more furniture. She said she did not want it and left to continue shopping on her own.

When she later returned home, the table was in their den. She couldn't believe Vic would do that and thought, "It's no wonder I feel that I'm living in *his* house." Deciding not to create a scene, she chose to surrender the whole situation. She was even able to avoid talking and commenting about the new purchase.

The next day, the neighbor who had sold Vic the table called him. The neighbor explained that it had been in her deceased husband's family for years, and she had offered it to their children some time ago. None of them were interested then. But now that she had sold it, they were angry with her. She asked Vic if she could buy it back. He understood the situation and returned the table later that day.

Lucy smiled, glad that God had worked this out so quickly and easily. She marked the experience as a memorable one, supporting the act of surrender. She was, thus, encouraged to continue the practice of surrendering on an even more regular basis.

In each of these last three stories, the actions of others seem to be magical: Ernie experienced but did not react to anger from others that he felt he had not instigated; Veronica was welcomed by her former co-workers with warmth that she could not imagine; and Lucy's problem with the table seemed to be resolved by people she didn't even know.

In reality, this "magic" is God working in what we sometimes call "mysterious ways." When we surrender the outcomes to God, God orchestrates an entire symphony of events that involve other metaphorical musicians over whom we have no influence. It is true that each of us is responsible for the sounds,

> *Self-development and co-creation are not mutually exclusive.*

either music or noise, that come from our individual instruments. But when we look to the conductor to lead us through a complicated score, we allow all musicians and instruments to blend into lovely harmony.

With an orchestra, we can see each musician and the conductor. In life, we don't. Rather, we surrender and then proceed to enjoy the outcome, trusting God, the Divine Conductor, to work "miracles" that extend far beyond our individual, human sphere of influence.

> *When we pilot our lives only with conscious goals, decisions, and actions, the outcomes we manifest might not resonate with our soul's flight plan for our highest good.*

Obstacles to Surrendering

Self-development and co-creation[96] are not

---

[96] **co-creation:** the inherent ability to manifest rewarding and blessed results in life

necessarily mutually exclusive, but they do move in somewhat different directions. This is why addressing spiritual growth and attainment only from ego perspectives, although potentially impressive, is not ideal and might be shortsighted. Our decisions to disregard guidance and exclusively pursue ego ambitions can be a serious mistake. Likewise, forsaking our karmic intentions and giving priority to less important needs can distract us from our life script and take us in a different, less desirable direction than what our soul intended prior to incarnation. And self-management, problem avoidance, or denial of our human emotions can intensify our spiritual karmic issues. In other words, when we pilot our lives only with conscious goals, decisions, and actions, the outcomes we manifest might not resonate with our soul's flight plan for our highest good.

ॐ Many people believe the best way to empowerment is through learning more spiritual concepts, enhancing brain capabilities, and working with mind-expanding techniques or occasionally even substances. They strive to control their own life and thoughts with brain-based measures. If they pursue spiritual growth, they look for modalities that focus on developing self-mastery. Some have become intellectually powerful and demonstrate significant concentration skills, psychic abilities, and/or the proficiency to manifest their physical, emotional, and seemingly spiritual goals. These people are a force to be reckoned with due to their strong personalities and auras.

ॐ Interestingly, however, persons who follow these paths have a significant tendency to fall into an ego trap. They might take credit for their accomplishments, even if they have been working with universal laws. They might decide or believe that their mental and spiritual control trumps God's will or guidance. Their truth is that they are not inclined to surrender anything in their life.

ॐ This is unfortunate because self-mastery life perspectives, interpretations, and applications represent an advanced version of the first floor operating system. Seeking spiritual completion from a control position reduces potential effectiveness and soul development.

> *Seeking spiritual completion from a control position reduces potential effectiveness and soul development.*

The next case typifies first floor spiritual development, which is operable—up to a point—but is, ultimately, a low-altitude flight plan.

Zach was a metaphysician who practiced spirituality and served clients from an intellectual, ego-based, head-controlled position. While maintaining eye contact, he would use well-developed mental strategies and techniques to address and assist others with their needs. He did not utilize prayer, guidance, intuition, or any energy treatments associated with Source.

Before realizing the full nature of his practice, D'Ann referred three clients to Zach. He was enormously helpful for one, had neutral results with another, and had a significant detrimental effect on the third. The reason, D'Ann later discovered, was that Zach approached each client from the perspective of his ego-defined viewpoint of what he had to offer rather than the open-minded view of his clients as individuals. He failed to consider that each person is unique and that all modalities have variable success rates depending on the people, their physical and spiritual situation, and their energies. When D'Ann realized Zach's ego-based approach to treatment, she no longer referred clients to him.

A few years later, Zach's sole reliance on his own energy caused him to experience an excruciatingly difficult phase in his life that manifested through an extramarital affair, divorce, and change of residence. He hit bottom.

This disturbing news about Zach was, in hindsight, not surprising. He was undergoing a traumatic life setup and an opportunity to heal, grow, and make a deeper connection with Source than he ever could through his previous professional practice or his personal management technique. Through his apparent downfall, God gave him a chance to rebuild his life with actual empowerment by making a spiritual commitment, surrendering, and working in partnership with Source.

The message for all of us is that God consistently

> *God consistently gives us the opportunity to transform.*

gives us the opportunity to transform. However, the stronger our ego identity, the more challenging our healing process, and the deeper we might fall into a state of apparent despair and destruction before we learn to trust God and rise again.

~ ~ ~

Some people approach life from a position exactly the opposite of self-mastery: they play the role of God's servant. They suppress their self-esteem and believe they are worthless sinners. They choose not to accept appreciation or compliments because they think doing so will inflate their ego. In an effort to be totally dedicated to God, they squelch everything in their personal life and deem themselves as valueless except as a vessel through which God works.

> Audrey had a strong, fundamental Christian background. She was outstanding at giving God credit for her blessings and taking personal blame for her shortcomings. "All that is good is because of God," she said, "and all that is bad is my fault." She instantly redirected any compliments that came her way with her pet phrase of "Praise God," which is actually a very vibrationally powerful statement. In Audrey's case, however, her belief restricted the inherent benefit she could have received by verbalizing "Praise God."

> Audrey came to D'Ann for only one session. Probably, the reason she didn't return was because she was not interested in becoming spiritually empowered, but only in being, according to her definition, "more holy." Rather than enlightenment, she desired information congruent with her belief system.

Audrey's view that life has only the two options of sinner or servant, while apparently sacrificing and humble, is actually an ego-driven lifestyle. Living from this vantage point thwarts spiritual growth and constrains development of our unique personalities because we strive to mold ourselves into the pattern we think God wants for us.

> *An ego-driven lifestyle thwarts spiritual growth and constrains development of our unique personalities.*

This approach to spiritual growth is different than surrendering because it is the epitome of living a head-directed and censured life. Although being a good servant takes extreme dedication and can foster blessings, the primary focus for such a person is on doing the right thing, which, although worthwhile, is exclusively a first-floor value that does not develop self-empowerment.

Getting out of our own way, even if that way appears to be self-sacrificing, is essential in order to release ego's grip as our dictator. Overcoming this ego-based mentality requires learning and k/Knowing what we accept to be God's Truth, which includes that we are inherently good and loving, and applying that t/Truth as often and in as many ways as possible.

ॐ In Truth, we are co-creators and inherently one with God. Therefore, we are already worthy and empowered. We are on earth to evolve by cultivating our inner attributes and potentials— and recognize them for the blessings they are.

> *We are on earth to evolve by cultivating our inner attributes and potentials—and recognize them for the blessings they are.*

> *In a challenging moment, any of us can default to old management habits.*

Ongoing Surrendering

ॐ No matter how well we learn to surrender, challenges can occur, especially in relationships, to really test us. In these most demanding situations, it's easy to fall back into old patterns. We might ignore, forget about, or override our previously successful surrender experiences and allow ego to take back control of our life. Usually, we do not consciously realize we are doing that and rarely do we formally state our intention or action to resume ego's control. The reason is that, in a challenging moment, any of us can default to old management habits; a comfortable way out is to let ego retake control.

🕉 Warning signs of pulling back from God can include worry, a feeling of burdensome responsibility, fear, and continuously heightened human dramas.

If the warning signs occur as rare exceptions, we might catch our shift from God to ego, learn from it, and reinforce our commitment to God. However, until we experience otherwise, most people trust themselves more than they trust God. Although this lack of trust is not wrong and might occasionally appear to be beneficial in some first floor way, it prevents and aborts spiritual growth at that opportune time.

The more enlightened decision is to re-express trust in God and continue with our surrendering activities, and then watch as life becomes a rewarding adventure.

28: FORGIVENESS

Heartfelt forgiveness is a process that results in emotional and karmic freedom from relationship mandates and scripted roles with other souls. Forgiveness can literally change our life. People have been known to heal emotionally, mentally, and even physically after they have released old energetic baggage that had been burdening them.

Forgiveness primarily addresses relationships and experiences. We might need to forgive ourselves, relationship partners, other people, conditions, career choices, companies, religions, social systems, events, clubs, or any other entity that has left painful scars.

The definitions of forgiveness are totally different at the first floor and fiftieth floor. Most of us have been raised to know the importance of forgiveness at the first floor, which involves a judgment: When someone did or said something to hurt us, we were told we need to forgive them. When we hurt someone, we were told to say, "I'm sorry."

Often, we truly do regret the hurt we've caused, but there are times when we are not sorry about our behavior. At those times, it does not feel good to have to apologize for something we thought was necessary or appropriate under the circumstances,

> *Forgiving does not mean we condone, excuse, or forget.*

even if it hurt or seemed wrong to the other person. When this happens, further discussion at a later time with the parties involved might be helpful to gain mutual understanding of each person's point of view or the basis for everyone's actions. At that time, we might or might not choose to apologize.

ॐ Forgiving does not mean that we condone, excuse, or forget. We don't condone because the offender might not have acted in the best possible manner. We don't excuse because the

> *Any unresolved, unreleased, and agitated emotional experience leaves seemingly dormant yet vibrationally active energies simmering somewhere in our system, usually in trash bags. Unless we release and resolve those energies in our current life, they will become karmic and affect future lifetimes.*

offender might have intended to do the offensive action. And we don't forget because the offender might do it again if given the chance. No wonder forgiveness is so difficult and unpopular.

However, some things people do are so excruciating or horrendous that most of us are not willing or able to forgive. E/go easily justifies this, which is why a person often waits to forgive until they feel ready.

Why Forgive

ॐ Yet, forgiveness, whether sooner or later, is necessary—for our own sake if not for the sake of the other(s.) That's because any unresolved, unreleased, and agitated emotional experience leaves seemingly dormant yet vibrationally active energies simmering somewhere in our system, usually in emotional trash bags in our chest. Unless we release and resolve those energies in our current life, they will become karmic and affect future lifetimes. Sometimes retention of residual energies creates physical symptoms, either in this life or a later life. When they are cleared, the body can heal.

The spiritual, fiftieth floor definition of forgiveness is devoid of judgment.

> *The spiritual, fiftieth floor definition of forgiveness is devoid of judgment.*

When we operate from a spiritual perspective and without judgment, we can:

- emotionally feel something painful or troublesome that happened but interpret it more neutrally;

- see that difficult events are spiritual setups to assist healing in our lives;

- determine that we likely needed the problem or

the offending person to play that exact role in our lives;

- understand that the other person is a "messenger" who will be held spiritually accountable for their behavior.

In fact, the absence of judgment helps us realize that we have probably played this same role back and forth for each other in other lifetimes.

When we choose not to forgive, we layer present life trash bags over past life emotional debris. Fortunately, we can discharge both types of energetic baggage by moving them up and out of our system. When we forgive, we clear our lives and bodies of emotional contaminants, boost our vibrational rate, and terminate and absolve karmic role-playing contracts. In other words, when we energetically forgive, we absolve the karmic contract with that soul. This release then allows us to symbolically enter the office of the karmic director who is in charge of our soap opera and actually resign from our scripted dramas.

> *Forgiveness is the most expedient, painless, and effective way to heal relationships.*

As we continue to evolve and forgive, we incrementally clear emotional debris from our present life, which disentangles us from becoming ensnared in the dramas of others. It usually is beneficial to forgive an offending party more than one time. Our higher vibrational rate and dimensional accessibility will connect to higher levels and dimensions in the other person. This allows previously unavailable, subtler energetic debris between each other to be liberated and cleansed. For this reason, forgiveness is the most expedient, painless, and effective way to heal relationships.

Loren, a minister, felt led to give a sermon on forgiveness. During the week prior, as usual, his thoughts frequently focused on his topic, how essential it is for spiritual growth, and what he would say.

Loren had been nursing a small flowerbed around the base of a tree in his front yard for four years. He had built a small brick border around it and each year planted additional flowers. This was the first year the area looked healthy and attractive. On Saturday morning as he was leaving to run some errands, he discovered uprooted and mutilated plants and flowers, the broken border, and beer bottles strewn around the site. He was heartsick and angry. He immediately thought: What senseless destruction! What would cause people to do such a foolish thing? Why now? After so much hard work, it was finally beginning to look lovely.

Within moments, he caught what he called "God's humor." He was being offered an opportunity to forgive. After several minutes of emotional confusion, followed by deep thinking, he realized he had no choice but to forgive if he was going to preach about that subject the next day.

Loren focused on the emotional pain the perpetrators must have felt to be so intentionally brutal, and he was able to summon compassion for them. He forgave them and cleaned up the flowerbed and border. The congregation heard and was moved by his story the next morning.

Who to Forgive

If our souls are to advance in this lifetime, we need to ask, "*Who* do I need to forgive?"

That answer is up to you. Some people might respond, "Everyone." Others might make a list of all persons who have ever angered or injured or frustrated them. Both answers tend toward being comprehensive—and that's good because unresolved energies don't go away on their own.

That leads to a second question, "*Why* haven't I already forgiven?"

We may not have realized how important it really is to forgive someone or something from a long time ago. Or more commonly, our ego feels justified in maintaining a grudge. Doing so

> *Our ego feels justified in maintaining a grudge.*

energetically affects both parties but is even more detrimental to the person who holds the grudge. Nothing good comes from that decision. Emotional residue creates karma. Unresolved energies wait patiently to be released, whether in this lifetime or another.

ॐ Karma also dictates—and this is important to keep in mind—that others have had to struggle because of things we have said, not said, done, or not done to them, whether intentionally or unintentionally. Karma and karmic release work both ways in relationships.

~ ~ ~

Sometimes Source nudges us to ask the same question, "Why haven't I already forgiven?" This thought, or even a setup to provide stimulation to forgive, might arise years or decades after an initial painful incident. The number of times that some setups continue to occur, even within a single lifetime, is a reminder that each soul is eventually given the opportunities necessary to heal.

Caleb was an outstanding employee for a large church. He handled his responsibilities with quiet efficiency, had a positive attitude, cooperated with others, and was generally highly respected. Although his boss, Matt, who was also the church's minister, recognized Caleb's proficiencies, he was working behind the scenes to hire a friend and former employee from another church for Caleb's position.

When Caleb accidentally found out about Matt's plans, he resigned. This action brought pressure from the church board of directors for Matt to rescind Caleb's decision. Matt met with Caleb and explained his ideas and plans to expand the present job description into something he felt Caleb was not equipped to handle. He asked Caleb to remain with the church at least for the time being until other arrangements could be made. Caleb decided he would not stay where he was not wanted, which was a logical ego decision, and quit.

Caleb was emotionally devastated. Because he had done nothing to deserve being treated that way, he blamed Matt for undermining him. Matt had not been up front with him and gave him no opportunity for input, to take further training, or be promoted or moved within the church. This made no sense to Caleb, and he did not even think of forgiving Matt. Fortunately, Caleb was able to easily find a new position elsewhere, but he never got over the painful experience because, to him, it was just so unfair.

Amazingly, nearly forty years later, through peculiar circumstances that a spiritual setup often provides, Caleb was asked to attend an out-of-town meeting to honor the former president of a church-affiliated college. He was reluctant to go when he found out Matt was the person to be honored, but he eventually decided, with internal nudging, that he wanted to see what had happened to Matt through the years. If nothing else, Caleb was curious to know how Matt had been able to move from ministerial work to academia.

At the program, Matt was recognized for all of his contributions to the institution during his tenure. Caleb saw that his elderly former boss was highly respected and liked. He forced himself to greet Matt at the end of the event in order to observe the other's response. Matt didn't even remember Caleb! He had dementia.

A cascade of excruciating emotions overcame Caleb. He was stunned. All of his righteous anger and blame for so many years was really to no avail. There was no way Matt was ever going to acknowledge the pain and suffering he had caused. Caleb would never receive an apology. Ancient ego thoughts of powerlessness and unfairness kept recycling and building until he couldn't help but release long-held, pent-up feelings. This purge happened in waves, over days and weeks.

By removing old, charged emotions, Caleb cleared enough energetic space for him to move beyond his ego view and reinterpret what had transpired so many years earlier. He did not know why the whole situation had occurred in the first place, but he had gained sufficient karmic knowledge to realize, apparently, the agonizing experience had actually been a spiritual opportunity to heal.

He considered that, perhaps, he had betrayed Matt in a former life and karma needed to be counterbalanced. Or maybe he needed to learn how to forgive. He knew he had benefited by becoming more empathetic for others whose employment had abruptly ended, and he had held better jobs along the way since that early encounter with Matt. He acknowledged that there could be other reasons, but knowing them now seemed irrelevant.

Basically, Caleb recognized that his unwillingness to forgive had stunted his own spiritual development. Although it took deep thought, weeks of reflection, and courage, Caleb eventually forgave Matt, an action that, of course, Matt was no longer able to cognitively know.

This story is about forgiveness without an intention to improve a relationship. Caleb's natural ego reluctance to forgive

Matt would eventually have become karmic if he had not chosen to go to the event to honor Matt. But by going, he unexpectedly placed himself in a situation that led to healing the defining, life-changing, grievous event and its perpetrator in his present life. He must have needed this exact and unique provocation to stimulate his old distress and force him to realize the futility of maintaining blame and hatred. Caleb's relationship challenge and situation was energetically and karmically resolved through forgiveness.

Matt had forgotten about the long-ago incident with Caleb, either because of his dementia or the simple passage of time, so we can assume that he was physically and possibly mentally unaffected by Caleb's presence at the event or by Caleb's later forgiveness process. But because souls resonate and energetically connect in nonlinear ways, we know that Caleb's soul benefited, and possibly, though unlikely without mental awareness and cooperation, Matt's soul energy might also have been boosted through Caleb's actions.

~ ~ ~

🕉 Occasionally there might be a situation, such as sexual child abuse, that might seem impossible to ever forgive, especially because the abused child might experience traumatic scars as an adult. Although there is no quick or easy fix for a person to remove these scars, he or she can heal rather than merely survive.

If the person, whether then as a child or later as an adult, can accept the idea of past lives, he or she can address forgiveness from the fiftieth floor view where souls better understand the concept of counterbalance or karmic debt. Karmic debt holds that the abused person's present life could be counterbalancing a past life in which he or she might have abused the person who is now the abuser. Or the abused person could have entered this life with the karmic need to be abused in order to learn forgiveness, heal some other karmic emotional debris, and/or receive motivation to help and serve others with this same issue of sexual abuse.

The challenge of physical life is that we usually live without consciously knowing our karmic background. This might be a drawback, but it is not a total obstacle, and abused persons can still profoundly heal if they desire to do so.

That healing includes not forgetting the childhood experience, because remembering provides ongoing incentive to heal the trauma. And the abused person does not need to accept, like, or love the abuser. Nor is it necessary to reestablish a workable relationship with the abuser. In fact, forgiveness can be totally one-sided and still be profoundly effective.

~ ~ ~

With these stories, we see that the scope of responses to the question, "Who to forgive?" might range from "Everyone" to "Well, maybe not those who commit heinous crimes," at least from the first floor perspective. From the fiftieth floor view, however, it's much easier to see that each soul is still one with God for all eternity regardless of actions in any particular physical lifetime. From that higher vantage point, it is easier to truly consider forgiving everyone.

How to Forgive: Overview

Knowing how to forgive is essential to karmic clearing and soul growth. In this overview, the main message is to be comprehensive.

➢ Compile a list of people, situations, or events that you know or suspect you need to forgive, as well as the people who you think need to forgive you. If you can't remember a name, list the incident or relationship.

> Begin your forgiveness list by naming all family members, birth through adult. If you were adopted or have never met your birth family for whatever reason, include them too.

> Then add the names of everyone you have lived with, dated, or been in personal partnership.

> Expand to include any past and present neighbors, friends, teachers, classmates, coworkers, bosses, employees, colleagues, clients, professional service providers, animals, and so forth so that you include anyone with whom you might have created unresolved energies.

Anyone who you have interacted with might have left emotional residue within you, and you within them, because of feelings that remain unreleased or unresolved. Past challenges within businesses, careers, circumstances, and major events in your life might also still be impacting you. You might be holding a grudge against your profession because you think you don't fit in with your coworkers, you don't philosophically align with your company or industry, your salary is inadequate, or you can't find the right job.

These feelings about work might be indirect. You might hate the man who fired your dad when you were ten years old, causing your family to move to a different house and you to give up friends and change schools.

> Be as thorough as you can when making your list. Keep your mind open to reminders from Source. You might be waiting at a red light and come up with an additional name or two.

➢ Keep paper and pen nearby and write down all who come to mind as you become aware of them. Don't be overwhelmed if you have over 100 names!

➢ And be grateful for your recollections because they will spur you on to make enormous vibrational progress.

➢ Next, expand your list beyond people and pets to include impersonal causes, events, or conditions that might cause you to carry energetic debris and hinder your spiritual status.

➢ Forgive each person or topic one at a time, using the Forgiveness Activity explained in the following pages.

➢ End every activity by pouring blessings onto your concern. Bless all positive influences.

➢ Ask for guidance, support, courage, means, and all other qualities you desire to benefit you and others in your efforts to forgive.

Each of us, individually, is not be able to save the whole world, but our prayers are potent and effective, and they do contribute to universal progress and growth. Our willingness and desire to work on forgiving everyone and everything not only helps our present life, but our past and future as well.

How to Forgive: Background

The person you are forgiving might be living or not. If he is deceased, forgiving might be easier because follow-up physical interaction is impossible. The person does not need to know you have forgiven him, unless you sense otherwise. In one healing period of time, you can work on one significant person or on two or three people who are more superficially connected to you. Space these episodes apart as you deem appropriate for your current position on your spiritual path, but keep in mind that it will typically take a few hours for you to notice the emotional shift and relief.

You might need to do more than one *Forgiveness Activity*[97] for some persons, especially if there is intense history or current turmoil between you. You might feel that your forgiveness is complete then find, in the future, that you repeat some of the same forgiveness statements you previously made, enabling a deeper emotional layer to move out.

This Forgiveness Activity follows a generic pattern that focuses on present life trash bags, (see Chapter 2, Section 8 of Karma,) and basic soul scripting. From this fundamental baseline, you will instigate improvements at other levels of your life.

The activity will work as described, but you are so unique that you might want to adapt it. At the same time, be alert for ego ploys that could deter your intentions. You could recognize the ego's presence by a reluctance to begin forgiving, or an internal debate about whether you need to forgive the other persons or they should forgive you first. If you continue to notice emotional landmines whenever you think about a person, you still have more energy debris inside you.

Perform this activity when alone, anywhere, and anytime, as often as you feel the desire or need. An ideal situation would be in the evening and in a warm bath because water is conducive to spiritual energies. If you have pets at home, love them before

---

[97] **Forgiveness Activity:** the process of applying forgiveness in our life concerning relationships and experiences with ourselves, other people, and organizations, in order to obtain freedom from all past, present, and future potential karma with its mandated role-playing

you get into the tub, reassure them that you are fine and will see them afterward, then keep them out of the room.

🕉 Because you initiate this Forgiveness Activity on your own, you are in complete control of who, when, how, and what to forgive. You can take the initiative to forgive when it is convenient for you, and you can say anything you want without the other person becoming angry or defensive, without interrupting or leaving. Alone, you finally can say all that you never could before. And if it doesn't feel appropriate to continue, you can stop at any time without having to explain.

Also be aware that, if the other(s) involved in your karmic contract choose not to forgive and release you, they will draft a different soul to play your role either in this lifetime or a future one.

How to Forgive: Forgiveness Activity

Step One: Remove First Floor Baggage

This first step in the Forgiveness Activity addresses stored memories and emotions from the *present* life. Energies move out of our system through our intention to heal, combined with supportive action. Forgiving provides a safe, appropriate, and timely way to purge our trash bags and burdens. Give this first portion as much time, attention, and emotional energy as needed.

> ➢ Imagine a holographic image in front of you of the person, (career, institution, and so forth) that you intend to forgive. Recall and state anything you remember about what he shouldn't have said or done, or what he didn't say or do that you expected him to say/do. Include statements you think he had no right to make, and actions you think he had no right to do, as well as your resulting emotions, including hate or other strong turmoil, for him when he said/did it. You can

even pose the question: "Why did or didn't you say/do such and such?"

➢ Recall all that you can of specific incidents in which he was "wrong." Speak it, cry, shout, blame, or swear. Say whatever it takes to help you expel stored feelings from your body and life. Be as specific, strong, or vicious as necessary. You are speaking your truth. The more emotions you release, the more potent your healing will be.

➢ Then, apologize to him for the wrongs you might or might not have said or done. Focus on when you disappointed, lied, hurt, behaved poorly, and so on. You can justify your behavior if you wish, but remember that you are trying to clear away any debt you are carrying, so be as honest and thorough as possible.

In the process of forgiving others, you might find yourself asking, "Just why did I act that way at that time?" The answer to that question might lead you to a more peripheral person who pushed a button for you. Include this person in your Forgiveness Activity.

> Emily had purchased carpeting for her home from a major department store. The salesman who took the order had told her the carpet would arrive in about two weeks, but it was on a backorder and kept being delayed.
>
> In the meantime, the carpet installers had already laid the padding, and its pink protective covering was coming loose from being walked on by Emily's family, leaving bothersome residue throughout the house. She had phoned weekly to check on the status of

delivery and was assured it would arrive "any day now."

After two months, Emily was overwhelmingly frustrated. She went to the store and located her salesman. She explained her situation, and he verbally assaulted her by defending himself and justifying his position. He told her that he was not responsible for the delay, he had done all that he could do, and he did not deserve to be treated the way she was treating him. Emily left the store in tears and went to her car and sobbed.

The next day, she went with a neighbor to a local carpet store, saw something she liked, bought it, and had it installed the following day.

Not until many years later when she learned about spiritual forgiveness did Emily recognize she was still carrying energetic debris about that carpet salesperson. She reinterpreted what had happened and realized that he had unconsciously volunteered to push a button in her to help her release trash bags that were ready to come out—trash bags that, on the surface, had nothing to do with carpeting, but with deeper emotions of frustration, powerlessness, unfairness, and an inability to speak her truth in other, unrelated circumstances.

Her crying, thanks to that incident, had moved those stored emotions out of her system and raised her vibrational rate. As she began her

Forgiveness Activity many years later, she did not know the salesman's name, but she asked for a generic image to represent that salesman's holographic energy to be placed in front of her, and she proceeded to forgive him.

Step Two: View Forgiveness from the Fiftieth Floor

Step two moves your focus past this present life's experiences to *soul relationships.*[98] To proceed effectively with this step, it is not essential to know any, some, or all of your past lives that you shared with the person you're forgiving. Nor is it necessary that you accept the concept of reincarnation, but it is helpful to at least be open to this possibility.

> ➤ To facilitate the ease of this step, realize that the following words are a guideline. Adapt them to say what you want in a way that will incorporate the essence of the words. As you do, trust that you are being further guided by your soul and by Source so that you might heal yourself to the greatest extent in the best possible manner.

The suggested words for forgiving someone with whom you share or shared a relationship are:

> *"I now understand that we each needed*
> *each other to be together in this lifetime,*
> *and that we asked or drafted each other to*
> *play the roles we've been performing for*
> *each other, even if we don't know why. We*
> *have probably played these same roles back*
> *and forth countless times in our past lives*
> *together. However, I am no longer willing*

---

[98] *soul relationships:* the energetic status between souls accrued from past and present life experiences

to keep doing this, and I also want to free
you from doing this any longer or ever
again. I want to completely heal our
relationship and resign from the dramas we
have been playing. Therefore, I completely,
freely, and permanently forgive and release
you. Please forgive and release me."

The person you are forgiving can respond with only three possible answers: yes, no, or remain silent. In your state of forgiving, you will very likely sense, see, or hear a response. If you notice nothing, that is fine too. Your forgiveness offers him an incentive to heal if he chooses to do so.

> ➢ If you feel that he forgave you, even though he would not have consciously realized anything changed, thank him for this decision. Suggest that both of you will now begin to heal, feel freer, and, if he is still living, be better able to relate in more fulfilling and gratifying ways.

> ➢ You might want to bless him.

> ➢ Be careful not to lie, even for a good reason. Do not tell him that you love him if you don't. Do not wish him well if you don't. But you could ask that he be protected, that his life might heal, and that he come to see and accept his life more clearly or honestly.

> ➢ Thank him for coming.

Afterward, you might sense his feelings have eased about you. You might recognize that he treats you slightly better or pushes your buttons less often or not as deeply as before. He could also behave in exactly the same way as before, but you will not feel the impact as strongly as you did in the past. You will still be aware of interaction dynamics with him, but your emotional response will have improved or even transformed. You will be less disturbed, more peaceful, and accepting.

If you received no response from him or sensed that he did not forgive you, you have still benefited from the activity.

> Tell him that you regret his silence but respect his position. State that you hope that sometime soon he might be willing to forgive you so that he will be freer. Ask God to help him. Thank him for coming into your life so you could heal your old karmic issues.

> Be aware that your forgiveness of him does not remove emotional blockages from his system, so be comfortable knowing that you are not doing his work for him, that you are not responsible for him or for his healing. Rather, you are setting yourself free from the binds that tie you to his soul in scripted, karmically challenging ways.

In everyday life, he might continue his actions as usual, or he might behave worse or better. Regardless, you will be better able to cope and heal than you were before, or you might decide to end the relationship.

You do not need to repeat the Forgiveness Activity with him simply because he did not release you. As a result of forgiving him, you will not need to play a scripted role with that soul in a future incarnation. However, he will need to work on his unresolved issue with some other soul until he clears his karmic script.

> If you want to forgive another person at this point, start over by feeling a true sense of emotional transition from the first person to the next, and repeat the

relationship forgiveness words.

~ ~ ~

If you need to forgive a "transient" person who pushed a button, such as the carpet salesman in the earlier story, know that the person does not have a karmic contract with you. Rather, he unwittingly volunteered to push a button to help you release trash bags and therefore to heal. Also be aware that you have undoubtedly performed the same "service" for others.

The suggested words for forgiving someone with whom you experienced a momentary encounter are:

> *"I now understand that you volunteered to*
> *serve me by pushing a button and triggering*
> *a strong emotional reaction in me. Because*
> *I now recognize a beneficial reason for*
> *what you did or said, I freely, completely,*
> *and permanently forgive and release you.*
> *Please forgive and release me."*

Step Three: Neutralize the Environment

> ➤ Ask for all the negative energies you released while forgiving to be neutralized from the environment and water, if you were in a bath. It will instantly be done.

You might feel lighter, but not empty. This is because you now have open spaces where the emotional toxins had been stored in your body. God's Light will fill these areas within you, but in the short term, you might be somewhat vulnerable to outside energies.

> ➤ To protect yourself, surround yourself with White Light.

313

➢ Finish with prayer, thanking God for life, healing opportunities, and support.

Step Four: Enhance Your Understanding

➢ Expand your view and interpretation of each person and relationship you forgave.

➢ Ask yourself:

- "What role did the person I forgave play for me?"

- "How well did he play it?"

- "What was my response?"

Do you see that he made your issues obvious and stimulated you to release unwanted energies? What did you learn from that person? How have you benefited as a direct result of the difficult issue between the two of you?

➢ If you cannot find an answer, at least know you are a survivor, and that you are probably stronger and have more stamina than you would otherwise have had.

➢ Reflect on how you might have helped the other person's life through the role you played.

How to Forgive Yourself

We must forgive ourselves, whether or not others forgive us, and even if we are not yet ready to forgive others. In fact, for some, self-forgiveness might be a prerequisite to forgiving others. Paradoxically, we might find it easier to forgive others than ourselves.

If you are struggling with excessive guilt or poor self-esteem, you might not even feel worthy to forgive yourself. Your perceived "sin" might have been nothing more than making an honest mistake or not realizing the full consequences of some action you took, or didn't take, which ended up hurting someone else. You might have been involved in something very serious, either accidentally or intentionally, that you have not been able to release. Perhaps the consequences of your actions are so awful that you feel you can't or shouldn't forgive yourself. A potential blessing of realizing karmic roles is the realization that, possibly, your behavior, action, or words were karmically prearranged and were precisely what the other person needed for incentive to help him or her heal.

ॐ As when forgiving others, you might need several sessions to fully forgive yourself. Therefore, perform the following activity with an open heart and in a fully alive moment with as much of you connected as possible and not while you are drifting off to sleep.

Step One: Become Still

> Get into a quiet, undisturbed, and solitary place. Talk to God. Tell Him your specific feelings, concerns, angers, and frustrations. Pour out your heart to Him.

> State out loud what you are releasing, whatever comes into your awareness in the moment. For example:

"I should not have treated my eight-year-old neighbor the way I did when I was ten. I slapped him and took his bike for an afternoon and told him I would beat him up if he told his parents. (Or I took her new bracelet or cell phone and then kept it.) I deeply regret my actions. I am so sorry. I forgive myself and ask him to forgive me. I release these feelings."

If you are or were a soldier, you might need to forgive yourself for killing someone. If you were unfaithful to your partner, you might need to forgive yourself for causing emotional hardships.

Step Two: Speak Your Forgiveness

➢ State your truth, the whole truth. Don't hide, soften, rationalize, or pretend. Face whatever you have to face head on. You might need to release yourself for violent emotional reactions, for times you said too much, or times when you did not say anything but wished you had. Be as true to yourself as you can be. You are finally facing the core of your being.

➢ When you have released as much as you can, make a few statements to God, such as:

"I claim that You love me, God. I claim that You hear me, forgive me, and are giving me peace. I ask for forgiveness from all souls who were involved in the experience. I trust that what happened had some positive eternal significance for all of us. I ask for all the courage and support necessary to avoid repeating any behavior that is not aligned with Your Truth."

Step Three: Affirm Your Soul Growth

➢ Then acknowledge your progress by saying,

"I am now free of guilt and self-blame. I know that God does not judge me. Only I judge myself. I will look at what I've learned from the experience and concentrate on producing positive results in

316

my life from this more advantageous perspective. I refuse to continue to beat myself up, deny my full potential, and carry this burden any longer. I claim that I now accept God's complete healing. I am stepping out confidently and with trust to improve my sense of worthiness and change whatever I can change. I receive blessings in my life. I follow an empowered path. Thank you, God. Amen."

You might or might not feel lighter or clearer immediately upon stating this prayer, but likely within several hours you will notice some improvement in vitality, freedom, and outlook. The extent of relief from guilt and pain is usually incremental and is an indicator of healing that is taking place.

Step Four: Resume Your Normal Life

➢ Repeat the activity anytime, even several times daily.

➢ Recognize the karmic implications of what might be taking place as you move along on your own healing path.

Benefits of Forgiveness

If you have been deeply offended, physically hurt, unfairly blamed, or intentionally victimized, your reactions might be strong, angry, and/or confused. It is likely that, in the immediacy of the moment or even short-term, you will not handle the instigator, event, or situation well.

This is because being treated poorly brings out the worst in human behavior—in all of us—and forgiveness is not usually our initial response. More likely, we feel that we don't deserve to be treated in that manner. We might know that we should not be judgmental, but the thought, "I was wronged," is stronger. We might think we should forgive, but we don't. And this unresolved emotional disturbance then perpetuates our ego management technique and delays our enlightenment.

ॐ Forgiveness, whether conducted solely or in concert with the perpetrator, will provide acceptance, peace, and freedom for the person or persons who forgive. The forgiver acknowledges that the past experience happened, but the energy is neutralized from that event so that it no longer drains, damages, or diminishes life quality. It

> *Forgiveness will provide acceptance, peace, and freedom for the person or persons who forgive.*

is also possible that the fiftieth floor forgiveness energy might have a life-altering effect on the perpetrator, but this potential benefit typically requires recognition and willingness on the perpetrator's part to accept responsibility for the violating action, and to do something to improve his viewpoint, life, or activities. Ideally he would also ask for forgiveness. The forgiver heals regardless of the perpetrator's response.

~ ~ ~

The following story about the power of forgiveness on the forgiver comes from Dr. Norman Sheeley, the Founder of The American Holistic Medical Association, who relates a story of a woman who was wheeled into one of his lectures on a gurney.

> The woman was placed at the side of the auditorium, near the front, clearly within Dr. Sheeley's view from the stage. Shortly after she arrived, he led the audience in a meditation

to discover what was holding each of them back in their life. As he scanned the group during the quietness, he wondered if the invalid had actually died. He left the podium and went to check on her. She had a weak pulse and was still breathing, although barely, so he returned to the stage.

Some months later as he was about to enter a store, a woman came running up to him, calling him by name. She asked if he remembered the woman on the gurney at a lecture he gave, and of course he did. She told him she was that woman. Shocked, he asked what had possibly happened to so totally transform her.

She said that during the meditation, she realized she was not responsible for her husband's unfaithfulness and that he would have behaved that way no matter whom he had married. She had wanted to leave him when their children were small, but stayed for their sake until they grew up. Later, she wanted to leave him but had no way to earn an income and sustain herself financially. So she stayed with him but began to physically and emotionally deteriorate. This realization during the meditation session had freed her from a life sentence of betrayal, anger, and futility.

She was now divorcing him and starting a new life. She was full of excitement and vitality. Her body had completely healed, and her life was now taking shape according to her initiative and ability. She was eternally grateful.

~ ~ ~

The following five examples highlight life experiences and the benefits of healing that resulted from forgiving. Some of them might seem trivial to an observer, but all were significant to the person who finally chose to forgive.

> Many years ago, Doreen was desperate for someone to sit with her very small children. She eventually called a teenager who lived across the street but who had never sat for her. The teen was available for the night in question, but she didn't want to babysit. Doreen's outer reaction was pleasant, but she was seething inside. She continued to hold a grudge against the girl.
>
> This incident came to Doreen's mind many years later as she was compiling her forgiveness list, and she realized that she had to finally release the would-be sitter and those buried emotions. She ended up realizing how childish she had been by carrying that anger around all of those years.

~ ~ ~

> When Holly turned twenty-five, her husband took her to a restaurant where they routinely sang "Happy Birthday" to the celebrants. Holly's new baby was only three weeks old, and she was still not feeling or looking her

best. The waitress called the diners' attention to Holly by announcing that she was celebrating her "Sweet Sixteen Birthday ... *the second time around!*" Holly was quite disturbed with this comment, and it took more than twenty years for her to finally emotionally clear the upsetting experience.

~ ~ ~

Bertha was a coworker with Clyde. Bertha found out that Clyde had taken a sick day from work when it should have been credited as a personal business day. She turned him in to the business office, and Clyde was docked his pay for the day. Both Clyde and his wife, Sheila, were angry that Bertha had done this and would stew about the situation whenever her name came up in conversation.

Several years later, Bertha apologized to Clyde. This apology helped Clyde forgive her, and he kindly assured her that he understood why she had done it and that she had been technically right. However, Sheila continued to harbor resentment toward Bertha for what she had done. The two families live near each other and Bertha's car is very distinctive. As Sheila was progressing in her spiritual life, she grew aware of her increased emotional and physical sensitivity whenever she saw Bertha's car and realized that she had to forgive her.

Sheila did the Forgiveness Activity on Bertha. A few days later, she again saw the unusual car and discovered that her reaction to it was neutral. She was delighted with this obvious improvement in her life.

ॐ This anecdote poses an additional possibility. If an action that we take results in some consequence to a person, our apology is even more thorough if we make an offer to compensate for or assist with the effect that we created. It would have been thoughtful if Bertha had offered to reimburse Clyde for the money he lost as a result of her tampering into his life. Very possibly, Clyde would have graciously refused her gesture, although other people would possibly choose to accept it.

~ ~ ~

Nate had a dog, Sammy, that he dearly loved. Sadly, Sammy had to be put down, and Nate grieved his passing for months. Not long after Sammy's death, a friend gave another dog, Whimsy, to him. Nate was not ready to have another pet so soon, and it took months for him to become comfortable with Whimsy. But even as he did so and as time went by, he noticed that he was missing Sammy more and more. He had no idea why. Whimsy was obedient, sweet tempered, gentle, smart, and a wonderful companion. Although it didn't make any conscious sense, he just couldn't seem to love her.

Nate finally asked a medical intuitive, Ted, if he could explain why he couldn't love his new pet. Ted stated that Whimsy had been Nate's dog three lifetimes ago. She had gone away with Nate's spouse, whom Nate dearly loved, and only the dog had returned. That is all Nate found out, but he decided to work with it.

As soon as he returned home from the reading, Nate sat down with Whimsy and looked into her eyes. He apologized to her for his emotional response several lifetimes ago. He explained that he had wanted his spouse to return home more than he wanted his dog and he might have blamed the dog for not keeping his spouse safe. Even without knowing the actual details, Nate forgave Whimsy and asked her to forgive him.

Nate immediately felt lighter, and by the end of the next day, he could finally feel love springing up within him for the sweet little creature who was now—and once again—his pet.

ॐ If forgiveness works this noticeably with an animal, imagine how it impacts a relationship with a person.

~ ~ ~

Lori had a tragic childhood of violent and frequent sexual abuse from about age four to ten. All of her siblings, including her brothers, suffered at the hands of their several abusers, but they never discussed it. The situation became like the metaphorical elephant in the room that no one acknowledged. In fact, Lori had so deeply buried her memories of the abuse that she had no idea anything unusual had happened to her.

Lori married at age eighteen and began to have disturbing and confusing nightmares. She could not understand why. Then her emotional closet opened wide, and all the skeletons fell out. She began to have flashbacks about her childhood and suffered such serious physical problems that she required many surgeries, including a hysterectomy. Her emotional traumas resulted in divorce.

Trying to find answers, Lori asked her siblings if any of her traumatic nightmare events had actually happened. They all validated her experiences because they had also been victimized. They confirmed that their grandfather, a minister, had physically and sexually abused his children, a deceit and hypocrisy that was not lost on her. Her father, brothers, brother-in-law, and even an uncle also became perpetrators, a case of generational sexual abuse.

A critically pivotal healing event occurred when Lori discovered that her mother had known all along what was going on in her home but had looked the other way and done nothing to support her young children. Lori was furious with everyone and distanced herself from her whole family for many years.

During her estrangement from them, however, she realized that, somehow, something had to change. So, at age twenty-four, she sought a spiritual path. She knew she had been violated, abused, taken advantage of, and betrayed by her mother and father, that she had been powerless to protect herself, and that she was a victim.

Over time, she grew to accept the reality of karma and how it functioned in life. She learned that she had selected her parents, her gender, and the life issues she would encounter. This fact was profoundly difficult to accept at first, but working with prayer and therapeutic Light workers, massage, and support classes, she went from anger, to grief, to blame, and finally to forgiveness.

Forgiveness, for her, occurred in layers and over time, but Lori kept doing it until she got to the core of her earliest abuse.

When she finished forgiving someone, she would picture that person as one with her. Then, when she felt they were whole and complete within God's Light, she knew she was finished forgiving.

In spite of her prolonged and agonizing path, Lori has forgiven everyone in her family, even her mother. She negotiated her return to the family by painstakingly talking to her siblings and parents about her own boundaries, what she was willing to accept and do with them, what topics were not to be mentioned, how often she would be in contact with them, and obtaining their agreement to her terms of reconciliation.

One brother began forgiving within two weeks of her decision to forgive. Another brother attended a counseling session with Lori and actually admitted abusing her as well as being abused by the men who should have loved him the most. He apologized to Lori.

Lori has come to see that she selected her birth family to support healing in the whole family and to be a catalyst for all of them to stop the cycle of abuse, which it has. Lori is grateful that they can now see each other occasionally and have healthier relationships.

Obstacles to Forgiveness

ॐ It is somewhat less effective to work on forgiveness if a person is still actively involved in a problematic relationship or situation. However, releasing disturbances while going through them can help us more easily handle our present state. When external

> *Releasing disturbances while going through them can help us more easily handle our present state.*

events stabilize or somewhat resolve, forgiveness can help us clear out the old issues more fully.

> ➤ To facilitate this, pray for guidance, courage, understanding, resolution, and love. And remember that you are likely as large a thorn in the side of others as they are in yours.

~ ~ ~

Too much of a good thing is still too much. Ironically, this also applies to the act of forgiveness.

Vivian was just beginning a spiritual path and was enthusiastically trying to do all of the right things with all of her ability. When she heard about the need to work on forgiveness, she automatically forgave everyone as soon as any issue began to arise.

Although it is never wrong to forgive, Vivian was actually short-circuiting her custom-designed, personal healing opportunities by deliberately overriding her natural and deeper emotions that she also needed to release.

During a session, when she asked about her new way of handling life, D'Ann told her that she could maximize the healing opportunities by allowing herself to more greatly feel the pain of those experiences, more emotionally express what was stored inside, and then forgive. In this manner, she would also come to realize a deeper sense of gratitude for her healing experiences.

Ongoing Forgiveness

At our spiritual core, there is nothing to forgive. We are clear, whole, Light beings. The more we forgive, the closer we move into a continual state of total acceptance and peace where forgiveness is no longer needed. After you have practiced forgiveness for an extended period of time, your Higher Self will assist you by, without any conscious thought, bringing into your awareness old, nearly forgotten remaining energies you still need to release.

Lydia had been married to her second husband for over twenty years and was working to forgive several adult members of her family. As she was washing dishes one day, out of the blue, she became furious with neighbors of her birth family because they had not attended her first wedding. Her startling thought and response caught her by complete surprise. Lydia had not seen, spoken to, or thought about any of those former neighbors for many years. She wanted to know why she was thinking of them now.

The answer is that Lydia had been energetically healing her life. Her Higher Self then began to exhume buried emotions and experiences that she would likely not have remembered on her own. Over the next several weeks, more old memories and reactions bubbled up into her consciousness. Lydia knew to follow through on each recollection with forgiveness. This took only a few minutes to do each time, and with each prayer of forgiveness she resumed her life with a higher vibrational rate.

29: E/GO VACUUM

E/go eyes and processes generate emotional turbulence and debris. Remember that when we only manage these emotions, rather than release or resolve them, they figuratively accumulate in trash bags in the chest area or are stored as actual, physical congestions in other parts of the body. These emotions collect during daily life, button pushing episodes, and especially, healing setups. The traditional ways of removing these deposits have been through emotional, verbal, or physical release, from benign to violent. Surrendering will also help to eliminate emotional trash bags.

> *E/go interpretation is the cause of spiritual immaturity that results in emotional debris.*

E/go interpretation is the cause of spiritual immaturity that results in emotional debris and disturbances that defy and delay development. To heal, we need to remove these energies as well as the functioning processes and systems—the ego mechanics—that are responsible for generating them.

Surrendering is particularly effective in regard to outcomes, but it also works on inner thoughts, energetic processes, and trash bags. Multi-dimensional energies, which enable us to operate at higher evolutionary energy levels, now provide an additional powerful, efficient, and life-changing tool that rids our system of ego mechanics and accumulated emotions. This tool is called the ego vacuum, (defined and referred to in Chapter 4 in the Releasing E/go Section.)

Why Vacuum

Intended to supplement surrendering and forgiving, the ego vacuum specializes in removing restrictive internal energetic processes and debris, suctioning out as many bits of debilitating energy residue as possible. Every time we use the ego vacuum, we raise our vibrational rate. To do that as efficiently, easily, and as powerfully as possible, we need to address whatever lingering emotional debris is causing our internal low vibrations.

Think of karma as disturbed emotions in your life resembling an ancient, ugly, extremely heavy chest of drawers stored in your basement. You don't want to go downstairs because this chest is repulsive, impossible to move, repair, or update, and painfully stuck. You have no idea where it came from because it was there when you moved into your home. You have been throwing emotional trash bags behind the chest all of your life because you didn't know what else to do with them, and they would be kept out of site as though they didn't exist. Whenever someone pushes your button, your attention is instantly pulled down to the chest of drawers. In order to profoundly heal your life, the whole chest and collection of trash bags, emotions and thoughts that we must touch and grab hold of, need to be taken from your basement and cleared away. They are far too heavy to move all at one time, so you need to break down the chest into small pieces and remove them incrementally before you can throw away the bags.

You figuratively go downstairs when you recognize the healing opportunity in a triggered moment. Rather than continue to merely manage your disturbed emotions, you choose to use the Three Pillars of Healing, your energetic hammer, screwdriver, and pliers, to remove one piece at a time of the hardware from the drawers. With many additional small steps to break down the chest, you gradually succeed in removing the whole unit, and then can finally begin to clear out your trash bags. Every removed portion of emotional debris raises your vibrational rate and improves your life.

As of this point in our spiritual evolution, there is no more effective tool to use to remove these inner low frequencies than the ego vacuum. It is the only tool that specializes in clearing anything and everything operating inside us that is holding us back from evolving, no longer working for us, or is old, immature, problematic, painful, redundant, limiting—anything we don't want any more.

Install the E/go Vacuum

🕉 In order to make the ego vacuum work to its maximum effectiveness, we need a high level of awareness of what is going on inside, and vacuum often and thoroughly.

Therefore, adapt the following visual image to suit you.

➢ Imagine an industrial, compact canister vacuum standing upright on the floor, extending to about waist height on your left side. This activity supports your powerful intent to heal because you are doing something physical to support your overriding spiritual and conscious intent.

This vacuum needs no attachments, only the suction hose and nozzle. It is in place there with you because of your intent.

> ➢ Use it to dispose of all ego filters, issues, emotions, thoughts, habits, attitudes, interpretations, opinions, management techniques, beliefs, expectations, and everything else that comprises your familiar, old system of operating.

> ➢ Use it to vacuum out anything that holds you back, is meaningless, redundant, negative, and unwanted.

Unlike a physical vacuum that sucks up and must be emptied of dust and dirt, the ego vacuum neutralizes all low-vibration energies it takes in.

> ➢ Therefore, use it as often as you desire, preferably many, many times a day.

What to Vacuum

Attempting to clean a dirty, cluttered, disorganized room can feel daunting. We might not know where to begin. Rather than toil haphazardly, we usually select one area to work on until, after a period of time, it is done. Similarly, when we vacuum out our emotionally charged energies, we need to identify the one issue, ego mechanism, action, or emotion that we want to clear at that time. We do this by stating the issue out loud as well as our intention to clear it. This statement determines what we want the vacuum to remove, and repeat it continuously during vacuuming.

When we use a physical vacuum to clean a particularly dirty surface, we can usually see where the cleaner head has tracked through and removed the dirt. If nothing else, we might see our progress by a change in the way a carpet nap lays, for example. With the ego vacuum, however, we do not need to track the issues we have been addressing, or the progress we are making. Our focus, instead, is on identifying ego-generated messages and trash bags of which we are aware in the moment, and on removing them from our system.

Because the trash bags are filled with emotional—and not physical—debris, we can suction out numerous old, debilitating feelings without ever filling the vacuum. And because so many energies will be suctioned out at each vacuuming, we will experience rapid release and healing, possibly within minutes or hours, or usually within days or weeks, depending on frequency of use and quantity of accumulation.

And we don't have to empty it. In fact, the emotional debris that it sucks need never again affect us.

How to Vacuum

➢ With your hand, take a hold of the imagined nozzle and place it at the top left hairline of your forehead.

Release any concerns about finding the exact right spot. As with the surrender statement instructions earlier in this chapter, it is your intent and follow through that activates the procedure. With more experience in using this tool, you will upgrade your technique so that you need not even physically hold the nozzle to your head, and situations will occur when you might automatically choose to locate it somewhere else on your body.

➢ But for now, take hold of the end of the vacuum hose. Move it to your forehead, and then use your other hand to reach across your body and turn the switch on.

➢ Identify the specific issue or unwanted limitation you intend to clear out, and state them aloud. (Ego mechanics was defined and explained in Chapter 1,

Resonator, under Urgent Messages.) You might say, for example,

"I am suctioning out all ego mechanics, emotional congestion, and trash bags concerning the issue of guilt. I am doing this because I don't want to feel this way anymore, and because I am so weary of feeling dragged down. I don't want and can't stand guilt in my life at all anymore. I know it is moving out of my system right now. I claim and trust that I am worthy, and that God forgives me for everything I have ever done that constitutes my strong and stubborn guilt. I want all debris about this issue cleared out now."

➤ Frequently repeat the statement about what you are removing.

➤ When you sense the need to stop vacuuming, usually within thirty to sixty seconds, honor that impulse, reach across your body again, take hold of the switch, and turn it off. If you miss this subtle cue, there is an auto shut off that will activate at the appropriate time.

➤ Return the hose to the vacuum where it will be conveniently available the next time.

Benefits of Vacuuming

ॐ There are two *profound* benefits to using the ego vacuum.

First, it will reduce and phase out your old methods of emotional release—strong physical movement, work, or exercise; yelling, crying, or throwing things—that were so grueling, exhausting, slow, and time consuming. You might still choose to process emotions out of your system in your old ways, but you will eventually find those old techniques to be less necessary and desirable as time goes on. You will simply tire of your old ways.

The second is that eventually ego vacuuming will remove charged energies *before* someone pushes your buttons. You will be increasingly aware of old thoughts and unwanted emotions in your ego head, vacuum them out, and preempt this old stimulus that was required to trigger blatant responses. This revision in your operating procedure will minimize and eventually eliminate your need to have healing setups and button pushers.

> *E/go vacuuming will remove charged energies* before *someone pushes your buttons. ... This revision in your operating procedure will minimize and eventually eliminate your need to have healing setups and button pushers.*

In short, you will experience a simpler, easier, smoother, happier, less stressful, and more joyful life. You will like more of what you do and more of the people with whom you interact. You might sleep better and laugh more. And you will willingly shrug off whatever no longer serves your soul growth.

These benefits will come more quickly and more easily when you combine vacuuming with forgiving and surrendering.

Christopher's issue was rejection and feeling unworthy.

He had been commissioned by the founder of a non-governmental organization involved with peace and environmental preservation to write its history. When the book was published, some people in the organization welcomed it and others expressed dislike for it, which Christopher believed was really a dislike for him rather than the book itself.

Each year, the organization held a large annual event for which Christopher felt he deserved to be one of the speakers. Yet, no invitation came. Eventually, Christopher asked members of the event organizing committee if they would allow him to speak. Some on the committee said yes and others hesitated. As before, Christopher felt that he was being snubbed and became angry. And he continued to wait for the invitation he believed he greatly deserved.

As the time for the current year's annual event approached, he became more forceful in his request, but seemingly still to no avail. Finally, he gave up and told himself, once again, there would be no invitation. Then, suddenly, only ten days before the annual event, he received an email from the committee, asking him to be on the program. He had twenty-four hours to decide if he could make it.

At first, Christopher considered not accepting the invitation. He felt it had come too late. He felt slighted that he would have to suddenly alter his work schedule and make travel reservations. And after having waited so long and then receiving an invitation only at the last minute, he felt justified saying no. Yet, he really did want to go.

On the morning he had to tell the committee of his decision, he called D'Ann with whom he'd had several previous sessions. First, they prayed for guidance, and then Christopher described the situation in general terms without providing specific details. She immediately received pertinent guidance and understood the situation. She explained to Christopher that he had been expressing his wants and needs from the standard ego view of a spiritual three-year-old child. "As soon as you let go of trying to control the outcome, you removed ego's blocking energy and made room for God to clear the way. That's when you received the invitation," she told him.

Christopher responded that he would go to the annual event, thus satisfying his desire that had been nagging him ever since the book was published. D'Ann said, "Choosing to go is the second step, and it's still ego-driven." Christopher then realized he was carrying an "I'll show them" attitude.

"First," she continued, "you must forgive everyone involved, including yourself, surrender the outcome to God, and use the ego vacuum to remove more blocking negative energy from your system." Christopher agreed and promised that he would, and he immediately began doing the ego vacuuming activity, which she had previously taught him.

The next day, in spite of being busy preparing for his trip, Christopher accepted an invitation to be a substitute bowler on an afternoon bowling league. He had once been a mediocre bowler with a league average of 160, and he still owned two custom-drilled bowling balls even though he hadn't used them in more than a decade. On that afternoon, he rolled three games close to or above 200, establishing an average of 206.

He associated his success to his conversation with D'Ann. In the past, he would concentrate on what he *wanted* in the way of a score or what he *needed* to win—and he often felt anxiousness and insufficient confidence to obtain those results. On this day, he simply focused on rolling the ball over a certain spot on the alley. "Everything else is physics," he told his teammates as the ball either knocked all the pins down for a strike or not.

Privately, however, Christopher was very much relaxed and in the moment. As he prepared to throw each ball, he would remind himself to walk steadily forward, stay balanced, focus on his target, let go cleanly, and trust that the physical outcome at the other end of the alley would be as good as possible. Later, he would confide to D'Ann his realization that steadiness, balance, focus, letting go, and trust are the keys to a positive spiritual life.

Ongoing Vacuuming

ॐ Using the ego vacuum provides immediate, effective, and noticeable energetic clearing, once you have vacuumed regularly for a few weeks. You might feel or see instant improvement, but this result depends on how much of your energetic issue still remains. The more often you vacuum, the more obvious your results will be.

ॐ How much of the issue remains after each vacuuming session is also dependent on how much emotional energy your system—or let's say, your ego—is willing to let go at any given time. As stated earlier in regard to forgiveness, too much of a good thing is still too much. Your inner Knowing knows this, which is why, for example, you don't let a physical vacuum cleaner stand still on one part of a carpet. Because you have lived with certain characteristics for a long time, your system cannot handle letting go of too much too quickly—that's too much instant change. Ideally you vacuum for no more than one minute at a time, even though you can vacuum again in five minutes if you like. You might even hear an inner voice say, "Okay, that's enough for now," or your head might shake a little bit as though it's trying to get away from the vacuum hose. Honor that and stop vacuuming—until the next time you get the urge to vacuum out a few more trash bags.

30: Implementing the Three Pillars

As stated at the outset of this chapter, the sequence and frequency with which you engage each of the Three Pillars of Transformation depends on you and the situation in which you find yourself. You probably easily understand when to apply forgiveness, even though you might not do so immediately or readily, and now you know how to forgive through the Forgiveness Activity. The idea of vacuuming out old emotional debris might be new to you, but, hopefully, you can accept the idea of removing negative energies and you can easily relate to the concept, the imagery, and the action of holding an ethereal vacuum tube to your forehead. Surrendering can be trickier for several reasons.

First, as stated earlier, the concept that surrendering is a sign of strength might be unfamiliar to you, especially if you were raised with the belief that "might makes right" and that surrendering—whether individually or as a nation at war—is an act of weakness and defeat. Then comes the question of how to blend surrendering with asserting yourself and speaking your t/Truth. Where is the line between surrendering and suppressing emotions, between speaking t/Truth and venting anger, between fiftieth floor responses and first floor reactions? Here is an ideal healing setup.

> Gregory is a professional writer who supplements his income as a speaker, presenting spiritual and travelogue messages to churches and organizations that pay him a modest amount in the low hundreds of dollars per engagement. Audiences throughout a multi-state area compliment him on the insights he brings to his presentations, yet he has not been able to command a great deal of attention within his home city, a situation that his ego doesn't like and can't understand.
>
> One day at a professional social gathering in his home city, Gregory conversed with

Maureen about his travels to various parts of the world and his first-hand experiences with people and celebrations of major faiths in other nations. Maureen said she was the director of a respected Catholic institution of which he was quite familiar, and she asked if he would be interested in presenting to public audiences as part of the institution's upcoming series on world religions. Gregory was delighted and said yes.

Over the next few months, Gregory and Maureen exchanged emails in which he presented topic ideas and she made selections that would be of interest to the institution's audiences. One day, he received an email from Maureen in which she asked if he was available to facilitate a six-hour seminar several months in the future. The email also included the statement, "Presenter stipends for this work are likely to be quite modest."

Gregory responded with embellished ideas to determine if they met with Maureen's expectations. He also asked, "How much stipend do you typically offer for a day-long event?" This exchange was the first time that either of them had brought up the subject of compensation.

Maureen's reply was, "We are looking at a $50 stipend plus lunch." Gregory was flabbergasted, then incensed; his buttons that deal with being respected and valued had been pushed. He fumed overnight, trying to decide how to respond. In the morning, he came up with an idea that pleased him. Perhaps Maureen had mistyped the amount. He sent an email back to her that read: "$50 is a very low stipend, especially for an all-day event by a professional presenter. Perhaps that's a typo and the third digit is missing?"

He found Maureen's response to be unsatisfying and dismissive, including the statement: "I forewarned that this might not be for you." Gregory was upset by this entire setup. He thought that not only had Maureen not forewarned, she had been inviting and encouraging. He found her assessment that the stipend would be "quite modest" to be a misrepresentation, labeling it instead as "obscene."

"What am I to do?" he thought. "I would like to speak at this venue in my home city, but I also feel like I'm being taken advantage of."

Gregory considered that most churches and organizations pay him much more than $50 to speak for twenty to ninety minutes. While the audience would never know how little he would earn from this seminar, he knew that he would feel unfairly treated, and that bothered him immensely.

Gregory was also angry at himself for not having asked about the compensation amount earlier, for assuming that the institution would offer something more than what amounts to minimum wage.

He became aware that the amount of money had become secondary, within his ego mind, to the way he felt he had been treated—or mistreated—by Maureen. He knew, deep inside, that this was a button-pushing setup to help him clear his karmic issues of feeling unworthy. The Universe was commanding him to speak his t/Truth, first to himself and, perhaps, to Maureen.

Gregory had had several sessions with D'Ann and was familiar with the Three Pillars. "But how am I to implement surrendering while I also speak my mind?" he asked himself, perplexed. "Should I simply not put any more thought energy into this situation and not reply to Maureen's most recent email? Or should I call her and tell her that I feel she misled me?"

Awakened in the middle of the night by these thoughts, Gregory initiated the Forgiveness Activity. He imagined a holographic image of Maureen during their first conversation at the social gathering. He asked why she had not been forthright regarding compensation. He also recognized Maureen as a "transient" button pusher and both forgave and thanked her for volunteering to play that role for him. Then he vacuumed out first floor energies— from past lives and this life—that had contributed to his anger and hurt.

When he finished and returned to bed, he felt lighter, more relieved, and freer. He sensed that more forgiveness, especially of himself for carrying these deep karmic issues, would be forthcoming, and at yoga class the next morning, he actually cried while in the downward-facing-dog pose.

But he still had the question of what to do in regard to further communications with Maureen. He felt a responsibility to himself and possibly to other speakers to express his disappointment and frustration. "But of what value would that serve?" he asked. "How am I to speak my truth without burning bridges? Do I even care if the bridges get burned?"

For these answers, he sent an email to D'Ann. He asked: "Should I remain quiet and walk away? Is that what it means to surrender? Or should I contact Maureen and voice my feelings? Is there a better course of action somewhere in between?"

Even as he composed these questions, he felt his internal instincts telling him that he would call Maureen. He told himself: "How can I expect others to listen to me and my stories if I don't speak up for myself?"

First, D'Ann confirmed that Gregory was experiencing a healing setup through which he had already made huge progress, energetically and spiritually, by using the Three Pillars. Then she told him, to grow further, he must address the situation at the first floor—and do so "with honesty, conviction, and tact."

She told him to verbalize—as well as emote—his feelings. "This will help you look at the situation differently than before, and this equates to healing," she said. She advised that he not associate the concept of "right or wrong" with whichever course of action he might choose, but to listen for inner guidance and trust that the entire situation was unfolding in divine order.

She said there is no contradiction between surrendering and speaking your t/Truth.

> *There is no contradiction between surrendering and speaking your t/Truth.*

She suggested that he first ask for God's assistance to determine the information he knows: what he heard Maureen say, what he said, what he read in her emails, and what he wrote in his. She told him that, when speaking with Maureen, it is okay for him to verbalize his hurt over not being treated appropriately and his desire to be treated better. Proactively telling Maureen he wishes she had discussed compensation at the outset—while also acknowledging to her his failure to bring up the subject—will be a huge step in his healing process because it will minimize the possibility that this type of setup will happen again.

Then D'Ann advised Gregory to surrender all of the unknowns: when the conversation will occur, what he will say, how long the conversation will take, how he will feel during and afterward, how Maureen will feel, how she will respond. She told him to say to God, "I surrender what I say, how I say it, and the outcome. You take over, guide my words, and work this out for the best of all concerned."

"This allows God to enter the conversation," she stated. "Even if you and Maureen decide that this is over and done— that you won't speak there—you will have benefited because you spoke up for yourself. This setup is designed to bring up: your old, habitual, painful, and immature emotions and default system of operating; to provide you with a new opportunity to release these emotions; to handle this issue differently and more wisely; and to help you heal."

She also interjected that, maybe, God has plans for Gregory to be somewhere else, doing something even greater on the day he would have, otherwise, spoken at the institution.

D'Ann confirmed that Gregory will probably talk with Maureen, that he is being led in that direction. "As you are dialing her number," she said, "again surrender the outcome to God. Then express your truth to Maureen. From your mouth will come words you hadn't planned to say. Those words will be accurate but not blaming. By standing up for yourself, you will express with exactness what you feel, including why you cannot, in t/Truth, speak for an entire day for $50."

D'Ann suggested that, if both Gregory and Maureen speak their t/Truth, some greater solution might evolve. Gregory might choose to remove the energy of money from the situation and speak for free or for voluntary love offerings from the participants, seeking instead compensation in the form of a higher energy and its resulting benefits.

On the other hand, God might lead Gregory to sense that further interactions with Maureen and this institution will only lead to additional insults. "This goes back to a religious concept that a servant doesn't deserve to be paid, and that people are supposed to selflessly or even sacrificially serve others with love in their heart. If people are willing to give away their gifts, there will always be organizations that will take advantage of them," she said. "Do you want to provide your energy to keep that system going?"

D'Ann cautioned that Maureen might be unwilling to admit a mistake, or actually think that she had been forthright about the stipend; she might become defensive.

The real issue, she repeated, is about Gregory's growth. "It is a requirement that you speak up for yourself; this is your chance to benefit from the setup," D'Ann said. "But," she emphasized, "speak up only *after you surrender.*"

As a lighthearted postscript, D'Ann also told Gregory that his disappointment about not being recognized in his home city is common. "In the New Testament, the disciples did not get respect in Jerusalem, which is one reason they went to spread the word of Jesus in other lands," she said. "That's not going to change. In order to become famous in your hometown, you almost have to leave and prove yourself elsewhere. Then you might—or might not—be welcomed back as a hero."

Gregory agreed to let go of expectations and surrender the outcome to God. He then performed the Forgiveness Activity again, surrendered, and held the symbolic vacuum hose to his forehead for a long time. He had the sensation that he didn't want to let go of some of his old pain, as though he were casting out a longtime friend.

So he turned his attention to making a list of "What I Know" and was surprised at how easily these ideas flowed.

I know that:

- I feel hurt at the way the situation developed.

- I am angry with both Maureen and myself.

- I have worthwhile messages to share with audiences.

- I am a worthy individual and I deserve to be treated with greater respect.

- $50 for six hours plus setup and teardown plus

preparation is not a "quite modest" stipend but is, in fact, less than minimum wage.

I now wish to know the answers to questions I could have asked at the outset:

- How many people might attend my session?

- How much will each person pay to attend?

- What is the size of the room and other logistical information?

In addition, I now see that my immature desire for acceptance had prevented me from asking these basic questions earlier. Therefore, I resolve that:

- If I speak at the institution, I will not accept an unprofessional amount of money.

- I might offer to be paid exclusively on the basis of love offerings from the participants as an expression of their appreciation for my message.

- I would make such an offer in the spirit of love and not with an "I'll show her" attitude.

- I would then accept whatever I receive, and I would be satisfied with my decision.

To further resolve this life healing setup:

- I desire to discuss the situation with Maureen and to express my feelings and further learn from this setup.

- I understand that even if she doesn't converse with me, I am ready and willing to let go of this situation in my own way, knowing that is how God intends for this setup to end.

- I am grateful that this situation has helped me further address the issue of not being worthy.

- I surrender the complete outcome to God.

A few days, including a weekend, passed while Gregory compiled this list and came to the time when he felt he was ready to contact Maureen. He sent an email to her, asking for a telephone appointment, but did not receive a reply. More days passed. A conversation between them did not occur.

A week later, Gregory considered attempting to reach her again, either by email or telephone, but felt a stronger sensation that the incident was over. He reasoned that he had initially responded from a position of ego consciousness and that he had been like a kid in a candy store too eager to satisfy an ego desire to present in his home community. He then committed himself to acting with greater self responsibility in the future. He also determined that God was telling him to surrender to the fact that a concluding conversation with Maureen was no longer necessary or likely beneficial for either party.

He did, however, envision speaking invitations in the future, and he mentally practiced asking for foundational details and identifying logistical parameters, including the amount of the stipend, prior to investing time and emotional energy into preparing for a presentation opportunity that was not completely confirmed. He thought about past speaking engagements in other communities when he had been more emotionally detached from the outcome and acted in this more professional manner. He contrasted those situations to this one, and noted the greater comfort he felt when the groundwork had been openly and forthrightly laid first.

Gregory continued to perform Forgiveness Activities, primarily on himself for acting with head authority rather than Source wisdom. He vacuumed, asking for clearing of whatever karmic debris from this lifetime or past lifetimes might have contributed to his feelings of being devalued and unworthy. And he again placed a holographic image of Maureen in front of him and thanked her for pushing his button and bringing this healing setup into his higher consciousness.

D'Ann also noted that experience is a great teacher. Gregory will now be on top of a potential speaking engagement with essential pertinent questions that answer his practical, personal concerns. He will not make critical assumptions again. Also he, in nearly any professional or personal situation, will be aware of an easier inclination to speak up for himself and will more quickly notice feelings and thoughts of self-doubt or over-confidence to be vacuumed away.

The setup with Maureen came in the ideal way and the perfect time to assist the next layer of his issues to be energetically released so they can no longer hold Gregory back from more empowerment in his life. There will no doubt be other setups as time goes on, but he will k/Know and trust, because of this specific event, that any future difficulties will indeed be spiritual blessings in disguise.

CHAPTER 6:
LIFE'S HEALING REMEDIES

The Three Pillars of Transformation—surrender, forgive, and vacuum—address three primary activities or tools that we can use to promote our own energetic clearing. These healing techniques are like divine gifts because they require no training, equipment, cost, or external trigger to use them. Yet, it seems that many of us forget to use or doubt that those Three Pillars will work. We then continue to search for additional methods to help us handle our situation or emotions, primarily when we are triggered. This chapter focuses on other activities, processes, understandings, and steps we can take to augment spiritual growth whether triggered or not.

We start with perspective, which is a foundational component of much of what is presented throughout *Life's Healing Setups*. Then we move to the topic of proactively healing ourselves physically and spiritually, which is also fundamental and beneficial.

31: PERSPECTIVES
What we experience as r/Reality depends on our perspective. To understand perspective in the physical world, think of various people standing miles apart at sunset on an ocean shoreline. From their individual vantage points, each will see something different: perhaps clouds, a storm, clear sky, crashing surf, gently rolling waves. Each view is accurate yet unlike the others.

Similarly, each person can have a different perspective

regarding the quality or value of the part of the ocean he or she is viewing. A person who finds beauty in serenity might find the storm to be unattractive while another might see a storm as exciting, invigorating, and also a thing of beauty.

This example regarding weather illustrates that each of us can have a different experience of everyday r/Reality as well as t/Truth, which is why even advanced spiritual leaders can have different views or understandings about how God works on earth. When we see these leaders contradicting each other, we must remember that none of them are necessarily wrong but only that their perspectives are diverse. This is why it is essential for each of us to follow what we sense to be our own t/Truth while we remember that God has the total omniscient view, which is Truth.

> *Even advanced spiritual leaders can have different views or understandings about how God works on earth.*

~ ~ ~

Perspective is a major factor in our life setups. Relationships form and marriages occur because people have seemingly compatible perspectives, and then problems and divorces often arise from conflicting perspectives. Children and parents naturally have varied perspectives if, for no other reason, than their different generations and the societal circumstances into which they were born. Emotions and personal truths are often based on perspectives. Likewise, people have dissimilar views of how to earn, spend, and invest money.

The fiftieth floor gives us a different perspective than the first floor. Life under the control of ego, including victimhood, judgment, and fear, are all influenced by perspectives. "Current perspectives" and "new perspectives" are a component of the Fear Setup Equation. Time is a convention, based on human perspectives, as are all business paradigms. Planetary transformation and the Three Pillars all require that we be willing to shift our perspective.

These already explained examples and the information about other healing remedies that follow demonstrate that perspective is profoundly crucial to the quality of our life. How we look at a situation or event not only determines what and how much we see but also our interpretation or meaning, our emotional reaction or

> *Perspective is profoundly crucial to the quality of our life.*

response, our perceived options, and our decision-making capability. Our view even sets our attitude, motivation, and the amount of effort we employ to follow through or accomplish.

For example, people who see themselves as a winner or hero will see, interpret, feel, and respond according to heroic views. When faced with adversity, they will "land on their feet" regardless of how difficult an experience might be. People who live with the position of victim or loser, however, will filter all experiences according to defeated or self-defeating viewpoints. Frequently, people with a victim or loser mentality become so fixated on what they perceive as an unfair and difficult position in life that they fundamentally close out any new information that could help them. These people will be either unaware of blessings or dismiss them as unimportant, be unable to sustain or adjust to more favorable circumstances, and rarely or never be able to thrive until or unless they shift their perspective.

~ ~ ~

Perspective is the second most significant and restrictive aspect in life after karma. As karma clears, our perspective gradually, safely, and automatically enlarges so that we see more alternatives, greater opportunities, and better solutions.

> *When we seek an energetic and spiritual path, our panorama of life and our vibrational rate expand and our interpretations, emotions, and responses instinctively grow to be wiser, more peaceful, and more effective.*

ॐ Our perspective depends on whether we function at the first floor, the fiftieth floor, or somewhere in between. At the first floor, many of us learn the coping mechanisms of putting on a smile, always doing the right thing, and/or constraining our emotions as ways to prevent an undesirable outcome from a difficult situation—and this is considered to be "positive behavior." However, the perspective from the fiftieth floor shows us that the difficult situation is really a karmic setup intended to heal according to our soul script. This fiftieth floor perspective enables us to at least accept, and hopefully welcome and embrace life's setups, for the opportunities they offer.

Perhaps one purpose of your current life is to overcome being a doormat, someone who people easily walked on in previous lifetimes. Perhaps Source is presenting you with difficult situations so that you will get some backbone and stand up for yourself, politely but firmly asserting your right to be you. People might look upon your assertiveness as "negative behavior," as though you have a bee in your bonnet, or they might ask, "Who do you think you are?" The answer, of course, is, "Myself."

Our view of ourselves and our circumstances changes as we

ride that elevator up from the first to the fiftieth floor. When we seek an energetic and spiritual path, our panorama of life and our vibrational rate expand and our interpretations, emotions, and responses instinctively grow to be wiser, more peaceful, and more effective.

~ ~ ~

An example of this message came to me through my interaction with my computer. So, after including stories about various clients, it is time for me to present a story about myself, which Source seems to have presented as if on perfect cue.

> I was writing this section on perspective when I ran into yet another computer glitch, an all-too-frequent occurrence, that prevented me from continuing to work. I could not locate the most recent version of the manuscript for this book that I had spent eight hours working on a few days earlier. The computer screen showed only a small, temporary file with that date on it. I was frantic.
>
> I am far from technologically gifted and have arranged for two people to assist me when I need them. I phoned each of them, and neither answered. I had only two hours to devote to writing that day, and I was stopped cold until I could get help. I was unbelievably frustrated and powerless to do anything to either rectify my situation or advance my manuscript.
>
> After a brief but strong talk with some of my guides, I realized that I needed to look at the situation differently. After all, I was presenting myself as being in a position of authority in

regard to perspective. I decided to change my view of what had happened. Perhaps there was a reason for me to put off writing for a day or two that I didn't know about. Maybe my inspiration would be better later. Or maybe deadlines for other responsibilities were actually more immediately necessary.

These were the possibilities that came to mind as I began to shift my perspective. And although my emotions did calm down to a more manageable level on that critical day, I was still not peaceful. But I made a decision to switch tactics. Instead of writing during that limited time frame, I chose to do other important chores that were waiting for my attention, and I felt good about getting those things accomplished. Later that afternoon, both of my "techie" people helped me —bless them!

A few days later, I came to the following conclusion, which was not generated from guidance, but from my own cognitive awareness of what was happening in my life and with my manuscript at that time. I realized that I needed to go through this personal experience so that I could include it in the book. With relief, I changed my frustration to gratitude!

The overall message here is that looking at a project deadline and attempting to fit a large amount of creative work into to a small time slot is a great life stressor. I had been so stressed that I blocked out all other subtler input, which is essential when writing about spiritual principles.

I was not able to work on the manuscript again for three days—until the weekend, which I had allotted entirely to writing. That Saturday morning, I applied all of the energy techniques I know to my own dilemma. I forgave the computer for its idiosyncrasies, myself for my ineptness, and both it and me for the long and difficult "relationship" we have had for so many years. I used White Light around and between each of "us."

I used the Three Pillars of Transformation, (surrender, forgive, vacuum,) prayed, and lit a candle with energetic charges on the flame. Then I had a talk with the guides who are helping me write, took a deep breath, and told myself this was going to be fun. And do you know what? It *was* fun!

I still need computer assistance to compensate for my lack of training, but my change in perspective and the energy work made a wonderful improvement in my approach and feelings, as well as my writing, which has more flow, ease, and clarity. Interestingly enough, the computer has actually "settled down!"

Another element of this story is that my editor, Robert Weir, who is also a client, was experiencing certain challenges at the same time he edited this chapter and the previous chapter on the Three Pillars of Transformation.

Robert's feelings were of being overwhelmed with details and having "too much to do" in regard to interactions with several other people. He and I conducted a session over the telephone and determined that the issue of "details" is part of his soul script that relates to a karmic debt that began in a previous life many centuries earlier and which he entered this life to remove.

Robert had already done much in regard to excessive details through interactions with a person in this life who was also part of that experience in the previous life. But now Robert was continuing to process out more of that old karmic situation.

Although paying attention to details is a valuable characteristic when editing, a recent setup had occurred in regard to his interactions with various friends in which he saw a need to be lighter and more flexible.

He utilized the Three Pillars by forgiving himself for getting caught up in this situation, surrendering the outcome with his friends to God, and vacuuming out the emotional debris associated with release of the past-life event. Then he shifted his perspective, which enabled him to see himself in a new way, identify what he wanted to change in himself, and determine a way to heal.

The irony of this issue arising at the same time Robert edited this part of the manuscript confirms the omniscient perspective and divine timing of Source to help us at exactly the right time and in ways that are impossible for us to see from our standard limited view.

Evaluating Your Perspective

If you are wondering about your perspective and whether you need to revise it, observe the following occasions in your life and pose the following series of questions.

> ➢ When you are having a difficult moment, ask yourself:

- Is this experience working for me?

If you answer no, then congratulate yourself for your powerful awareness and knowing that now is the time for you to activate a personal change.

> ➢ Then ask:

- "When I experienced this situation in the past, did I merely manage and, thus, perpetuate the condition?"

- "How can I use the situation to now see a larger view of what is really transpiring?"

- "How else can I shift my viewpoint and look at the situation in a different way?"

Usually the first and easiest step is to actually reverse how you have always seen the challenge. If you look at something as work, now look at it as play. If it is hard, address it as being easy. If it is a problem, see it as an opportunity to work out a new and better solution. If it seems impossible to heal, look at it as an opportunity to remove barriers to healing.

➢ Finally ask:

- "How can I (or we) change or even overcome and improve?"

- "What fears are blocking me (or us) from seeing this challenge as an opportunity?"

Try this idea and see the improvement it will make for you. With enough practice and spiritual growth, you will expand your perspective and see increasingly more options.

32: PHYSICAL AND SPIRITUAL HEALING

In everyday life, problems get our attention, are difficult to ignore, and can be great motivators to take action. First floor occurrences will continue to need repairing, replacing, or maintaining, and not all of our decisions or efforts will produce the desired results. In the following poem, God is saying that this is good, that what appears to be tribulations are really temporary trials, and that what we perceive as problematic has potential to be beneficial.

I asked God to take away my pain.
God said, No.
It is not for me to take away, but for you to give it up.

~

I asked God to make my handicapped child whole.
God said, No.
Her spirit is whole, her body is only temporary.

~

I asked God to grant me patience.
God said, No.
Patience is a by-product of tribulations;
it isn't granted, it is earned.

~

I asked God to give me happiness.
God said, No.
I give you blessings. Happiness is up to you.

~

I asked God to spare me pain.
God said, No.
Suffering draws you apart from worldly cares
and brings you closer to me.

~

I asked God to make my spirit grow.
God said, No.
You must grow on your own, but I will prune you,
to make you fruitful.

~

I asked for all things that I might enjoy life.
God said, No.
I will give you life so that you may enjoy all things.

~

I ask God to help me LOVE others, as much as he loves me.
God said ... Ahhhh, finally you have the idea.

—Claudia Minden Weisz (mother of a Rett Syndrome child)

> *We seem to require pain or discomfort in order to know what we need to work on.*

The t/Truth is: In our personal lives, we seem to require pain or discomfort in order to know what we need to work on. If we were totally comfortable, we would be unaware of a need to heal anything. If everyone were wonderful, our buttons would not get pushed, and there would not be a catalyst for our improvement.

Earth is uniquely designed to help us heal. However, we do not consciously want these

> *Life management postpones healing.*

difficulties, and we try to avoid or be prematurely rid of them, both in others and ourselves. With intentional effort, we learn ego management skills to cope with, accept, deny, withdraw, avoid, blame, or in some other way handle our issues. But life management postpones healing. God's Truth is that we, at the soul level, have the inherent ability to proclaim, "My problems are healed and released," and they will instantly disappear. However, this potential has not yet manifested for us due to our lack of understanding and our

> *It is helpful to understand the origin of our karma and how that affects our relationships and issues, but it is not essential. We only need to learn how life is structured and how best to respond in ways that promote soul growth.*

ego-based, low-vibration frequencies.

ॐ Most of us prolong this condition of operating at lower energies because we do not understand that past-life karmic experiences create present life challenges. Learning the connection between present and past life issues can nudge us to investigate this fact and the energetic tools available to release karma. Once we have utilized the Three Pillars of Transformation, the next most fundamental and beneficial approaches to healing are for us to reinterpret our difficulties and energetically clear our programmed thoughts and unwanted emotions. It is helpful to understand the origin of our karma and how that affects our relationships and issues, but it is not essential. We only need to learn how life is structured and how best to respond in ways that promote soul growth.

The following two stories illustrate these principles.

> Dick and his wife, Dora, had a young daughter, Beth, with emotional challenges. She was to begin kindergarten in a few months, and they were concerned that she would be placed in a special needs classroom because of her behavior. They were doing everything they knew how to do to change her conduct so she could avoid that educational classification and stigma. As most caring parents would do, they had been focusing on controlling and moderating her outbursts by trying to help her develop self-control, understand their expectations, and learn more appropriate social skills. Nothing seemed to help, and they were feeling desperate.

During a session with D'Ann, Dick learned that the emotional displays were necessary because Beth had brought karmic, disturbed energies into this life that needed to be released. He understood that if he and Dora changed their approach to their daughter's behavior, she would actually heal. Guidance encouraged them to provide a safe, convenient place and appropriate items, toys, or props that would assist her to move the energies out of her system. Anything she was interested in doing would work well, they were told. She could kick or throw a ball against a wall, pound her fists on a bed or cushion, run around their basement, jump on an indoor trampoline, or hit a punching ball. Dick and Dora could ask her what she felt like doing and provide a way to make it work. She needed to release every time she overreacted. She could go on her own to the safe place and do the activity as long as she wanted. The parents took the recommendation and set up an appropriate place and materials for their daughter.

A few months later, Beth was able to successfully handle a traditional classroom, and her behavior at home was almost normal. She was using the safe place less and less often.

~ ~ ~

Sidney incarnated in this life to not only clear karma but also to develop his gifts to inspire, serve, and assist others. One of his present life challenges is excessive responsibility. He is the state president of a large nonprofit organization that fund-raises and provides for needy families. He used to work fifty to sixty hours a week, had little time for his personal life, and was lacking in vitality outside of work, much to his family's dismay.

Once Sydney began an energetic spiritual path, he focused on clearing his responsibility issue. He looked for areas in his work life where he could reduce or eliminate his involvement, and he withdrew from some national boards. He practiced surrendering and forgiving, and he gave himself permission to release his deepest emotions. He committed to improved communication and cooperation in working through his issues on the job and at home.

All of this change and effort took time and determination, but he is reaping great rewards. He now works thirty to forty hours a week and is even more effective than before. He cannot explain how it is possible to work less and accomplish more, but he is delighted. He is especially happy that his personal and family life have also significantly improved.

ॐ Cutting back on responsibilities that cause us to be unbalanced can be helpful or necessary, but we need to also make other changes and improvements. Frequently saying no to others or our duties without consideration for the well being of ourselves and others is not a healing position but another ego management technique. But taking steps to reassess, reprioritize, and readjust old life patterns and responsibilities will promote congruency.

It is precisely at the point in our life when things appear and feel the bleakest, most critical, and most painful that we are being offered a prime opportunity to clear a specific issue. This is a signal that it is finally time to face and release the internal emotional baggage that has been restricting our growth, a time when we can jump-start healing by enlarging our perspectives and interpretations of life's difficulties. When we remove emotional baggage, we drive the momentum of healing and see that releasing charged emotional energies is a key to our spiritual growth.

~ ~ ~

> *When things appear and feel the bleakest, most critical, and most painful, we are being offered a prime opportunity to clear a specific issue.*

Almost all people have come on earth to heal, and we attract soul-healing needs at an early age well before we are able to consciously choose our wants as adults. When we pray for relief, understanding, or to be spared from the difficult experience and yet nothing improves, we often feel that our prayers are not being answered. This is a logical ego conclusion, but it is incorrect. As so aptly stated in the poem a few pages earlier, if we need a specific setup experience to help us discharge and heal energetic debris from our system, God is not likely to give us a

> *Almost all people have come on earth to heal, and we attract soul-healing needs at an early age well before we are able to consciously choose our wants as adults.*

reprieve or miracle. Our soul scripted plan of work takes priority over our conscious desires.

~ ~ ~

Healing is a vast and ancient topic that has been addressed through folk medicine, home remedies, and old wives' tales in every society throughout time. There have always been accidents and illness that have necessitated remedial measures, and people have sought healing for obvious physical, emotional, or mental symptoms, pain, and trauma. Historical procedures originated from inspiration and trial-and-error experimentation. Then, over time, even primitive doctors recognized certain steps as being more effective, and these became the standard treatments. Whether these were based on mystical faith, plant-based remedies, biological research, or scientific advances depended on the nature of societal beliefs and the available technology.

The classic American allopathic medical model has followed the path of technology and pharmaceutical chemistry, but does not yet recognize that illness has an energetic dimension. The scientific, first floor canon requires observation, investigation, and research. In order for modern Western doctors to change, new processes need to be controlled and results must be replicated in dependable, laboratory fashion, including the use of double-blind studies.

All too often, prescription medicines are touted as the latest and greatest fix for managing conditions or diseases. Yet after some years, large-scale, unpredicted, detrimental consequences have prodded or forced the medical/pharmaceutical industry to either modify or reverse the earlier protocol. Class action suits have resulted from the victims suffering serious, critical, or fatal side effects. Even foods are subject to the back-and-forth reversal of medical opinions. For example, avocados have long been considered healthy to eat. Then, sometime during the early years of Americans obsessing about cholesterol levels, doctors said to avoid them because they are high in saturated fat. Now, many physicians are again suggesting eating avocados because they are deemed to be a healthy food that provides good cholesterol.

In spite of contradictory medical opinions and practices, we still benefit from science. If we are injured in an accident, we need to get to a hospital, have x-rays taken, broken bones set, infections treated, stitches and sutures placed, or whatever procedures emergency medical personnel define. For this reason, energetic healing will likely not eliminate a need for allopathic treatment—at least in the current societal paradigm.

Ideally, however, medical technology and healing energy will blend to create the new holistic medical model of

> *Ideally, medical technology and healing energy will blend to create the new holistic medical model of the future.*

the future. Emerging modalities, techniques, and technological breakthroughs are moving us into an ever-expanding world of possibilities in every facet of our lives, especially in healing. While these advancements might strengthen the belief of some that only science has the answers to good health, in modern societies many holistic practitioners and patients prefer the perspective of a connection between body, mind, and spirit. A growing number of people accept that, instead of relying so exclusively on pharmaceuticals, it is to our ultimate benefit to clear medical conditions and symptoms by addressing energy flow in the body. As energy healings become increasingly more common, accepted, and recognizably effective, holistic treatments, including those based on soul-related energy, will become more readily available.

~ ~ ~

The first story below is about significant physical healing, and the second is of emotional improvement. Both are the result of energy work, and both helped to clear karmic issues.

> Abby was having long-term, painful, and serious stomach difficulties. Her doctor recommended surgery, but she wanted to avoid that if possible. Seeking alternative, holistic answers, she met with D'Ann for the first time.
>
> The issues that came up revealed that Abby had an intense desire to please others as well as a fear of how they would react to her. These energies were karmically based and intensified by other present life factors to a crisis point, peaking and harvesting in order to be released. Abby was also told about the connection between her emotional life crisis and the resulting physical symptoms, a relationship that she had not been able to see on her own.
>
> Two hours later, after that session, Abby became quite physically ill. She assumed she had the flu. Primarily throwing up, she did not realize her stomach was cooperating with the shift in healing energy and was actually detoxifying. The symptoms lasted for a week. After that, Abby was physically healed and no longer required surgery.

In addition, Abby knew that she had energetically released

her issues, a situation that she would have liked to discuss with her physician even though his view was strictly allopathic. She also began to be more forthright, standing up for herself and speaking her t/Truth, and noticing when she ignored her own feelings, opinions, or needs in order to please others. Her new approach might have rocked a few boats, but she did not let potential or actual unpleasant reactions stop her very often anymore. In essence, she was better able to keep her emotional plate clean.

~ ~ ~

Missy was a lovely, kind, and gentle person who was married to a doctor. Her life focus was almost completely and constantly on what she could do to help others. This worked well for everyone except her. As a result of sacrificing her happiness, she also lost her enthusiasm for life and accrued much anger and frustration that made her extremely depressed.

Based on guidance, D'Ann encouraged Missy to do regular physical exercise to move the disturbed emotions out of her system. Because she owned a stationary exercise bicycle, she decided to use that whenever she could, and worked out about thirty minutes a day.

Within two months, Missy was feeling greatly improved, and a few friends had even commented on the brighter look in her eyes. Being very careful to take baby steps, she was also able to reform her behavior and speak up for herself. She still helped others but not as constantly or intensely as before. This gave

her more opportunities to do what she really
wanted to do in her own life.

~ ~ ~

Starting with René Descartes in the 1600s, the scientific
medical model has held that the body works like a machine,
while the soul, being non-material, does not follow the laws of
nature. Today, fortunately, we generally interpret a person as
more than a body machine that, when sick, needs fixing. The
spiritual view extends beyond correcting a physical ailment or
mental/emotional condition, and addresses both the inner and
outer health and life of a person. We acknowledge healing as an
endeavor that encompasses improvement in any facet of our
lives.

This comprehensive perspective reveals a more complete,
holistic system of attitudes and beliefs that motivates us to
consider a fuller scope and range of possible factors when
assessing an ailing person's condition. These factors include
emotions, areas of life frustration, life style influences, education
and employment satisfaction, physical and psychological needs,
religious or spiritual perspectives, karmic effects, and life
situations. Such a broad view provides a high-level examination
greater than what we can achieve with any single *modality*,[99]
whether based on ancient traditions or the most modern scientific
development.

The holistic health model is based on our relationship with
Source and our recognition that each and every person is a
unique and prime participant in the whole life equation. As we
perceive this equality among all people and viewpoints, we see
that the doctor—or any other authority figure for that matter—is

---

[99] ***modality:*** a particular healing practice, such as massage, reiki, or energy
healing

no longer the exclusive expert with all of the knowledge and answers based only on limited scientific research and symptomatic variables.

🕉 With this broader perspective, we can then assume our privilege and responsibility to be our own patient advocate and have a better, more open exchange of respect, rapport, and information between physician and patient that allows for a more effective diagnosis and treatment.

> *Healing is more art than science.*

People on both sides of the stethoscope can realize that healing is more art than science. Providentially, more conventionally trained physicians are coming to new realizations and accepting this viewpoint. Some are even endorsing these other complementary, alternative, and integrative healing approaches.

Incorporating multi-dimensional modalities allows us to address individual and exceptional conditions, challenges, or symptoms in ways not available through allopathic medicine alone. Because multi-dimensional approaches are not limited by scientific studies, we are able to access much more information from higher, non-physical realms. We can then interpret and address additional healing possibilities with a more complete, thorough, and subtle energy field.

The healings I've seen in my practice throughout the years extend far beyond the realm of typical medical and physical potential. The following topics are a brief sampling of successes even after a single session:

- Energy shifts that occasionally result in immediate intuitive breakthroughs that enabled some clients to hear guidance and see auras, non-physical colors, and spiritual guides and beings.

- More commonly, improvement or clearing of physical conditions that include back pain; curled toes from childhood polio; allergies (one woman was finally able to have her own puppy); infertility; asthma; painful joints; dizziness; sciatica; cancers; Bell's palsy; and expeditious recovery from surgeries.

- Healing of a wide variety of additional concerns: addictions; anorexia; anxiety; bashfulness; breaking hair; difficulty concentrating; depression; fears; hate; panic attacks; rage; sociopathic, bipolar, and obsessive compulsive disorders; and unfaithfulness. One woman was no longer a shopaholic.

When karmic energy causes an emotional/mental issue and/or physical symptom, removing the karma improves or clears the concern to whatever extent is possible and most appropriate for each person's spiritual healing and soul growth. The healing process then shifts

> *When karmic energy causes an emotional/mental issue and/or physical symptom, removing the karma improves or clears the concern to whatever extent is possible and most appropriate.*

from the exclusively physical, medical realm to being under the guidance of the Higher Self. Personal initiative, efforts, and consistency are still under the conscious mental and physical worlds of influence and responsibility, but the Higher Self, with its subtle yet powerful wisdom and energy, determines the degree of improvement. Therefore, this fuller scope of healing includes each unique soul history, timing during this life, intent, actions, and spiritual connection, as well as karmic and physical needs.

ॐ When we treat a person energetically, we must always keep in mind that wellness and

> *Wellness and energy healings are not just about the alleviation of symptoms. ... The scope of karmic coverage also includes causative agents and issues.*

energy healings are not just about the alleviation of symptoms. Even if a specific concern is addressed and disappears, the scope of karmic coverage also includes causative agents and issues. Because each person is so unique, not everyone with a similar symptom or condition will experience the same healing order or results.

To actualize the greatest benefit, we must be ready to hear

and accept our t/Truth and make changes in our life. We might need to be courageous, take responsibility for our issues, and/or be willing to finally make difficult decisions. If we are not ready to face the implicated problem or are closed or skeptical, we will block the release of the generating energies and prevent ourselves from healing.

~ ~ ~

Beliefs are powerful and limiting. Believing that an unscientific energetic modality cannot possibly be effective will assure that it is not. Because complementary healing processes are not based on scientific research, it is extremely easy for ego to discount and reject them. This next example shows what often happens when one person wants to change someone else who has a closed mind.

> *Beliefs are powerful and limiting. Believing that an unscientific energetic modality cannot possibly be effective will assure that it is not.*

Burt had been on a spiritual path for many years. His wife, Sylvia, was completely turned off to the whole idea. Their marriage was in serious difficulty because of many factors. Burt had received so much insight, understanding, and benefit from his sessions with D'Ann that he gifted Sylvia with an appointment. He had hoped that she would learn some important ideas that would open her mind, shift her attitude, and begin better communication between them. She resisted the offer for months but finally gave in only to stop Burt's persistence.

Because Sylvia was not ready to change her life or hear a broader interpretation of what was happening, she remained closed, agreed with nothing that was said, and felt it had been a waste of her time and Burt's money.

D'Ann had recorded the session, as she always does. When Burt listened to the recording, with Sylvia's permission, he validated the t/Truth that Sylvia was unwilling to see, hear, or face any idea other than what she believed or had already preconceived.

The old adage, "You can lead a horse to water but you can't make him drink," is applicable to many things, even energy work. If a person is not interested in learning, growing, or accepting new ideas, they will not give time, energy, or thought to anything out of their realm of comfort. Sylvia will not change her life until or unless she is ready to. Their marriage ended several months later.

~ ~ ~

Humans are eternal energy beings in a physical body for a brief time. For this reason,

> *Some people die more spiritually healed than they had ever physically lived.*

physical health, while important to life on earth, is less important than spiritual development. Some people die more spiritually healed than they had ever physically lived.

When the body improves after an energy treatment, it is a blessed benefit of physical and spiritual healing. It is a sign that the original energetic cause of the condition had, in some way, been connected to unseen or even karmic challenges that the person was ready to address and release. It helps for us to recognize and accept that everything important serves us in some way, even if we have no answers as to why it occurred, why it hurt so much, or how it went away.

Therefore, it is always wiser to place no expectations or assumptions concerning the outcome of an energy healing or any other spiritual activity, event, or situation. The results are often different from what we might have wanted or hoped for because restoration happens at such a deep level.

True healing of any kind gets to the fundamental root. There is a time lag on earth for our external, physical form to react and reflect

> *Healing takes time, and sometimes we understand it best and appreciate it most only in retrospect.*

a difference relative to our inner, soulful change. An example is that of a pregnant woman; no matter how spiritually advanced she is, her body will typically need a full, nine-month gestation period to birth a baby.

Likewise, physical, emotional, energetic, and karmic healing takes time, and sometimes we understand it best and appreciate it most only in retrospect. With full karmic healing, the end result might prove to be more significant, better, or more complete than we could have originally anticipated, especially from the perspective of illness.

Finally, when you seek spiritual healing, remember that some energy modalities, such as cranial sacral, kinesiology, and hypnosis, might be especially helpful in improving certain physical conditions. Find out the primary specialty of a healer before booking a session.

33: HEALING INDICATORS

All healing is safest when accomplished incrementally. We

grow and learn to eat, walk, and speak at a small yet steady pace. Once in a while, a breakthrough or miracle occurs that propels a person into a totally different level from where he or she was, but that is the exception to the norm. We can usually manage and adjust our lives more easily with small changes that allow us to live our normal life without feeling threatened or overwhelmed.

Similarly, we need to grow into an experience. If we were unexpectedly presented with a doctorate degree in a subject for which we had no training, we would not have the background and knowledge to be effective with it and we would not favorably compare with someone who had worked hard to earn his or her degree. This explains the frequent failure of the lottery to successfully and permanently change lives. Most large winners spend their entire prize within two years of receiving it. Many end up bankrupt because they do not have the financial consciousness or money management skills to wisely spend and invest money for the long term.

Yet, many people seem to have a lottery-like, make-it-better-now attitude in regard to any kind of health concern. Healing might seem slow, frustrating, and costly, but the t/Truth is that we progress only according to what we can handle. At the same time, because time seems to be speeding up, events seem to be compacting and moments of relaxation are fleeting. In like fashion, the presence of advancing spiritual energies are enhancing the availability and potency of many healing modalities, especially those that involve working with energy, and are cultivating our ability to more fully and more quickly benefit from these higher concentrations.

As these advancing energies enter our systems, we still have to deal with emotional debris that has required us to cope with and modify our lives around their low-level vibrations. But it would not be wise for us to remove these low frequencies all at once. In the same manner as being presented with a spontaneous doctorate degree, our whole life would be thrown out of the precarious first floor balance we have worked so hard to create.

However, with patience and incremental energetic shifts, we can more easily and gradually adjust to boosts and changes in ways that promote integration and wholeness within ourselves as well as our connection with other people. As we advance in this manner, we encounter experiences and situations that serve as healing indicators, marking our progress on our journey.

> *With patience and incremental energetic shifts, we can easily and gradually adjust to shifts and changes in ways that promote integration and wholeness.*

Ron was continuously berated and verbally abused by his spouse, Mona. Whenever she felt incapable of coping with him, his actions, or inactions, she would order him to go to their basement. He had learned the hard way that it was wiser to not even comment when she behaved like that, so he would retreat with no verbal response. After only one session with D'Ann, he determined he would no longer meekly accept her dominating, insulting behavior. He would stand up for himself, even if it made her more vicious for a while.

Ron worked on healthier, more appropriate reactions to Mona's antagonism. He began to state his t/Truth with one or two comments before retreating, and he changed his escape location. Later, he more actively addressed his own concerns with her and was gradually able to have a discussion or argument before withdrawing. Over time, he began to draw personal boundaries, verbally support himself, and only rarely backed away from her.

He became more aware of being mistreated, dismissed, and/or not receiving emotional support from others as well, not just Mona. He continued to take small steps to improve his position with everyone in his life.

As overwhelming as this healing process seemed, Ron made tremendous progress with his issue in all of his relationships. D'Ann does not know how Mona accepted his more assertive behavior or if they are still married.

~ ~ ~

Sometimes others see changes in us before we do or even see changes that we miss entirely. Occasionally others might adapt or amend their behavior as a result of our efforts to heal ourselves. This next account shows incremental healing that started with one person and affected the dynamics of a whole family.

Tanya had a life issue of excessive responsibility. She was raised to always complete her obligations first before playing, relaxing, or doing something she wanted to do. Work was first. This pattern continued well into adulthood, and she raised her children to be the same way. However, her children were less compliant than she had been, and her buttons were frequently pushed by their occasionally casual behavior. Additionally, her husband did not have the same level of discipline as Tanya, and he prioritized experiences more than duties. This caused her to feel unsupported, and she carried enormous resentment that all of the housework and family management was in her lap.

Being a spiritually connected person, Tanya determined she needed to heal this issue. She surrendered everything and forgave everyone involved in her issue. These activities cleared and moderated many of her charged energies. She began to be more honest in the moment when something needed to be done and she could not easily do it or others could not help in some way. She was able to leave some tasks unfinished. She learned to avoid a project if it was someone else's responsibility. Even this new pattern alone made a profound improvement in her life. These incremental changes were not easy but became possible.

This increased the amount of time that Tanya could engage in fun activities with her family, and over time, others in the family increased their participation in home cleaning projects. Because they became more responsible for their own tasks, she felt almost no resentment, and the family shared more enjoyable experiences and social opportunities.

Just as significant was the relaxation Tanya saw in her own life. Saturday mornings used to be her chore time. Sometimes they could now be playtime, and while she was away from home, she would not feel burdened or anxious to get back to work. She was able to do some housework at other times during the week. Her heavy responsibilities were spread out over more days, were less forced, and easier to face and accomplish.

Her healing created a win-win solution for the entire family.

~ ~ ~

Everyday living generates happenings that we do not necessarily cause but are responsible to handle or fix. The more empowered we become, the more we will automatically recognize inherent potentials and benefits that stem from a problem even as we are involved with it.

> *The more empowered we become, the more we will automatically recognize inherent potentials and benefits that stem from a problem even as we are involved in it.*

Barb had finished packing her van to go on a trip. When she was ready to leave, the van would not start. The battery was dead. Fortunately, the other family car was available for a jump-start.

Barb could have complained about being inconvenienced, about having to get her hands dirty, about the fact that no one was there to help her. Instead, she realized how fortunate she was to still be at home. She reasoned that the battery could have failed on the freeway or in an inconvenient or unsafe location, that she could have needed help from strangers, that the repair could have taken hours. Even so, because the situation occurred on a Sunday morning, she assumed it would be difficult to find an open repair facility.

After starting the van, she drove to the nearest large store with an auto service department. It was open twenty-four hours a day, no one was in line, and the service clerk was available immediately. Twenty minutes later, she was on her trip with a new, extended-warranted battery that had been on sale.

Most of the time when something difficult happens, we have two choices: to look on the dark side or see a hidden advantage. Some people even say that being delayed doesn't make them late but helped them avoid the accident that didn't happen because they had not been somewhere earlier. With a spiritually healed attitude, we can look for the gift in any situation.

> *With a spiritually healed attitude, we can look for the gift in any situation.*

~ ~ ~

Indications of our healing can manifest in various ways, all of which boost us beyond our old predictable patterns.

Controlling life is no longer a goal as we continue to surrender everything to God. From this freer and less burdened position, we become more energetically congruent with Source.

In this desired condition, all of our mental, emotional, physical, and spiritual components integrate into similar and compatible views, processes, goals, and attributes. All facets of our functioning align with Source Truths to stimulate our lives and our spiritual growth.

Healing can mean that undesirable emotional states lift. Emotional scars and pains release. Internal emotions, responses, and decisions to external situations moderate and improve. We notice more personal support or feel less need to receive it. We become more easygoing and comfortable with ourselves and others. Our sense of humor improves. Self-confidence and acceptance of all that life brings us strengthens. We become more open, receptive, creative, optimistic, and empathetic. Peace and hope emerge. Fears subside. We experience more love, vitality, and joy in our life.

Healing affects our appearance and behavior. We exude more peace and happiness and could even stand taller. We might stop procrastinating and lessen other unproductive management techniques. We have more ability to successfully work with our responsibilities, accomplish more meaningful goals, and follow through with our projects. We have a larger array of response options, handle our life in more rewarding ways, and make personal decisions more easily and with improved outcomes.

Healing demonstrates its presence in practical ways. We experience fewer and less intense life challenges. Our difficult events are briefer, and we enjoy longer periods of less stressful time in between occurrences. Our relationships improve and our life dysfunctions decrease or disappear. We shift away from obsessing about money and reprioritize our financial goals so that we become free of debt, more frugal, more generous, and better at money management. We become more conscientious about our residence and workspace by cleaning and clearing clutter from closets, drawers, and shelves. We might decide to rearrange or replace furnishings, redecorate, or even move.

As we evolve, we shift our priorities. We bring forth our talents and spiritual gifts by developing new interests or rekindling our fondness for a long-forsaken hobby that brings a profound component of soul delight. We receive guidance and inspiration more often and more clearly, and we grow to understand our life more fully.

34: HEALING VARIABLES

Major factors influence healing. These include spiritual and life actions and inactions, our perspectives, decisions, and management techniques, and whether or not we choose to surrender, forgive, and vacuum. No matter what our beliefs, expectations, opinions, history, judgments, or options, we do have free will choices. We decide what to do with each of these expressions in daily life. Our decisions determine the quality and development of our present life and future lives.

Suppose two people are critically injured in a car accident. Although each survives, neither one will ever walk again. One victim turns bitter and resentful, deciding that he will never be normal and will need to rely on others for the rest of his life. "If only the accident hadn't happened!" he bemoans. His view discourages others from visiting and helping him, and maintaining such negativity will make his life even more frustrating and difficult.

The other victim is grateful to be alive, appreciative of all the support he gets, becomes involved in other's lives, and decides not to live with self-pity. This second person's outlook encourages friendship, support, and admiration. Although permanently physically debilitated in some way, this person's mental and emotional attitude might be stronger than before the accident.

In these two examples, we see that our healing variables are the decision to complain or not to complain, to be bitter or be grateful, a matter of choice so well summarized in the ditty: "Two men looked out through prison bars; one saw mud, and the other saw stars."

~ ~ ~

The following three stories introduce another variable: the decision to act or not to act.

> *We are empowered beings. There is no substitute for action.*

God wants us to remember that we are empowered beings, and that there is no substitute for action, even when we are in dire straits. Yet, even so, some people choose to rely on the security of ego consciousness, functioning under the oppressive conditions of ego control.

People who employ emotional ego management techniques in their everyday life are usually liked and respected. They give the impression that acting positive, brave, and strong is a fine course of action. And it is, as long as we also deal with our more deeply felt emotions. When we don't, our actions become pretend actions or surface actions, part of a façade that fails to heal the inner traumas. When we merely manage—rather than process out—our emotions, we allow an energetic dilemma to develop through which held-in-check toxic energies can create illness.

> Rose was a warm, loving, gentle, and positive person who *never* complained, even though she sometimes wanted to. She always focused her conversations on other people's lives, even

when she wished to also express her own feelings.

Rose's situation occurred during and after World War II, and money was tight. At age thirty-five, she married into a family with two young children who had lost their mother to pneumonia. The mother's maiden sister had wanted to marry the children's father. Because that didn't happen, Rose was under constant criticism and resentment from the mother's family after the wedding, a situation that persisted for as long as she lived because the relatives kept in close contact with the children. Rose gave birth to two children, and one of the step-siblings had a difficult time with the blended family. Rose's greatest joy came from being a talented singer in church choirs, an activity in which she had engaged since being a young woman.

Even though Rose had never smoked cigarettes, she developed cancer of the larynx (voice box) when she was only forty-five. The surgery left her with a permanent hole in her throat through which she had to breathe, speak, cough, and sneeze. She had to avoid boats, swimming, and even showers because of the danger of taking water into her lungs. Imagine how difficult her life must have been to live and raise her family without a voice—and to never sing again.

Rose used esophageal speech for the rest of her life and could only mouth the words to music. She volunteered to meet with hospital patients who had their voice boxes removed to give them comfort and encouragement. When any disappointment or challenge came along, she would usually claim, "It could be worse."

Rose lived until the age of ninety-three, finally succumbing to esophageal cancer. Even at the end of her life, when she could no longer see, hear, speak, walk, or even eat, she never complained.

As a singer and a wife and mother, Rose's throat had been her primary source of physical expression, the area of the body that holds the energy of willpower and communication, most meaningfully associated with those she especially loved dearly. When she chose never to complain, her throat became vulnerable to her energetic buildup. Under ego influence, she exerted tremendous self-discipline to stifle her significantly intense emotions and remain positive, even about the difficulties in her life. Likely, the cancer that caused her to lose her larynx as well as the cancer that finally claimed her life was energetically caused from the accumulated emotional toxins that she had felt but had suppressed in her efforts to respond so positively and optimistically to others.

~ ~ ~

Monica, a woman in her early seventies, had been married to the same man for over fifty years, at least forty-eight of which were unhappy. They had only one child, a daughter who had married, bore three children, and died of cancer in her early forties.

Monica and her husband had such a difficult

relationship that they communicated primarily through notes, each cooked their own food and did their own laundry, and rarely ended a conversation without an argument. They ignored their home, which was cluttered and disorganized.

Although Monica was living an emotionally blighted life, she took excellent physical care of her mind and body, and was seeking more understanding of her life and spiritual healing from many sources. She had been a client of D'Ann's for many years, and it was frequently recommended that she reduce her stress level at home and make changes in her life. Monica, however, still listened to her resistant ego and was not willing or was too overwhelmed at home to make personal changes.

Because Monica felt unable to apply spiritual understandings to her daily life, her stress level did not improve. D'Ann's guidance even encouraged her to leave her husband and the chaos and tension of their home for a significant period of time. Even a long vacation would help.

However, Monica maintained that she was not able to leave her husband even though she received that message through a healer. She held on to her good reasons for staying with him: he was older than she, and she was concerned that he was mentally deteriorating; she had nowhere else to live and didn't have funds to live separately; she could not afford a long vacation and didn't have enough clothes to visit friends for an extended period of time; and so on. Wintering in a warmer climate was not a workable solution, and she couldn't even imagine getting away for one weekend.

One winter, Monica fell on the icy sidewalk in front of her home and broke a hip. This forced her to finally be away from her husband for an extended period of time, but in a nursing home rather than in a relaxing or enjoyable location. After she recuperated, she of course returned home, required therapy, and used a cane for a few years. The relationship with her husband did not improve.

In a subsequent session, guidance stated that Monica had a six-month window of opportunity during which she could still make important life changes to reduce her stress level. If she did not do so, stress would become so overwhelming that the option to improve her life would lapse.

Monica continued to live her normal life at home but within a year could no longer handle her physical and mental challenges and was unable to write checks, shop for groceries, launder her clothing, or even read books, which was her favorite pastime. She lived the rest of her life in a senior care facility for the mentally impaired.

Monica's story helps us understand the critical message that we have free will choice, but only to a degree. If we are not willing to make any changes in our life, we might get to a point where Source intervenes, often through a crisis, accident, injury, or illness. Monica's life healing setup was the broken hip that took her away from her husband for an extended time. Nothing before the accident had worked to reduce home stress. Our soul cares more about our karmic life script and is less concerned if we are happy and enjoying what is going on, or are in pain or misery. In order to progress spiritually, we must remember that there is no substitute for taking action, especially at critical times. Monica's physical fall and mental decline was an inevitable result of her free will choice of inaction.

> *Not making a decision is a decision.*

Not making a decision is a decision.

~ ~ ~

Joan had been raised in a large, extremely dysfunctional family. On her eighteenth birthday, which was Christmas day, her mother ordered her to leave home. She had several more difficult years on her own trying to make life work and developing her artistic and musical gifts. Eventually, she joined a devout spiritual organization, incorporated their teachings into her life, and meditated daily for several hours.

She married a loving and wonderful church musician, and they had two children. A few years later, without knowing anything about a life-turnaround for her mother, they unexpectedly ran into each other at a spiritual retreat and re-established a minimal relationship with both of her parents.

After becoming a mother, Joan had begun to

have flashbacks of bizarre scenes, including one of a dead body in the basement of her birth home. She had no conscious memories to relate to these terrors, only hazy and disturbing recollections.

Joan went into intense conventional therapy with a psychiatrist and realized that her upbringing had been horrendous. All of the children had suffered tremendous abuse. When she asked her siblings about the dead body in the family basement, which her siblings affirmed had been there, they were all frustrated because none of them knew anything else about the deceased person or the circumstances surrounding this morbid scene.

At that point, Joan and her husband knew they were no longer willing to have anything to do with her parents, even though her mother had supposedly changed her life. They wrote a letter to them and permanently severed any possibility of reconciliation.

When D'Ann asked Joan how she could spiritually handle the karmic ramifications of such a dramatic step, Joan replied that she and everyone in her family had probably been performing a similar drama, alternating roles back and forth, for lifetimes. Joan realized that it had to stop somewhere, sometime. For her, this was the time.

Joan and her husband had already taken the first step with the letter to her parents. They completed the healing—and eliminated future karma—by forgiving her parents.

A person would typically have an overwhelming aversion to even consider forgiving anyone, let alone their own parents, for such gross behavior. But Joan and her husband drew upon a highly evolved and spiritual view of life as an incentive to forgive her parents. As difficult as this was to accomplish, it physically, emotionally, and spiritually liberated Joan from her past. To maximize her healing potential, she added cranial sacral work and crystal healings to her treatment regimen.

35: COMMITMENT TO HEALING

Whenever we commit to anything spiritual—whether to evolve our life, learn a quality like giving more freely, or undertake an activity like healing—Universe quickly responds by presenting a healing setup, a challenge, usually emotional or financial, that is perfectly and uniquely designed for us. The earlier story in the section on forgiveness about the minister and the mutilated flowerbed demonstrates this process.

The obvious, outward reaction to a life-empowering claim resembles a homework assignment. We need opportunities to practice and apply more advanced energetic concepts, work toward spiritual goals, and prove whether we mean what we say about our commitment. Merely reading another book or taking a class rarely sets this response in motion.

We learn more readily and completely when we commit to a life change, knowing that the energy of change will come to us from invisible sources, according to our life blueprint, which, as you remember, is our karmic script. Then it is up to us to watch what happens and respond in proactive, energetically healing ways. Knowing this aspect of the life blueprint concept ahead of time allows us to ironically smile through our discomfort when the setup arises. It also helps when we keep in mind that talk is easy—that it's easy to say what we're going to do or would do under certain circumstances—but it takes action and follow-through to actually improve life.

Spiritual Experimentation

🕉 If you want to experiment with any of the spiritual tenets in this book, this is the place to begin, trusting the words you can readily see on the pages in front of you. Learning more is always helpful, but you will only develop when you draw upon the invisible energies around you to make the changes you say you want make in your own life.

> Clara decided to pursue a spiritual path. Although she didn't have the money in her budget to spend at that time, she booked an appointment with a healer near her home. She had the session on a Wednesday night and used a charge card for payment. Immediately afterward, she scheduled a few more sessions because she recognized how beneficial the therapy was for her.
>
> The next day, Clara had car trouble. The repair bill was over $1500, and this created a serious financial predicament for her. Although the following day, Friday, was payday, she did not have the funds to fully pay for even the first appointment. How could she possibly cover the repair bill too? This seemed like a visible sign that she should not yet pursue spiritual growth through the healing sessions.
>
> But Clara also understood that this could be a test to see how determined she was to prioritize a new path that could turn her life

around. Unsure of what to do, she forced herself to spiritually reprioritize her life, trusting that the benefits of this shift would be invaluable and worthwhile, no matter how difficult it might originally be to enact.

Because she used a budget, Clara had been regularly paying her bills, so she reviewed her expenditures and cut out nonessentials. After extensive examination of her finances, she decided to temporarily postpone additional healing sessions. She did not give up her interest or determination to follow a spiritual path but concluded fiscal responsibility was also part of her commitment. Over the next several years, she continued to seek spiritual growth by reading many helpful books and applying t/Truths in her life to the best of her ability.

Clara made the best decision she felt she could by combining her prioritized fiscal responsibility into her goal of spiritual growth. Some people might need to make that same choice for a period of time. A first floor view embraces financial responsibility, and Clara acknowledged that it is prudent to clear up debt and spend wisely.

> *To an advanced soul, abundance is not a goal but a byproduct of our full commitment to a spiritually vital and rewarding life. ... Abundance might appear as financial wealth or in other forms such as love, relationships, adventure, humanitarian endeavors, or creative expression.*

Clara's decision to cancel her appointments was not a

mistake according to conventional wisdom, but it did minimize and delay the potential for her dramatic personal growth. This concept might be hard to grasp with a mind powered by 110 energy, but the fiftieth floor view knows that money challenges will ease when we support and follow spiritual understandings. To an advanced soul, abundance is not a goal but a byproduct of our full commitment to lead a spiritually vital and rewarding life. Spiritually committed persons also know that abundance might appear as financial wealth or in other forms such as love, relationships, adventure, humanitarian endeavors, or creative expression.

To activate the highest power of the healing blueprint energies in her life, Clara would initially have kept her appointment and paid a portion of all of her bills on that next payday. The method for transforming our ego life into a life of spiritual growth is not about becoming irresponsible, recklessly spending money on things or any spiritual process available, nor is it about not paying bills, but on prioritizing spiritual growth over the action of bill paying—and this is the pledge that Clara took at her decisive moment. Ideally, she would attend more healing sessions because they are the means for her to fulfill her energetic pledge. She could also have practiced more prudence by spacing the sessions further apart, paying for them over a longer period of time, and perhaps asking for a reduced rate.

With this plan, she would have been financially over-committed for a while, but her life blueprint would see that her financial situation would ease. This change could take a few more paydays or it could begin to happen right away in some unexpected manner.

By following through on her commitment to heal, Clara would receive some boost that would compensate her to a degree for the present hardship she incurred when reprioritizing her life.

She might notice needed items on sale, find and use coupons, receive a surprise refund, or learn that she could reduce a regular bill, such as an insurance premium or telephone contract. When tapped into these higher, invisible Source energies, she could unexpectedly receive a pay raise, promotion, or a new job opportunity. She might find that her money would seem to stretch further than it had before. Someone could offer a loan with little or no interest or give a gift of needed items. The possibilities of abundance are truly boundless.

If Clara keeps her original spiritual promise and responsibly prioritizes spiritual growth above everything else, she will have passed this particular monetary test. Her finances will become more stable and likely more abundant.

Source Support

ॐ When we make the commitment to heal, Source supports us by first addressing our spiritual needs over our conscious desires, such as for money. In a sense, humans are each a large magnet sending out karmically charged energies. The results that come to us are in direct response to the energies we emit. This is why we continuously and unconsciously attract the people, events, and circumstances that Source knows we need to further our soul growth. When we respond according to our t/Truth instead of

> *To resolve our dilemmas, we need to be aware of and clear out—vacuum—our tainted energies, which will then stop attracting those specific challenges to us.*

management, things get worse or harder, to offer greater emotional release for healing. The better life manager we are, the more intensely we need to be triggered to overwhelm our coping skills, which will diminish ego authority.

So these programmed impulses bring challenges that are really opportunities, incentives, and motivations to release old issues. To resolve our dilemmas, we need to be aware of and clear out—vacuum—our tainted energies, which will then stop attracting those specific challenges to us.

ॐ Once we know about the karmic magnetic attraction of life's blueprint and the resulting setups, we have at least three advantages when faced with a challenging situation:

1   In spite of our emotional reactions, we will recognize that we are being offered something beneficial, intended to serve us in some way.

2   We will know we need the dilemma in order to stimulate healing of an issue.

3   We will understand that we apparently are ready to heal that issue because it is peaking and demanding our attention.

In short, we will comprehend, as presented earlier in the section on Relationships, that important things happen *for* us, not *to* us.

> *First floor scenes and challenges are illusions that we conveniently take at face value with no awareness of the causes that form them.*

Our grasp of these concepts is essential in order for us to reinterpret life's difficulties and spur ourselves to release karmic energies. This knowledge will help prevent us from repeatedly handling things in our old and ineffective ways. But it is still up to us to recognize what is happening and make wiser decisions.

🕉 As explained earlier in the section about Fear, appearances are deceiving. All our ego interpretations, mechanisms, emotions, and responses have been generated from insufficient, three-dimensional input. When using that low-level perspective, we only see and work with the results of the blueprint energies that are creating our physical world. From the highest Truth, first floor scenes and challenges are illusions that we conventionally take at face value with no awareness of the causes that form them.

When we reinterpret each situation and energetically cooperate with it by doing what we know to do in order to heal, our experiences and manifestations will amend and prosper. This idea resembles asking a magician to perform a different act. He or she will be happy to do so, but it will take different behind-the-scene techniques to provide the new result. Addressing the invisible, causative energies and clearing them will reduce the strength of our magnet. We will heal and gradually strengthen our

> *What we are energetically working on to heal during a dark night is the exact opposite of what it looks and feels like.*

ability to trust God's unseen, beneficial energy more than the world's physical appearances.

🕉 Our awareness, understanding, and trust in our life blueprint are necessary because our conscious conclusions about difficult, everyday life experiences are not accurate enough. It is the contrast between ego night and Source Light that we don't yet understand.

Ironically, ego night refers to that which we can see in the spiritually darkened physical world, and Source Light is the energy we can't see but is constantly with us and guiding us *when life isn't working go to*

toward our higher good. What we are energetically working to heal during an ego challenge is the exact opposite of what it looks and feels like.

For example:

- Dealing with death means new life awaits.

- Feeling powerless means empowerment awaits.

- Feeling isolated means unity awaits.

- Feeling out of control means the ability to trust God awaits.

- Feeling betrayed means karmic freedom through forgiveness in that relationship awaits.

- Feeling poverty means abundance awaits.

- Feeling fear means greater spiritual attributes await.

The message in all of these examples—and there are others too—is that whatever conclusions ego prods us to jump to about our challenges, God wants us to turn them inside out and discover what is actually occurring spiritually.

> *Whatever conclusions ego prods us to jump to about our challenges, God wants us to turn them inside out and discover what is actually occurring spiritually.*

~ ~ ~

good news

ॐ Occasionally we experience situations, not designed primarily for our own healing, in which we are called on to be a more passive participant. These difficult situations essentially involve someone else, but we can permit or find ourselves pulled into the drama to some degree. The intensity of our response determines who will

> *The intensity of our response determines who will most benefit from the setup, us or the other person for whom we play a temporary role.*

most benefit from the setup, us or the other person for whom we play a temporary role.

When we remain connected to Source, trust that all is well, and reinterpret what is happening through spiritual understandings, we remain true to our blueprint even when we don't know about it. This enables us to see the absurdity of the situation when someone acts up, throws a tantrum, or behaves strangely. If we genuinely maintain a calm or clear response or have only a brief or mild emotional reaction, it indicates that we are a guest actor in someone else's show.

> D'Ann once phoned Lulu, a well-known metaphysical practitioner, to gain some professional information even though they had never spoken to each other before. Lulu's manner was offensive, condescending, impatient, and disinterested. D'Ann found this peculiar response so weird that she actually held the receiver in front of her face, looked into it, and softly said to herself, "What in the world is this all about?" Then she hung up as quickly as possible and asked Source for clarity.

Guidance said that Lulu's response was like a navigational buoy to show how crucial it is to be open, kind, and genuine to everyone regardless of what else is transpiring. It also highlighted the need to communicate what is appropriate for the situation at hand; for example, Lulu could have stated that it was an inconvenient time to talk and asked to delay the conversation until later.

Evaluating the situation from Lulu's perspective, D'Ann surmised that her call at that moment had apparently unintentionally pushed a button for Lulu, probably ego defensiveness, and had served D'Ann is a less obvious but equally important way.

Experiential Markers

ॐ Another component of a healing blueprint is *experiential markers* or *signposts*,[100] which we recognize by their unexpected, exaggerated, and strange appearance that stands out from our norm. These markers provide an opportunity to:

- measure, according to the intensity of our emotional reaction, how much we have already healed;

- enlarge our range of reaction and behavior possibilities;

- remind us of essential life elements; and/or

- sample expanding energetic sensitivities and awareness that are beginning to manifest as we close

---

[100] *experiential markers* or *signposts:* events that when spiritually interpreted, signal progressive healing

in on a new vibrational level.

To understand this, think about driving a car with a standard transmission up a steep mountain road, an activity that requires you to downshift the vehicle into a lower gear and consumes more gasoline. Once you crest the peak, the car will increase speed and pick up momentum so that

> *Life nearly always presents us with a downshift before we receive the next major boost, accomplishment, or*

you can shift back into a higher gear and reduce your gas consumption. In spiritual healing, the mountain represents a significant life challenge that forces you to downshift and exert more energy just to get over the hump. On the other side of the crest, you can re-employ the natural force of gravity to help you regain momentum and regain a boost from rolling smoothly along again.

🕉 Life nearly always presents us with a downshift before we receive the next major boost, accomplishment, or breakthrough. This is a healing characteristic of our life blueprint. When we address a problem, like the loss of momentum when going uphill, we can energetically promote its removal and place ourselves at the top of the mountain. Arriving at this new, elevated vibrational frequency shifts us into a more advanced level of life operation. Each experience bolsters us to a higher dimension with more efficient flow and vitality. After one or two episodes of downshifting, followed by improved and increased life movement and satisfaction, we will feel less consumed by our difficulties and more focused on potential upcoming benefits.

While in the uphill, downshift situations, however, we are often caught in a first floor perspective. We do not seem to know any specific information about the difficulty. We do not know what to do, how long it will last, or where we will be when we are past the trouble. We do not have any practical answers—all we know is what we can see from the first floor. Yet, we can observe and remember this patterned aspect of our life design, and that can help us through each new tribulation even as we continue to function, the best we can, without any immediate answers.

> Cassandra, a single mom, is a powerful, intuitively gifted woman who had a wretched childhood with verbal abuse, no emotional support, and intense dramas. Once she embraced her soul path as an adult, her whole life began to open up. She discovered her spiritual mission and was able to intuitively serve others through her profession.

> However, every month or two, Cassandra has a painful, overwhelming crisis in her life that knocks her out of commission for several days or even a few weeks. Several times, she has unexpectedly become extremely ill and unable to work. Her daughter was critically ill and she needed to take time off work to nurse her. Her home was broken into three times and money and valuables were stolen by, she was certain, a family member. And she was sued by a neighbor over a petty dispute. Although she could see this pattern, she could not understand the need for or purpose of the dilemmas.

> After learning about the downshift pattern to attain higher frequencies, she could appreciate

and see the progress she was making, and she began to work more cooperatively with the intermittent challenges.

She now anticipates a noticeable boost in her personal and especially her professional life just on the other side of each setback, and she always notices a spiritual breakthrough or significant inspiration for new ideas in treating her clients. This understanding enables her to get through these episodes, which are becoming shorter, further apart, and more continuously beneficial. Each breakthrough seems more inspired, effective, delightful, and powerful than the previous one.

~ ~ ~

ॐ All life-impacting events happen according to divine timing. We might never understand why it takes so long to find the best life partner, a better job, clarity to make a major decision; why we feel stuck in unwanted circumstances; or why we have accepted the assignment to care for an invalid who is in severe pain and wants to die but lingers for months or years. These kinds of life experiences are in our karmic life blueprint and serve our soul in some essential way. It is less important for us to work on finding answers for our questions and more beneficial to, as neutrally as possible, accept what is happening.

> *It is less important for us to work on finding answers for our questions and more beneficial to, as neutrally as possible, accept what is happening.*

We need to recall that we signed on for the challenge. It is

what it is. Forcing our conscious will in life resembles the constant irritation of a nail file wearing us down. Our resistance is not helpful and wastes energy, effort, and time.

> ➢ To handle these unwanted situations, trust the unseen energies around you, keep praying, and ask for guidance, strength, resolution, wisdom, support, relief, understanding, divine intervention, and blessings.
>
> ➢ Remember to focus on gratitude and use the Three Pillars of Transformation: surrender, forgive, and vacuum.
>
> ➢ Do things differently, seek support groups or healing modalities, and get readings.

You might see only minimal options, but sometimes even a small shift can reap great benefits.

~ ~ ~

🕉 Because issues are spiritually and energetically mandated, the larger perspective and Truth of life's structure is out of sight, blocked from our conscious awareness. This inaccessibility allows only ego to control and manage our life, and with helpful additional response options seemingly not available, we often resort to the counter-balancing technique of rebelling from an issue.

> Paul came into this life programmed as an excessive giver. He not only wants to help others, he is compelled to give, not financially so much as in reaching out to others and doing whatever he can to help them. He might grocery shop for someone, take someone else on a needed errand, and help someone else with a work project. He enjoys socializing

with others and helping them, yet he wishes he didn't have to give so thoroughly and so often. But his mandated issue is like a switch that is always on and, because there is no dimmer switch, his only other option is to turn the switch off.

When Paul turns the switch off, he withdraws from people by regularly taking long, hot baths. Although a bath is normally beneficial to the body and the spirit, it is mainly a management tool for Paul because his decision to take an unneeded bath is his way of shutting his switch off to allow freedom from responsibility for those who have come to depend on him.

When even the baths don't help him enough to counterbalance his fatigue, he rebels. He refuses requests to help others, avoids answering the phone unless it is someone who does not want something from him, stays home as much as possible, finally does something good for himself like take a nap or read a book, and doesn't talk to anyone for an extended period of time. Paul easily justifies these reactions. He says he needs rest from his burdens, and time alone helps him restore his usual coping ability.

However, Paul almost always experiences a backlash when he returns to his usual routine, a sign that the issue continues to be active in his life. Someone he could have helped and didn't might have developed a more serious need or condition. Other people might be angry with him for not being there when they needed him. He might have missed a deadline. A situation might have developed adverse consequences that he could have prevented. These repercussions agitate Paul, and he nearly always feels some remorse, guilt, or self blame even though he knows he needed time out.

Paul usually concludes that these reactions to his time away are more difficult to handle than it would have been had he just kept up his normal level of giving. He resolves to continue excessive giving, switching himself back on, because that seems easier for him in the long run.

Paul does not heal when he merely manages his issue, and temporarily withdrawing from life only prolongs his continuation in this switch-on, switch-off pattern. He does not heal because he is not open to healing. He is not interested in opening his mind to the larger understandings of energy and spiritual growth, so he has not been able to find any other workable options to improve his programming.

Help versus H-E-L-P

ॐ Another invisible concept in our spiritual blueprint involves the word "help." When we pray for help with a first floor situation, we are asking for assistance, relief, solutions,

> *Because our souls are our top priority, "help" from the fiftieth floor means that we are asking to become vibrationally boosted into further empowerment.*

improvement, or clarity. When this involves a life concern or issue, a higher dimensional process clicks into place that is different from the responses we were consciously asking for. Because our souls are our top priority, "help" from the fiftieth floor means that we are asking to become vibrationally boosted into further empowerment. We then enhance the meaning of "help" into the acronym H-E-L-P, which stands for **Heal Energetic Life Patterns**.

Universe then responds to our request by presenting a challenge—a healing setup—that appears and feels like the exact opposite of what we asked for. In the short term, life becomes more difficult, not easier, and we have to downshift to get through. But when we realize that releasing low frequencies raises our vibrational rate, just like a car engine revs up in a lower gear, we can choose to energetically cooperate with the presenting challenge by using the Three Pillars of Transformation. In this way, we will, in fact, receive soul help.

ॐ If you are not interested in or are unwilling to work with this higher level of response and involvement, then do not use the word "help" in your prayer request. Substitute a word that more specifically addresses your desire, such as being aware of an answer, more insight, relief, or something to be easily removed, solved, softened, or even stopped. This different approach will rarely trigger more challenges.

Blueprint Realities of Life's Healing Setups

It's important to remember that our life's healing blueprint is our karmic script. We can't see this configuration, but we can see its visible effects. This can be confusing because what we see as trials and tribulations are really potential blessings.

ॐ The following, therefore, is a summary listing, in general terms, of three-dimensional manifestations that typically occur according to your blueprint, how to transform your struggles into peace, and steps to take to live beyond your ego. Understanding these concepts is critical. When you're in doubt about whether or not a particular situation is a healing setup, assume that it probably is. Use these lists to remember, confirm, and heal. It also appears in the Appendix where you can easily make a copy for future reference and use, which will be profoundly helpful when you are in a setup.

Realities of Your Life Blueprint

1. You learn your karmic issues through interactions and experiences with your birth family. Your adult family provokes these same issues to offer healing opportunities.

2. Spiritual commitment, intent, claims, and prayer elicit challenges to see if you mean what you say.

3. You are a magnet that attracts people, circumstances, and events to push your issue buttons.

4. What you focus on grows: problems, health, gratitude, blessings. What you focus on is your choice.

5. Appearances are deceiving. What you experience at the first floor is usually the exact opposite of what is occurring spiritually.

6. The intensity of your inner disturbance and the degree of your involvement in dramas determine whether the arising issue is primarily yours or someone else's.

7. Your internal and external responses in difficult situations are the experiential markers that show the extent of your healing progress.

8. Downshifts precede spiritual boosts.

9. All life-impacting events and situations happen according to divine timing.

10. The initial on/off switch for issues restricts you from seeing and employing better options; by using energetic release to incrementally remove issues, you open yourself to a larger context with additional and wiser response possibilities.

11. Asking for "help" on the first floor is an SOS call; spiritual help has a higher purpose—to Heal Energetic Life Patterns (H-E-L-P.)

Transform Struggles into Peace

1. Accept full responsibility for your life just as it is and be willing to make changes.

2. Surrender your life to God, and cultivate a spiritual path.

3. Apply spiritual and energetic understandings to everything in daily life.

4. Be aware of setups, button pushing, mirroring, and projecting.

5. Reinterpret each difficult experience as a beneficial opportunity.

6. Safely, appropriately, and in a timely way, release your emotions.

7. Use the Three Pillars of Transformation and other energy-based techniques and modalities.

8. Speak your t/Truth.

9. Seek to develop and use guidance.

10. Finally make a decision to move beyond a stalemate. Sometimes ANY decision will help.

11. Change your response pattern when triggered, even if initially in only trivial ways, to gradually open, shift, and heal your issues.

Live Beyond Your E/go

1. You experience fewer, less intense, and shorter setups and personal issue challenges as you energetically heal; eventually you will have no need for them to occur.

2. You are free from the limitations of three-dimensional methods of operating, perspectives, interpretations, emotions, and responses. You are clear of restrictive processes and programming.

3. You keep your emotional plate clean.

4. You are beyond temptation and don't even think about anything that is not beneficial. Your thoughts are powerful, manifesting prayers.

5. You are a whole-brained, multi-sensory, multi-dimensional Light being.

6. You are internally congruent and continuously attuned to Source.

7. Guidance is normal, and you easily receive, recognize, and utilize it.

8. Your empowered Ego fosters wisdom and peace.

9. Miracles, synchronicities, and blessings are standard. You overflow with gratitude and praise.

10. You are one with all creation, and you exude understanding, compassion, and unconditional love.

11. You desire to be—and are—a channel of blessings for others.

36: HEALING TESTS

Just as mathematics involves many different processes at various levels of competency from learning to count to advanced calculus, healing also engages a panorama of possibilities presented to us in levels, layer upon layer. The more evolved we become, the more we will recognize healing opportunities, cooperate with them, and move through them more efficiently and less brutally. We will spot them more readily in our own life and in the lives of others, grow in our ability to identify and label the targeted issues we chose to address in this incarnation, and handle them more expertly in shorter periods of time. We will likely find that these issues are still painful, difficult, and confusing. But we will accept that too because we will have learned that, until we evolve beyond the need for emotional responses, our anger and/or outbursts are necessary to stimulate an energetic release.

Each button pushing experience we have resembles taking tests in school. After several quizzes, (buttons,) we will have an energetic exam, (setup,) which is more thorough, extensive, intense, and challenging than having any single button pushed. Although the idea of taking a test is unappealing, going through the spiritual setup is intended to benefit us and/or to establish our greater ability. We do not literally pass or fail these tests, but they give us a chance to release more old energies and demonstrate wiser responses. As we develop a stronger internal connection to Source, our understandings enlarge about what is taking place in our life, and we expand our abilities to respond more maturely.

ॐ Testing is necessary. On shore, anyone can claim to know how to swim. It is only by getting into water over our head that we demonstrate competency and overcome hesitation, concern, or lack of confidence. If we cannot swim well enough and need to be rescued, that is a sign that we need more training or practice. If our life tests show that we need more spiritual practice to heal our issues, we can be assured that someone or some situation will enter our lives to push our same buttons again.

Self-Initiated Tests

Sometimes when we give ourselves a test, we might do so with a snap decision to simply do something new and different. It is as though life leads us to a fork in the road with a deeply entrenched, detrimental self-belief, habit, or pattern in hot pursuit. There we are, faced with an instant decision, and suddenly we choose to take the path we haven't taken before.

If you are ready to proactively jump into situations that will heal your life, you might invite a healing event to begin. Because you recognize the energetic benefit of the challenging experience you will have as a result of the forthcoming test, you can take comfort or even solace from the fact that you chose to initiate the test and that you have spiritual options available that will vibrationally boost you forward during the challenge.

> To begin, talk to God and state that you are ready to heal your issue of (and then fill in the blank), which has been especially frustrating or painful for you.

Depending on variables, the test could begin to manifest almost instantly or might take a day or so to activate.

~ ~ ~

The following story is about a life issue of time pressure.

> Although Wesley was almost never late for any deadline or appointment, he too often would squeeze in one more task that he could have left to do later. His issue was feeling caught in a time crunch, always trying to pack in too much in too little time. But he could never seem to catch this common situation in time to make a conscious change.

> One day as he was leaving work for a doctor's appointment, he glanced at the clock and realized he was going to be late, something he could barely tolerate. Because he was so very uncomfortable with this situation that occurred too frequently, he recognized an opportunity to help himself heal.

> As he walked to his car, he stated out loud that he would not pay attention to time during his drive. Universe immediately assisted his intent by making every traffic light red!

> While waiting for the first few lights to turn green, Wesley kept affirming that he would not look at the clock. He noticed he was gripping the steering wheel harder and harder, and finally his knuckles started to turn white. At one fateful red light, he realized that, for as simple as this exercise sounded, the old energies owned him. He could not stop himself from turning his head to see the time, a very small physical movement in a car.

He put his right hand in front of the clock to block his view. When he turned his head, he stuck out his tongue, and said to no one, "Ha ha! I had to look, but I didn't have to see!" The rest of the ride was easier.

A few weeks later, a similar opportunity presented itself. He was able to resist looking at the car clock but did have to keep telling himself not to do so. The next time he had an episode, he was able to maintain the affirmation that he would get there in divine timing. He hardly thought about the time.

For people who can structure their daily life to routinely handle responsibilities in a timely way, the decision not to look at a clock might seem trivial, but for people like Wesley who build their days on the foundation of time, the decision is huge. People like Wesley, in his condition at the beginning of this story, go through life as if they were pulling Big Ben on a cart behind them. Time is always looking over their shoulder.

Wesley was able to cure himself of stuffing too much in too little time by labeling his issue, demonstrating a new and different response, and releasing his emotions. Fortunately, he was able to use his old nemesis, his car clock, in a quick and painless way. Wesley still experiences time-related stress in other areas of his life, but not when driving himself to appointments. In that regard, his healing was incremental but noticeable, welcome, and permanent.

~ ~ ~

The following story shows a more complicated and frustrating test that lasted for five agonizing and exhausting days. The healing benefits were enormous and profoundly welcomed.

Devon realized that he had always felt like a martyr, claiming that all responsibility and work ended up on his plate. He plodded through life with the belief that everything was up to him to handle because it wouldn't get done otherwise, deadlines would not be met, or the quality would be lacking.

He had learned it was not effective to complain about his problems because either nothing changed or the other people's reactions made the situation worse. He felt overburdened and resentful, and he had resigned himself to sacrificing easier and happier activities in order to stay on track with his life's demands. He finally decided to ask God to help him heal this life theme during his upcoming stay-at-home vacation.

The following day, over about a two-hour period, he felt an internal dimmer switch begin to turn on and reach a high setting. This, as it turned out, was God responding and testing him in ways that Devon had not anticipated.

For the next five days, Devon was absolutely inundated at every turn with the perfect setup to push his collection of martyr issues to the forefront of his awareness. He felt so overwhelmed that he missed about 50 percent of his healing opportunities. When he did catch himself making his typical, tried-and-true reaction to what was happening around him, he consciously made the tiny changes he was able to make in his response.

His spiritual examination impacted his whole vacation week, which turned into eighteen-hour days of non-stop work. He did not need more martyr experiences to raise his awareness about his old habits, but he did require more occasions to change his responses to those experiences. During that week, he swore, shouted, complained, threw up his hands in despair, had conversations with himself, rebelled, cried, and continued to express his frustration over the emotional debris he had allowed himself to carry.

At the end of the five days that would have been his vacation, everything in every aspect of Devon's life had been tested, addressed, cleaned, organized, and completed. Over about a two-hour period, the dimmer switch that symbolized his intense triggering, dialed down and turned off. Devon noticed that everything around him was eerily quiet. He leaned against a wall and said out loud, "Finally it's over. Well, of course. Work hard enough and eventually everything gets done." But he knew the results were much deeper than that. He had taken care of the business of being busy before, but that hadn't resulted in healing. This time, it had.

A few days later, Devon felt like he had taken a final exam when God presented him with one more pop quiz. He had company for dinner on a Sunday night. Enjoying conversation with them, he did not do any kitchen cleanup while his guests were there.

They stayed later than he had thought they would, and he became quite well aware that he had to get up early the next morning for work. When his guests finally left, he stood looking at his disheveled kitchen, and for the first time in his life, he gave himself internal permission to leave the dirty dishes on the table and in the sink rather than automatically cleaning up the mess and grumbling in the process.

His reaction was new and remarkable! He saw himself faced with the opportunity to make a decision that had never been possible for him to make before. He saw that he was now free to do—or not do—the cleanup. Standing at that fork in the road, he decided to clean up that night—not because it was his normal martyr-like way but because he chose to.

Within a week, a close friend commented that Devon's martyr syndrome seemed to be gone. Devon also knew that he felt more liberated. His behavior didn't completely change and he still performed many of the same tasks he had before, but he did so with a different attitude and perspective.

Over the next several months, four more experiences appeared as signposts to indicate Devon's healing. The first time, he verbalized some comment like, "I suppose I have to do this now because if I don't, it won't get done." Immediately afterward, he recognized that he had spoken like a martyr. The second time, he began his response with a new awareness of what was actually processing in his head and he said, "My martyr wants to say something." The third time, he only thought some observation similar to, "Why did I even ask her to help me? Of course I will have to do it myself." The final experience involved the inflection in his voice when he began to make a statement with the word, "Well," in a martyr-like tone that Devon caught immediately and restated with a straighter pitch. With each of these moments, Devon was aware that he was healing himself of his previous martyr syndrome.

Devon was clearly aware of the improvement in his life with the martyr role removed. He originally had no idea what he would endure when he initiated his healing test, but he will be forever grateful that it only took five days to heal a lifetime or even lifetimes worth of martyr energy.

Emergency Tool Kit

The following four steps are an emergency tool kit we can use when a button is being pushed or during a test when we feel backed into a corner. Other healing options are more efficient and powerful, and will surpass the need for these tools, but these are basic, handy, and effective when needed.

Step One: Don't Shoot the Messenger

When someone or something pushes your buttons, Universe is providing a custom designed, essential, spiritual opportunity—a setup—for you to

> *Your messengers truly are assisting you. ... Hard as this is to hear and learn, you need them to do exactly what they are doing.*

heal and grow. The situation likely won't look or feel beneficial, but the issue will be familiar. An immediate cluster of thoughts will rush through your head: "Here it goes again." "Why does this keep happening to me?" "I don't deserve this." "When will it end?"

You will experience a strong and instinctive emotional reaction to handle the problem in your customary way because that technique has worked before. However, your prior responses merely managed the issue, which in a crisis is sometimes all you can hope for. While in crisis-management mode, you might explode at the person who pushed your button. In fact, that response is unwise not only because it can harm your first floor relationship with the person and lead to greater problems or even animosity, but exploding your emotions at the messenger will not discharge enough of your energetic debris because you might still be attempting to somewhat manage what you are saying.

When you have learned to swim in spiritual water, you will remember that the experience is intended to benefit you. You will remind yourself: "Don't shoot the messenger." Your messengers truly are assisting you, although they are consciously unaware of their role. Hard as this is to hear and learn, you need them to do exactly what they are doing. If they don't, someone else will.

Step Two: Label the Issue or Emotional Button

Labeling the issue is like writing the name of something you've cooked on its container before you put it into your freezer for storage. It helps you identify what you're looking for when you retrieve it later. Spiritually, the label gives you more information to hold onto and another piece of understanding as you progress along your path. If you can't label it there in the moment, move on. Perhaps in a few hours or days, you will make more sense of what transpired. The wording for the label and further insights might come to you later, unexpectedly, or when you journal your experiences.

Step Three: Demonstrate a Different Response

As you gain insight about the value of having your buttons pushed, you will realize that you can respond differently than you have in the past. The change in your response might seem trivial or strike you as being significant. Regardless of the dimension of change, be assured that it will produce noticeable benefits.

Any change in your response will lead you to see that you have developed a specific method to handle a pushed button. Merely rebelling about the situation or doing nothing new might offer short-term management help, but those options do not promote healing. Likewise, do not create a new, supposedly improved tactic and use that all the time; doing so only substitutes a new management technique for an old one.

> ➤ To really fuel your success, respond—there, in the moment—in some different way that you've never done. Your new novel action might be something strange, meaningless, or even funny: walk around a chair before you sit down; get a drink of water before you do anything else; twiddle your thumbs; sit on your hands; pull your earlobe; or any other fresh activity you can think of in the moment.

> ➤ If you become angry while driving a car or operating machinery, park it or shut it off, and walk away from whatever might harm you physically.

At first, you will probably still need to deal with the issue in substantially the same way as you always have—like wading before you try to swim—but you will have added this unusual step to your response repertoire. And this is what you want because every time you change your standard habit, you remove a portion of your old reactive energetic template. Each fresh response resembles removing a nail from the issue wall that has been holding you prisoner all of your life.

> ➤ When you demonstrate a new response,
> congratulate yourself. You passed that test!

You are making progress in incremental degrees to minimize your strong emotional reactions! And the next time you are challenged, you will find that you have more viable or meaningful options to work with.

> Betty learned about the helpfulness of changing her routines at a time of professional desperation. Her job was becoming overwhelming, and she felt no support from other employees or bosses. Not having any other ideas and deciding to give something different a try, she chose to alter her typical patterns.
>
> The next day, Betty changed everything she possibly could. She got out of bed on the other side, dressed in a different than normal order, and held silverware in her opposite hand. She drove to work a different way, put her wastebasket in the middle of the floor, and threw her trash around it rather than into it. It was an odd day.
>
> By the following day, Betty noticed internal shifts that she found encouraging. She was aware of more helpful possibilities to ease her burdens at work. She felt less trapped and

handled everything noticeably better.

A few weeks later, Betty forged another unusual day and reaped even more benefits. These weird but fun experiments paid obvious dividends.

Step Four: Release Emotions in a Safe, Timely, and Appropriate Way

When you are energetically triggered, it is critical that you recognize a healing situation immediately or as soon as possible and give yourself permission and opportunity to release the charged energy from your system. Although you might be tempted to lash out at the person who sparked your emotions, that isn't necessary.

> ➢ Instead, go someplace where you can be alone: an office, closet, field, parked car or parking lot, or even a bathroom. Dislodge your energies with strong physical movements and/or emotional or verbal venting. Cry, yell, tell the provoker off, complain, stamp your

There is nothing you can say that God has not already heard, and God will continue to love you and support you no matter what you say.

feet, rip paper towels, kick something soft, beat a pillow on your bed, or even swear.

As peculiar as it sounds, swearing or any other volatile discharge permits you to experience an intense release. If you were raised not to use profanity, swear anyway. There is nothing you can say that God has not already heard, and God will continue to love you and support your healing no matter what you say.

> To move out more and deeper inner energies, utilize physical movement, exercise, aerobics, sports, laughter yoga, and hard work such as splitting wood. Pulling weeds or cleaning out a catchall drawer in your kitchen or office are also effective because of the metaphysical symbolism of getting rid of unwanted stuff.

> While you physically move, invite karmic debris and other internal, emotional toxic energies to come up so you can vacuum them out.

If you are running, you might feel compelled to run harder, longer, farther, and faster, pushing and pushing and pushing yourself just to prove you can—knowing that if you can do that with your body, you can also push yourself to even greater nonphysical healing. You might become emotional with deep laughter or flowing tears that will also remove old energies and make your life easier to handle.

By venting emotions, you are releasing your reaction to what just transpired as well as processing out older, causative energies buried deeper in your energetic system.

> After your activity, whether verbal or physical, ask Source to neutralize the environment. Be assured that all released energetic debris will be cleaned up and that you have raised your vibrational rate.

37: HEALING SUGGESTIONS

We have countless ways to heal, and new processes constantly emerge and develop. This allows us to take initiative to heal in any way that feels appropriate. Work with the following basic and foundational ideas. They are readily available, free-of-cost, and vibrationally uplifting.

➢ Make a commitment to heal and follow through regardless of possible temporary fallout.

➢ Review major life crises with a broader understanding to determine the issues and roles involved.

➢ Place fewer restrictions on how you think the Universe should work and be more aware of what is actually occurring.

➢ Stop procrastinating and make necessary decisions. While indecision prolongs your old patterns, resolving something can literally shift you away from worrying and frustrating management processes and improve your life.

➢ Be aware of what draws your attention. Guidance can occur through anything and anyone, at any time, and in any place. You might receive clues, nudges, and actual answers in unexpected ways: overhearing a conversation, reading billboards, scanning media broadcasts, or seeing meaningful signs or coincidences.

To heal: ask, listen, trust, and apply.

ॐ The summation of these healing suggestions is to ask, listen, trust, and apply.

➢ Ask Source for healing, solutions, and further understanding.

➤ Listen to the still, small voice within.

➤ Trust the response that comes up.

➤ Then apply the information in your life.

When you follow these suggestions, you can move mountainous obstacles, one clump of dirt and emotional debris at a time.

~ ~ ~

The following story illustrates a seemingly random supportive God hug that came in an easy and synchronistic way.

> Ellie was in the depths of feeling worthless and had determined that nothing she had ever done amounted to anything of lasting value, that her opinion didn't matter, and that her feelings didn't count. Although this had been a lifelong issue, she had never felt it so intensely. To her mind, life was not worth living.
>
> One day, Ellie was buying a gift for a friend. Another shopper in the store checkout line was holding a lamp identical to one Ellie had in her office. Ellie told her that she loved the lamp and that it fit very well with the traditional décor in her office. The stranger said she was purchasing it as a gift for a friend who also had traditional decor and liked formal furniture. The shopper expressed her hope that her friend would appreciate the lamp. Ellie assured her that it would fit in beautifully.
>
> The woman's next response shocked Ellie. She

loudly asked for Ellie's name. After Ellie told her, she stated, "I'll tell my friend that if Ellie says so, it has to be true." Although she laughed in the moment, Ellie did not miss the deeper purpose of the comment: God had spoken through this stranger to boost her self-esteem.

~ ~ ~

We can only take the next step from where we are. Lingering on past mistakes is unproductive, and regret inhibits progress unless we alter it into motivation. Any movement, shift, or decision on anything could start our healing and energy to flow. Ideally, we will also incorporate prayer, spiritual principles, and outside supportive resources to assist us along our healing path.

ॐ It is also absolutely not true that there are no alternatives in a crisis. Our choices might appear limited, unappealing, or overwhelming, yet we can always add, remove, or do something to assist ourselves or another, even when energetically

> *Lingering on past mistakes is unproductive, and regret inhibits progress unless we alter it into motivation.*

blocked, depressed, handicapped, or dying. Progress might be slow or seem miniscule, but remember the tale of the tortoise and the hare and keep moving, no matter how laboriously.

~ ~ ~

A concern that nearly everyone has at some point on a healing path is when to take initiative and when to surrender and wait for God to work things out. There are two distinctly different positions to this matter: first floor versus fiftieth floor.

First floor conclusions create the initial uncertainty. When we make no decision, miss an opportunity, or do not become invested in an outcome, the results lead to passivity that prolongs our predictable default system of operating. Surrendering our will

> *The more evolved we become, the more we will know what, when, and how much to do. ... God won't do for us what we won't do for ourselves.*

and trusting God, on the other hand, will help us clarify the situation. Surrendering does not mean that we do not take action. First of all, the decision to surrender and making the statement to surrender is an action. The high-level view that we gain by surrendering enables us to rely on Source for guidance, from which we will intuitively sense or know when to wait, when to act, and what action to take.

The straightforward answer to action versus inaction is this: the more evolved we become, the more we will know what, when, and how much to do. We will see new doors open and vistas to embrace. God's gentle stream of wisdom gently urges us to realize that God won't do for us what we won't do for ourselves.

> ➤ When in doubt about what to do, ask God for specific guidance or signs.

> ➤ Check with the resonator, our internal energy detector that alerts us to timely and/or critical messages.

> *Applying guidance activates high-dimensional voltage and effortlessly improves results.*

> ➤ Then trust and work with the response you receive.

➢ And remember that applying guidance activates high-dimensional voltage and effortlessly improves results in all areas of our lives.

~ ~ ~

The following story shows a surprising, satisfying, and very obvious external change as a result of surrendering a lifelong issue.

> Carole had been living with an issue of excessively helping others. Much of the time, she was happy to do something that would make someone else's life better, but she was also worn out. She recognized a healing crisis when her activity level went through the roof and she was not reaping rewards from her efforts. She felt that too many demands were being placed on her time and energy. Her quandary was how to stop this pattern, get her life under control, and assist her own healing.
>
> Just avoiding personal interactions or refusing to get involved in everyone else's dramas were not healing options for her. Carole had tried these tactics before to no avail, so she prayed for guidance to clear her issue. The inspiration that came to her was to surrender both her interpretation of what she thought was going on in other people's lives as well as her ego-based mandate to become involved.
>
> Every time she caught those old, familiar thoughts and tendencies begin to stir, she surrendered them. Over some time, she noticed that she felt compelled to help others

less often. When she did choose to become involved, she freely wanted to do so. She realized that she was now being motivated by desire rather than a sense of obligation.

Near the end of Carole's healing of this issue, she began to notice that friends were reaching out to her more often rather than she always taking the lead by phoning them, speaking first, or offering assistance.

Significant improvement became very apparent to her when she went to a resort where she had frequently stayed but had not visited for several months. Usually she would make the first step to greet neighbors, phone others to see how they were doing, and extend an invitation to socialize. When she arrived that year at the end of a crisis period, she chose to just sit back and see what developed without her initiative.

As a result of the change in her issue energy and different posture of waiting for whatever God had in mind, she soon saw that her old friends were coming to her rather than she initiating contact with them. One neighbor, who had never come first to visit her, came over almost immediately. Within another day, two different families invited her to dinner. Within her first week at the resort, she received five phone calls from people she had typically reached out to first but who had rarely called her. The difference was startling and most welcome, and it brought a smile to her heart because she could see how the shift within her was leading to incredibly different responses from her friends.

This simple healing step of surrendering can be effective for all of us when we apply it frequently and consistently to our own issues, and not necessarily only one issue at a time! The benefits for us far outweigh any seemingly short-term inconvenience or uncertainty we might sense or feel.

> *The degree of conscious, ego-based strength that binds us, along with our resistance to change determines how difficult, long, confusing, and emotional the healing process is.*

38: E/GO DEATH[101]

Spiritual growth requires that we monitor and review our day-to-day flow of life as well as life's affairs so that we can energetically heal and improve. The degree of conscious, ego-based strength that binds us, along with our resistance to change determines how difficult, long, confusing, and emotional the healing process is.

If Source is to control our life, we must surrender our conscious, head-controlling ego. E/go resists this transference of power because it has functioned as our exclusive survival system since we originally chose to leave Source eons ago. In our early years under karmic mandate, ego initially favors us with its protection. Over time, as ego either struggles to accept its non-spiritual limits or resists higher vibrations that are beyond its ability to accept, it becomes like a dictator who will not accept

---

[101] *ego death:* ego's excruciating stage of defeat when it realizes it must abdicate its life dictatorship to Source, yet its default systems remain with reduced authority

being overthrown. It will fight for its life.

When ego sees that we will not let it win that fight and that we intend to heal and more fully identify with Source, it has no other recourse than to incrementally adjust to our higher frequencies. When we have evolved into some level of multi-dimensionality, it realizes that it is over-extended and begins to run out of answers, options, and diversionary ploys to maintain its separate, controlling existence. It gradually loses its ability to hold us back from integrating with Source.

E/go cannot survive at that new power level and accelerates into a high gear of deviousness as it attempts to maintain its existence and control. Many people have succumbed to these distractions, which make it extremely difficult for them to see how their head rules their life. Some convince themselves they are spiritually advanced while still living incongruent lives. Some trust no one but themselves. Others who have read or studied many higher spiritual concepts become mentally overconfident and are no longer open to receive t/Truth. Some are stubbornly locked into self-righteousness, claiming to know they are right and that they do not need to change but others do.

These positions are incredibly common among spiritual seekers, and they effectively stop spiritual growth. A person can succumb to ego's ploys and opt out of an empowered life by ignoring his or her responsibilities, being self-absorbed, living as a recluse, rebelling, or in some other way shutting down to a higher profiled, more involved, or advanced life.

ॐ However, when we see through ego's tricks and choose to continue on our evolutionary spiritual path, ego will eventually cease to dominate. At that point, ego, not remembering its home base is our congruently empowered Ego, realizes its demise is imminent and sends its terminal message, like a death rattle, to us. Because ego has been our whole conscious identity and in charge of our method of operating, we cannot distinguish between its message and our own thoughts. We interpret these repeating death statements literally. It is common at this difficult juncture for some people to have passive thoughts of, or active desire for, suicide.

This is because we do not understand that the dissolution of ego's authority, domination, and identity—and not the end of our physical life—is upon us. The thought that suicide is the way out of our painful life is merely an illusion, ego's final attempt at control by destroying the body and mind that is its host. Our test at this time is to move through this essential and liberating phase, not opt out of it. This

E/go death is a standard stage of vibrational healing.

process resembles the metamorphosis of a caterpillar, which when it realizes it's dying and the world is over, transforms into a butterfly. E/go is merging with Source. E/go death is a standard stage of vibrational healing. Our challenge is to realize that this excruciating experience is actually good for us because it is removing ego from our lives and bringing us back into greater, fuller association with Source.

~ ~ ~

Many people have gone through ego death with all of its confusing and painful trials and discovered there is no need to repeat this critical portion of healing. Without exception, they emerged as a significantly more empowered being. Each felt grateful that they survived the experience and were glad when it was over. They all concurred that their resulting new life was worth everything they had endured.

Our attempt to attain this higher vibrational energy that is the Higher Self does not start out as conscious awareness for most of us. Therefore, ego death transitioning hastens the thinning of the veil between our conscious state and unconsciousness.

This evolution is necessary because we are becoming more whole-brained beings. This evolutionary process progressively removes the barriers that have blocked us from truly k/Knowing that Source is always accessible and forever manifesting all forms of goodness and abundance in our life. Progress is still incremental, but momentum accelerates. Life moves on more smoothly, effortlessly, and peacefully. It is not so much that we can easily see that all is externally well yet, but we will know internally that all is becoming well and that we can handle whatever happens externally in a more effective and less burdened way than before.

39: DARK NIGHT OF THE SOUL

In the recent previous pages, we've seen that the healing remedies of life have progressed through varying degrees of difficulty, from simply altering our perspectives by recognizing our healing opportunities and healing tests, to the highly powerful and profound ego death. We've examined our healing indicators, the many variables to healing, and our life's karmically mandated

> *Distinguishing characteristics of a Dark Night of the Soul: duration, depth, and extent of demolition.*

healing blueprint. We've seen how we can use healing suggestions, experiential markers, and our emergency tool kit to aid and chart our spiritual progress.

Similarly, spiritual evolution consists of many steps and levels, filled with various stages of trials and challenges all along the way. Humankind has traditionally required the dramas of setups, mirroring, projecting, and button pushing to assist our spiritual progress. After many of these quizzes and tests, we typically have a major exam to move us into the next profound higher tier of vibrational frequency. Some levels represent greater shifts than others, similar to entering grade school, middle school, and high school. When a person is spiritually ready to enter college, there will likely be an extended bombardment period, usually referred to as the *Dark Night of the Soul.*[102] As the name suggests, this is also a profound and highly evolutionary experience. If a soul is seeking a spiritual doctoral degree or was not able to sustain an earlier vibrational boost and reverted back to old patterns, it might go through more than one Dark Night siege. Prior experience might help to build some trust that the eventual results more than compensate for the relatively short-term difficulties.

~ ~ ~

Whether seeking a spiritual path or not, you and almost everyone else has had an extended period of time when everything seems to go wrong. Although brief episodes of problems are a regular part of normal life, this extended Dark Night phase feels like someone is holding your head underwater until you almost die, allows you to come up ever so briefly for a gasp of air, and then immediately plunges your head under again and again. When this stage happens, you do not know how long it will last, what you will have to face before it is over, or even who you are or where you will be when it is completed.

A Dark Night of the Soul typically lasts many weeks to months and sometimes longer—as long as needed to break apart and remove the unwanted, old, defiant, and preprogrammed karmic and present life energetic debris and patterns that have been restricting you from living the rewarding life you desire.

---

[102] ***Dark Night of the Soul:*** a prolonged period of experiential and emotional assault, intended to dismantle ego's spiritually immature identity, personal history, agendas, and behavior

During this time, you will have doubts about everything. You might be pushed to your literal brink, where you wish you could be put out of your misery—this is the suicidal tendency of ego death.

You might feel that you are failing at everything because your old operating systems can't survive evolution's higher frequencies. Your ego filters and issues will go through a real-life bombing to leave the limitations of the three-dimensional world behind. This transition time is incredibly difficult to cope with and endure.

As in all other aspects of spiritual work, many variables exist. The distinguishing characteristics between a prolonged difficulty and something more significant and comprehensive are: how long the experience lasts; the depths of pain you encounter; and the far-reaching scope of demolition that impacts nearly every area of your life. Just as in school, a final exam can target everything you need to know and learn.

Because we are energetic beings, the purpose of this

> *The Dark Night of the Soul is valuable because it exquisitely, totally, and thoroughly breaks down and destroys old ways of operating that no longer serve us.*

first floor life assault is to break apart the old, resistant, and limiting ego barriers so we can expand beyond them. Removal of these energies will transform us into a more fully dimensional being so that a new and advanced version of ourselves will emerge. It is not yet possible for either us or ego to prevent this magnificent stage of development. The soul's need to evolve will override our conscious beliefs, goals, and agendas. When we, as spiritual seekers, undergo this siege, our primary advantage over the general population is our potential to consciously yet

lly understand what is taking place and, by cooperating
Source energies involved, hasten the results.
Surrendering, forgiving, and using the ego vacuum can minimize
the duration of the Dark Night. The Three Pillars of
Transformation and higher dimensional energies even have the
inherent potential to eventually eliminate the need for the Dark
Night.

The Dark Night of the Soul is valuable because it
exquisitely, totally, and thoroughly breaks down and destroys old
ways of operating that no longer serve us. This is why things are
going wrong in every aspect of life—from relationships,
situations, and problems that keep popping up to fatigue,
physical symptoms, and loss of interest in life, hobbies, and
activities—all of which can lead to hopelessness and depression.

We feel helpless. We did not ask for this, do not want it,
have no control over what is happening, and see almost no
answers for our first floor questions as to why it is happening
and what to do about it. We are under continuous emotional and
psychological assault, receive little or no relief or help, and are
overwhelmingly confused. Yet, ironically, in spite of all this
internal pain, to a casual observer, our life might appear the same
or as normal as ever.

As I've stated before and want to do with more emphasis
now, this *tremendous hardship is actually a blessing*. A Dark
Night gives us the opportunity to shed much in relatively little
time. Afterward, we might be able to assist others when they are
in need.

If we make the
intended life
responses and
adjustments

> *A Dark Night is a blessing that
> gives us the opportunity to shed
> much in relatively little time.*

during the taxing time, we enter the next vibrational grade. If we give up, cannot, or do not make the leap, then Source or our Higher Self allows us to stay in the present level and gather more preparatory, healing experiences before giving us another opportunity at a later time to undertake the ordeal again. Either way, the Dark Night is necessary. It is designed to boost our elevating energetic competency so we can enter the next higher stage of personal empowerment. Fortunately for us, the Universe is infinitely patient, so we will have as many opportunities and lifetimes as we need to accomplish our spiritual development.

See the Appendix for typical symptoms while in the Dark Night of the Soul, and personal benefits that emerge after becoming free from that experience.

~ ~ ~

ॐ The purpose behind a Dark Night of the Soul is always to assist our highest good, and the Higher Self uniquely designs a Dark Night for each soul. Some people might need remedial work if a critical area is not as developed as the rest of their being, and that deficit will be targeted first. An example of this tutorial need would be a person who has never been able to draw healthy personal boundaries. He or she would repeatedly and excessively experience turmoil as a result of others' behavior, offering recurring opportunities to see and "get" his or her enmeshed issue, respond differently, remove standard emotions, and revise typical responses. These changes will help the person see formerly invisible, inappropriate, and unwise behaviors and patterns. This person will also promote more personal freedom from being ensnared in dramas he or she doesn't want.

Sometimes people who have been rebelling or making unwise or harmful decisions will undergo a Dark Night to assist them in breaking free from the chains that have bound them. They or others close to them might have to hit bottom before they make a substantial life change. Other persons might have been resisting or ignoring their t/Truth and might require intense physical or emotional disruption to help them wake up. Others might have no awareness of the deeper meaning of life and need some

> *The purpose behind a Dark Night of the Soul is always to assist our highest good.*

experiences to sensitize them to the inner subtler and simpler realms. And still others might be so stubborn or full of hate, anger, blame, selfishness, and so on that they need a complementary "collision" to stop them in their tracks.

Sandy was in a Dark Night of the Soul. Many things were coming to a head within a few weeks. A new grandchild had been born, a son was moving out of state, a second daughter was getting married, and Sandy's mother was deteriorating with dementia in a distant nursing home. She was involved in a special project at work that required her participation each day and some evenings every week for an extended period of time. She had personal health concerns, and additional projects and personal deadlines were all culminating at about the same time.

Also during this unbelievable time, Sandy accidentally discovered that her only sibling, Kent, had not been paying their mother's bills or taxes, had gotten a second mortgage on their mother's home, and owed more than he could ever possibly repay. What had been a sizable estate was now in jeopardy.

Kent placed a distressed call to his sister and

threatened suicide. Sandy later learned that he went into the woods to end his life, and as he pulled the gun's trigger, an invisible movement from a being who was probably one of his guides, literally pushed the gun away in a safe direction. He was not supposed to kill himself. Instead, he ended up in jail.

A few days before co-hosting her daughter's shower, Sandy had to take off from work and make a trip to take care of some legal matters concerning her mother. During the two days she and her husband were away from home, they felt divine intervention assisting them. Every single person they dealt with went way beyond the bounds of their position to help. The banker gave them his home phone number in case they needed him. A man at the courthouse literally ran a few blocks to check on something for them to be sure he was accurate. Their attorney spent over two hours with them instead of the allotted thirty minutes and offered many possibilities concerning her mother, brother, and the estate. On their way home, they stopped at a favorite fish store and discovered the building was vacant. A car pulled alongside them as they were leaving, and the driver escorted them to the new business location. They were so grateful for the obvious assistance from so many people and for the temporary reprieve.

Their arrival home dropped them back into their problems and concerns, and it took all of their energy and focus to get through the onslaught. Eventually things were resolved. Her mom passed away, and the estate was settled, leaving no inheritance. Sandy regretfully broke off her relationship with Kent.

The larger perspective and deeper, more specific meaning of Sandy's Dark Night was an opportunity for her to demolish her karmic roles of rescuer and slave. She had frequently bailed Kent out of his dilemmas. In spite of her well-paid position, she had been unable to enjoy abundance due to ongoing financial needs of others around her. Sandy had always carried burdens that she could never entirely fulfill or accomplish. She held more than her fair share of responsibilities and received little acknowledgment, personal benefit, or support in return for her efforts, hallmarks of her slave role.

Her Dark Night had been an excruciating life experience that opened a new operational level with many benefits and joys. Sandy and her husband moved into a new home in a different state, began their own business, and Sandy was also able to maintain a very prestigious full time job. This desirable stage lasted for many years.

Yet, over time and as a result of many more healing opportunities in which she reverted to default patterns, she again began to rescue others and then felt enslaved. She was overwhelmed and unable to sustain the advanced vibrational level she had earlier attained. As a result, nearly ten years later, she experienced another Dark Night of the Soul. A repeat experience of this ordeal may occur more than one time in any person's life even if they have not reverted to default systems. It will produce a thorough cleansing of the system in preparation for a significant vibrational boost and life change.

40: NAVIGATIONAL CRUTCHES

There is no magic formula to hanging on through a Dark Night of the Soul. It is designed to break us up, tear us down, and take us to the emotional brink. If we think of standing on a very high precipice, there will be times when our feet are almost off the edge. Or think of being lost at sea in a raging storm. Then remember these two insightful quotes, stated in various ways by several sources, that represent a beneficial perspective for this metaphorical yet common challenge.

> *"When you come to the edge of all the Light you have known and are about to step out into the darkness, TRUST is knowing one of two things will happen. ... There will be something to stand on, or you will be taught how to fly."*

And

> *"Sometimes He calms the storm, and sometimes He calms us in the midst of the storm."*

~ ~ ~

Almost everyone through the ages has suffered at least one severe life ordeal. What doesn't break us makes us stronger. If we really cannot cope, we can insist on God's intervention, which will be given either immediately or within a brief period of time.

If we really cannot cope, we can insist on God's intervention, which will be given either immediately or within a brief period of time.

ॐ Resembling a child who constantly throws tantrums, if we overuse our demand option, it loses its effectiveness. But if we have a critical need, we can stop what we are doing and, in a sense, quit. We can express to God what we feel, why we feel that way, what we need, and how difficult it is for us to keep doing whatever we've been doing. We can demand that something internal or external change now. We can insist on it. But then we must be prepared for something extraordinary to happen, which might come about in an unexpected way. This spiritual declaration usually provides significant relief. Then the next move is up to us.

When Stephanie was in her Dark Night of the Soul, which lasted eighteen months and took another year to restructure afterward, she was frequently at the brink of her endurance. She was being stalked and threatened by someone at work, and her car tires had been slashed. She feared a bomb either in her office, car, or home, and was concerned about her own safety and that of her family.

One Thursday evening, she crossed the line. She had just realized that she no longer had the patience or ability to competently read a map and concluded that her stress level was on overload. Right after that upset, she was standing by the stove when the timer buzzed. She couldn't remember why it had been set, so she just turned it off. A few minutes later, she began to smell something burning, opened the oven door, and saw the cookies that she was baking were now blackened. That was it. Obviously something had to change.

She finally exploded at God with strong language that portrayed her plight. She shouted and told God in no uncertain terms that she could not continue on the way things were going. If she would be a better help to others by being glued back together after breaking apart, then keep it coming. If not, then this stuff had better stop happening immediately because she was done.

During breakfast the next morning, a loving being appeared in her kitchen. He told Stephanie that she had been walking through the valley of the shadow of death. "How about that," she thought, "God really did know!" She immediately remembered the Biblical text that follows those words: "I will fear no evil, for Thou art with me." She had indeed feared evil.

The being assured her that she and her family were safe. Yet she wondered why she hadn't been told that weeks earlier. That would have made her life so much easier. The being said two protectors would be posted at her office door until they were no longer needed. He told her that all was well, she was doing well, and God loved her. Stephanie thanked him and cried.

When she arrived at her office that morning, two of the most threatening, huge, sentries— energy beings—she could ever imagine were standing in the hall on both sides of the door. She was glad and comforted to know they were her security force for as long as necessary. They remained on duty for several weeks and told Stephanie when their last day approached. She thanked and blessed them from the depths of her heart.

Stephanie's Dark Night did not end the day the being came. However, that was her emotional turning point. She did not have to demand intervention again, although she did ask for and received help at many other points. Sometimes, she felt like a discarded tube of toothpaste on a freeway run over by every truck. Even when she knew there was nothing left inside the tube, more trucks continued to strike her, so she concluded there must have been a speck of toxic energetic toothpaste left that hadn't been removed yet.

The day the ongoing hits felt only like a bee sting rather than being flattened, Stephanie knew she must have rounded a corner. The sting only lasted a few minutes, and from that point on, she gradually became aware that the bombing blitz was ending. She found that looking around at her life was an overwhelmingly sobering experience, similar to assessing the ruins after a tornado. She needed to address the damage in her life and make many first floor decisions. Having never experienced and survived a Dark Night of the Soul before, she felt ill equipped to move forward. She had no clear plan of action because her reliable default system wasn't operating as it always had, and she didn't even know where to begin. Yet, her life inexorably moved on—one improving day at a time.

ॐ It is usually easier and more accurate to assess things in retrospect. Healing is no exception. Stephanie gradually came to see the benefits of having gone through her Dark Night experience, and she made step-by-step changes to improve her life. She was able to see better alternatives when she needed to make a decision, realized that her default system was less obtrusive, learned to trust guidance more than ego, and shift her focus to treasure life qualities more than accomplishments. This is what Source wants for all of us.

~ ~ ~

During a Dark Night of the Soul, it helps to cling to a few mental lifelines such as:

- remembering that everything happening is intended to assist your healing;

- knowing that the assault will eventually end; and

- accepting that you will be more evolved on the other side of the siege.

It is very beneficial to continue to release emotions, surrender, forgive, and use the ego vacuum.

You can also:

- simplify your life, responsibilities, and clutter;

- reprioritize; and

- keep only the most essential of whatever is important.

> *Internal and external clearing influence and support each other.*

These relate to the spiritual principle that if you have been stuck and want to heal, start by cleaning out your house. Also, after you have completed a major healing, it is common to work on your house, redecorate, or even move. Internal and external clearing influence and support each other.

Priorities

Consider our top three priorities: God, others, and ourselves. Most of us are raised to place these in that order: God first, others second, and ourselves last. This is a first floor idea based on the notion that we are selfish if we place ourselves above others in our own life equation. In actuality, we are irresponsible if we don't take care of ourselves physically, mentally, and spiritually first. Once we are in a more complete and healthy personal status, we can better serve others. We see this demonstrated when we fly in a commercial aircraft and the flight attendant instructs us, in the event of a loss of cabin pressure, to place an air mask on ourselves before assisting the person next to us.

Because we are all a portion of God and we can only change ourselves, we need to place ourselves second on our priority list, just under God, and ahead of all others, including our family and loved ones. We would only be selfish if we stop at that point and do not attempt to also focus on others. Fiftieth floor priority is God, us, then others.

~ ~ ~

As you reprioritize yourself into your rightful position, you will notice a greater desire to:

➢ Take good physical care of your body.

➢ Eat healthfully, rest more, and sleep as much as you need.

> Focus on any benefits, blessings, or advantages that you do have.

> Identify what you want, which might be difficult during a challenging time, and what you don't want in life, which will be easy to do.

> Talk to someone who is supportive. A good friend, family member, or even a crisis center might help. Ideally, seek a professional energy worker who specializes in moving and releasing energies, which will facilitate clearing internal debris.

Transformation is in process, and benefits await. As you progress, you will set aside your crutches and stand on your own two feet—in oneness with God, and in union with all other persons.

41: PERSONAL RESTRUCTURING

The energetic demolition of a Dark Night of the Soul is usually followed by an intense period of restructuring. We are not the same person we were at the beginning of the healing episode, and we need to discover and possibly seek assistance while developing our new identity.

> *Restructuring renovates our life to more authentically align and harmonize with our advanced vibrations and capabilities.*

Restructuring requires courage and determination. We will need to make changes in our life, rebuild, or even in some ways seemingly start over. There will be opportunities for new choices. Decisions might be difficult. We might have different interests than those of people who were previously important to us, and we might, perhaps, even set aside formerly meaningful relationships and/or activities.

Restructuring renovates our life to more authentically align and harmonize with our advanced vibrations and capabilities. We are making tremendous spiritual progress, even if life still feels or appears to be confusing.

We will probably feel somewhat like an adolescent again. Life might seem to be an ongoing experiment with many mistakes, so we will make allowances, forgive ourselves, and move on. We will need time and many different experiences to become aware of who we now are, and to clarify our enhanced attributes, priorities, and goals. Usually we shift our taste in clothes and life-style. One morning a woman spontaneously looked at all of her carefully selected purses and said out loud, "Why do I have all of these? I don't like any of them!" It was time for her to make some changes.

We tend to think of healing as meaning that things are getting progressively better. That is not always true in the physical world when we are healing spiritually. In the larger Universe picture, we indeed are getting better and more healed, but in our everyday lives, sometimes things get worse before they get better, and we might be strained in unforeseen ways.

Whatever we have been avoiding we must face, and whatever we have accommodated we must remove and make resulting adjustments.

> *Healing is a journey. The most difficult parts are the most crucial.*

We need to break the blocks that have been holding us back and discard them.

Healing is a journey. The most difficult parts are the most crucial. Our goal is to remove all of the energetic debris from our system so that we can begin to develop and mature into our full potential. If we are the seed of a daisy, we will not grow into a rose in this life, but we have a grand internal design that longs to blossom in all divinely possible ways.

~ ~ ~

Most people are able to restructure their life with little pain. Although it takes effort, time, and some serious decision making, life after a Dark Night of the Soul responds more efficiently to our efforts and activities. We might increasingly experience more hope, potential, enjoyment, and fulfillment.

Regretfully, it is also possible for us to encounter an exception to these benefits.

> Mable had spent all of her life striving to be a success by working and networking very hard and by investing wisely. She had completely bought into common material trappings such as dressing for success, accepting only the highest quality in everything, owning several homes, vacationing in exotic areas, and driving high-end luxury cars. On the surface, she had her life rather well in control, but her spiritual reality was that she had sold out to external, limited, skewed belief systems. She believed that appearances impress others, that more things mean more success, that it's okay to be whoever you must be to make a sale, and that it's wise to say what the other person wants to hear.

> Then God took over. Mable's materialistic, conforming life did not reflect her inner self. When she got on an active spiritual path, her life with all of its structures started to crumble around her. She eventually lost her business and her savings. She downsized to one modest home and drove a less expensive car.

This dismantling period was unbelievably painful for her, and it lasted for many years. The breakdown process finally stopped, and it then became a matter of her deciding what she wanted to build into her life to more accurately reflect her new inner self.

However, she still continued to listen to her battered ego, which stalled her self-discovery, the rebuilding process, and her ability to fully apply spiritual principles. Until and unless she derails ego messages, she might remain stagnated in her currently confused and unhappy life.

Mable had not been wrong to have all of those material blessings, but she had placed them at the top of her priority list. She had let external possessions determine her identity and self-worth. She had, in essence, made them her god. She ignored her inner life, and she inwardly craved peace, love, and acceptance to stop the rat race and enjoy simple things.

She would likely have never volunteered to give all of her possessions away and start over, so God intervened to move her in a healthier and more fulfilling direction, but in a different lifestyle than she was used to.

Before God stepped in, Mable had blocked herself from spiritual growth due to her fear of losing what she had worked so hard to accomplish. Even after Mable experienced a major materialistic crash, she felt stuck, confused, and frustrated about her life and her future. She is gradually becoming more peaceful and accepting of her life as it is, and is trusting God more than she ever thought was possible.

Not everyone requires this degree of external hardship. A spiritual path is more about seeking God's will in our life and working with whatever God might bring to us as a result. That is why a Dark Night of the Soul is so essential for our transformation.

42: VIBRATIONAL HEALING

We can follow any of six pathways to address and move beyond karmic, low-vibration components in our present life. The first two of these routes are not desirable, the third occurs randomly and intensely, and the remaining three are becoming more mainstream, available, and powerful.

Pathway One: Accident and Injury

In the first pathway, the Universe might gift us with a physical concern. This neither looks nor feels like a present, but it can help us dislodge low vibrations and relieve energetic congestion.

An accident is an occurrence while performing an activity that leaves a physical injury. The accident might be as simple as stubbing your toe on a chair, or bruises caused by physical exercise, or an impact with an automobile, or a major piece of industrial equipment that leads to hospitalization.

After an accident or injury, we might choose to reprioritize, stop procrastinating, or make important revisions in our life. We might relieve some karmic issue.

If we suffer impairment, the soul, with its karmic blueprint for soul growth, is unconcerned about our pain, inconvenience, financial distress, or our opinions or excuses. Its position is, "You are going to work on your issues. Whether you do it the easy way or the hard way is your choice."

The easy way is to take advantage of this opportunity during our recuperative period to release and heal. The hard way is to refuse to release, fail to see and understand the opportunity, claim that we don't know what to do about the causative situation, or simply express our unwillingness to change. If we choose the hard way, karmic energy might very well move us onto the next healing path.

Pathway Two: Illness

Each soul wants and needs to be clear and free of karmic and present life energetic residue. If these energies remain, they typically backlog, congest, and create the breeding ground for illness, whether temporary, chronic, or life threatening.

Even though genetics, environment, and lifestyle are also causative factors or agents of illness and none of our bodies will get out of life alive, many physical conditions are energetically issue-based. We often have physical symptoms, conditions, or illness that manifest in places in the body where dense energies are stuck. As our life issues come to a peak for healing, we might see the appearance of new, unusual, or painful physical responses.

Once we release these charged energies, the physical symptom, condition, or illness might be relieved or even cured— at least most of the time. However, the physical issue might also be caused by other, deeper, karmic or other concerns. In this case, removing the initially apparent cause is only a first step, to be followed by additional clearing. Regardless of what is the main cause, we will not clear the problem if we are not ready to handle and resolve the issue.

For this reason, it might be necessary for us to merge conventional allopathic medicine with complementary energetic healings for an optimum health and healing program.

Pathway Three: An Intense Spiritual Experience

This pathway can offer a life changing opportunity that might occur in many ways: a profound forgiveness or salvation event; an angelic intervention, rescue, or message; a miraculous healing; a near-death or out-of-body experience; a visit from a deceased loved one; or a spiritual breakthrough.

These milestones are not predictable, do not occur on demand, nor do they happen to everyone. They often occur at, or create a point of, personal crisis. If we wait for this type of experience to begin our healing process, many of us would never heal.

Pathway Four: Access Untapped Brain Potential

In the over 90 percent of the brain we haven't been using, we possess the latent capability to overcome nearly all human limitations. We have and can access advanced Knowledge and wisdom; gain the abilities to transcend the wheel of reincarnation; *bi-locate*[103] and *tele-transport;*[104] and manifest and materialize our heart's desires.

Our challenge is to find ways to safely and consistently access these remote areas of the brain. We are not yet evolved enough to easily, broadly, and specifically reach or target these highly powerful areas.

However, a few modalities have had some success in certain ways that are helpful in expanding our spiritual experiences. The tried-and-true methods are: hypnosis; certain drugs (not recommended;) vibrational frequencies, such as drumming, tapping, or playing rhythmic instruments, chanting, humming

---

[103] *bi-locate:* to physically be in two locations at the same time

[104] *tele-transport:* to move from one location to another with no physical effort

certain pitches, listening to percussive music; working with quartz crystals and other healing stones; meditation; yoga; breathing techniques; martial arts; color and light stimulation; visualization; bioenergetics, and many others.

Our lives will be enriched when we combine these developmental options with the Three Pillars of Transformation. Although we are evolving at an unprecedented rate, we still have a long way to go before we manifest our full powerful potential.

Pathway Five: Spiritual and Energetic Assistance

This benefit occurs from outside of us. Praying or meditating for relief might bring healing or possibly spiritual beings to us to answer our prayer. However, the primary external sources of assistance are a person, tool, or modality.

God reaches and helps each of us in countless ways, and humanity has always been able to receive spiritual aid. Throughout time, there have been mystery schools, avatars, masters, yogis, gurus, spiritual leaders, and healers. In our present era, the need for, recognition of, and acceptance of a deeper spiritual connection for each of us is gaining a wider audience. Any assistance that targets an energetic level has a greater possibility of reaching our energetic core.

Pathway Six: Energy Clearing

This advancing field can rapidly and somewhat easily promote spiritual and vibrational development. It is based on the understanding that we are, at our core, eternal empowered energy beings, and we simply need to remove low frequency, energetic blocks to manifest our internal divinity.

More people are discovering and embracing this healing approach. This book covers this approach in detail.

~ ~ ~

It is never too late to spiritually heal. Actual results might or might not include physical healing.

CHAPTER 7:
SPIRITUAL EVOLUTION

When we take initiative to address and apply the principles presented in *Life's Healing Setups*, we eliminate the need for dramas and someone to push our buttons. Then we begin to use more advanced concepts in energetically proficient ways to develop our spiritual ascension. We don't necessarily eliminate all low vibrations, but we learn to add and incorporate techniques and practices that will raise our vibrational rates. We move away from resistance and force and into God's flowing stream of unconditional love. We spiritually soar into empowerment.

43: SPIRITUAL PATHS

Whether motivated by desperation, hopelessness, crisis, curiosity, or desire, we can radically shift and enhance our life by embracing a spiritual path. Because we've honed our views and interpretations by first floor daily life, we now need to open our understandings to larger realms of possibilities. Every internal area of our identity and how we function is involved in this process.

> *To walk a spiritual path is to intentionally practice a process of advancing from ordinary life to a vibrationally ascended position.*

To walk a spiritual path is to intentionally practice a process of advancement from ordinary life to a vibrationally ascended position. This is a common goal of persons who actively seek to realize our natural unity with God. However, because we are individuals, following a spiritual path means different things to different people, and there are endless possibilities of what we might do, as well as variable levels of effectiveness that result from our actions.

The *standard* spiritual path and the *energy* spiritual path are completely different. The solution is *not* about knowing *what* to do consciously in a positive way to *resolve* the situation, even though that is what many modern gurus have espoused in recent years. Our soul's evolution occurs when we identify *how* energy cleansing works and *apply* the powerful techniques to release the low vibrations and clear them from our system.

With the standard spiritual path, we work from the head down. We think that once we learn something, we need to discipline ourselves to apply it in our life to grow and make this new practice become second nature. Then we go on to the next lesson, and the next, and the next. That's head-down thinking. It is linear, three-dimensional, and ego-based.

When we work with an issue energetically however, we work from Source-up. We identify the fact that, at our core, we are one with God, and we were born into this life with soul chosen emotional contamination as low frequency energetic debris. As we regularly release this karmic collection, our wholeness and connection with Source and all the attributes that we want in our life *automatically* appear. We don't have to force solutions from the head-down to heal; we simply let our inherent soul qualities bubble up

> *We don't have to force solutions from the head-down to heal; we simply let our inherent soul qualities bubble up according to God's and our co-mingled divine nature.*

according to God's and our co-mingled divine nature. This is what your soul at its most basic level *already knows*, and what God wants you to remember.

~ ~ ~

Generally, on a spiritual path we seek answers to these primary questions:

- Who am I?

- Who or what is God?

- What is my soul's purpose?

- Why am I here at this time and place?

By seeking answers to these questions, and desiring spiritual benefits such as receiving guidance, we explore ways to create a more meaningful,

> *When we decide to pursue a spiritual path, the rules of life do change.*

rewarding, deeper life. We instinctively desire quiet, contemplative, and inspirational time, opportunities, and experiences. We hope to develop our potentials, improve or restructure our values, and reprioritize our spiritual understandings, goals, and efforts. Above all, we are willing to change in order to support our new direction.

This is critical because when we decide to pursue a spiritual path, the rules of life *do* change. Our normal life and purpose refocus to address and heal our personal concerns or areas that need our attention and remediation. This shift represents a new beginning. If we are fortunate, we launch our new life out of curiosity or a desire for deeper connections. More often, we are spurred by challenging times, by not knowing why or what to do to make them better, and because we feel overwhelmed and confused.

Our old views, opinions, and management techniques no longer serve us. We often need help, support, and guidance from others. Those closest to us in our family or personal relationships might not understand nor want to support us in this new endeavor. Those people might walk away from us or push us away from them. Yet, developing a spiritual support system is important even though the healing process is bumpy, uncomfortable, chaotic, and lengthy. When we connect with others who are going through similar experiences or who have helpful input and feedback, we find comfort and encouragement.

When we focus on internal growth and development, our outer life eventually responds and manifests greater ease and fulfillment.

> *When we connect with others who are going through similar experiences or have helpful input and feedback, we find comfort and encouragement.*

~ ~ ~

To begin or boost spiritual development:

➤ Verbalize your commitment to prioritize your spiritual life and to pursue and employ energetic t/Truths and concepts. This does not require any specific technique, philosophy, belief, dogma, discipline, or action.

➤ Read inspirational self-help and spiritual books.

➤ Look for appropriate workshops or classes.

➤ Browse a local health food store and read ads posted on their bulletin board.

> Research topics of interest online.

> Sample an assortment of healing and reading modalities.

> Pay attention to synchronicities, routines, and encounters, knowing that, in spite of recurring challenges, you will be led and encouraged on your new path.

Prayer is one of the most powerful and available tools for empowerment. It can be a strong catalyst for spiritual intervention and grace.

44: PRAYER

Prayer is one of the most powerful and available tools for empowerment. It can be a strong catalyst for spiritual intervention and grace. Yet, the power of prayer is often misunderstood and the tool is underused.

Most of us have memorized prayers. When we rattle these off without thought, they lose their effectiveness. But when we recite the words with an open heart and focus on their meaning, we sense some personal response.

More often, we ask for assistance, protection, guidance, intervention, help with decisions, and healing for any areas of concern. We

The most powerful prayers are "Thank you, God," "I love you, God." And "Praise God."

might sometimes feel we are giving God a list of our opinions, wants, or needs for ourselves or anyone or anything. These prayers actually focus our attention on the adverse condition we want to avoid or be rid of. As we learn to trust more fully, we will begin to focus our prayers more on attributes and gratitude than outcomes. We will learn that the most powerful prayers are

"Thank you, God," "I love you, God," and "Praise God."

Many people state that God knows us so well and, therefore, question the necessity of prayer. It is Truth that we are always connected to God, but on the human level, using words to express heart and head petitions, whether thought or spoken, helps relieve the weight of our burdens, and opens us to receive and transmit higher frequencies. Then the higher our vibrational average, the easier, more effective, more obvious, and more immediate our prayer results will be. Eventually, we come to see that every thought is literally a prayer. As we think, so also do we pray.

> *Every thought is a prayer. As we think, so also do we pray.*

ॐ When God receives our prayers, either for beneficial events or relief of our worries, energies are activated. However, we frequently miss or misinterpret God's answers because we are so focused on first floor appearances, objectives, reactions, behaviors, and outcomes. Functioning linearly tremendously reduces our ability to see God at work. When we look at incidents as isolated and separate events rather than connecting them with a broader view of the situation, we often miss guidance or life patterns that would be helpful or even necessary for us to understand. If we do not receive an obvious answer to our prayer, we have another opportunity to surrender ego and practice trust in God. When we are alert for God's greater wisdom, we see that,

> *When we look at incidents as isolated and separate evens rather than connecting them with a broader view of the situation, we often miss guidance or life patterns that would be helpful or even necessary for us to understand.*

sometimes, the results from our prayers are different than we expected or hoped for. We might even think that God is working against us.

A perfect example of prayer seeming to backfire occurs in a scene from the film, *It's a Wonderful Life*. George Bailey, the lead character played by Jimmy Stewart, is sitting at a bar next to an angel disguised as an old man, Clarence, whom he had recently rescued from a supposed suicide attempt. George is in a state of profound personal and financial desperation. Not knowing what else to do to solve his dilemma, he finally prays for help. Within minutes, the husband of his child's teacher enters, discovers that George is the man who had ruthlessly just bawled out his wife, and punches George in the face. George concludes that his prayer backfired. Clarence says that he is the answer to George's prayer, having come to tell George what a difference he has made in so many people's lives. The assault is a healing setup that happened because of George's former words against the wife. The rest of the movie, however, reveals how Clarence helps George open and alter his viewpoint, interpretation, and appreciation of his life. Things work out differently but better than George could have possibly imagined. The solution becomes less about money and more about receiving help and support from those he had been selflessly serving for so many years.

The logical conclusion that George initially had about the results of his prayer are, unfortunately, all too common in real life. Some people don't believe in prayer because it often brings about harder, unwanted, or

We might not procure what we want, but God answers our prayers according to what we need and are ready to handle for our soul's growth.

different results than requested or expected. And they choose to stop there and simply endure continued hardship. Yet in the largest picture, we might not procure what we want, but God answers our prayers according to what we need and are ready to handle for our soul's growth.

Answers to Prayers

If we interpret prayer as our part of a phone conversation, meditation is silently listening for God's input. Many spiritual seekers practice meditation for peace, inspiration, and growth. Answers to prayer arrive in divine timing and in diverse methods. Until we are able to spiritually hear, God responds to us in any way we are open enough to receive.

> When Bridget was seven years old, she devoutly prayed for her doll to come alive and turn into a baby. She fervently repeated this prayer for several days and was terribly discouraged when nothing happened. Bridget finally said that if her doll didn't come alive, she wouldn't believe in God anymore.
>
> When she went to Sunday School that same week, her teacher made a casual reference to God knowing what is best for us. As an example, the teacher referred to a child asking for her doll to be brought to life. The teacher said God would not fulfill that request because little girls are neither ready nor equipped to raise a baby.

Bridget was jolted enough by this synchronistic example to realize that her prayer had obviously just been answered. God had said no and, through the teacher, explained why. Bridget continued to believe in God in spite of her disappointment and learned to care less about getting her own way.

Prayer Energy

ॐ The energetic intensity of prayer is boosted when someone leads a group of people in prayer and everyone verbally or even silently and mentally repeats the words. Each individual exponentially adds potency. For example, four people praying the same words are conceptually equal to four to the fourth power: 256.

> *The energetic intensity of prayer is boosted when someone leads a group of people in prayer and everyone verbally or even silently and mentally repeats the words.*

ॐ It is important that we be specific when praying for someone, something, or our self, especially if we are part of a prayer group that communicates from afar, such as through emails or a telephone chain. If the objectives are not specific and coordinated, the prayers could negate each other. For example, one person might ask for a patient to be healed while another prays for the subject to pass easily and be removed from pain and suffering. However, when many people offer unified prayers, regardless of the timing, the effects can be profound.

ॐ Whether praying alone or with a group, we must remember to phrase prayers with positive words. Instead of asking for, "Relief from anxiety," ask for "Peace" or "Resolution." Rather than saying, "I need help through this crisis," rephrase to something like, "Send me comfort, guidance, strength, support, relief, understanding, courage," and so forth. If you need money, it is more effective to affirm, "I am receiving guidance, prosperity, and abundance," rather than to express lack with the words, "I need money."

ॐ Be careful of the word "need." When used in a prayer, the Universe will reinforce it, and you will continue to need.

~ ~ ~

Prayer can literally be the means to manifest a miracle. The following story relates an outcome that could not be planned, worked for, hoped for, or even thought of.

> Keith and Kate were watching her mother's dog, Fifi, so the mother, Donna, could stay with an ill relative for a few days. The couple also owned a dog, so having two in the house was not an inconvenience.
>
> One morning, Keith took their dog and Fifi for a walk. They were on a sidewalk along a busy road when a neighbor jogged past them. Fifi bolted off behind the jogger. Keith yelled her name and chased after her. The dog ended up dashing into the street and getting run over. Fortunately, there were no car accidents involved, and the dog died immediately.
>
> Keith and Kate were now faced with a huge problem. Donna had often stated that she didn't know what she would do without Fifi because they had been constant companions for years. How could the couple possibly tell her Fifi had been killed? Knowing Donna as they did, they anticipated that her response could be extreme grief, anger, and blame, or even suicidal thoughts or action. The best reaction they could hope for would be that she would be in grief, not blame Keith or the jogger, and otherwise handle herself

responsibly.

They spent nearly an hour weighing all of the possible scenarios and how to best handle this tragic situation. They decided they had to tell her that evening when she was to come by and pick up Fifi. They asked several family members to pray for her and her reaction to and acceptance of Fifi's death. At the last minute, Donna called and told them she had decided to stay at the relative's home one more night.

The couple had an excruciating day and night but kept praying. Donna arrived just after lunch the next day. When Keith told her what had happened, her response totally shocked them and all of those who had been praying for her. They witnessed a miracle. She barely used one tissue for her tears. She said Fifi was getting old and might have had cancer and arthritis. Although she would miss her dog, Donna thought it must have been her time to go. She said it was not Keith's fault, and told him to tell the jogger that she didn't blame him either. Then she brought up other discussion topics.

Both Keith and Kate were amazed at the power of prayer and the marvelous result. Donna's reaction was entirely out of character for her and was better than they could have possibly imagined. Even Donna admitted she couldn't believe how well she was taking the news. She continued to feel incredibly normal during her grieving period. Her reaction doesn't make logical sense, based on Donna's past behavior or what might be an expected reaction by anyone who lost a pet, but this is how the setup and drama played out.

~ ~ ~

🕉 Elizabeth Kubler-Ross, a psychiatrist and pioneer in near-death studies, tells of a story in which a woman was involved in an almost fatal car accident and had a near-death experience.

As the woman's soul left her body, she was aware of the frustrations and comments being expressed by so many of the nearby inconvenienced drivers. However, she noticed a glow surrounding one particular car behind her. As she moved toward this light, she heard the driver praying for her. She took mental note of the license plate number.

Later, this woman was revived, recovered, and released from the hospital. As soon as she was able, she located the driver's address through her license plate and took flowers to the woman who had prayed for her. It was an emotional meeting.

This story is a beautiful and heart-warming example of the reality of the spiritual world and the evidence of prayer energy in the physical world.

45: SACRED PERSPECTIVES

The two primary perspectives of humanity's relationship with God are distinct from and quite oppositional to each other, not even reaching the plateau of being dualistic. Yet both, in their disparate ways, tend to serve people, depending on each person's current state of evolution.

One perspective is that of *religion*,[105] which states that people, by following prescribed, established protocols, will attain eternal salvation, but only through the intercession of an external savior, a direct intermediary with God-like powers. The other perspective is that of *spirituality*,[106] which holds that souls already have an innate, internal, eternal, universal connection with God that has never been broken. Therefore, as life changing as it often is for a person because of the massive conscious infusion of divine love, the soul itself does not require an external savior or a salvation experience.

Religions, especially those that are well established and fundamental in nature, traditionally focus on beliefs, rituals, traditions, and compliance based on official interpretations and consensus. Mainline religions throughout the world profess that God is outside of us and must be obeyed and worshipped. Their basic tenet is that if we live a good enough life and are in a state of grace at the moment of death, we will connect with God in a place called Heaven. With this view, God has all the power and authority, and people are sinful beings who face judgment and the possibility of eternal damnation. Religions generally don't accept the idea of reincarnation, and tell us that we must do good things and please God in this one and only lifetime, in order to be worthy of being in His presence after we die.

---

[105] *religion:* a specific system of beliefs and worship based on human-created tenets about God

[106] *spirituality:* that which concerns internal, unseen energies of God or the soul in contrast to the everyday material, physical world

Spirituality is primarily concerned with our personal healing and inner evolution. Through spiritual practices, we learn that we are energy beings more than physical bodies, that God is within us and also outside each of us, and that we are already One with Source as are all other souls. With spirituality, we seek God's

> *Religion teaches faith, which is passive. Spirituality encourages trust, which is active. Faith is believing God can. Trust is Knowing God will.*

will and can receive guidance and inspiration individually, and not need a priestly or ministerial intermediary. We do not require any beliefs in an invisible God to guide our decisions and actions, rather, we see God in all beings, creatures, and things throughout nature and the cosmos. As Source-based souls, we desire to see all people as Light beings and we seek to unveil and manifest God's Light on earth. This universal love is our guiding beacon to "Do unto others as we would have them do unto us."

Religion teaches faith, which is passive. Spirituality encourages trust, which is active. Faith is believing God *can.* Trust is Knowing God *will.*

Interestingly, religion and spirituality might intersect or coexist, and one need not exclude the other. In fact, even with the oppositional aspects of these perspectives, it is sometimes beneficial for a person to experience religious salvation as a significant boost toward spiritual empowerment. That is because *both of these contrasting perspectives derive from inspiration,* which is a divine influence directly and immediately received by the mind or the soul, whether it comes from reading books or observing nature, whether from praying to God with fellow brethren or going within in meditation.

Likewise, a vital spiritual path might not include religion, and a religious life might not include deep spirituality. It has been said that religion is for people who do not want to go to hell. Spirituality is for souls who have been to hell and do not want to go back. This statement, while humorous, is also an oversimplification. So, let's take a closer look at the characteristics of religion and spirituality and at how each of them serve souls in their unique ways.

Religion

Religions both unite and separate people.

ॐ Religions are one of the few cultural institutions that attempt to serve humanity and help those in need, especially in times of local or national emergencies or natural disasters. A person might find God and have a complete spiritual life change as a result of a religious conversion. Shared beliefs within a congregation offer a sense of belonging and can bond people together, especially by serving on church committees or singing in the choir. Holy Scriptures contain powerful, timeless, spiritual Truths. We can be inspired and learn these Truths in a worship setting in a way that reinforces our connectedness to others, even if only temporarily. We might also be recipients of needed assistance through the charitable giving of religious organizations.

People of a religious faith affirm that their religion is right and rely on their authoritative scriptures to prove it. Separation occurs when they believe that other religions and texts are not as right or are even wrong. People kill and die in support of their religious beliefs, upholding their doctrines with required commitment and loyalty. To the believer, eternal life is at stake. When these tenets become entrenched over generations and centuries, religious beliefs rarely evolve or get revised. Over time, they become traditions. As American humorist Will Rogers stated, "There is no argument in the world that carries the hatred that a religious belief does."

Religions usually encourage dogmatic training, faith in the scriptures, missionary evangelism, and zealous conversion of people of other religions or the "unsaved" who do not have religious connections or dedication. These religious teachings represent a first floor paradigm that holds God as a separate, all-powerful external being, whom mankind is to revere and serve. Religions encourage, and sometimes even require, group worship with prescribed rituals and prayers ideally within a consecrated building.

~ ~ ~

Most of today's active, well-established religions are relatively old. The sacred texts on which these religions rely were written, screened, and standardized hundreds or thousands of years ago. These holy books not only establish but also chronicle the religion's long-standing beliefs, doctrine, and dogma. Committees of ecclesiastic clerics who shared almost identical views of God and worship determined these official policies and sanctioned writings, which are human interpretations of spiritual Truths as Source had revealed them to the people at that time. The clerics' decisions were made by mutual agreement in a process that was likely long, intense, difficult, and occasionally agonizing. Their agreed-upon conclusions formed the foundation of a religion. The sacred texts became their exclusive and permanent holy writ.

~ ~ ~

Religions' primary goal is survival. Therefore, religious groups have hierarchical organizational structure. More members mean a more intricate political system. Policies must align in order for the group to keep functioning. Staying in the God-business also requires funding. While tithing might or might not be emphasized, there is continuous need for income.

Because religions operate exclusively at the first floor, their beliefs cause people to make understandable yet erroneous assumptions and conclusions about God. Divine benevolence seems to occur in rare situations or to only a few chosen people. Some ministers use this to their advantage, reminding the "sinners" of their congregations to keep repenting, believing, and tithing. The spiritual interpretation, however, would not focus on "sin," which means behaving against God's laws and requires confession, but encourages us to accept that humans are on a healing journey. We make mistakes from which we learn. At a spiritually advanced level, we will not even mentally process any incongruent thoughts or have self-serving agendas, so the idea of sin becomes irrelevant. How often do we need to remind ourselves not to kill someone? The idea is not even on our conscious radar. Our more evolved awareness might recognize that a "sin" occurred through a healing setup, but it might also stem from ego-based responses of anger, hatred, revenge, or other dark motives or uncontrolled behavior. Regardless of the background cause, forgiveness in the present is always appropriate.

Seeing serious problems, pain, inconsistencies, and deficiencies in life lead some to believe there is no God. Others express rational opinions such as:

- "God doesn't love me."

- "I must always be good in order to earn God's love."

- "I am not good enough for God to ever care about or listen to me."

- "God must enjoy punishing me for my sins."

- "If there is a God, He does not intercede in my life."

Although these views might seem logical and obvious in the physical world, they are also based on what people have observed, learned, and experienced through interactions with religious groups. However, these conclusions are the result of living with karmic mandates. They represent first floor responses and are inaccurate within the larger scope of fiftieth floor Reality: they are not Truths. The more rigidly we adhere to our primary beliefs, whether within a religion, when observing religious people, or even everyday beliefs such as "I must always do the *right* thing," the more opportunities we miss to heal and develop spiritually. Instead, in order for our souls to evolve, we would be wise to be open and receptive to the understandings of others, especially the Truth that God is within *all* of us *now*.

Low-vibration beliefs are only one of several factors that can obstruct us from knowing that God is already part of our life. Other common impediments, which are frequently preached in some religions, are fear-based judgment, resistance, close-mindedness, self-righteousness, and even prejudice. These are all ego conclusions, opinions, and maneuvers. The Truth is that, except when we block Source energy through fear or belief systems, God constantly blesses everyone at all times, regardless of our religions.

E/go doesn't want us to understand that. E/go's cleverness and its ability to distract perpetuate its elementary and dominating control over our life. It takes a spiritually advanced person to catch and not fall for these ego charades. This relates to ego death, which we've already learned about in the previous chapter. Just as ego fears its demise within an individual, it also craves to thrive within the leaders and members of any organization that preaches and promotes teachings that, in effect, steer people away from or block their awareness of Source Truths.

~ ~ ~

When a member of a religious group defies established behavioral beliefs or expectations, some groups have established a procedure to handle the violators. In the Amish community, the practice is called shunning. In Catholicism, excommunication. In the secular world, it is cutting the heretics off from the community or family until or unless they change their ways and meet the requirements to be reinstated.

Regrettably, these protocols, with variations that have included torture and death, have been played out too many times throughout the ages. The crisis topics vary, but the reactive, trauma-creating decisions wreak havoc in the lives of those involved and perpetuate judgment, separation, and even karma.

Divisive actions by both the rebellious person and the religious group generate ethical, moral, emotional, physical, psychological, and spiritual consequences that don't easily go away. The beliefs that justify this practice are man-made, three-dimensional, and are based on we're-right-and-you're-wrong views that corrupt spiritual Truths. Usually the people facing these decisions emotionally struggle with them, but they are following what they have accepted to be the right thing. Their beliefs validate their conclusions and their actions.

> Jeremy was raised in a large, devout Catholic family. He was a good natured, cooperative young man who did his best in all endeavors. He was a gifted church organist. He was also gay.

Jeremy was in the homosexual closet throughout his teen years, but after college, somehow his parents found out. Because Jeremy's sexual lifestyle is considered such a grave sin in the Catholic Church, his parents and siblings permanently severed all ties with him. It was excruciatingly painful for the whole family, but they prioritized their beliefs over their relationship with their son. In their minds, he was behaving immorally and was obviously wrong. They felt that if they allowed him to remain in the family, they would be endorsing his lifestyle. They felt they had no choice in the matter because the church was so emphatic in its position of labeling homosexuality as sin.

Jeremy lived an extremely conflicted life. He continued to be employed as a full time musician in Catholic churches, hiding his sexual identity. At the same time, he no longer had any family to emotionally support and interact with him. Of course, he never changed his sexual orientation, and died in his middle forties from AIDS. He had lived a difficult life that spiritually offered his family the opportunity to evolve by choosing love over beliefs, judgment, and fear.

Not knowing the profound significance of this opportunity, they chose the standard first floor protocol for dealing with someone who violated their dogma. Their family relationship never did resolve. Only God knows the ultimate damage—or possible future karmic challenges—that all family members and close friends who are tragically faced with this or some other religious crisis or dilemma will experience.

ॐ Debating both sides of this judgmental, painful, communal violation policy and dilemma can be an endless and frustrating experience. In this story, Jeremy's lifestyle, as stated above, offered his family the opportunity to choose love over beliefs, judgments, and fear. But ego eyes prohibit broad-scale consensus and acceptance. This first floor approach is closed, absolute, self-righteous, and the epitome of conditional love. Where is God in this description?

> *Jeremy's lifestyle offered his family the opportunity to choose love over beliefs, judgment, and fear. But ego eyes prohibit broad-scale consensus and acceptance.*

Even logically considering spiritual repercussions and possible resolutions to this custom are difficult and inconclusive. At the bottom line, the only applicable Truth that brings an opening for transformation is acceptance of the fact that Source loves unconditionally. When we move beyond the need to impose conditions or live under the influence of imposition, we promote spiritual growth.

Spirituality

Spirituality states that we came into this life to seek empowerment but, because we were born with God's divine energies, we need not

When we move beyond the need to impose conditions or live under the influence of imposition, we promote spiritual growth.

search externally for them. They are within and awaiting our discovery and manifestation.

Spirituality, therefore, is a fiftieth floor Reality in which ultimately unconditional love is a constant and there are no judgments or traditions to uphold. With spirituality, we exist beyond the scope of specific beliefs, rituals, or standardized texts or readings. We replace limiting protocols with understanding. We easily

Spirituality is a fiftieth floor Reality in which ultimately unconditional love is a constant and there are no judgments or traditions to uphold.

adopt new or revised insights or information as Source personally reveals them to us, and we see that this happens frequently.

Those on a spiritual path see that ego eventually merges with Ego, which means that we are beyond fear, anxiety, separation, and agendas. We live in a flow. Miracles are normal. Life is rewarding. When real life difficulties happen, we form our interpretations from a place of trust and peace. This advanced understanding does not, however, mean we are to be unaware of or daring in the face of potential first floor concerns. It remains advisable for us to keep doors locked and use care in unfamiliar places. We do not want to rely on our guides to exert excessive protective measures to compensate for our lack of caution.

The founders of early spiritual-based groups in the 1700 and 1800s relied on their individual soul connection with God. This was primarily because, traditionally, relatively few spiritual organizations offered regular group opportunities to feed the soul and provide spiritual bonding and networking. When people gathered, they did so in small groups, often in people's homes, just as the early founders of today's well-established religions did centuries or millennia earlier.

In recent years, more groups have formed to support and assist personal growth and development. These include organized New Age or New Thought churches with relatively small congregations, drumming circles, sweat lodge practitioners, meditation groups, and philosophical discussion assemblages centered around books such as *A Course in Miracles*, and those written by spiritualistic, holistic, and humanitarian keynote speakers of modern times and the recent past. The primary concept within these foundling groups is that we are walking our individual path of self-development, pursuing our particular soul scripted agenda forever in connection with Source, and always seeking harmony with all other souls.

> *Spirituality is innate, quiet, and soul fulfilling.*

With this foundation of both individuality and unity, the journey into spirituality is innate, quiet, and soul fulfilling. God's Oneness is internally and externally inclusive. We are co-creators with Source and are, therefore, loving and fearless. Sacrifice is meaningless and unnecessary when we resonate to joy. Our internal altar connects with our beingness. God is the Source, Guide, and Conductor of our lives. We receive personal guidance and Truth as Knowingness. God's will is for us to be abundant, fulfilled, peaceful, and wise, to know that we have a generous, serving spirit that blossoms and blooms with freedom and inspiration.

~ ~ ~

Inspiration and guidance are available to everyone, can occur in any place, and can be piqued by any internal or external means. We can receive inspiration and guidance in many ways but most constantly by listening to the quiet knowing in our heart. Some factors promote the availability of spiritual input: being mentally and

> *We become more attuned to insight by recognizing, utilizing, and appreciating guidance.*

emotionally open and alert, desiring to receive, having a need or purpose for guidance, working with and taking steps to implement previous input, and viewing life from the fiftieth floor. We become more attuned to insight by recognizing, utilizing, and appreciating guidance. Inspiration might change us, or it might change the direction or quality of our life.

When we write uplifting ideas into our journal, diary, stories, poetry, or musical lyrics, we capture them in time as

> *Words and ideas have little meaning until they merge with experience.*

we also try to explain them from our current understanding using words available to us. Our account is our attempt to communicate our experience, awareness, or perception. Because language evolves over time, historical mystics described their spiritual experiences and concepts in ways that we might consider to be archaic or unclear today. If you imagine a person who lived 500 years ago attempting to describe a computer or microwave oven, you would see that it would be impossible. That's because people of that era had no experience with those twentieth century inventions, and because words and ideas have little meaning until they merge with experience.

This is a fundamental concern when reading sacred texts. They are probably accurate, yet limited notations, altered through various translations that often appear obscure to us today because our advanced knowledge surpasses the literalness of those ancient writings. Yet, the principles found in those texts are still valuable, which is why we can best find answers to eternal questions through our direct, personal experience of Truth. As *A Course In Miracles* tells us, "A universal theology is impossible, but a universal experience is not only possible, but necessary. Here alone consistency becomes possible, because here alone uncertainty ends."

Our Attuned Perspective

Our perspectives, goals, and the audience we are trying to reach with any message determine how we explain something to others. A teacher will address her first grade students in a totally different manner than she would doctoral candidates. A child's explanation of marriage would only somewhat resemble an adult's, with the child's views probably not being wrong, just over-simplified. We very specifically teach a young child how to safely cross a street with the simple commands, "Stop. Look. Listen." Adults know this procedure but do not follow it to the letter because they have learned to be careful in a more casual manner. With maturity and development comes a natural relaxation and expansion of rules and training, and that's all right because we need to move beyond rigid protocols in all areas of our lives. This is especially applicable to spiritual growth.

Some persons feel very much at home within the rigid structure of organized religion; they find comfort with the simplicity of being told what to believe, how to pray, and how to act both within the church-based rituals and in their daily lives.

Other persons feel restless, bored, or confined by religious dogma and, thus, turn away in order to attain and manifest what they believe is their true spiritual association with God.

Therefore, whether we are religious or spiritual, our perspective, at its roots, is based on how we view God.

> *Whether we are religious or spiritual, our perspective is based on how we view God.*

Our ancestral understanding of God is that of an exaggerated human father figure who is autocratic, dictatorial, harsh, and judgmental. This God watches our activities and behaviors and metes out punishment when we are bad and grants forgiveness when we confess our sins. This figure somewhat resembles Santa who only rewards us when we are good.

Mankind created and interpreted God in our image. But now it is time for us to revise this inferior, limited, first floor version of our Creator—and come up with a new image of both God and ourselves. By maintaining a first floor judgmental view and holding expectations regarding God's actions toward us, we create incalculable pain and problems, some of which have become so enmeshed in people and cultures that they have often led to wars and ongoing transgenerational trauma.

God's identity and intervention with humankind has primarily been revealed to us through, and based on, Holy Scriptures. These Scriptures have not been officially upgraded since ancient times, and

> *In order to survive, religious groups must retain and uphold their sanctioned and sacrosanct beliefs, which is the same philosophy that ego uses to maintain steadfast, inviolable control of our individual minds.*

the reason why is obvious to the ego mind. In order to survive, religious groups must retain and uphold their sanctioned and sacrosanct beliefs, which is the same philosophy that ego uses to maintain steadfast, inviolable control of our individual minds. When disenchanted members of a particular religion crave different or more current, more relevant, or more advanced spiritual thoughts and views, their only alternative is to break away from the main church and form a different branch or sect, which has historically proven to eventually align again with ego thinking.

Whether we worship within a religion or follow an individualistic spiritual practice, Source works in *everyone's* life. Regardless of how different or even contradictory religious and personal belief systems are from each other, we can manifest blessings and spiritually turn our life around by following whatever form of worship, practice, or attunement God calls for us. God enters our awareness and guides and fashions us in any and every way we allow, no matter how few possibilities there are, or how tiny these openings might be.

> *God enters our awareness and guides and fashions us in any way and every way we allow, no matter how few possibilities there are, or how tiny these openings might be.*

~ ~ ~

Accepting beliefs, such as those espoused by religion, is necessary and healthy at an early stage of personal development. This practice provides guidelines for personal attitudes, values, mores, and decisions within social interactions and relationship dynamics. However, being locked into preordained or prescribed beliefs eventually holds us back from evolving our own spiritual connection with God. This is also an ancient Truth found in an anonymous quote from the early fourteenth century: "The nearer the church, the farther from God."

ॐ Once we mature to a level of being in which we would not even think of harming others, breaking laws, or violating ethics, we have moved beyond the need for the restrictions imposed by religious belief systems. The fewer beliefs we have, the less resistance we feel and the more capable we become of employing our own guidance. After we set aside our predetermined, restrictive features, God can then work in our life with more potent thoroughness and effectiveness.

> *The fewer beliefs we have, the less resistance we feel and the more capable we become of employing our own guidance.*

46: GUIDANCE

Messages from guidance can come to us in numerous ways, depending on our sensitivity of reception, the degree to which we've developed our intuitive sensors, and our current state of evolution on our spiritual path.

When we operate with first floor methods, we practice meditation in order to clear our mind of thoughts and to receive guidance. Meditation can be helpful to anyone and is always an option to still the mind and resonate with Source. Yet, developing this skill with the first floor mentality takes significant self-control, discipline, effort, and time, which some people are not willing or even able to do.

The fiftieth floor view does not require that we sit silently as we attempt to train our

> *We evolve more effectively from our core up rather than from our head down.*

mind to let go of all thoughts in meditation. Rather, the perspective from the penthouse shows that we merely need to remove the mental and emotional energetic barriers that have been blocking us from connecting to our divine soul. Doing so might require courage and diligence, but both the activity and the results are practical and experiential rather than theoretical or mentally contrived. Self-discipline is not required. Instead, we watch for incongruencies in our life and use the Three Pillars of Transformation to clear them. We also listen for our t/Truth and seek broader understandings from a wider scope of possibilities. We evolve more effectively from our core up rather than from our head down.

We can receive guidance symbolically, synchronistically, or experientially. Guidance comes to us through circumstances, events, ideas, inspirations, people, thoughts, readers, and psychics. It comes through spiritual conversations with deceased visitors or loved ones, guides, angels, the resonator, our Higher Self, and God. Some people know or have a hunch about something. Some receive visions, have profound dreams, channel guidance, use

> *Our spiritual gifts are fascinating and rewarding as we practice and develop them.*

automatic handwriting, read tea leaves or tarot cards, or use pendulums or other divining methods. Some physically feel a sensation, become aware of a particular smell, or hear or see a message. And others might need to experiment in order to learn how to interpret and work with their gift.

Our spiritual gifts are fascinating and rewarding as we practice and develop them. As our vibrational rate increases, we access higher energies that stimulate guidance more powerfully, constantly, and accurately.

~ ~ ~

Some people become skilled enough to be able to determine who their guidance is coming from. This can make a difference. All guidance comes *from* God, but might be revealed *through* lower vibrational means, such as the ways given above. These various possibilities are not the same as guidance directly from God, which is the "still small voice" within. Realizing this, some people feel that receiving messages from anyone other than God is a waste of their time, and they don't bother with any messenger other than the highest possible source. Although that is *theoretically* accurate, this view is also *ego driven*. In Truth, God utilizes beings, people, circumstances, events, and anything and everything else available to work His purpose. If the message you receive rings t/True, begin to trust and work with it in whatever ways or to whatever extent feels appropriate to you.

Be aware that hearing guidance will rarely occur through our ears from an audible, external sound. Nor does seeing necessarily refer to visual sight. Receiving a spiritual message, in whatever way it happens, is "hearing" and "seeing" in the spiritual sense. Some people find that the actual process of acquiring input

> *Receiving a spiritual message is "hearing" and "seeing" in the spiritual sense.*

might vary at times or become so natural that the method is irrelevant. The main intent is to apply what we receive, regardless of how it is delivered.

~ ~ ~

We all have the "still small voice" within. Nearly everyone has heard an occasional urgent message, and most people heed this unusual alert, while others learn the lesson the hard way.

At age fourteen, Tammy was primarily concerned with social activities and her friends. One day, she was going to ride a bus to an ice skating rink. Although her home was near a bus stop for a particular line that would take her to the rink, her girlfriends were going to take a different bus and route. As she walked past her own bus stop, she heard a voice say, "Stop. Get on the bus here." Even though this was a strong, internal directive, she dismissed it in favor of being with her friends. When she was stepping onto the other bus, she again heard the word, "Stop." She again dismissed it. As her group walked toward the back seats, she felt a wall of fear overcome her but said nothing to her friends and acted normally.

Five stops later, a group of young men, dressed in typical casual clothing, got on the bus and gave her a significant beating. They targeted only her. Tammy felt she had been selected because she was so small and vulnerable. Her friends were not able to stop the beating, but eventually the bus driver broke up the fight. She received medical treatment and it took some time for her to physically and emotionally recover, but she learned a valuable and unforgettable lesson. She promised herself that she would never again ignore guidance.

~ ~ ~

ॐ When we first begin to receive guidance, we might find that it is not 100 percent accurate 100 percent of the time even though that degree of purity is an eventual goal. The Truth is that guidance is 100 percent accurate, but our receptors and discernment are rudimentary. Therefore, obtaining reliable guidance is not an absolute. There are many variables, and time and practice are required for us to hone our subtle skills. We will make mistakes. The possibility for error, however, is not a reason to avoid seeking and developing our ability to receive.

Pursue spiritual guidance in spite of occasional glitches. Multi-dimensional energies are facilitating the opening of our receivers to access Source energy for clear, constant, powerful, timely, and wise advice. It is up to us to look for it, listen, trust, and put the pieces together. Source

> *Source energy is never wrong. As our understanding of Truth evolves, guidance adjusts to changes in our free will choices.*

energy is never wrong. As our understanding of Truth evolves, guidance adjusts to changes in the free will choices that others and we have made that would impact us. That is why guidance, in order to protect us, might interrupt our thoughts and actions in any given circumstance, or it can even occasionally reverse itself in response to outside factors that have altered the situation.

When in doubt about the accuracy of the guidance you receive, check in with the resonator. If you still need more clarification, consult an intuitive for a reading and input. When an external source validates the counsel, we can rely on it more fully. On occasion, different readings will seem to contradict each other. At one time in her life, a woman had a serious question about how to handle a challenge in a relationship, and received five seemingly unrelated answers from five intuitive people. Initially, she was perplexed and disappointed, but ultimately all five answers proved to be accurate.

~ ~ ~

The following three experiences illustrate more about how guidance can work.

Peter continuously and effortlessly receives daily, specific guidance about his life, what to do and say, what is happening, and where to go. This input is not a command or directive for him to follow, but it is given as helpful and wise suggestions that he has learned will enhance his day, productiveness, and fulfillment. This system works very well for him.

~ ~ ~

Kirk has developed such complete trust of guidance that he relies on it for everything. Many years ago, his guides told him that he doesn't need to buy books or rely on anyone else for assistance, that he will hear everything he needs to know. Although his gift did not exempt him from studying for exams when he was in school, he continues to receive important and specific details, such as a page number in a book for a needed or corroborative reference. Now, as an intuitive chiropractor, his gift has produced significant results for some of his patients.

~ ~ ~

Within two days, Cora heard three friends talk about themselves or people they know who went to a dermatologist and were diagnosed with possible skin cancer. She had been aware of a spot on her arm for years, but it hadn't changed very much, and it was easy for her to ignore. However, the remarks she heard were so specific and peculiar that she decided to go for a skin checkup.

The lab report stated that Cora had basal cell carcinoma. Although that is the least injurious type of skin cancer to have and is not life threatening, she would not have thought of going to have the spot checked out without having been nudged by guidance to pay attention to the words of her friends.

It is also possible to hear of several similar events and not have it pertain to you personally, but by paying attention and responding appropriately, you might realize that you are receiving guidance intended to benefit others. It is then up to you to follow guidance's urgings

> *Whether or not we pay attention to God's will is an indicator of our true desire for spiritual evolution.*

or nudges to speak up and carry the message forward to those who need to hear it.

47: GOD'S WILL

God's will, if you recall, is a process, experience, or outcome that comes from God and serves our highest good. Whether or not we pay attention to God's will is an indicator of our true desire for spiritual evolution.

Before seeking a spiritual path, we might have only occasionally been interested in a divine being or haphazardly allowed God into our life. We might have given only lip service to the concept of God's will.

Even when on a spiritual path, what we know as true might not necessarily be Truth. The mistakes we think we made might have, in fact, been fulfillment of God's will for us to enhance our spiritual evolution. This phenomenon demonstrates that, no matter how much we study or attempt to practice spiritual ways, we will not know all we want to know, we will have occasional doubts, and we will experience some confusion as a natural part of our life.

Some people struggle with

> *We will be most fulfilled when we merge our will with God's will.*

insignificant areas of God's will, such as whether or not He cares if we drink orange juice or milk, or turn right or left at a particular intersection. Getting caught in this kind of thinking clouds up the larger scope of life. The greater distinction to make is whether we are seeking our own will instead of God's. The Truth is that we will be most fulfilled when we merge our will with God's will.

God's will is sometimes more easily determined in retrospect when we have the hindsight to see the wisdom and beneficial results of what has transpired. Sometimes we need to learn the hard way because practical experience is the best teacher. We might miss the easier or simpler path that God provided, but if we eventually benefit from the detour, then we will go farther and accomplish something else probably just as or possibly even more important.

As long as we are significantly tied into a scripted life path with its burden of karma, life will present challenges. These difficulties are also part of God's will to assist our

> *God understands, loves, and accepts us—warts and all.*

spiritual development. Because God has infinite patience, there is no need for us to hurry through life, struggle with fears, or anguish over decisions. God understands, loves, and accepts us —warts and all.

God's will is not always the easy path. Some life challenges might remain in our life, but we can deeply and peacefully accept them and not be stuck with the old views and emotions. Even when we are in God's flow, we will still work very hard. The life quality difference is in our interpretation and integration of the word "work." Once we are significantly congruent with God, we take delight in the beneficial resonance of any resulting activity, regardless of the name we apply to it. Work becomes non-work, or joy-filled play—not because it is always fun but because we feel privileged to be involved with God as we generate the rewards of our highest calling.

> *Work becomes non-work because we feel privileged to be involved with God as we generate the rewards of our highest calling.*

Initially, God's will is different than ours, and with first floor energy, we might even conclude that God's will is in conflict with our will. As we advance toward empowerment, we crave God's will for us, and we want to honor God's presence in our life. Over time, we learn to know God's will with significant clarity, but, as with comprehending guidance, we need practice in order to achieve this level of discernment.

When we see that inner attunement is always leading us, we will have finally learned to trust Source. Our life is then permanently changed and upgraded. We are whole, enlivened, and emotionally

> *At the fiftieth floor, God's will is ours.*

nurtured. Our deepest spiritual longings are fulfilled. We live in a state of gratitude and appreciation. Life becomes more of an adventure in discovery because we no longer merely manage challenges but are led through and beyond them. We participate in activities with little or no resistance, and we emanate light. At the fiftieth floor, God's will *is* ours.

48: MIRACLES

ॐ A *miracle*[107] is a memorable and divine gift, defined in the dictionary as "an event inexplicable by the laws of nature and so held to be supernatural in origin, or an act of God." A miracle can be a single episode or several clustered segments of experiences, situations, or events. Miracles are the substance of stories in which angels appear, outcomes are illogically altered, spontaneous healing takes place, valuable information or guidance is provided, or other unpredictable and extraordinary experiences happen that cannot be replicated, easily explained away, or denied. These miracles might occur with or without prayers for divine assistance or even when the recipient of the miracle is unaware of a critical need. Often a person's life is spared from a tragedy or permanently changed, or someone's behavior or response is so wonderfully atypical that the only conclusion possible is that a miracle transpired. For all of these reasons, miracle stories are meaningful and inspirational.

> One summer, Dave and Erin were driving home from a vacation. They decided to take a less busy road in order to see small towns. Dave was at the wheel, Erin was sleeping in the front passenger side, and their dog was in back in her car seat.
>
> Erin woke up when she heard a person whistle.

---

[107] *miracle:* a profoundly beneficial, multi-dimensional event or experience that rarely occurs at the first floor, but is normal on the fiftieth floor

She was perplexed because Dave didn't whistle. She asked him if he had tried to wake her up that way. He said he had not whistled but had heard it too. Erin whistled the pitches she had heard, and he agreed they were the same. They looked at each other with confusion because the only other creature in the car was their dog, and of course, she couldn't whistle. They were driving about 60 miles an hour with the windows closed, and it made no sense to conclude that someone outside had managed to project the sound in their direction.

When Erin asked what had been going on, Dave admitted that he had been starting to fall asleep, but was hesitant to wake Erin up to drive. Because there was no logical explanation for the whistle, and they were now both wide awake, they concluded that God had prevented a serious accident by sending a being who intervened in such a simple, quick, and effective way.

Erin expressed their deepest appreciation to God for the protection and miracle. They were obviously not supposed to die that day.

Miracles happen frequently on earth but not on a recurring basis to the same person unless the person is empowered. The higher our vibrational rate, the more miracles we perceive and experience.

49: BLESSINGS

> *The higher our vibrational rate, the more miracles we perceive and experience.*

Blessings are on-going conditions or situations that provide a quality of life and spiritual advantage beyond what we can accomplish on our own. Some people identify their blessings as "good luck" or say "things worked out well." The larger Reality, however, is that they were blessed by Source. When we congruently follow our t/Truth, God works through and with us in inestimable and abundant ways.

> *When we congruently follow our t/Truth, God works through and with us in inestimable and abundant ways.*

We can't earn blessings, yet we can achieve goals that provide a beneficial position in which blessings manifest, such as earning a college degree that leads to us obtaining rewarding employment. Blessings can also occur without any effort and might be a byproduct of other endeavors. People might volunteer to assist us, we might unexpectedly receive an inheritance, or find an incredible bargain on a necessary item. Blessings can occur as a result of praying, speaking, assisting another person, or doing something so thoughtful or so well that others bless us in return.

ॐ We seek to be a channel of blessings for others when we function with an open heart and loving intent,

> *No matter what we do in the spirit of love, we get more back than we give.*

and by displaying our willingness to serve. No matter what we do in the spirit of love, we get more back than we give. Our blessed returns might come from different people or in diverse ways, but that blessing is always of a higher vibrational frequency than the blessing we gave out. That is the uplifting element of blessings.

~ ~ ~

ॐ At the fiftieth floor, blessings abound. However, with an exclusively first floor view, we are unable to see the full scope of abundant blessings that a larger context would offer.

First floor fairness claims that if we spend a certain number of hours working, we should earn a specific amount of income—a tit-for-tat arrangement. When we operate at the fiftieth floor, we experience abundance, whether in money or other blessings that extend far beyond the effort that we exert. Yet, many or even most spiritual workers have challenges concerning adequate earnings, and there are various karmic reasons for this life issue. Yet it is possible for some Light workers to heal beyond their predicament. If they do not earn according to their worth, they will be taken care of in other ways.

> Russ is an experienced, dedicated, and gifted healer. He has attempted to support himself and his family through his profession but has struggled financially. Although family circumstances provide a comfortable lifestyle, he always feels inadequate because of his meager contribution to the household money supply. He tried every spiritual and practical technique he knows to develop abundance in his life. In spite of these efforts, as time went on, he grew more aware of and perplexed by his extensive selfless service that did not yield anything close to what he knows he deserves. This inequity defied logical and spiritual principles and created deep resentment that something is wrong somewhere.

One of the healing methods Russ learned was to say the words "Praise God" on a continual basis regardless of what was occurring in life. He decided to work with this simple mantra and diligently and frequently thought and stated the phrase. At times, Russ felt ridiculous saying "Praise God" when he was in pain or handling a difficult situation or problem, but he kept up his commitment.

A few years after he began to use the "Praise God" statement, Russ received an unexpected inheritance. His financial circumstances substantially improved and shifted his perspective about how God works. He could finally see that God was providing for him and his family in a way beyond what he could have accomplished on his own. He might or might not ever earn an appropriate or adequate income from his professional efforts and time, but God answered his prayers for abundance from a direction and in a way totally unrelated to Russ' service. He was being taken care of and blessed beyond belief.

As a result of the obvious financial blessing in his life, Russ no longer held resentment about his work. He interpreted "earning" in a radically different way. Income from his career became nearly irrelevant in his mind, not because he was independently wealthy but because he lived knowing God was taking care of him beyond the old linear equation that time at work equals a specific monetary compensation.

Serving others became a privilege rather than a job. In addition, Russ repeatedly saw that items he needed were on sale in stores, that physical things broke at the most convenient time for easy replacement at affordable prices, and that he effortlessly saw innumerable blessings everywhere in his life. He could authentically praise God for his abundance.

"Praise God" is a phrase that adds extra credit to our overall vibrational average. It has extremely high frequencies that, over time, accrued enough clout to eventually manifest a major life change for Russ. Of course, not every Light worker will receive

God will supply our needs, and the freer we are from ego's grip, the more liberated, abundant, and empowered our life will be.

an inheritance or even have a significant financial event that marks a more advanced developmental level. However, God will supply our needs, and the freer we are from ego's grip, the more liberated, abundant, and empowered our life will be.

Energetically congruent spiritual workers are blessed in more ways than they can comprehend. Like Russ, an initial typical situation might present a conundrum if we feel resentment from what we perceive as

As long as we surrender ego, follow our inner t/Truth, and serve others, blessings will continue to pour forth.

inadequate income from work—until we learn otherwise.

Counting Our Blessings

ॐ Abundance means so much more than financial wealth or wellbeing. We can be abundantly blessed with friends, hobbies, radiant health, and an active lifestyle. We can enjoy a supportive family, rewarding employment, opportunities, travel and cultural experiences, living close to nature, peace of mind, and seeing nonmaterial fruits of our labors.

When we more fully appreciate loving attributes and aspects of our lives and relationships, we will recognize how blessed we are. We will notice deeper, fuller, easier, happier, and enhanced benefits in our lives. As long as we surrender ego, follow our inner t/Truth, and serve others, blessings will continue to pour forth.

~ ~ ~

Almost all of us have many blessings in our everyday world. Looking for them during a typical day is a worthwhile activity that helps us refocus our attention, amp up our gratitude, and open ourselves to see more blessings to appreciate.

➤ Notice your thoughts and feelings while rereading the preceding paragraph.

➤ Make a list of what is working well in your life.

➤ Scan for any area of abilities, activities, assistance, experiences, health, provisions, relationships, responsibilities, time, or even elements in nature that you appreciate.

ॐ The degree of reluctance you notice about doing this activity, and/or the resentment or anger you feel about what is or is not on your list will highlight the areas where ego is still ruling your life.

> ➢ Begin to clear these ego energies, using the Three
> Pillars of Transformation—forgiving, surrendering, and
> vacuuming—and then concentrate more on your
> blessings.

The supportive and beneficial energies you transmit will
attract more blessings to you.

50: EMPOWERMENT

Empowerment and transformation are words that have
already been defined and used extensively throughout *Life's
Healing Setups*. They are similar but distinct, and I bring them
together into your consciousness to make my final point.
Transformation is the *process* of activating a higher vibrational
energy in order to incrementally evolve as we ascend from the
first floor to the fiftieth floor. Empowerment is the augmenting
result of transformation, and means that we vibrationally attain
the fiftieth floor attributes so that we can better interact in
unified co-creation with God.

On the fiftieth floor, our internal lives are so improved—so
transformed—that the external shifts and benefits are obvious
and welcome, we are
more aware of our
powerful thoughts
and prayers, and we
receive support in
previously unheard
of ways. Because we

> *Dynamic transition is so critical
> and powerful that physical
> symptoms usually occur as our
> body adjusts to accommodate
> these life-changing energies.*

can choose and are now able to avoid performing some or many
of the activities and responsibilities of our formerly mandated
roles, we have freedom—we are empowered—to select when,
how much, and with whom we interact. We are blessed with a
fuller array of other behavior options free from emotional,
mental, or obviously unwanted consequences.

We are more spiritually attuned to God's will. As taxing and confusing as our path might now be, we know that each soul—including your soul—intentionally chose to be on earth at this time, and in some way, experience these escalating transformative energies. We see that we have more free will choice in regard to how we respond to healing opportunities. From our endeavors to seek enlightenment, we learned how to spiritually interpret experiences, and apply and activate these principles in our life. In this way, we placed ourselves in an advantageous position for profound soul growth in this incarnation.

We see that we can merge with Source though our Ego while still in a body, although physical density does limit the vibrational frequency we can attain and sustain. Our cell structures are adapting to these increasing potencies as our DNA evolves. This dynamic transition is so critical and powerful that physical symptoms usually occur as our body adjusts to accommodate these life-changing energies. Gratefully, no matter how difficult, painful, confusing, long, and symptomatic this time is, the results will be far greater than we can imagine.

> *Humanity's integration with God is so thorough at this empowered level that we no longer live resisting our t/Truth or fearing anything.*

ॐ Humanity's integration with God is so thorough that at this empowered level that we no longer live resisting our t/Truth or fearing anything. Our transformation leads us to continuously trust Source. Our liberated ego and divinely merged wholeness activates personal mastery while we completely surrender to and become co-creative with God. The effectiveness, quality, and flow of our life blesses ourselves and others. We are empowered.

We bless our healing setups for providing the means for us to arrive at this profound level of life. We emerge as Light beings who radiate our unconditional loving essence to the world.

~ ~ ~

ॐ May we all be blessed with Truth, love, and peace. Amen!

APPENDIX

GLOSSARY

Akashic Records: a high dimensional energetic library that stores all histories of all souls and all lives

aura, prana, chi (qi): a vital essence that arises from and surrounds all life forms

beings: advanced spiritual entities or souls, not presently incarnated on earth, who promote divine intervention and/or assistance for humanity

beliefs: resolute, judgmentally screened, and predetermined guidelines that are intended to shape life, and often require allegiance, prescribed behaviors, and self-discipline

bi-locate: to physically be in two locations at the same time

blessings: on-going conditions or situations that provide a quality of life and spiritual advantage beyond what we can accomplish on our own

button: an energetically charged issue that is emotionally inflamed and easily provoked

co-creation: the inherent ability to manifest rewarding and blessed results in life

congruent or *congruency:* a state of mental, emotional, physical, and spiritual integration in which all facets of our functioning align with Source Truths

control: exercising command over inner and outer aspects of life, causing disharmony, urgency, incongruency, anxiety, and other disturbing emotions

Dark Night of the Soul: a prolonged period of experiential and emotional assault, intended to dismantle ego's spiritually immature identity, personal history, agendas, and behavior

default method of operating, default system, default response(s), default executive system: uniquely developed, well-practiced, automatically triggered, three-dimensional coping strategies and self-management techniques that we formed through karmic issues and present life emotions and experiences in order to survive life's stresses and challenges

dharma: personal blessings, advantages, qualities, and traits that manifest from past life attainments

divine: that which pertains to or comes from God; Godlike

divine guidance or *guidance:* timely, appropriate, and beneficial awareness, messages, inspiration, or advice that originate from beyond conscious, logical thought

divine intervention: God's active involvement in life, either directly or through an angel or a messenger; often considered to be a miracle

divine timing: synchronistic experiences that occur at the best possible moment to maximize potential benefits or outcomes

Ego (capital E): the congruent state of empowered consciousness attuned to God

ego (lowercase e): a small segment of our divine core that is responsible for our safety but which also functions exclusively with a rational, limited identity as though it were disconnected from Source

ego agendas: self-serving views and behaviors

ego consciousness: our exclusive awareness of and reliance on the self-created remnant of our divine identity, that is more associated with fear and protection of the human form and mind than with Source energy

ego control: a state of being in which we allow ego to rule our life, distancing us from our inherent trust in God

ego death: ego's excruciating stage of defeat when it realizes it

must abdicate its life dictatorship to Source, yet its default
systems remain with reduced authority

ego filters: three-dimensionally programmed screens used to
interpret and understand life and curtail higher functioning
potentials

ego games: repetitive roles and behaviors that stimulate
repetitive responses and dramas

ego input: consciously processed, unenlightened messages that
are based solely on what we've learned from our past three-
dimensional experiences

ego interpretation: personal opinions of our world based on
ego's isolated, limited, and resistant view of life

ego management techniques: three-dimensional interpretive and
response skills through which a person maintains an ego-induced
façade of being in control of his or her life, but which actually
signifies that ego is in control

ego mechanics: thought processes that create disturbing
emotions, defy spiritual growth, and perpetuate spiritual
immaturity

ego vacuum: an etheric tool that suctions out ego mechanics,
trash bags, and energetic emotional congestion, instantly
neutralizes all removed energies, and raises vibrational rates

emotional debris: a collection of unreleased, unresolved
emotions from present life experiences accrued from merely
managing challenges and minimizing, avoiding, or denying
reactive feelings; these might be stowed anywhere in the
physical body and create symptoms or health challenges

emotional trash bags: the energetically charged emotional
accumulation from the present life that is typically stored in the
chest area with little or no apparent physical implications

emotional t/Truth: honestly recognizing, admitting, and
expressing emotions to assist congruency

empowerment: the benefits of incremental integration of ego into Ego that stimulates whole brained functioning and manifests Source congruency in our will, thoughts, emotions, decisions, and actions

energetic debris: any undesired, unreleased, and unresolved energies in our system; these can be karmic or emotional, but might also include other "low energies" such as environmental residue and strongly persistent, limiting mental filters that manifest as three-dimensional thoughts, habits, beliefs, judgments, and so on

etheric: a non-physical, energetic, intangible state or existence

expectations: deeming that the actions, responses, or results of someone or something should conform to our self-defined interpretation of rightness or appropriateness

experiential markers or *signposts:* events that when spiritually interpreted, signal progressive healing

fear: absence of trust, the foundation of ego, a paralyzing emotion

forgiveness: the process of reinterpreting painful experiences and relationships, and clearing their stored, negatively charged emotional energies

Forgiveness Activity: the process of applying forgiveness in our life concerning relationships and experiences with ourselves, other people, and organizations in order to obtain freedom from all past, present, and future potential karma with its mandated role-playing

Foundation of Life: the Source of all that is, commonly referred to as God, Allah, or Yahweh in ancient religions and with words such as Creator, Prime Energy, or Universal Energy in modern times

free will: the ability to make choices in life, which expands as we remove karma and address our soul script

God consciousness: our awareness and integration of Source attributes, energetic resonance, and Knowing that transcend present life limitations and awaken empowerment

God's will: a process, experience, or outcome that comes from God and serves our highest good

grace: the ability to allow for the unknown

gratitude: feeling and expressing emotional and mental appreciation

head authority: the habitual ego voice that overrides and masquerades as genuine guidance, and which we often choose to obey

healing: improvement or resolution in any aspect of a person, including the holistic mind/body/spirit connection, and the karmic roots of past and current life experiences

Higher Self: an inborn, divinely attuned essence that is a single portion of Source

incongruent or *incongruency:* portions of inner emotions, thoughts, and functioning that significantly differ from each other and require ego management to handle

inspiration: a divine influence directly and immediately received by the mind or the soul

interpretation: the meaning one derives from personal experiences, events, observations, and understandings

issue(s) or *life issues:* karmically caused recurring challenges that trigger illogically harsh emotions and elude permanent resolution

issue potencies: the force or concentration of a karmic issue that presets the prevalence of button pushing and intensity of emotional reaction

judgment: the act or practice of screening life through a filter that depicts all events, circumstances, and issues as good/bad, right/wrong, black/white

karma: unreleased and unresolved issues and emotions from past lifetimes

karmic burn: a soul script that includes all or a difficult portion of accrued karma to address in one lifetime and results in profound, recurring challenges that often prove to be unsolvable through conventional means

karmic carryovers: issues that have been active in many earlier lifetimes

karmic clearing: removing the low energy vibrations of karma to enable spiritual evolution

karmic or *life script:* soul-chosen areas to address in the upcoming life

karmic restrictions, barriers or *energy blocks:* soul-mandated requirements imposed by karma that, until they are energetically cleared, prevent us from attaining some specific desired accomplishments or attributes in this life

karmic retribution: a self-chosen life circumstance in which a situation we posed on others in a previous life is imposed on us in this lifetime

karmic reward: an infrequent soul-selected lifetime to enjoy blessings with a minimum or absence of karma

Knowledge (capital K): Source-based understandings

knowledge (lowercase k): consciously learned information

latent karma: emotional energetic debris acquired during this present life that is unreleased and unresolved

life between lives: multi-dimensional, continuous stream of soul life between incarnations

life blueprint: the unseen energetic configuration of life that offers healing opportunities and generates visible effects; how the karmic script functions

life lens: the filtering system, preset with our karmic issues, through which we view and process our life and world; this filter skews our behavior and limits internal and external support, ease, and blessings

Light (capital L), *God's Light,* or *Source Light:* the actual radiant Source essence of all life, centered physically in the solar plexus

Light being: a person who exudes the glow of his or her divinity

Light worker: a person who contributes to humanity's energetic advancement

light (lowercase l): physical illumination or realization

merge: to gradually blend your limited ego into a whole brained Ego as your new personal identity

miracle: a profoundly beneficial, multi-dimensional event or experience that rarely occurs at the first floor, but is normal on the fiftieth floor

mirroring: grating interactions with others who reflect or display our own issues

modality: a particular healing practice, such as massage, reiki, or energy healing

oath or *vow:* a decree or consuming mental commitment without a fulfillment or expiration clause, made in a previous lifetime or earlier in this lifetime, to do or not do a particular act, that energetically remains active throughout incarnations until the decree is consciously released

peace: a state of harmony within oneself and in personal relations between people or groups; absence of urgency; congruent acceptance of all aspects of life

perspective: the point of view from which a person sees a situation, experience, event, or even life itself

primary constructs (PCs): the notion that we can accept an energetic view and apply a spiritual interpretation to our existence and experiences

projecting: inappropriately attributing our opinions and

expectations onto another person as his or her own

Reality (capital R): perspectives, interpretations, actions, and outcomes based on divine, universal Truths

reality (lowercase r): perspectives, interpretations, actions, and outcomes based on human truths

reincarnation: rebirth of a soul in a new body to clear karma, learn lessons, foster new experiences, serve others, and spiritually evolve

religion: a specific system of beliefs and worship based on human-created tenets about God

resonator: an internal energy detector that alerts us to timely and/or critical messages that originate beyond our conscious scope

roles: soul-scripted behavior

set up: to put someone or something in a particular place, order, or condition

setup or *spiritual setup:* a spiritually planned, unexpectedly triggered, interactive issue-healing crisis, that is perfectly orchestrated for all involved to push specific buttons, stimulate acute emotions, and provoke intense dramas

sigil: a symbol that holds energy

soul: our unique, eternal Source energy that animates life

soul endowments: attributes that emanate from Source to enhance our soul and life evolution

soul growth: the process of healing, evolving, and blossoming into our potential divine empowerment

soul relationships: the energetic status between souls accrued from past and present life experiences

Source: the Prime Energy of our creation, a portion of which remains eternally accessible whether we are incarnated or not

Source energy: divine vitality that feeds the soul and provides guidance and opportunities to enhance spiritual evolution

Source wisdom or input: synonyms for divine guidance; antonym for head authority

spirits: souls that are earth-bound and only one level beyond physical life

spiritual path: seeking development of an inner divine nature

spiritual principles: energetic virtues, guidelines, and understandings that help us heal and transform

spirituality: that which concerns internal, unseen energies of God or the soul in contrast to the everyday material, physical world

surrender: to release three-dimensional ego processes, functioning, allegiance, identity, and resulting outcomes in order to expedite empowerment

tele-transport: to move from one location to another with no physical effort

tenet of karma: the principle of "cause and effect" that directly influences, molds, and restricts our present existence due to unreleased and unresolved past life energies

three-dimensional: a view of life based exclusively on that which can be seen, touched, and measured, and which compels and directs human activities; this outlook represents spiritual immaturity

transform or *personal transformation:* a gradual energetic healing process that replaces three-dimensional operations with divine functions and attributes

transmigration: incarnating from one kingdom to another

Truth (capital T): the ultimate, universal, and transcendent Reality that is miraculously accessible to all

truth (lowercase t): the conclusions that we, as humans, have come to accept as reality in our individual lives

unconditional love: an ever-present state of nonjudgmental acceptance, support, and radiance that is embedded in Source and is consistently all encompassing and all forgiving

understandings: concepts, perceptions, and assumptions intended to guide, assist, and enrich life, individually accepted and applied, and effortlessly revised and expanded

vibrational frequencies: scientifically measurable oscillations that emanate from all divine and human creations; frequencies increase as we spiritually develop

victim: a person who is abused by life, feels powerless, and is typically unable to foundationally improve or thrive

White Light: an intentionally visualized, milky-white energy field placed around an object, life form, or person for protection, comfort, and blessing

BLUEPRINT REALITIES
OF LIFE'S HEALING SETUPS

Realities of Your Life Blueprint

1. You learn your karmic issues through interactions and experiences with your birth family. Your adult family provokes these same issues to offer healing opportunities.

2. Spiritual commitment, intent, claims, and prayer elicit challenges to see if you mean what you say.

3. You are a magnet that attracts people, circumstances, and events to push your issue buttons.

4. What you focus on grows: problems, health, gratitude, blessings. What you focus on is your choice.

5. Appearances are deceiving. What you experience at the first floor is usually the exact opposite of what is occurring spiritually.

6. The intensity of your inner disturbance and the degree of your involvement in dramas determine whether the arising issue is primarily yours or someone else's.

7. Your internal and external responses in difficult situations are the experiential markers that show the extent of your healing progress.

8. Downshifts precede spiritual boosts.

9. All life-impacting events and situations happen according to divine timing.

10. The initial on/off switch for issues restricts you from seeing and employing better options; by using energetic release to incrementally remove issues, you open yourself to a larger context with additional and wiser response possibilities.

11. Asking for "help" on the first floor is an SOS call; spiritual help has a higher purpose—to Heal Energetic Life Patterns (H-E-L-P.)

Transform Struggles into Peace

1. Accept full responsibility for your life just as it is and be willing to make changes.

2. Surrender your life to God, and cultivate a spiritual path.

3. Apply spiritual and energetic understandings to everything in daily life.

4. Be aware of setups, button pushing, mirroring, and projecting.

5. Reinterpret each difficult experience as a beneficial opportunity.

6. Safely, appropriately, and in a timely way, release your emotions.

7. Use the Three Pillars of Transformation and other energy-based techniques and modalities.

8. Speak your t/Truth.

9. Seek to develop and use guidance.

10. Finally make a decision to move beyond a stalemate. Sometimes ANY decision will help.

11. Change your response pattern when triggered, even if initially in only trivial ways, to gradually open, shift, and heal your issues.

Live Beyond Your E/go

1. You experience fewer, less intense, and shorter setups and personal issue challenges as you energetically heal; eventually you will have no need for them to occur.

2. You are free from the limitations of three-dimensional methods of operating, perspectives, interpretations, emotions, and responses. You are clear of restrictive processes and programming.

3. You keep your emotional plate clean.

4. You are beyond temptation and don't even think about anything that is not beneficial. Your thoughts are powerful, manifesting prayers.

5. You are a whole-brained, multi-sensory, multi-dimensional Light being.

6. You are internally congruent and continuously attuned to Source.

7. Guidance is normal, and you easily receive, recognize, and utilize it.

8. Your empowered Ego fosters wisdom and peace.

9. Miracles, synchronicities, and blessings are standard. You overflow with gratitude and praise.

10. You are one with all creation, and you exude understanding, compassion, and unconditional love.

11. You desire to be—and are—a channel of blessings for others.

DARK NIGHT OF THE SOUL

The following list identifies the typical inner feelings, reactions, thoughts, and conclusions that a person might encounter while undergoing the Dark Night of the Soul. Some of these statements might describe challenges you have had for your whole life, or some that you might have never experienced before. Usually most things on this list are incredibly intense for an extended period of time. As you process out the inner pain and charged energies, you eventually manifest the results of tremendous healing.

Typical Symptoms

- You feel as though nearly everything is wrong, difficult, neutral, or bad.

- You feel as though you have no personal control in your life and that no one else can help you with these problems.

- You feel alone, even if others are around you and are trying to help.

- You don't care about much of anything or anyone.

- You feel frustrated and life appears so futile that you commonly think or say, "Whatever!" or "Oh, well!" perhaps accompanied by a deep sigh.

- You are hit with compiled crises. Many normal irritations, problems, or unwanted events are condensed into a short period of time, and the end is not in sight.

- Your problems look and feel exaggerated.

- You experience financial strain and drain, sometimes for the first time or in an unusual fashion.

- You are challenged in social conversations. Most everything you think, feel, and say is negative. It is tempting to avoid groups of people or situations where you must interact with others.

- You feel temporary relief when you are away from your natural environment, such as when you are on vacation, visiting a close friend, going to a movie, and so on. However, because you need this change so much and so often and because God is so thorough in presenting the setups from which you can learn, even TV, movies, novels, magazines, or other pastimes will often trigger an issue that pushes your button.

- You might feel an occasional, overwhelming desire to run away, leave your career, spouse, family, or other long-term commitments. You might know you won't leave because you have been effective or rewarded in the relationship before. You might feel that your coworkers and loved ones don't deserve your difficulties or that your thoughts are unreasonable. Your immediate anguish could feel like you are pinned to a wall and can't change anything. You might feel ashamed for having escape thoughts.

- You feel remorse and grief when you think about your life. Everything is so hard that you feel: "I'm wrong," "Life isn't fair," "My life is a failure," or "I'm worthless and undeserving of anything better." You might compare yourself to others who you think have a better life, more money, or a happier existence.

- You have intense feelings of being betrayed, resented, unsupported (even spiritually,) constantly pushed by others, and that you are a victim.

- Your thoughts about the world and people around you might cause you to feel overwhelmed, confused, furious, hopeless, helpless, stressed, resentful, exhausted, tearful, angry, and over-emotional.

- You might have thoughts of giving up, wondering how you can possibly go on, or of suicide.

- You might question your sanity and have to work harder than usual to appear sane.

- You form harsh conclusions and often berate yourself. You might even purposefully injure yourself.

- You have difficulty concentrating and very little gets finished or not finished to your satisfaction.

- You are depressed and feel the need to cut back on optional activities such as classes, therapies, and social activities. You might even want to avoid necessary activities such as grocery shopping, and cooking.

- You might have physical symptoms or health conditions arise. Your weight might gain, drop, or fluctuate.

- If you have previously been able to receive guidance, you might now be blocked or misunderstand the messages, whether they come to you directly or through healing messengers.

- You have a continuous, excessive need for White Light, and are vulnerable to attracting undesirable low life forms, forces, experiences, and events.

- You feel as though you have few or no blessings in your life.

Personal Benefits

There are enormous personal rewards as a result of going through the Dark Night of the Soul transformation process. Individual awareness of these improvements will vary, but the following list represents typical improvements.

You might:

- Be able to clear challenges as they arise and not accumulate energetic debris.

- Be able to see a larger view of life with fuller and clearer awareness.

- Be aware of more flow and assistance in your life.

- Be able to heal your physical body faster by intentionally focusing on your health.

- Be able to cleanse karmic patterns and be aware that you might still need to clear present life effects from the karmic issues.

- Be aware of when contradictions become wholeness, for example: become more sensitive to higher understandings, guidance, energies, and blessings from Source and less sensitive to ego reminders about old unresolved pains, perspectives, and personal history.

- Have the desire to live a clearer and simpler life.

- Become more emotionally disentangled, detach from outcomes, and feel less reactive and triggered by people and events around you.

- Feel connected to all living creatures and enjoy a sense of unity and oneness with all.

- Be receptive to changes in guidance, that is: as you become one with God, your guidance team ceases playing the role of taskmasters to help you heal and shifts into primarily facilitating blessings and providing answers to prayer in your life; you then gradually expand your ability to withstand the high energy of direct input from the Higher Self.

- Improve personal relationships, although this might take time, effort, courage, willingness to change, and forgiveness by others as well; it might be excruciatingly painful for any or all of the parties involved.

- Increase personal empowerment along with an internal awareness of congruency, wholeness, peace, stability, Truth, guidance, spiritual connectedness, and integration.

- Have a less crowded personal agenda and see time constraints ease as you increase your trust of divine flow and your understanding that things will happen at the best time and in the best way.

- Have less desire and need to control and manage your life as you allow God to lead you.

- Be more appreciative of life and notice more blessings.

- Realize more freedom to allow desirable outcomes and responses.

- Be drawn toward nature and become "green" with your usage of earth's resources.

- Manifest, recognize, and acknowledge greater intuition, guidance, and extrasensory perception (ESP.)

- See more options and, thus, be in a greater state of peace.

- Enjoy greater synchronicity and manifestation of abundance in all forms.

- See that personal efforts are more effective and the results more obvious.

- Live in constant communication with God and realize that the practice of spiritual disciplines is becoming increasingly optional.

- Notice how prayer changes, that is: as you become more aware that you are one with God, you also see a decreasing need to utilize formal prayer because you know that your every thought is a prayer; you also become more careful about what you think, choosing only thoughts that are beneficial, kind, and generous.

- Question less and Know more.

- Experience relief from concerns and burdens as you surrender control, trust God, and Know that all is well.

- Realize freedom from the need to play roles and have others play roles for you.

- Desire to serve others because doing so is a blessing and not an obligation.

- Speak more personal truth and be more honest and forthright, regardless of historical or anticipated consequences.

- Know that external changes will result from internal healing.

- Be in a state of unconditional love and enjoy bliss as divine attributes effortlessly blossom.

FREQUENTLY ASKED QUESTIONS

Q: Why is it important for me to know about past lives?

A: Past lives created the majority of your present life conditions, situations, relationships, and issues. You can have greater insight into what is happening now when you are aware of certain elements from past life experiences. Knowing backgrounds can help you understand, accept, and heal in ways that have defied traditional efforts. You can also better appreciate talents, blessings, and advantages from a larger perspective, that is, from the perspective of many lifetimes rather than only a few years in this lifetime. If you are seeking energetic healing, it is extremely helpful to consciously understand what caused your present life challenges so that the karmic energies can be removed. Fortunately, it is not essential to know all of your past lives in order to heal, only enough of them to reveal the overview of your foundational issues and their primary origins.

Q: **Do all people have karma?**

A: At this time on earth, nearly all people bring in karma from past lives. However, a few blessed people, and a growing percentage of babies and very young children, are coming onto earth free of karma. They are very wise beings and will help create our new society when we are ready and their gifts are needed.

Q: **Must I accept the concept of reincarnation in order to fully heal?**

A: There are no required beliefs as you heal, but having an open mind might allow significant energetic healing. You might not be ready to open up to possibilities that you at this point could interpret as threatening, wrong, or weird. Ideally you will follow where you feel led, trusting that your best interests are guiding you toward fruition. But it is crucial that you accept the differing beliefs of others as valid for them, even if you do not resonate to the same t/Truth.

Q: **Do I need to know about my past lives?**

A: Fortunately, it is not essential. Although helpful, a spiritual path does not require knowledge of past lives. Even if you live an exclusively three-dimensional life, you can still have some spiritual growth.

Q: Can energy modalities benefit everyone?

A: There is nothing on earth that works equally well for everyone. There are many factors that might prohibit a person from working with or healing from any energy modality. A few of the possibilities that could defeat your, or anyone's, success in energy healing are: fear of change or the unknown, the need for security, hidden perks in the present dilemma, coping at maximum capacity, inability to accept personal responsibility, confusion, stagnation, outdated beliefs, the need to blame, and inappropriate timing. Strong motivation and effort to heal could nudge you into a healthier place where your healing could begin.

Q: If I go to an energy session with a particular concern, will it be addressed?

A: Most likely. However, since guidance is in charge of the topics during a session, a different issue might be covered. You might know of a problem in your living room, but Source might decide you first need to work on something in the basement.

Q: Why is energy healing so important? Aren't there more tested and scientific ways to heal?

A: Energy healings focus on the subtlest level of the body. At this level, disturbances and illness energetically manifest before becoming physically obvious. Some conditions might be prevented from developing into symptoms or illness. Healing is an art more than a science because every single body is different. We need traditional allopathic medicine, but that modality comes with tremendous practical limitations in the methodology, practice, conflicting research results, side effects, costs, and so forth. So often, allopathic remedies merely manage, rather than cure, the condition, disease, or illness. Energy healings might offer fuller relief and even cures because the root cause of the condition is being addressed, shifted, and released.

Q: Why is energy so important?

A: You are an eternal energy being in a physical body, not a body who happens to have a soul. You will experience a greater likelihood of success in healing by addressing the fundamental cause of the condition rather than treating only the symptoms. Healing from this energetic standpoint might or might not transform the physical state; that's because we all die at some time. The *energetic* definition of healing transcends the physical dimension to cover all aspects of a person and his or her life, including the holistic mind/body/spirit connection as well as the karmic roots of current life experiences. Energy healings focus on physical, emotional, mental, psychological, and spiritual conditions in your current body, which is why there can be profound healing in a short time and why, often, physical pain rapidly diminishes or even permanently disappears. Life comes with no guarantees. Many variables, unknowns, and possibilities exist with everything, including energy work.

Q: Is there one spiritual path we are all meant to follow?

A: Yes and no. All of us are ultimately seeking enlightenment and full connection and reunion with God, so we are all traveling in the same basic direction. However, the work we do on ourselves to move us along toward this goal is unique, which is why we all have a different spiritual path. To walk our individual path, we must honor our own individual t/Truth, and also everyone else's t/Truth, especially when it is different than ours.

Q: **Must I give up traditional Christianity or other religious beliefs in order to make great spiritual advancement?**

A: Giving up your religious practice is not a requirement. Some people from all walks of life, whether from agnostic, atheistic, disinterested, or religious-based backgrounds, come to embrace spiritual principles. Religious decisions and involvement are uniquely individual, and as you progress spiritually, you might find delightful or surprising events and changes in many areas of your life, including whether or not you want to begin or continue your connection with religion. After being away from religious institutions for a dozen years, I have, nearly miraculously and with obvious guidance, actually joined a church, something that came about by surprise and with delightful benefits. You might also find that you begin to view your religious practice with a greater degree of joy and acceptance because of your spiritual practice.

Q: **How important is it that we speak our t/Truth?**

A: Speaking our t/Truth is perhaps the straightest path toward healing because, when we do, we stop acquiring emotional debris and might also move out stored trash bags. However, without spiritual awareness, you might be inclined to assume that speaking your t/Truth means constantly giving your opinion, or that you have the right to say anything you want to anyone at anytime. That is not so! This ego-based, self-absorbed behavior generates relationship challenges. If you subscribe to the value of speaking your t/Truth, it is essential that you also be willing to hear, listen to, accept, and work through the expressed t/Truths of everyone else, especially those closest to you.

Q: **What is the value of surrendering?**

A: Surrendering helps us immensely when we desire spiritual growth. It facilitates honest, deep, and meaningful communication and improved outcomes. As we acclimate ourselves to this higher purpose and energy, it will become easier for us to recognize our t/Truth, and k/Know when and how to apply it.

ABOUT D'ANN

My name is D'Ann Rohrbach, and I have been on a personal spiritual path since 1973, as a result of discovering reincarnation through a book my husband was reading. This new awareness opened doors to vast ethereal and sacred concepts and launched a new direction for me. Meditation, healing modalities, intuitive readings, and related books created a solid foundational background that enriched my life and developed my skills. The guided revelations I receive help my clients reinterpret, understand, enhance, and heal their life's journey. I feel privileged to be part of the energetic evolution of humanity during these eventful times.

As a National Merit and later a Returning Woman Scholar, I earned a Bachelor of Science degree in Education, Cum Laude, from Wayne State University, Detroit, Michigan, in 1989. I am a retired professional church organist, carillonneur, and former substitute public school teacher.

I began my professional clairvoyant and clairaudient clinical practice, Harmonic Vibrational Therapy®, HVT®, in 1987 as a direct result of a spiritual breakthrough while working with a quartz crystal. Initially, I primarily tapped the Akashic Records for past life readings and healings. The process I use evolved and continues to evolve, and now I specialize in clearing karmic issues and assisting the emerging human.

I was guided to establish a healing center, train associates, and teach spiritual development classes. My frequent talks, readings, and therapy sessions receive consistent enthusiastic response. I mentor innumerable clients across the United States and Canada through this process. I spearheaded the founding of a growing spiritual network, Northern Light Seekers, in Petoskey, Michigan. Serving as the first President of the Board for four years, I moderated the monthly meetings.

A native of Michigan, I am married with two children and three grandchildren. My enjoyments include music, long walks, reading, nutrition, spiritual study, traveling, and relaxing in my northern Lake Michigan vacation home.

ABOUT HARMONIC VIBRATIONAL THERAPY®

After nearly fourteen years of diligent meditation, my spiritual breakthrough with a channeling record keeper quartz crystal instantly enabled me to feel, hear, see, and know guidance. I began to develop this gift by meeting weekly with a few local members of the Detroit Chapter of A.R.E. With this group I received a constant stream of insights that led to greater understanding of the unseen world and how God works on earth, and also produced diverse and obvious healing for each of us. My friends gave me encouragement and referrals, and I activated my soul's purpose and established this spiritual ministry.

HVT® is an intuitive, energetic, spiritual, and multidimensional modality. It identifies life issues and their origins, explains how and why they are manifesting, and releases a portion of their physically held, energetic charge. This removal promotes healing of specific issues, and elevates spiritual development.

This healing process is based on revealing guidance from the client's Higher Self, (an inborn, divinely attuned essence proportionately less than the level of Source.) This profound personal core determines what is covered in every session. My guidance translates this information from the Akashic Records and other resources, and a group of divine beings energetically assist me in clearing these specific issues, one dose at a time. Issues manifest as predetermined perspectives, illogical, strong, and easily triggered emotions, and recurring patterns and responses that we wish we could alter. We are rarely able to heal our issues through conventional means, because these karmic challenges require energetic and higher dimensional approaches. Our karmic need to spiritually heal is the preliminary reason most of us are on earth at this time.

As a result of another breakthrough in 2004, I also draw sacred sigils (pronounced sijils,) symbols that hold energy. These profound, unique, and potentially limitless tools constantly send energy to a client and amplify spiritual growth and healing. One of these sacred sigils clears a client's karma and Akashic Record, and has even occasionally physically healed in seemingly miraculous ways. I am so incredibly blessed to love what I do, and feel so privileged and awed to see God at work in everyday life.

Harmonic Vibrational Therapy® advances harmony within the body, emotions, life, and soul. The healing concepts, patterns, and processes I have seen through these many years in my practice are the basis of LIFE'S HEALING SETUPS.

(Please turn the page.)

LIFE GOES ON.

NOT JUST IN EVERYDAY

PHYSICAL LIFE,

BUT THE LIFE OF YOUR SOUL

GOES ON AND ON AND ON.

BLESSINGS!

NOTES

NOTES

NOTES